lonely planet

# Miami
# & the Keys

The
Everglades
p125

Miami
p38

Florida Keys &
Key West
p142

# Contents

## PLAN YOUR TRIP

Welcome to Miami
& the Keys............ 4

Miami & the Keys Map ...6

Miami & the Keys'
Top 15................8

Need to Know ..........16

If You Like....... ........18

Month by Month....... 22

Itineraries ............ 26

Travel with Children.....31

Regions at a Glance.... 35

## ON THE ROAD

MIAMI............ 38
Sights..................39
Activities ..............82
Tours...................87
Festivals & Events ......88
Sleeping...............90
Eating..................99
Drinking & Nightlife..... 110
Entertainment.......... 116
Shopping.............. 119
Information ........... 121
Getting There & Away ... 122
Getting Around......... 123

THE
EVERGLADES ..... 125
Everglades
National Park ........ 128
Tamiami Trail........... 128
Homestead
to Flamingo Point....... 135
Biscayne
National Park ........ 140

SHRIMP CEVICHE,
KEY WEST

LIFEGUARD STATION,
SOUTH BEACH P45

# Contents

## FLORIDA KEYS & KEY WEST ...... 142

**Upper Keys** .......... 143

Key Largo
& Tavernier ............ 146

Islamorada ............ 150

Long Key .............. 152

**Middle Keys** .......... 153

Grassy Key............. 153

Marathon.............. 153

**Lower Keys** .......... 156

Big Pine, Bahia Honda
& Looe Keys ........... 156

Sugarloaf
& Boca Chica Keys...... 158

**Key West** ............ 159

## UNDERSTAND

Miami
& the Keys Today ......174

History ...............176

Multicultural Miami... 184

Food & Drink .........193

Outdoor Activities .... 201

Environment ........ 208

Art-Deco
Architecture ..........217

## SURVIVAL GUIDE

Directory A–Z ........ 222

Transportation ....... 232

Index................ 240

Map Legend.......... 247

GREAT BLUE HERON,
THE EVERGLADES

## SPECIAL FEATURES

Art Deco Miami........ 43

Multicultural Miami... 184

Outdoor Activities .... 201

Environment ........ 208

# Welcome to Miami & the Keys

*Beauty is the name of the game here. From fashion models to deco hotels, beach sunrises to wetland ecosystems and alluring islands, South Florida is an aesthetic masterpiece.*

## The Magic City

South Florida is a land of dreams and Miami is known as the Magic City. Imagination and innovation are big here, manifest in art, architecture and festivals. You'll see it in the extravagance of Lincoln Rd, the ephemeral neon beauty of Ocean Dr, the cloud-kissing skyline of downtown Miami and in the mid-century modern design on N Biscayne Blvd. From the pink castle walls of a Coral Gables mansion to sun-dappled marinas in Coconut Grove; from the Fabergé-egg interior of the Vizcaya Museum to experimental art in Midtown – stay in Miami long enough and you might believe magic is real.

## Eat, Drink & Be Merry

In Miami and the Keys, nothing succeeds like excess. People take indulgence to Roman Empire levels, from the music-video-like pools of Miami Beach's extravagant super-hotels, to buckets of beer and fried shrimp in the Florida Keys, to expertly shaken cocktails mixed under a Little Havana moon. Even the skyscrapers are a testament to the region's push for size and extravagance. Fortunately, the best purveyors of food and fun are realizing the good times can't roll at overdrive forever, and are incorporating sustainable business models.

## Everglades Encounters

South Florida is full of natural beauty, especially the spectacular wetland ecosystem of the Everglades. A colorful cast of characters inhabits the fringes (and occasionally, the heart) of these swamps, marshes and rolling prairies. Alligator wrestlers and Bigfoot hunters share a beer at crab shacks, while panthers prowl the backyard, and environmentalists document the magic of this unique wilderness. The Everglades shows nature at its most alluring; witness the ripple of bubbles as a gator submerges into the blackwater bayou, and the fish-dive of waterfowl hunting the sparkling sloughs.

## The Keys to Quirk

America's eccentricities (and quite a few eccentrics) coalesce in the southeast corner that is South Florida. And the truly unconventional are found in the sun-dappled isles of the Florida Keys. This lovely island chain is connected by the Overseas Highway – one of the nation's great road-trip byways. Here you'll find drag queens working as insect exterminators, 'No Name' islands inhabited by miniature deer, and colorful Key West: a tolerant pot of gold at the end of a rainbow flag. And all ensconced within the natural beauty of shimmering bays, serene tidal flats and emerald islands.

## Why I Love Miami & the Keys

By Adam Karlin, Author

South Florida is an American original. The emphasis on beauty, presentation, style and color is intoxicating and comes in a million shades, from graffitied Wynwood Walls to extravagant high-end hotels. There's often a sense of whimsy about and, more so, a palpable feel of cultures colliding; no other place merges Anglo America, Latin America and the Caribbean so completely. Throw in some sunny islands to chill out on and a heart-wrenchingly beautiful wetland wilderness and I'm sold.

**For more about our author, see page 248**

Above: Sunbathers on Miami Beach (p39)

# Miami & the Keys

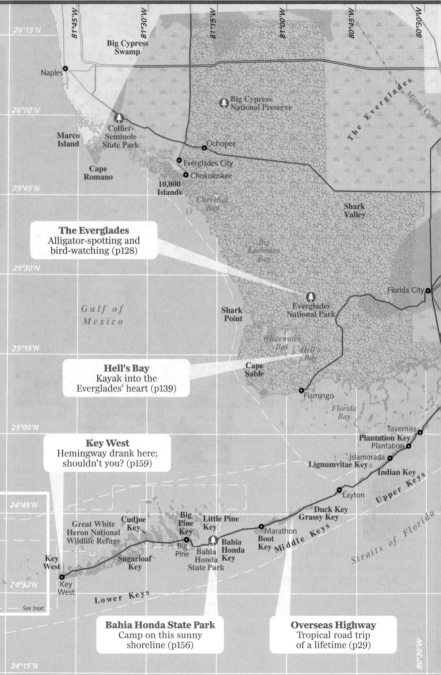

**The Everglades**
Alligator-spotting and bird-watching (p128)

**Hell's Bay**
Kayak into the Everglades' heart (p139)

**Key West**
Hemingway drank here; shouldn't you? (p159)

**Bahia Honda State Park**
Camp on this sunny shoreline (p156)

**Overseas Highway**
Tropical road trip of a lifetime (p29)

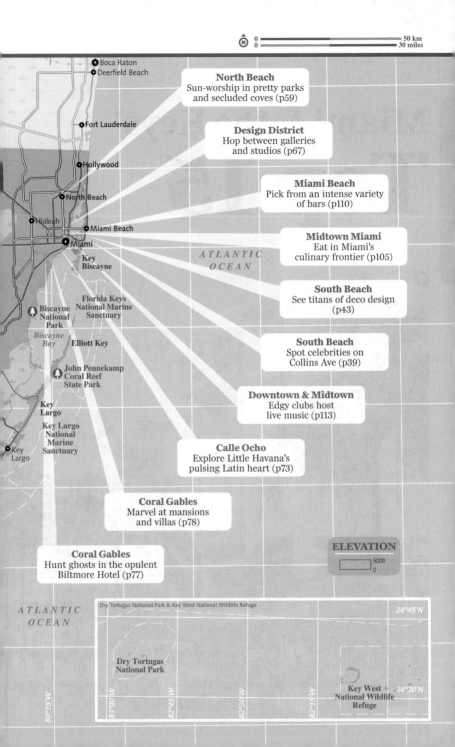

**N** 0 ————————— 50 km
0 ————————— 30 miles

Boca Raton
Deerfield Beach

**North Beach**
Sun-worship in pretty parks
and secluded coves (p59)

Fort Lauderdale

**Design District**
Hop between galleries
and studios (p67)

Hollywood

North Beach

**Miami Beach**
Pick from an intense variety
of bars (p110)

Hialeah

Miami Beach

Miami

Key
Biscayne

ATLANTIC
OCEAN

**Midtown Miami**
Eat in Miami's
culinary frontier (p105)

**South Beach**
See titans of deco design
(p43)

Florida Keys
National Marine
Sanctuary

Biscayne
National
Park

Biscayne
Bay

Elliott Key

**South Beach**
Spot celebrities on
Collins Ave (p39)

John Pennekamp
Coral Reef
State Park

**Downtown & Midtown**
Edgy clubs host
live music (p113)

Key
Largo

Key Largo
National
Marine
Sanctuary

Key
Largo

**Calle Ocho**
Explore Little Havana's
pulsing Latin heart (p73)

**Coral Gables**
Marvel at mansions
and villas (p78)

**Coral Gables**
Hunt ghosts in the opulent
Biltmore Hotel (p77)

**ELEVATION**

500ft
0

ATLANTIC
OCEAN

Dry Tortugas National Park & Key West National Wildlife Refuge

24°45'N

Dry Tortugas
National Park

Key West
National Wildlife
Refuge

24°30'N

# Miami & the Keys'
# Top 15

## Checking Out Art-Deco Giants

**1** Like all great cities, Miami and Miami Beach have a distinctive architectural style. Actually, art deco isn't just distinctive in Miami. In places like South Beach (p39), it's definitive. The style is an early 20th-century expression of aesthetic that embodies seemingly contradictory impulses – modernity with nostalgia for the beaux arts; streamlining coupled with fantastic embellishment; subdued colors and riots of pastel. Whatever your take on deco may be, you'll be hard-pressed to find a better concentration of it outside of Miami and Miami Beach. Below left: Ocean Drive (p39), South Beach

## Alligator-Spotting in the Everglades

**2** South Florida loves to embrace fashion, culinary trends and whatever the world thinks is hip. But look beneath the region's surface (literally) and you'll find a landscape and inhabitants who are ancient. How old? It doesn't get much more primeval than alligators, designed by nature to be perfect, leathery carnivores; predators whose engineering was so flawless, they haven't seen fit to change much since dinosaurs roamed. Spot dozens of gators from the boardwalks of the Royal Palm Visitor Center (p137).

PAWEL GAUL / GETTY IMAGES ©

NANCY NEHRING / GETTY IMAGES ©

M. TIMOTHY O'KEEFE / ALAMY ©

## Overseas Highway Road Trip

**3** The Florida Keys (p142) are linked by Hwy 1, also known as the Overseas Hwy. Heading over the road's many bridges and pulling over intermittently to admire the Gulf of Mexico or Florida Bay is simply one of the great pleasures of Florida travel. If you don't feel like driving, you can cycle much of the 127.5-mile route; most of the way is flat, shoulder lanes are established throughout, and more than 70 miles of the Florida Keys Overseas Heritage Trail (p148) are there for cyclists to enjoy.

## Eating Up Midtown Miami

**4** Miami is a city that loves its indulgences, and the greatest of these is a fine meal. If you really want to play with your taste buds, come to Miami's culinary frontier: Midtown (Wynwood, p105, and surrounds). In restaurants that range from the rustic to the violently indulgent, you'll find the best in local ingredients – a rich banquet of decadence plucked from Florida's fields and oceans – prepared Miami-style, with plenty of tropical flair and fun. Above: Seafood meal, Delano Hotel (p95)

## Miami Nightlife

**5** Miami is a fun, good-looking city, and the best way to accept this truth is to head out on the town. In places such as Midtown (p114), Miami Beach (p112) and Coral Gables (p109), you can find laid-back bars – even dives – where the clientele is glamorous, sexy and shiny, yet friendly and down to earth. Even the megaclubs on Miami Beach, with their occasional restrictive red ropes and sky-high cover charges, are worth checking out for their sheer dedication and innovation in the field of creating bacchanalian excess. Top right: Colony Hotel (p46)

## Sun-Worshipping on North Beach

**6** When people think of fun in the sun and Miami, their mental Rolodex often flips to two words: South Beach. And don't get us wrong! South Beach is stupendous. But if you're interested in escaping the crowds and the pressure to look fabulous, head to North Beach (p59). People-spotting aside, this is generally a higher quality of beach. Places such as Haulover Beach Park (p61) are pretty enough to serve as your screensaver, and if you really fancy a complete tan, there's a clothing-optional beach here, too.

### Celebrity-Sighting in South Beach

**7** South Beach (p39) is all about glamour, in its original, Old English meaning: a spell. Magic. So many celebrities come to South Beach that their lifestyle rubs off on we mere mortals who chase them around, hoping to spot them strolling Lincoln Rd or sipping a drink at the Shore Club's Skybar (p112). There is a self-fulfilling magic to the paparazzi atmosphere of South Beach. Lose yourself in the swooning crowd, because as you search out celebrities and hang in their hot spots, you start feeling like one yourself. Top left: Skybar (p112)

### Exploring Calle Ocho

**8** *Ellos llaman a este barrio 'Little Havana' pero no son solo Cubanos los que viven aquí.* Sorry. We're just pointing out that Little Havana (p73), nominal heart of Miami's Cuban community, is populated by more than Cubans. Spanish speakers from all over line Calle Ocho, otherwise known as '8th St,' one of the most colorful, culturally vibrant thoroughfares in the country. It helps to speak some Spanish, but it doesn't matter if you don't. Just grab a cigar, a tall fruit juice and place your finger on Miami's multicultural pulse. Top right: Cigarmaker, Little Havana

### Hunting the Biltmore's Ghosts

**9** Miami doesn't lack impressive buildings, and some say the grandest jewel in the city's crown is the Biltmore (p77) in Coral Gables (even the name rolls aristocratically off the tongue). Built in 1925, this hotel encapsulates the two initially disparate vibes of the Jazz Age: brilliant flashiness and elegant dignity. Today the majestic grounds are prowled by the well-to-do and the ghosts of guests past. And we don't just mean the Biltmore captures the essence of its heyday; some say spirits haunt the halls.

## Partying in Key West

**10** Key West (p159) is many things: counterculture icon; southernmost tip of the continental USA; and sun-drenched haven for the gay community. But for all these things, it is also, like it or not, a floating bar. Thousands of folks come here annually to cut loose. Join 'em! Start with a sunset over Mallory Square, watch a dog on a tightrope and fire-eaters, then embark on the infamous 'Duval Crawl' and get ready for the night of your life. Just don't plan much for the morning after. Below: Sunset at Mallory Square (p159)

## Gallery-Hopping the Design District

**11** Miami's hippest residents pop into South Beach clubs occasionally, but for years the loci of cool-kid activity has been Midtown (the area north of Downtown that includes Wynwood and the Design District, p67), once a working-class 'hood. Many buildings are now galleries, studio spaces, art warehouses or all of the above. Every month these art outposts throw open their doors. Wine flows. The artsy and just plain glamorous dance from gallery to gallery. And new frontiers in Miami cool are pushed. Bottom: Wynwood

## Marveling at Coral Gables' Mansions

**12** Coral Gables (p77) is called the 'City Beautiful', and with good reason. America in general and Miami in particular are often associated with gaudiness, but Coral Gables turns this cliché on its head. Yes, houses here are opulent, and some are admittedly over the top, but many are gorgeous executions of a Mediterranean-revival style that blends Iberian villas, Moroccan *riads* and Roman pleasure domes. We highly recommend gawking.

## Kayaking Hell's Bay

**13** Good old Glades boys – who once lived in what is now one of America's most beautiful national parks – dubbed one stretch of water 'Hell's Bay.' Why? The waterway, part of a complicated capillary network of Glades streams, was 'hell to get into, hell to get out of.' But it's also heavenly once inside, shaded and shadowed by a tunnel of vegetation that cools you while water runs past your paddles. Forget fearsome titles; kayaking Hell's Bay (p139) is one of the most romantic exploratory experiences in South Florida.

## Camping on Bahia Honda

**14** Everyone assumes the Florida Keys are ringed with beautiful beaches, but this is actually not the case. The Keys are mangrove islands, and as such their coasts are often a tangle of bracken and vegetation – pretty, but hardly a traditional beach. Not so at Bahia Honda (p156), where a pretty smear of buttery sand is spread along the coastline. Book early and you can camp here, waking to perfect salt-water breezes and the glimmer of a new day dancing on the nearby waves.

## Exploring Nightlife North of Downtown

**15** There's a feast for all seasons when it comes to partying north of downtown Miami (p114). The bars, pubs and clubs here, which stretch from rough Overtown to artsy Midtown to the vistas of Biscayne Blvd, run the gamut of styles, from posh lounges where models sip chardonnay, to gay dive bars where karaoke is often on the menu, to studio spaces converted into kickin' live-music venues; quite a few eccentric examples that sample all of the above.

# Need to Know

**For more information, see Survival Guide (p221)**

## Currency
US dollars ($)

## Language
English and Spanish, and, in Miami, Haitian Kreyol

## Visas
Required for most foreign visitors unless eligible for the Visa Waiver Program

## Money
24-hour ATMs widely available across Miami, the Keys and the towns that border the Everglades. Credit cards accepted at most businesses.

## Cell Phones
Local SIM cards can be used in European or Australian phones. Europe and Asia's GSM 900/1800 standard is incompatible with the USA's cell-phone systems.

## Time
Eastern Time (GMT minus five hours)

## When to Go

Tropical, wet & dry seasons
Tropical climate, rain year round
Warm to hot summers, mild winters
Mild to hot summers, cold winters

Miami Beach
GO Jan–Apr

Miami
GO Oct–Dec

The Everglades
GO Jan–Apr

The Keys
GO Jan–Apr

Key West
GO Oct–Dec

### High Season
(Jan–Mar)

➡ Winter weather in South Florida is dry, sunny and practically perfect.

➡ You'll need to book well in advance to line up rooms at this time.

➡ A preponderance of festivals equals lots of fun – and crowds.

### Shoulder
(Apr–May & Oct–Nov)

➡ The early end of spring resembles late winter; by May the weather gets humid.

➡ October is still hurricane season, but things dry off later in the month.

➡ Festival season gears up in late fall.

### Low Season
(Jun–Sep)

➡ Sure, it's hot as hell, but sea breezes are cooling.

➡ Mosquitoes are at their worst, especially in the Everglades.

➡ Did we mention hurricanes? Fortunately there are good early-warning systems on hand.

## Useful Websites

**Art Circuits** (www.artcircuits. com) Gallery maps.

**Everglades National Park** (www. nps.gov/ever) Maps and info.

**Beached Miami** (www.beached-miami.com) Arts website.

**Visit Florida** (www.visitflorida. com) Official state tourism website.

**Florida State Parks** (www. floridastateparks.org) Primary resource for state parks.

**Miami Herald** (www.herald. com) News.

**Florida Keys & Key West** (www. fla-keys.com) Keys visitor info.

**Lonely Planet** (www. lonelyplanet.com/usa/miami) Destinations, hotel bookings, traveler forums and more.

## Important Numbers

You need to dial the area code for all calls, including domestic. The only exception is the emergency number.

| Miami & the Keys area code/ Everglades area code | ☏305 or ☏786/ ☏239 |
|---|---|
| Police/Fire/ Medical Emergency | ☏911 |
| Miami Beach Patrol | ☏305-673-7714 |
| Hurricane Hotline | ☏305-468-5400 |
| Everglades National Park | ☏305-242-7700 |

## Exchange Rates

| Australia | A$0.93 |
|---|---|
| Canada | C$1.08 |
| Europe | €1.37 |
| Japan | ¥0.99 (¥100) |
| New Zealand | NZ$0.86 |
| UK | £1.68 |

**For current exchange rates see www.xe.com**

## Daily Costs

**Budget: Less than $120**

➡ Hostel dorms: $30–$50; cheap rooms: $70–$90

➡ Self-catering or cheap eats: $20–$40

➡ Bicycle rentals: around $15

➡ Walking is free!

**Midrange: $120–$250**

➡ Hotel rooms: $100–$150

➡ Midrange meals: around $20–$30 per person

➡ A night at a bar: $25–$60

**Top End: Over $250**

➡ Cover at bigger nightclubs: starts at $20

➡ Mains at upscale restaurants: at least $50 per person

➡ Room service: $20–$100

## Opening Hours

**Shops** 10am–6pm Monday to Saturday, noon to 5pm Sunday; shopping malls keep extended hours.

**Banks** 8:30am–5pm Monday to Friday, to noon or 2pm Saturday

**Restaurants** Breakfast 7am–11am, lunch 11am–2pm, dinner 5pm–10pm, later on weekends

**Bars** Around 5pm–3am

## Arriving in Miami

**Miami International Airport** (p122) Metrobus runs every 30 minutes from 6am to 11pm; it heads to Miami Beach every 35 minutes. Shuttle vans are available for $15-24. Taxis to South Beach cost around $32.

## Getting Around

**Car** Most travelers in South Florida rent cars. Traffic is always an issue in Miami and its surrounding suburbs. Rental cars generally come equipped with Sun Pass transponders. These devices carry credit to get you through the region's many tolls. This charge is usually added to your rental fee; contact your rental agency or visit www.sunpass.com for more information.

**Bus** Miami and Miami Beach have reliable bus systems, but getting around can be time consuming; see www.miami-dade.gov/transit/routes.asp for detailed route information.

**Walking & Cycling** If you're staying in South Beach you can walk most of the time, or use the extremely convenient and cost effective DecoBike bike-sharing program (p82), but this won't help if you're heading to Miami proper. That's because Miami and Miami Beach are two different cities separated by the blue waters of Biscayne Bay. Key West is very walkable and bike-friendly, but getting to Key West requires either a car or bus.

For much more on **getting around**, see p233

**PLAN YOUR TRIP** NEED TO KNOW

# If You Like...

## Beaches

When many people think of Miami, they're really thinking of Miami Beach – that's how synonymous South Florida and beaches are. The coastline starts at South Beach and extends over 100 blocks of cityscape.

**South Beach** Normal folks come here to sight models, celebrities and lifestyles of the fabulous. (p39)

**Bahia Honda State Park** A windswept, serene spot that exemplifies the forested, sun-bleached beauty of the Keys. (p156)

**Crandon Park** A gorgeous beach that mixes nature and fun on offshore Key Biscayne. (p70)

**Haulover Beach Park** In North Beach, Haulover provides privacy, quiet – and birthday suits at the nude beach. (p61)

## Nightlife

Is it any surprise that a region so famed for its sex appeal knows how to let loose and have a lot of fun come evening? Latin American sensuality, European hipness and the raw American ability to have fun mash up in some fantastic bars and clubs in Miami. The Keys abound with fun joints that attract tourists, fisherfolk and cheerfully insane pirates.

**Midtown** Miami's most innovative, interesting bars attract artists, the creative class and, of course, the glam crowd. (p114)

**The Keys** Key West gets the glory, but the other Keys, such as Islamorada, have their own self-contained party scenes. (p152)

**Key West** This island of eccentrics at the end of the rainbow does not lack for good times. (p170)

**South Beach** Lovely local bars and lounges mix it up with a more red-rope scene of models and celebrities. (p110)

## Cuisine

South Florida is a magnet for immigrants, and as such it has an international palate, supplemented by a local bounty of tropical citrus and sea life. Many flavors are Latin American, but jet-setters demand – and receive – fusion cuisine from Europe and Asia. Heartier home cooking can be found in small towns around the Everglades, while the Keys balance local flavor and cosmopolitan tastes.

**Little Havana** Miami serves up some of the best Cuban cuisine outside actual Havana. (p107)

**Midtown** Some of Miami's most original menus are served in some of its most beautiful eating spaces. (p105)

**North Beach** It may not be as glamorous as South Beach, but there are great multicultural eateries up this way. (p102)

**Everglades** Fried gator, fried frogs' legs, hot sauce and a cold beer – it's not *haute cuisine,* but it's damn delicious. (p133)

**Key West** For an island of this size, there's a fantastic variety of food on offer. (p169)

## Outdoor Activities

South Florida's tropical landscape is unique in the continental USA. From the mangrove islands of the Keys to gentle grasslands, beaches and palm hammock (forest), to the great wetland wilderness that is the Everglades, there is plenty of distinctive beauty here.

**Everglades** The 'River of Grass' is a uniquely beautiful ecosystem that can easily be the highlight of a visit to South Florida. (p128)

**Crane Point Museum** On the island of Marathon, this outdoor

**Top:** Conch fritter stand, Mallory Square (p159), Key West
**Bottom:** Sunbathers on South Beach (p39), Miami

museum is a great introduction to the ecology of the Florida Keys. (p154)

**Oleta River State Park** Drive past the condos of North Miami Beach and slip into wilderness serenity on a canoe or kayak. (p61)

**Hell's Bay** Canoe into the bracken heart of the marsh in this attractive series of small streams. (p139)

**10,000 Islands** To truly appreciate the Zen of South Florida, camp in this lovely barrier archipelago. (p132)

## Music

Miami is arguably the greatest entrepôt in Latin America, a region that – forgive us the stereotype – likes its music. From samba to salsa to reggaeton, the rhythms of the Caribbean and Central and South America resound here, alongside Euro techno, indie rock, Haitian pop and local hip-hop. Needless to say, the beat is infectious.

**Bardot** Live acts occasionally grace this hip Midtown joint. (p115)

**Green Parrot** Local live bands regularly rock the scene at Key West's oldest, funkiest bar. (p170)

**Churchill's** If you think Miami can't rock, check out the Mohawks at this hard-bitten British pub. (p115)

**The Stage** Live music and performance art takes, well, the stage here on a regular basis. (p118)

**Big Night in Little Haiti** The monthly party at the Little Haiti Cultural Center is a Caribbean and Kreyol feast for the ears. (p69)

# Wildlife

Discover dinosaur descendants in the Everglades, huge fish in the Keys and plenty of wildlife sanctuaries in-between.

**Royal Palm Visitor Center** Wander onto the boardwalk here and stare down hundreds of gators prowling the water. (p137)

**John Pennekamp Coral Reef State Park** In the continental USA, diving simply doesn't get better. (p147)

**Big Pine Key** Tiny deer – cute as all get-out – are the inhabitants of the largest island in the Keys. (p157)

**Biscayne National Park** Come to Biscayne, a national park that's almost entirely underwater, to catch or spot fish. (p140)

# Shopping

Miami unabashedly loves consumerism. Fashionistas flaunt Milanese levels of bling and sophistication thanks to a heavy European and Latin presence, alongside more artsy labels and indie boutiques.

**Books and Books** The best independent bookstore in Miami is a bastion of good taste and great literature. (p120)

**Pepe Y Berta** Slip by this Little Havana tailor and slip into the guayabera, Cuba's coolest shirt. (p120)

**Metta Boutique** Get your karma balanced at this cute shop of sustainable, fair-trade gifts. (p120)

**C Madeleine's** This is vintage clothing so beautiful it can rightfully be classified as classic couture. (p119)

# Arts

From events such as Art Basel to venues including the Adrienne Arsht Center and intimate galleries of Wynwood, the arts have paved the way for much of Miami's renaissance.

**Adrienne Arsht Center for the Performing Arts** Resembling a series of seashells, the Arsht Center is a performance space par excellence. (p64)

**New World Center** Not to be outdone, Miami Beach's concert hall hosts both edgy art and mainstream productions. (p51)

**Studios of Key West** A one-stop gallery-gazing spot for those into the artistic output of Key West. (p161)

**Cuba Ocho** This Little Havana spot hosts visual and performing arts that showcase Miami's Cuban creativity. (p73)

**Wynwood** Drop by on the second Saturday of each month for an open-house peek into Miami's best galleries. (p88)

# Architecture

From deco to the Design District, South Florida's architecture sets it apart as a region unlike any other in the USA.

**Art Deco Historic District** South Beach's heart is clustered with hotels, promenades and other prime examples of the art-deco movement. (p39)

**Freedom Tower** Downtown Miami is known for skyscrapers, and this classic tower was one of the first. (p66)

**Coral Gables** The mansions of Coral Gables run the gamut, from Mediterranean wedding cakes to neo-Arabic palaces. (p79)

**Key West** There's a shady joy to strolling under the eaves of Key West's French Caribbean and Spanish-revival homes. (p159)

**Vizcaya** This fairytale estate is the most opulent, over-the-top jewel in Miami's considerably sparkly architectural crown. (p75)

# Quirky Florida

Many eccentrics are attracted to this part of the world. Be it for weather, gators or hedonism, what follows are some of our favorites from the 'Only in Florida' category.

**Everglades International Hostel** The backyard of this fantastic hostel resembles the trippy art of '60s psychedelic album sleeves. (p137)

**Skunk Ape Research Headquarters** It's a 'reptile zoo–museum' dedicated to hunting the Everglades' Bigfoot. Why aren't you here yet? (p132)

**Coral Castle** A Latvian hewed this palace from coral and now it doubles as a monument to lost love. Why not? (p136)

**Robbie's Marina** Like an aquatic petting zoo, except the pets are enormous monster tarpon fish. (p151)

**Florida Keys History of Diving Museum** PADI people, check out possibly the most complete collection of diving paraphernalia in the USA. (p151)

# Old Florida

'Old Florida' is a bit of an invented affectation, but the term is also a byword for ecofriendly, preservation-

Key deer, National Key Deer Refuge (p157), Big Pine Key

minded attractions that are well worth your time.

**Robert Is Here** At this farmers market, taste the bounty of the region – sometimes shipped direct to your home. (p137)

**Turtle Hospital** At this Keys institution, visitors can see injured and sick sea turtles cared for by dedicated volunteers. (p154)

**Rod & Gun Club Lodge** Smooth paneled wood, spirits at the bar and photos from hunting and fishing trips of the past. (p134)

**Florida Keys Wild Bird Rehabilitation Center** This sanctuary for injured avian creatures has long been an attraction in the Keys. (p147)

**No Name Key** This quiet island boasts miniature deer and some of the best pizza in the Keys. (p157)

## Multicultural Encounters

The Keys are a crossroads of the Caribbean, while Miami is one of the most immigrant-rich cities in the country. Diversity is more than a buzzword here – it's the cloth that the social fabric of South Florida is cut from. These sites speak to the tropical cosmopolitan nature of this region.

**Viernes Culturales** Little Havana transforms into a Cuban street party on the last Friday of the month. (p117)

**Goombay Festival** In late October, Key West explodes into a celebration of Bahamian music, food and dance. (p166)

**Little Haiti Cultural Center** Pick up a beaded purse from Port-au-Prince or original art by young Haitian Americans. (p69)

**Miccosukee Village** In the Everglades, learn about the folkways of Florida's indigenous people. (p129)

**Arthur Godfrey Road** Also known as 41st St, this Miami Beach road is the heart of the city's sizable Jewish population. (p59)

# Month by Month

## TOP EVENTS

**Art Basel Miami Beach**, December

**Winter Music Conference**, March

**Carnaval Miami**, March

**Hemingway Days**, July

**Fantasy Fest**, October

## January

The beginning of the new year is also the height of the tourist season. Expect fair weather, crowds, higher prices than usual and a slew of special events.

### ⊙ Martin Luther King Jr Day Parade

This parade, held on the third Monday of January, celebrates the legacy of the USA's most iconic civil rights hero. The procession runs along NW 54th from NW 12th Avenue to Martin Luther King Jr Memorial Park. A Caribbean twist gives this event a distinctly Miami feel.

### 🏃 Orange Bowl

Hordes of football fans descend on Miami for the Super Bowl of college football, the infamous Orange Bowl (www.orangebowl. org). The entire city gets an injection of energy, while team rivalries simmer in sports bars. (p88)

### ☆ Key West Literary Seminar

Key West has long been a haven for writers escaping the real world, and its expat authors have turned the annual Key West Literary Seminar (http://keywestlit-eraryseminar.org/lit) into one of the premier festivals of letters in the USA.

### ⊙ Art Deco Weekend

Art Deco is Miami's signature style and this weekend fair features guided tours of the city's many clusters of deco structures, concerts, classic-auto shows, sidewalk cafes, and vendors of arts and antiques. Held in mid-January (www.artdecoweekend.com).

### ☆ Miami Jewish Film Festival

This international film festival (www.miamijewish filmfestival.com) gets a lot of attention outside Miami. It's a great chance to cinematically *kibitz* (chat) with one of the biggest Jewish communities in the USA.

## February

The last hurrah for northerners escaping the harsh winter, February brings arts festivals, street parties and excellent wildlife-viewing in the Everglades.

### ⊙ Coconut Grove Arts Festival

This late-February fair features more than 300 artists from across the globe. It's one of the most prestigious festivals of its kind in a city that doesn't lack for an artistic calendar (www.coconutgroveartsfest.com).

### 🔒 Original Miami Beach Antique Show

This show unearths an attic of all the world's quirky, cool stuff crossed with an archaeology dig. It attracts some 800 dealers from more than 20 countries (www.originalmiami-beachantiqueshow.com).

### 🍴 South Beach Wine & Food Festival

A festival of fine dining and sipping that has become a fixture of South Florida's social calendar (www.sobefest. com). Expect star-studded brunches, dinners and barbecues. This is the best time of year to brush shoulders with a celebrity chef.

# March

Spring arrives, bringing warmer weather, world-class golf and tennis festivals, and St Patrick's Day. Expect some spring breakers to behave badly on the beach.

## ☆ Jazz in the Gardens

This late March music festival celebrates old- and new-school R&B, soul, funk and dance music. It primarily attracts an older African American crowd, but if you have groove you are welcome. Held in Miami Gardens, a suburb just north of Miami proper (www.jazzinthegardens.com).

## ✵ Carnaval Miami

Miami's premier Latin festival takes over for nine days in early March: there's a Latin drag-queen show, in-line-skate competition, domino tournament, the immense Calle Ocho street festival, Miss Carnaval Miami and more (www.carnavalmiami.com). (p88)

## ✵ Spring Break

Throughout March to mid-April, American colleges release students for one-week spring breaks. Coeds pack Florida beaches and there is plenty of debauchery – but hey, it's all good fun. Fort Lauderdale to the north is popular, but Miami attracts its share of students too.

## ✵ St Patrick's Day

Ireland's patron saint gets his due across Florida on March 17 (any excuse to drink, right?). Miami turns the greenest, with huge parties held across town; check the *New Times* for a list.

## ☆ Winter Music Conference

Party promoters, DJs, producers and revelers come from around the globe to hear new artists, catch up on technology and party the nights away. If you've any interest in electronic music, it would be criminal to miss WMC (www.wmcon.com).

## ☆ Miami International Film Festival

The Miami International Film Festival (www.miamifilmfestival.com), sponsored by Miami-Dade College, is a two-week festival showcasing documentaries and features from all over the world. Spanish-language films are an important component of the event.

## ☆ South Beach Comedy Festival

March may not be the happiest month in Miami, but during the South Beach Comedy Festival (www.southbeachcomedyfestival.com) it's hard to leave town without a smile, as excellent talent performs stand-up in venues across the city.

## ◉ Miami Fashion Week

Vogue, darling. Models are like fish in the ocean in Miami during most of the year, but they're simply ubiquitous during Miami Fashion Week (www.miamifashionweek.com), when designers descend on the city and catwalks become disconcertingly commonplace.

# April

Welcome to shoulder season: lower prices, balmier temperatures and some choice events. This is Miami's best transition period between winter crowds and summer swelter.

## 🏃 Miami Beach Polo World Cup

It may surprise you that polo is a big thing here, until you consider the sport's connections to the fashionista scene, celebrities and the European and South American upper crust. Teams come from across the world for the La Martina Trophy (www.miamipolo.com).

## ☆ Billboard Latin Music Awards

This prestigious awards show (www.billboard-events.com/latin) in late April draws top industry execs, star performers and a slew of Latin-music fans. The ceremony includes live music sets by Latin performers from across the world.

# May

Spring in South Florida can either mean pleasantly subdued heat or sweaty soup. This is when mosquito season begins in earnest in the Everglades.

## ☆ Aqua Girl

Aqua Girl (www.aquagirl.org) is the biggest party of the year for Miami's lesbian population, and by any measure, is a pretty exhausting kick-ass event.

DJs, jazz brunches, comedy nights, beach parties, rock concerts and art exhibitions add up to a lot of fun.

### ☆ Jazz in the Park

Weekend gigs are a civilized way to soak up art, culture and some chilled white wine, which tends to complement Miami's late spring swelter. There are free shows in Hialeah, at Hialeah Park casino. (p80)

### ☆ Sizzle

This weekend party, which celebrates gay men of color, brings all the boys to the yard. Structured as a multiday dusk-to-dawn party across the city, you can expect lots of debauchery at this popular circuit event (www.sizzlemiami.com).

### ☆ Miami Gay & Lesbian Film Festival

Held late April to early May, this annual festival (www.mglff.com) is screened at various South Beach theaters. Lesbian, Gay, Bisexual and Transgender (LGBT) visitors will find fun events bracketing the event, generally of a more cerebral bent than is normal for Miami's scene.

### ☆ Sweatstock

Every year, Sweat Records (www.sweatrecordsmiami.com), one of the best record shops in town, puts on a festival aimed at locals with headline acts performing indie rock, punk and electronica. Visiting will throw you into the Miami music scene. (p121)

### ◉ Miami Museum Month

Miami Museum Month (www.miamimuseum-month.com) makes the entire month of May a good time to visit. It's an excellent chance to experience happy hours, special exhibitions and unique lectures in some of the best museums in the city.

## June

In June the real baking heat and wet humidity begins in Miami, and the events calendar tones down a little as a result.

### ☆ Goombay Festival Coconut Grove

Bahamas Mama. One of a few Goombay festivals held in South Florida, this massive fest, held in the first week of June, celebrates Bahamian culture in Coconut Grove. Expect music, street food and *lots* of dancing.

## July

OK – not only is it hot, it's hurricane season. Yay! But seriously, this is a good time to visit. There are less crowds and locals are friendlier and more accessible to tourists.

### ◉ Independence Day

July 4 features an excellent fireworks and laser show with live music that draws more than 100,000 people to breezy Bayfront Park. The pyrotechnics light up the sky above Biscayne Bay in an oddly romantic way. (p65)

### ◉ Hemingway Days

One of Key West's more (in)famous annual rituals is Hemingway Days, a party that celebrates all things Hemingway (our way of saying: expect drinking, if not game hunting). The highlight is the yearly running of the Ernest-lookalikes (à la the running of the bulls).

## August

August is sweltering and it's the deepest dip in the low tourist season. Many visitors head to the Keys, where cooling sea winds are a regular phenomenon.

### ✕ Miami Spice

Top restaurants around Miami participate in Miami Spice's Food Month (Ilovemiamispice.com), offering prix-fixe meals to lure folks out of the air-con. For most tourists, this is an easier festival to appreciate than the celebrity-focused South Beach Wine & Food Festival.

## September

The weather is still steamy, and autumn brings back college students – expect lots of revelry in the university 'hoods such as Coconut Grove and Coral Gables.

### ☆ International Ballet Festival of Miami

While much of Miami's arts calendar is given over to modern visual art and music, the International Ballet Festival of Miami (www.internationalballetfestival.org) is the main event for the city's considerably active patrons of classical dance.

### 🏃 Great Grove Bed Race

With a pajama pub crawl and drag-racing beds through Coconut Grove, the Great Grove Bed Race (www.thegreatgrovebedrace.com) is one of Miami's wackier celebrations. It's held around Labor Day Weekend (the first weekend in September).

### ◉ Womenfest

Womenfest (www.womenfest.com) gives ladies the chance to seize the large LGBT spotlight in Key West. This is the premier event for the island's lesbian population, attracting thousands of lesbian visitors from around the world.

## October

As hurricane season ends and the weather gets properly pleasant again, Key West takes over the events calendar with two raucous street celebrations.

### ☆ Fantasy Fest

Held in late October, Fantasy Fest (www.fantasyfest.net) is by far the highlight of the Keys social calendar. The body paint, glitter, feathers and crazy floats come out, inhibitions are left at home, and a seriously decadent time is had by all.

### ◉ Goombay Key West

In the heart of Bahama Village, one of the most vibrant Caribbean neighborhoods in the country, the Bahamian Goombay Festival (www.goombay-keywest.org) serves up music, food, singing and dancing in late October, the same insane week as Fantasy Fest.

## November

Tourist season kicks off at the end of the month, bringing more crowds and cooler days. Festival time starts in earnest with the White Party.

### ☆ White Party

If you're gay, and you love music, excess and naughty fun, don't miss the White Party (www.whiteparty.net). This weeklong extravaganza draws thousands of gay men and women for nonstop partying at clubs and venues all over town.

### ☆ Miami Book Fair International

In mid to late November, the Miami Book Fair International (www.miamibookfair.com) is among the most important and well-attended book fairs in the USA. Hundreds of nationally known writers join hundreds of publishers; Latin American authors form a considerably strong contingent.

## December

Tourist season is in full swing. Northerners book rooms well in advance so they can bask in sunshine and be here for holiday festivities.

### ☆ Art Basel Miami Beach

One of the seminal international art shows in the world, Art Basel (www.artbaselmiamibeach.com) can reasonably claim responsibility for putting Miami Beach on the map of the international jet-setter crowd. Gallery showcases, public installations and parties appear throughout Miami and Miami Beach.

### ◉ King Mango Strut

Held each year just after Christmas, this quirky 24-year-old Coconut Grove parade (www.kingmangostrut.org) is a politically charged, funfair that began as a spoof on current events and the now-defunct Orange Bowl Parade.

### ☆ Art Miami

Held in January or December, Art Miami (www.artmiami.com) is a massive fair that displays modern and contemporary works from more than 100 galleries and international artists. It may not have Basel's big name, but the talent is still very impressive.

# Itineraries

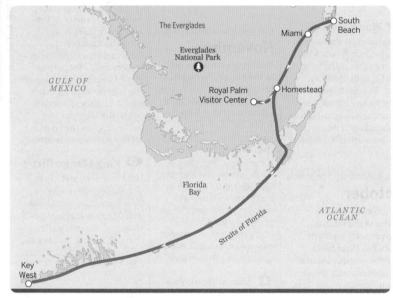

 **10 DAYS** Essential South Florida

On this trip you'll have a chance to explore Miami's beaches and back alleys, from white sand to classical architecture. It covers a diverse range of neighborhoods that encapsulate the nationalities of Latin America and the Caribbean, as well as the unique wetland and mangrove ecosystems of the Everglades and the Florida Keys.

Start your trip in **South Beach, Miami** which encapsulates the best of what South Florida has to offer. Exclusive hotels such as the Delano, Tides and the Shore Club capture the sheer aesthetic innovation of the South Beach experience. Enjoy people-watching on Lincoln Rd and a tour of the Art Deco Historic District.

Using South Beach as a base, spend the next four or five days exploring some of **Miami's neighborhoods**, including the Latin flavor of Little Havana, the Euro-style cafes and mansions of Coral Gables and the art galleries, excellent food and bumping nightlife around Wynwood and the Design District. Next head to the Everglades, either west along the Tamiami Trail through Hialeah or through Florida City, and visit the **Royal Palm Visitor Center**. **Homestead** is the jumping-off point from Miami to the Florida Keys. Spend at least a day and a night in **Key West**.

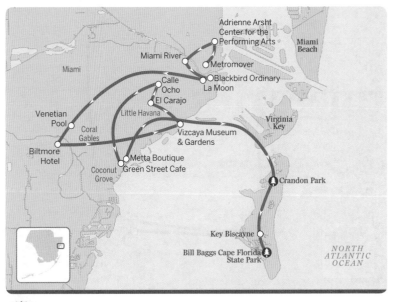

 **Downtown to South Miami**

On this trip you'll experience some of the best of Miami's multicultural enclaves, hobnob in some of its wealthiest neighborhoods and witness firsthand the opulent magic that gives this city the nickname 'The Magic City'.

Start in Downtown, a glittering fist of steel and glass that shadows rough alleyways and cheap international flea markets. Take a long ride on the free **Metromover**, hopping on and off to see downtown sites such as the gorgeous **Adrienne Arsht Center for the Performing Arts**. Have a stroll along the **Miami River**, taking in the sunset and romantic seediness (try not to walk too far from the Metromover station, for safety's sake). At night, have a beer at **Blackbird Ordinary** before doing as the locals do and having a Colombian hot dog at **La Moon**.

The next day, head to Coral Gables, making sure not to miss the **Venetian Pool** (possibly the loveliest public pool in the USA), the **Biltmore Hotel** and a shopping stroll down Miracle Mile. If that isn't opulent enough, see what happens when Mediterranean revival, Baroque stylings and money get mashed together at the **Vizcaya Museum & Gardens**. Afterward, top off a visit to these elegant manses with dinner at one of the best restaurants in Miami in – no kidding – a gas station at **El Carajo**.

On the third day, head to Little Havana and have a stroll down **Calle Ocho**, making sure to watch the dominoes at Máximo Gómez Park. Have a Cuban lunch, browse the local cigar shops, then pop over to Coconut Grove, where the hippies of yesterday have been utterly replaced with the yuppies of today. Well, there's still some good karmic vibe under the banyan trees in the form of stores such as the **Metta Boutique**. Grab a bite at **Green Street Cafe**.

Spend your last day exploring Key Biscayne, enjoying beaches, sunbathing and bliss in areas such as **Bill Baggs Cape Florida State Park**. Before you leave, head to **Crandon Park** and stroll along the sand, or do as locals do and take a nap. Is there a quiet, serene beach in manic Miami? You just found it.

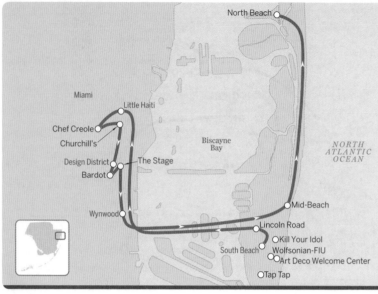

# 5 DAYS  Miami Beach & North Miami

See some of Miami's glitziest glamour honeypots, filled with celebrities and the opulent infrastructure that has been built to accommodate them. Then immerse yourself in some of the city's most fascinating cultural enclaves, as well as hipster gentrification zones.

Start your trip in South Beach and use this region and its excellent hotels as your base. Make sure you visit the **Wolfsonian-FIU** design museum to get background on the surrounding art deco. Head for **Lincoln Rd** to people-watch and browse the trendy shops; afterward, you'd be remiss to not take a tour with the lovely folks at the **Art Deco Welcome Center**. For a nice dinner try **Tap Tap** (psychedelic Haitian). When you're ready to hit the town (and the rails), have some beers at **Kill Your Idol**.

The next day, check out **Little Haiti**. This is one of the most colorful, recognizably immigrant neighborhoods in Miami. It can be edgy at night, but by day you're fine to explore. Feast on ox-tail and other Haitian treats at **Chef Creole**. A half mile south of here you'll find Sweat Records and **Churchill's**; the former is one of Miami's best music shops, while the latter is a down and dirty British punk pub.

You can easily make a day out of visiting Little Haiti, so the next morning go to the trendy **Design District** and the art galleries and studio spaces of **Wynwood**. Taken together, these neighborhoods constitute Midtown Miami, the most self-consciously artsy and creative section of the city. The Design District is a compact area that's easy to walk around and good for shopping (assuming you're loaded; these aren't starving artists, apparently). If you're hungry, head to one of the new restaurants flowering just north of here in shady Buena Vista or along Biscayne Boulevard. At night, Bardot or **The Stage** are great spots to wet your whistle, watch DJs and live music and get your dance on.

After a few days of exploring Midtown and South Beach, head north along Collins Ave to **Mid-Beach** and **North Beach**. To get here you'll pass through the Condo Canyons – rows and rows of glittering residential skyscrapers, all testament to the power of real estate in Miami. In Mid-Beach, near the north end of South Beach, you'll find an excellent boardwalk where you can stroll by the sand.

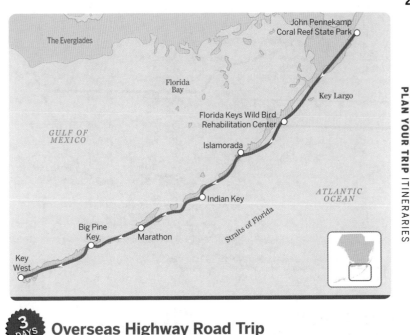

## 3 DAYS  Overseas Highway Road Trip

The Overseas Highway (Hwy 1) runs from the tip of the Florida mainland all the way to the famed Mile Marker 0: Key West, the end of the road and the end of America. As you tick the mile markers down, you'll be treated to some of Florida's oddest attractions and the ever-inspiring view of Florida Bay on one side, the Gulf of Mexico on the other.

Well, OK, you'll get to that view, but first you have to go through the Upper Keys, larger islands that block the view of the water via big fields of scrub pine and mangroves. On northerly Key Largo, check out the diving options at **John Pennekamp Coral Reef State Park**, or visit the injured birds at the **Florida Keys Wild Bird Rehabilitation Center**. After a day's activities among fish or birds, tear into some lunch at the lovely Key Largo Conch House.

Sleep in **Islamorada** on your first day in the Keys – if you can afford it, splurge at excellent Morada Bay. Wake up the next morning and feed the enormous tarpon at Robbie's Marina, and if you're feeling fit, hire a kayak and paddle out to **Indian Key**. When you have finished, you'll likely be feeling a little sapped, so make sure you caffeinate yourself at the excellent Midway Cafe.

By midday you'll easily have arrived at **Marathon**, geographic center of the Keys. If you're curious about the unique ecological background of the Keys and fancy a walk in the woods, head to the Crane Point Museum; if sea turtles happen to be your thing, a visit to the good doctors at the sanctuary Turtle Hospital may be in order. Eat dinner over the water at Keys Fisheries, then grab a beer at Hurricane.

Wake up and cross the Seven-Mile Bridge onto **Big Pine Key**, where tiny Key deer prance alongside the road.

Another hour's drive south and you're in **Key West**. Truly, this island deserves its own itinerary – just make sure you don't miss the sunset show in Mallory Sq, the six-toed cats at Hemingway's House and a night out at the infamous Green Parrot, the mother of all Keys bars.

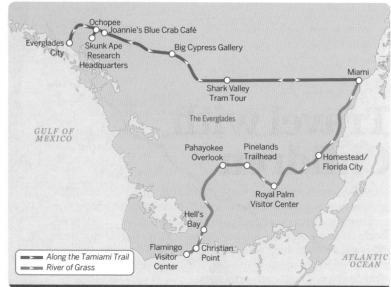

Along the Tamiami Trail
River of Grass

## Along the Tamiami Trail

**2 DAYS**

This route takes you into the heart of the stereotypical Everglades: airboat tours through waterlogged wetlands and cypress swamps crawling with gators, with a stay in a fishing village.

Go west on Tamiami Trail (US 41) past the airboat tours to the Shark Valley entrance. Take the **Shark Valley Tram Tour** or rent a bicycle from the front kiosk and ride back on an asphalt path (the same one used by the tram) that curves into the swamp. You're almost guaranteed a glimpse of alligators and wading birds.

Push on to **Everglades City** (the other Tamiami Trail sights can be visited on the return trip to Miami), a warm hamlet once known for smuggling into the swamps but today more tied to the tourism trade.

The next day head back toward Miami. Stop at the **Skunk Ape Research Headquarters**, a delightfully weird zoo, gift shop and Bigfoot hunting camp; have lunch at the excellent **Joannie's Blue Crab Café**; check out the country's smallest post office in **Ochopee**; and stop by the **Big Cypress Gallery**, which contains some of the finest photos of the beauty of the Glades.

## River of Grass

**2 DAYS**

This route into the Everglades takes in vistas of long prairies and cypress domes.

Drive south from Miami to the adjoining towns of **Homestead** and **Florida City**, and pull over by the Coral Castle, a maudlin monument to unrequited love. You're now just outside Everglades National Park, where you'll find Robert Is Here, a fantastic farmers market and petting zoo. Continue to the Everglades Outpost, an animal hospital for exotic critters.

Push west to see the most impressive points in the park, including the **Royal Palm Visitor Center**, where walkways lead over dark waterways prowled by enormous alligators; the **Pinelands Trail**, which takes you through a grove of skeleton-thin swamp pine; and **Pahayokee Overlook**, with views over the Zen quiet of the greater Glades.

Spend the night back in Florida City at the fantastic Everglades Hostel. The next morning head back into the Glades and push further south. There's great kayaking and canoeing at **Hell's Bay**, good low country over the windswept mud flats at **Christian Point** and boating in Florida Bay at the **Flamingo Visitor Center**.

Plan Your Trip

# Travel with Children

South Florida doesn't possess the reputation that child-friendly Orlando has, but sheesh, where does? This region still knows how to care for your young ones. South Florida has a plethora of parks, nature trails, megamalls, beaches, zoos and family-friendly hotels and restaurants to keep your kids happy on holiday. With the obvious exception of our nightlife listings, Miami's seedier neighborhoods and a few high-end restaurants (and OK, the nude beach at Haulover State Park), we don't list places we would consider unfriendly to children, although some are naturally more friendly than others.

## Miami & the Keys for Kids

There is a plethora of kid-themed activities in Miami. Just remember: this is Florida, and every tourist town in Florida has already anticipated the needs of every age in your family. With increasing skill and refinement, nearly every Florida museum, zoo, attraction, restaurant and hotel aims to please traveling families of all stripes.

Your only real trouble is deciding what to do. Florida offers so much for kids and families that planning can be tough. Simple itineraries can suddenly become a frantic dawn-to-dusk race to pack it all in.

### Eating Out

Most midrange Florida restaurants have a dedicated kids' menu, along with high chairs, crayons for coloring, and changing tables in restrooms. Even cheap ethnic eateries – a delicious, ubiquitous constant in the Miami dining scene – are good at accommodating children. Most restaurants, even high-end ones, are happy to make a kids' meal by

## Best Regions for Kids

**Coconut Grove**
Big malls, mainstream cuisine and a pedestrian-friendly center.

**Everglades**
Kid-friendly National Park exhibits. And big alligators. Kids love alligators.

**Florida Keys**
Active families with older kids will adore the snorkeling, diving, fishing, boating and all-around no-worries vibe.

**Key Biscayne**
An enormous, central park devoted to kids and surrounded by child-friendly nature trails and public beaches.

**Coral Gables**
More malls, midrange restaurants that are happy to host children, and the fairy-tale Venetian Pool.

**Miami Beach**
Lincoln Rd, South Pointe Park, Ocean Drive neon and the sandy beach will keep your kids grinning.

request. As a rule, families with infants or toddlers will get better service earlier in the dinner hour (by 6pm). Some high-end restaurants may look askance at young diners; simply ask when making reservations.

Our favorite restaurants for kids are:

➡ Big Pink (p100)

➡ Boater's Grill (p107)

➡ 11th St Diner (p99)

➡ Los Pinareños Frutería (p108)

➡ JT's Island Grill & Gallery (p134)

➡ Jerry's Famous Deli (p101)

➡ Steve's Pizza (p103)

➡ Shuckers (p102)

➡ Tap Tap (p99; not so much for the ambience as the amazingly colorful hand-painted interior.)

## Animal Parks

Some visitors expect Disney World and Universal Studios to be just outside Miami (they're actually a few hours away). South Florida isn't a theme-park contender, but what it does possess, in oddly high numbers, are animal parks. Some are grassroots volunteer outfits that rescue injured beasts, such as the Turtle Hospital and Bird Sanctuary in the Keys. Others more closely resemble hybrid zoo/theme parks, such as Monkey Island and Jungle Island in Miami. These locations are a hit with kids, although you can expect more child-oriented infrastructure and exhibits in the Miami examples. There's also easy wildlife access at Royal Palm Visitor Center in the Everglades.

## Beaches

The prototypical Florida family beach is fronted by or near very active, crowded commercial centers with lots of water sports and activities, tourist shops, grocery stores and midrange eats and sleeps. Admittedly, the region's most popular beach, South Beach, is a bit more sophisticated and snooty. But c'mon – this is still Florida. Lots of families hang out on the southern end of South Beach. Mid-Beach and North Beach are also more traditionally family-oriented, as are the beaches on Key Biscayne.

The Keys lack beaches, despite being islands. However Bahia Honda State Park on Bahia Honda Key is safe, reasonably nature-focused while still fun in a beachy way, and has a small, kid-oriented science center on-site. Sombrero Beach on Marathon is near a playground and has good food options.

## Museums & Attractions

Miami and the Keys holds its own in the 'Stuff Kids Love' stakes. In addition to all the animal life in the Everglades National Park and outside of it, there is decades worth of only-in-America kitsch. Hard to define 'sites' such as the Coral Castle in Homestead wow kids if only for their unique weirdness. The visitor centers of the area's many parks all have child-friendly interactive exhibits.

Some of the art museums may not jive with your kids (although the more cerebral children will appreciate the trip), but institutions such as the Bass Museum directly and indirectly sneak learning right into a child's day.

## Getting into Nature

Much of your time here is spent in air-conditioning, but don't overlook unpackaged nature. Florida is exceedingly flat, so rivers and trails are ideal for short legs and little arms. Raised boardwalks through alligator-filled swamps make perfect pint-sized adventures. Placid rivers and inter-coastal bays are custom made for first-time paddlers, adult or child. Never snorkeled a coral reef or surfed? Florida has gentle places to learn. Book a sea-life cruise, a manatee swim, a nesting-sea-turtle watch or a glass-bottom boat tour. At Oleta River State Park and almost every state park we review in the Keys, there's family-accessible kayaking and boating.

# Children's Highlights
## Beaches, Pools & Parks

➡ **South Pointe Park** Ice-cream stands, soft grass and plans to install a water feature. (p51)

➡ **Mid-Beach Boardwalk** Fronts a family-friendly stretch of sand. (p59)

➡ **Arch Creek Park** Has nature walks and ghost walks. (p61)

➡ **Crandon Park** Pretty Key Biscayne spot with sand and nature trails. (p70)

➡ **Venetian Pool** One of the most beautiful public pools in the country. (p77)

➡ **Jacob's Aquatic Center** Small Key Largo water park with plenty of kiddie pools. (p148)

➡ **Bill Baggs Cape Florida State Park** Picnic tables front a pretty sweep of beach. (p71)

➡ **Biscayne Community Center & Village Green Park** Playgrounds, sports fields and a packed kids' activities schedule. (p71)

➡ **Barnacle Historic State Park** Outdoor paths and frequent family-friendly outdoor concerts. (p75)

➡ **Fruit & Spice Park** Pretty trails wind past freshly fallen fruit. (p81)

➡ **Biscayne National Underwater Park** Glass-bottom boat tours, snorkeling over epic reefs. (p140)

➡ **John Pennekamp Coral Reef State Park** Same great coral reefs, by snorkel or glass-bottom boat tour. (p147)

➡ **Harry Harris Park** In Key Largo, this small park is one of the best in the Keys for kids. (p147)

➡ **Sombrero Beach Park** Sugar-soft sand lines calm water on one side, playground facilities on the other. (p154)

## Animal Encounters

➡ **Zoo Miami** In Miami, this extensive and wide-ranging zoo has all the big-ticket species. (p80)

➡ **Marjory Stoneman Douglas Biscayne Nature Center** Kid-friendly intro to subtropical South Florida on Key Biscayne; has great hands-on programs. (p71)

➡ **Monkey Jungle** The tagline at this Miami zoo says it all: 'Where humans are caged and monkeys run wild.' Unforgettable. (p81)

➡ **Jungle Island** This Miami zoo has tropical birds and exotic species such as the liger, a tiger-and-lion crossbreed. (p81)

➡ **Everglades Outpost** This volunteer-run animal sanctuary is essentially a great small zoo. (p136)

➡ **Miami Seaquarium** One of the state's biggies on Key Biscayne; has various swim-with-the-fishes programs. (p71)

➡ **Shark Valley** Bike or take a tram tour along the paved road of this Everglades park. Wading birds and alligators are practically guaranteed. (p128)

➡ **Royal Palm Visitor Center** Take a boardwalk trail over some of the Everglades' most beautiful wetland landscapes. (p137)

➡ **National Key Deer Refuge** Kids love spotting these cute-as-Bambi minideer on Big Pine Key. (p157)

➡ **Florida Keys Wild Bird Rehabilitation Center** Injured birdlife is sheltered along several windy paths at this refuge on Key Largo. (p147)

➡ **Turtle Hospital** In Marathon, turtles get tender loving care from a staff of dedicated volunteers. Visitors welcome (and appreciated). (p154)

➡ **Robbie's Marina** In Islamorada, a sort of 'working' harbor and aquatic petting zoo. (p151)

➡ **Robert Is Here** The Everglades' favorite farmers market has a petting zoo and fresh juice. (p137)

## Quirky Fun

➡ **Metromover** See the city from the sky via this free elevated train. (p64)

➡ **Mallory Square** A carnival for the crowds that pops off every evening as the sun sets. (p159)

## Museums

➡ **Miami Children's Museum** Extensive role-playing environments. (p81)

➡ **HistoryMiami** Bookish kids will appreciate the thoughtful exhibitions. (p65)

➡ **Miami Museum of Science & Planetarium** A bit old and dated, but still fun and child-oriented. (p75)

➡ **Gold Coast Railroad Museum** Little train-spotters will get their fix here. (p81)

---

### DATE NIGHT

Traveling with kids doesn't necessarily mean doing *everything* as a family. Want a romantic night on the town? Several child-care services offer in-hotel babysitting by certified sitters; a few run their own drop-off centers. Rates vary based on the number of children, and typically they require a four-hour minimum (plus a $10 travel surcharge). Hourly rates range from $14 to $25. These services generally apply to Miami; in the Keys you may have to ask the folks at your hotel front desk about local babysitting options, although larger resorts should have sitter staff in-house.

**Kid's Nite Out** (www.kidsniteout.com)

**Sittercity** (www.sittercity.com)

**Sunshine Babysitting** (www.sunshinebabysitting.com) Statewide.

---

**RULES OF THE ROAD**
...........................................................................

Florida car-seat laws require children under three to be in a car seat, and children under five in at least a booster seat (unless they are over 80lb and 4ft 9in tall, allowing seat belts to be positioned properly). Rental-car companies are legally required to provide child seats, but only if you reserve them in advance; they typically charge $10 to $20 extra. You can also rent them from baby-gear-rental companies.

---

➡ **Florida Keys Eco-Discovery Center** In Key West, fantastic and entertaining displays pull together Florida Keys ecology. (p160)

➡ **Crane Point Museum** Excellent alfresco introduction to the ecology of the Keys at this museum in Marathon. (p154)

➡ **Vizcaya Museum & Gardens** Older children will appreciate the whimsy of this fairy-tale mansion. (p75)

➡ **Coral Castle** Kids may not appreciate the kitsch, but they still love the weirdness of this odd structure. (p136)

➡ **Miami-Dade Public Library** Flagship library for Miami. (p66)

➡ **Miccosukee Village** On Tamiami Trail in the Everglades, this Native American village has culture shows and alligator wrestling. (p129)

## Planning

If you're a parent, you already know that luck favors the prepared. But in Florida's crazy-crowded, overbooked high-season tourist spots, planning can make all the difference. Before you come, plot your trip like a four-star general: make reservations for every place you might go. Then, arrive, relax and go with the flow. Family-friendly accommodations in this guide are marked by a family-friendly icon (👪).

### What to Bring

If you forget something, don't sweat it. Just bring yourself, your kids and any of their can't-sleep-without items.

That said, here are some things to consider:

➡ For sleeping, a pack-and-play/portacot for infants and/or an inflatable mattress for older kids can be handy, especially if you're road-tripping or sticking to amenity-poor, budget-range motels.

➡ Bring light rain gear and umbrellas; it *will* rain at some point.

➡ Bring water sandals for the beach, water parks, and play fountains.

➡ Bring sunscreen (a daily necessity) and mosquito repellent.

➡ Prepare a simple first-aid kit; the moment an unexpected cut or fever strikes is not the time to run to the drugstore.

## Accommodations

The vast majority of Florida hotels stand ready to aid families with cribs (often pack-and-plays), rollaway beds (some charge extra), refrigerators, microwaves, adjoining rooms and suites. Ask about facilities when you book. Large hotels and resorts can go toe-to-toe with condos for amenities, including partial or full kitchens, laundry facilities, pools and barbecues, and various activities.

While some high-end boutique hotels in Miami Beach and adult-oriented B&Bs in the Keys may discourage young kids, they aren't allowed to discriminate and ban them. If you're unsure, ask about their minimum age preference. In general, the best Miami neighborhoods to stay with kids are South Beach (despite the mad party scene, it has the best hotels in town), North Beach, Coconut Grove and Coral Gables. Children should be fine at most of these places, except for South Beach's priciest hotels – these hotels generally attract a celebrity-party crowd rather than families. Good family-style motels and B&Bs can be found in the Keys, Marathon, Islamorada and Key Largo.

## Travel Advice & Baby Gear

If you prefer to pack light, several services offer baby-gear rental (high chairs, strollers, car seats etc), while others sell infant supplies (diapers, wipes, formula, baby food etc), all delivered to your hotel; book one to two weeks in advance.

These websites provide family-centered travel advice and services:

**Baby's Away** (http://babysaway.com)

**Babies Travel Lite** (www.babiestravellite.com)

**Jet Set Babies** (http://jetsetbabies.com)

**Travel For Kids** (www.travelforkids.com)

# Regions at a Glance

Miami is the urban heart of this region, filled with the best dining, nightlife and shopping – plus, of course, some very fine beaches. In the past, travelers gravitated to Miami Beach over Miami, but today the city on the mainland can give the beach a run for its money when it comes to culture (and it has always been a bit more cosmopolitan). The Everglades are a wet wilderness filled with some of the best wildlife-spotting in Florida, along with pools, rivers and lakes that constrict and expand with the moon and tides, and nearby funky roadside attractions. The islands of the Florida Keys are particularly good for idiosyncratic attractions, tasty dining, fun bars, tolerance and diversity, as exemplified by Key West.

## Miami

Food
Nightlife
Architecture

### Edible Exploration

Be it Colombian hot dogs with plum sauce or Thai-Japanese fusion dishes, the shabbiest Central American shack or Italian *osterias* prepping truffles and pasta, this city has a taste for international cuisines and their budgetary evolution from cheap eateries to high-end, four-star restaurants.

### Club Kids

With a large Latin population, warm tropical evenings and money to burn, Miami doesn't like to sleep. Bump shoulders with students in Coconut Grove or dance to EDM and trip-hop in the clubs that adjoin Midtown and Downtown.

### Deco Decor

In North Beach, the Miami Modern movement is keenly felt in the shadows of enormous condos. In South Beach, deco rules the day. Take a few hours to wander the Art Deco Historic District, one of the most distinctive pockets of architectural preservation in the USA.

p38

# The Everglades

Wildlife
Quirkiness
Camping

### Gator-Gawking

Wildlife-viewing is good in the Glades any time of year, but if you visit in the winter dry season, you'll see a *Jurassic Park* landscape of prehistoric reptiles plus an avian rainbow of wading birds.

### Only in Florida

From a blue-crab shack across the street from the USA's smallest post office, to a giant Coral Castle located next to a sanctuary housing armadillos, timberwolves and tigers, the Everglades attracts America's eccentrics.

### Kayaking & Camping

There is something simply magical about paddling a kayak or canoe over sheets of sunrise-dappled water, be it a slow marsh tinkle or the wide teal expanses of Florida Bay. This is how mornings were made to be spent.

**p125**

# Florida Keys & Key West

Environment
Arts
Food

### Mangroves & Hammocks

The Keys are an ecological anomaly in the USA, a series of mangrove islands that conceal hammocks (groves) of palm, pine and tropical hardwoods found nowhere else in the country (and in some cases, the world).

### Authors & Artists

Thanks largely to its historical toleration of the homosexual community, the Keys (especially Key West) have long been an artist colony. Authors, from Hemingway to Frost, have been attracted to the island and its piratical, creative cast as well.

### Fish & Mango Salsa

Folks here are mad for fishing and the natural culinary accompaniment to said hobby. If the fish you eat here isn't fresh, there's something wrong. Land food exists as well, of course, accompanied by tropical garnishes and the famous Key lime pie.

**p142**

# On the Road

The Everglades
p125

Miami
p38

Florida Keys &
Key West
p142

# Miami

### Includes ➡

Sights . . . . . . . . . . . . . . .39
Activities . . . . . . . . . . .82
Tours . . . . . . . . . . . . . . .87
Festivals & Events . . . .88
Sleeping . . . . . . . . . . . 90
Eating . . . . . . . . . . . . . .99
Drinking
& Nightlife . . . . . . . . . .110
Entertainment . . . . . . .116
Shopping . . . . . . . . . . .119
Information . . . . . . . .121

---

### Best Places to Eat

➡ Exquisito Restaurant (p107)
➡ Chef Creole (p105)
➡ Blue Collar (p105)
➡ Choices (p104)
➡ Steve's Pizza (p103)

---

### Best Places to Stay

➡ Shore Club (p94)
➡ Gale South Beach (p94)
➡ The Standard (p94)
➡ Raleigh Hotel (p94)
➡ Pelican Hotel (p92)

## Why Go?

Miami is so many things, but to most visitors, it's mainly glamour, condensed into urban form.

They're right. The archaic definition of 'glamour' is a kind of spell that mystifies a victim. Well, they call Miami the Magic City. And it is mystifying. In its beauty, certainly: the clack of a model's high heels on Lincoln Rd, the teal sweep of Biscayne Bay, flowing cool into the wide South Florida sky; the blood-orange fire of the sunset, setting the downtown skyline aflame.

Then there's less-conventional beauty: a poetry slam in a converted warehouse, or a Venezuelan singing Metallica *en español* in a Coral Gables karaoke bar, or the passing *shalom/buenas días* traded between Orthodox Jews and Cuban exiles.

Miami is so many things. All glamorous, in every sense of the word. You could spend a fun lifetime trying to escape her spell.

---

## When to Go
### Miami

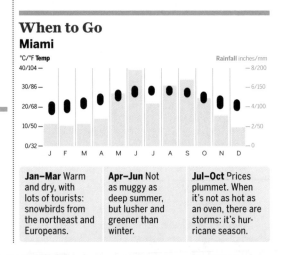

°C/°F Temp · Rainfall inches/mm

**Jan–Mar** Warm and dry, with lots of tourists: snowbirds from the northeast and Europeans.

**Apr–Jun** Not as muggy as deep summer, but lusher and greener than winter.

**Jul–Oct** Prices plummet. When it's not as hot as an oven, there are storms: it's hurricane season.

# History

It's always been the weather that's attracted Miami's two most prominent species: developers and tourists. But it wasn't the sun per se that got people moving here – it was an ice storm. The great Florida freeze of 1895 wiped out the state's citrus industry; at the same time, widowed Julia Tuttle bought out parcels of land that would become modern Miami, and Henry Flagler was building his Florida East Coast Railroad. Tuttle offered to split her land with Flagler if he extended the railway to Miami, but the train man didn't pay her any heed until north Florida froze over and Tuttle sent him an 'I told you so' message: an orange blossom clipped from her Miami garden.

The rest is a history of boom, bust, dreamers and opportunists. Generally, Miami has grown in leaps and bounds following major world events and natural disasters. Hurricanes (particularly the deadly Great Miami Hurricane of 1926) have wiped away the town, but it just keeps bouncing and building back better than before. In the late 19th and early 20th centuries, Miami earned a reputation for attracting design and city-planning mavericks such as George Merrick, who fashioned the artful Mediterranean village of Coral Gables, and James Deering, designer of the fairy-tale Vizcaya mansion.

Miami Beach blossomed in the early 20th century when Jewish developers recognized the potential American Riviera in their midst. Those hoteliers started building resorts that were branded with a distinctive art-deco facade by daring architects willing to buck the more staid aesthetics of the northeast. The world wars brought soldiers who were stationed at nearby naval facilities, many of whom liked the sun and decided to stay. Latin American and Caribbean revolutions introduced immigrants from the other direction, most famously from Cuba. Cuban immigrants arrived in two waves: first, the anti-Castro types of the '60s, and those looking for a better life since the late 1970s, such as the arrivals on the 1980 Mariel Boatlift during a Cuban economic crisis. The glam and overconsumption of the 1980s, as shown in movies like *Scarface* and *Miami Beach,* attracted a certain breed of the rich and beautiful, and their associated models, designers, hoteliers and socialites, all of whom transformed South Beach into the beautiful beast it is today.

Political changes in Latin America continue to have repercussions in this most Latin of cities – as former mayor Manny Diaz once said, 'When Venezuela or Argentina sneezes, Miami catches a cold.' In the last half of the 'aughts,' Miami embarked on a Manhattanization of its skyline that – barring a brief pause from 2008 to 2010 due to the financial crisis – hasn't really let up. Miami has, as of this writing, the third-biggest skyline in the USA (after New York and Chicago), most clearly evident in the area around Brickell.

## Maps

McNally, AAA and Dolph's all make great maps of the Miami area. The best free map is from the Greater Miami & the Beaches Convention & Visitors Bureau (p122).

## Sights

Miami's major sights aren't concentrated in one neighborhood. The most frequently visited area is South Beach, home to hot nightlife, beautiful beaches and art-deco hotels, but you'll find historic sites and museums downtown, art galleries in Wynwood and the Design District, old-fashioned hotels and eateries in Mid-Beach (in Miami Beach), more beaches on Key Biscayne, and peaceful neighborhood attractions in Coral Gables and Coconut Grove.

Water and income – canals, bays and bank accounts – are the geographic and social boundaries that divide Miami. Of course, the great water that divides here is Biscayne Bay, holding the city of Miami apart from its preening sibling Miami Beach (along with the fine feathers of South Beach). Don't forget, as many do, that Miami Beach is not Miami's beach, but its own distinct town.

### South Beach

The most iconic neighborhood in Greater Miami, South Beach encompasses the region south of 21st St in the city of Miami Beach, though hoteliers have been known to push that up as high as 40th St and on our maps it is below 23rd St. Collins Ave, the main artery, is famous for its long string of art-deco hotels. The chic outdoor cafes and restaurants of Ocean Dr overlook the wide Atlantic shorefront, while pedestrian-only Lincoln Rd Mall is a shopper's heaven. Anything south of 5th St is called 'SoFi.'

★ **Art Deco Historic District**  NEIGHBORHOOD
(Map p52) South Beach's heart is its Art Deco Historic District, from 18th St and south along Ocean Dr and Collins Ave. It's ironic that in a

# Miami Highlights

**1** Mingling with the beautiful hipsters amid the jaw-dropping **Wynwood Walls** (p69) murals.

**2** Cigar smoke and dominoes; saying *bienvenido* a Little Havana in **Máximo Gómez Park** (p73).

**3** Taking in a show at the gorgeous **Adrienne Arsht Center for the Performing Arts** (p64).

**4** Splashing about the faux grottoes and coral cliffs in the magnificent **Venetian Pool** (p77).

**5** Dancing to Caribbean beats and chowing down on curried conch and goat at the monthly **Big Night in Little Haiti** (p69).

ATLANTIC OCEAN

Golden Beach

Aventura

Collins Ave

Collins Ave

Ojeta River State Park

Indian Creek

See Northern Miami Beach Map (p60)

Ives Dairy Rd

NORTH MIAMI BEACH

Southern Memorial Park

NE 163rd St

Biscayne Blvd

W Dixie Hwy

Alton Rd

Dade Blvd

Collins Ave

Julia Tuttle Cswy

JFK/79th St Causeway

Morningside Park

NE 6th Ave

Griffing Blvd

NE 2nd Ave
N Miami Ave

DESIGN DISTRICT

See Wynwood, Design District & Little Haiti Map (p68)

NW 2nd Ave

NW 7th Ave

NW 119th St

OPA-LOCKA

NW 27th Ave

Little River Canal

NW 79th St

LIBERTY CITY

Big Night in Little Haiti

NW 54th St

MIAMI

NW 36th St

NW 37th Ave

Palmetto Expwy

N Le Jeune Rd

E 4th Ave

CAROL CITY

Gratigny Pkwy

W 4th Ave

NW 57th Ave

HIALEAH

Palmetto Expwy

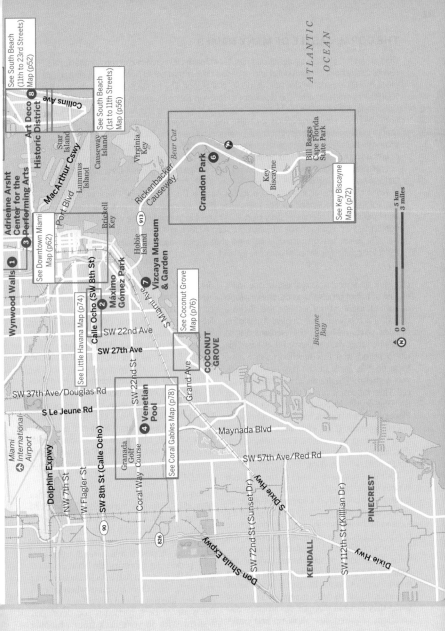

**1** Wynwood Walls
**3** Adrienne Arsht Center for the Performing Arts
**8** Art Deco Historic District
**2** Máximo Gómez Park
Calle Ocho (SW 8th St)
**7** Vizcaya Museum & Garden
**4** Venetian Pool
Crandon Park **6**
**5**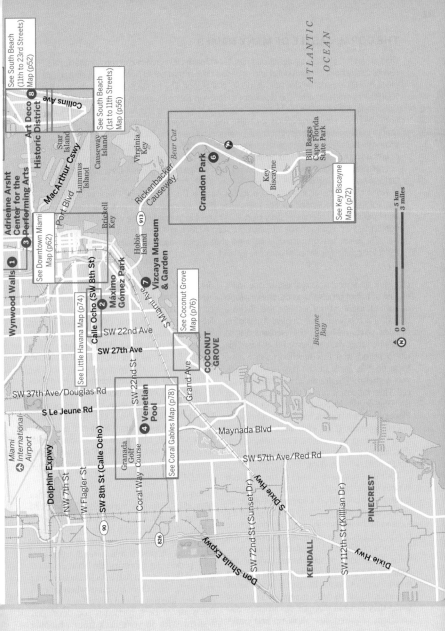

*ATLANTIC OCEAN*

See South Beach (11th to 23rd Streets) Map (p52)
See South Beach (1st to 11th Streets) Map (p56)
See Downtown Miami Map (p62)
See Little Havana Map (p74)
See Coral Gables Map (p78)
See Coconut Grove Map (p76)
See Key Biscayne Map (p72)

Collins Ave
MacArthur Cswy
Star Island
Causeway Island
Lummus Island
Port Blvd
Brickell Key
Hobie Island
Miami Ave
SW 22nd Ave
SW 27th Ave
SW 22nd St
Granada Golf Course
Coral Way
SW 8th St (Calle Ocho)
NW 7th St
W Flagler St
Dolphin Expwy
Miami International Airport
SW 37th Ave/Douglas Rd
S Le Jeune Rd
Grand Ave
Maynada Blvd
SW 57th Ave/Red Rd
SW 72nd St (Sunset Dr)
S Dixie Hwy
SW 112th St (Killian Dr)
Dixie Hwy
Don Shula Expwy

Virginia Key
Rickenbacker Causeway
Bear Cut
Key Biscayne
Bill Baggs Cape Florida State Park

Biscayne Bay

COCONUT GROVE
KENDALL
PINECREST

90
826
913

5 km
3 miles

**6** Relaxing far from the celebs while still appreciating the beautiful Miami skyline in **Crandon Park** (p70).

**7** Exploring the opulent **Vizcaya Museum & Gardens** (p75).

**8** Wandering through the architectural heritage of the **Art Deco Historic District** (p39).

## THE CORAL CASTLE OF MANY NAMES

On a street full of fairly opulent buildings, 1114 Ocean Dr, a cream-colored Mediterranean-revival castle built of hewn coral and exposed timber that could rightly be the center set piece of a *Pirates of the Caribbean* movie, stands out. The three-story palace, built in the 1930s, was modeled after the Governor's House in Santo Domingo, where Christopher Columbus' son once laid his head. For years it was known as the Amsterdam Palace – until one day, in the early 1980s, it caught the eye of a certain fashion designer named Gianni Versace. Versace bought the property, renamed it the Versace Mansion and promptly locked horns with local preservationists after announcing plans to tear down a neighboring hotel so he could build a pool. After a battle, the moneyed designer won – but also struck a deal that would allow for law changes, saving more than 200 other historic hotels in the process.

None of it mattered in 1997, when stalker Andrew Cunanan gunned Versace down in front of the beloved mansion. For years after, the house was known as Casa Casuarina and operated as a members-only club. Currently it is the site of The Villa by Barton G hotel (p93). Ironically, the death of a European fashion guru here has attracted lots of, well, European fashion gurus. Tourists still shuffle by, armed with morbid curiosity and a thirst for celebrity-related photos of any kind.

city built on speculative real estate, the main engine of urban renewal was the preservation of a unique architectural heritage. See, all those beautiful hotels, with their tropical-Americana facades, scream 'Miami.' They screamed it so loud when they were preserved they gave this city a brand, and this neighborhood a new lease on life. Back in the day, South Beach was a ghetto of vagrants, druggies and retirees. Then it became one of the largest areas in the USA on the National Register of Historic Places, and then it attracted models, photographers, hoteliers, chefs and...well, today it's a pastel medina of cruisers, Euro-fashionistas, the occasionally glimpsed celebrity and tourists from Middle America.

Your first stop here should be the Art Deco Welcome Center (p122), run by the Miami Design Preservation League (MDPL). To be honest, it's a bit of a tatty gift shop, but it's located in the old beach-patrol headquarters, one of the best deco buildings out there. You can book excellent $20 guided walking tours (plus audio and private tours), which are some of the best introductions to the layout and history of South Beach on offer. Tours depart at 10:30am daily, except on Thursday when they leave at 6:30pm. No advance reservations required; just show up and smile. Call ahead for information on walking tours of Lincoln Rd and Collins Park, the area that encompasses upper South Beach.

★ **Wolfsonian-FIU**  MUSEUM
(Map p56; ☎305-531-1001; www.wolfsonian.org; 1001 Washington Ave; adult/child 6-12 $7/5; ⊙noon-6pm Thu & Sat-Tue, to 9pm Fri) Visit this excellent design museum early in your stay to put the aesthetics of Miami Beach into fascinating context. It's one thing to see how wealth, leisure and the pursuit of beauty manifests in Miami Beach, it's another to understand the roots and shadings of local artistic movements. By chronicling the interior evolution of everyday life, the Wolfsonian reveals how these trends were architecturally manifested in SoBe's exterior deco. Which reminds us of the Wolfsonian's own noteworthy facade. Remember the Gothic-futurist apartment-complex-cum-temple-of-evil in *Ghostbusters*? Well, this imposing structure, with its grandiose 'frozen fountain' and lion-head-studded grand elevator, could serve as a stand-in for that set.

**Lincoln Road Mall**  ROAD
(Map p52; ⊙farmers market 9am-6:30pm Sun) Calling Lincoln Rd a mall, which many do, is like calling Big Ben a clock: it's technically accurate but misses the point. Yes, you can shop, and shop very well here. But this outdoor pedestrian thoroughfare between Alton Rd and Washington Ave is really about seeing and being seen; there are times when Lincoln feels less like a road and more like a runway. We wouldn't be surprised if you developed a slight crick in your neck from whipping around to check out all the fabulously gorgeous creatures that call 'the road' their natural environment. Carl Fisher, the father of Miami Beach, envisioned the road as a '5th Ave of the South.' Morris Lapidus, one of the

*(continued on p51)*

GLOWIMAGES / GETTY IMAGES ©

# Art Deco Miami

South Beach may be known for celebrity spotting, but the area's original cachet owes less to paparazzi and more to preservation. The art-deco design movement, the architectural and aesthetic backbone of SoBe, is powerfully distinctive and finds expression in soft lines, bright pastels and the integration of neon into structural facades.

**Contents**

➜ Classical Deco
➜ Deco Elements
➜ 'New' Deco Hotels
➜ Quirky Deco Delights

**Above** Detail of a carved art-deco wall, Miami.

MAISANT LUDOVIC / HEMIS.FR / GETTY IMAGES ©

1. Cardozo Hotel 2. Lifeguard station on South Beach
3. Essex House Hotel

3

RAPPY VINIKER / GETTY IMAGES ©

ESSEX HOUSE

# Classical Deco

In the past, South Beach architects distinguished themselves through decorative finials, parapets and neon signage. Miami Beach deco relies on 'stepped-back' facades that disrupt the harsh, flat Florida light. Cantilevered 'eyebrows' jut out above windows to protect interiors from the sun.

## Cardozo Hotel

This lovely building (p95), along with the neighboring Carlyle Hotel, was the first to be rescued by the original Miami Beach Preservation League when developers threatened to raze South Beach's deco buildings in the 1980s.

## Carlyle Hotel

Located at 1250 Ocean Dr, the Carlyle comes with futuristic styling, triple parapets, a *Jetsons* vibe and some cinematic cachet: *The Birdcage* was filmed here.

## Essex House Hotel

Porthole windows lend the feel of a grand cruise ship, while the hotel's spire looks like a rocket ship, recalling art deco's roots as an aesthetic complement to modernism and industrialism. Terrazzo floors cool the lobby (p93).

## Lifeguard Stations on South Beach

Besides being cubist-inspired exemplars of the classical deco movement, with their sharp, pleasing geometric lines, these stations are painted in dazzling colors. They're along the beach from 1st St to 17th St.

## Jerry's Famous Deli

Housed in the Hoffman Cafeteria Building, this spacious 1939 gem (p101) has a front that resembles the prow of a *Buck Rogers*-inspired ship. The carved owls on the roof scare off pigeons – and their poo.

# Deco Elements

As individualized as South Beach's buildings are, they share quirks and construction strategies. Canopy porches provide cool places to sit. To reflect heat, buildings were originally painted white, and later, pastels, with accent colors highlighting smaller elements. Some hotels resemble Mesoamerican temples; others evoke cruise liners.

## Crescent Hotel

Besides having one of Miami Beach's most recognizable neon facades, the Crescent (at 1420 Ocean Dr) has signage that draws the eye down into its lobby (the better to pack guests in), rather than up to its roof.

## Waldorf Towers Hotel

Deco guru L Murray Dixon designed the tower of this hotel (at 860 Ocean Dr) to resemble a lighthouse, surely meant to illuminate the way home from drunken Ocean Dr revels.

## Colony Hotel

The Colony, at 736 Ocean Dr, is the oldest deco hotel in Miami Beach, and has what may be the most iconic facade on Ocean Dr. It was the first hotel in Miami to incorporate its sign (a neon wonder) as part of its overall design. Inside the lobby, a space-age interior includes Saturn-shaped lamps and *Flash Gordon* elevators.

## Cavalier South Beach

The step-pyramid sides and geometric carvings that grace the front of this classic (p93) are some of the best examples of the Mayan or Incan-inspired 'temple-as-hotel' school of design.

## Wolfsonian-FIU

The lobby of this museum (p42) contains a phenomenally theatrical example of a 'frozen fountain.' The gold-leaf fountain, which formerly graced a movie-theater lobby, shoots up vertically and flows downward symmetrically.

**1.** Colony Hotel **2.** Waldorf Towers Hotel **3.** Cavalier South Beach

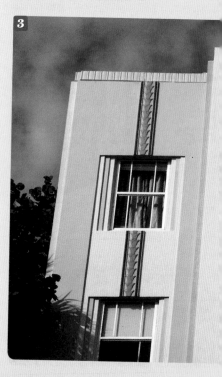

**1.** Hotel Victor **2.** James Royal Palm Hotel
**3.** Delano Hotel among the Collins Ave streetscape **4.** The Tides

DENNIS K. JOHNSON / GETTY IMAGES ©

# ② 'New' Deco Hotels

Hoteliers such as Ian Schrager combine faith in technology – flat-screen TVs, Lucite 'ghost chairs,' computer-controlled lobby displays – with an air of fantastical glamour. Newer hotels such as the W and Gansevoort South have deco roots, but have expanded the architectural sense of scale, integrating deco style into Miami Modern's (enormous) proportions.

## Hotel Victor

Forward-thinking management (who give a nod to the past) have done an excellent job of turning this L Murray Dixon original (p92) into an undersea wonderland of jellyfish lamps and sea-green terrazzo floors.

## Delano Hotel

The top tower evokes old-school deco rocket-ship fantasies, but the theater-set-on-acid interior is a flight of pure modern fancy. The enormous backyard pool mixes Jazz Age elegance with pure Miami muscular opulence. (p95)

## Tides

The biggest deco structure of its day was a temple to the deco movement. Today, the lobby of the Tides (p95) feels like Poseidon's audience chamber, while rooms exemplify contemporary boutique aesthetics.

## James Royal Palm Hotel

There's no better place to feel a sense of sea-borne movement than the *Titanic*-esque, ocean-liner themed back lobby of this massive and beautifully restored hotel (p96). The mezzanine has enormous modern dimensions but classic deco styling.

## Surfcomber

One of the best deco renovations on the beach is offset by sleek, transit-lounge inspired lines in the lobby and a lovely series of rounded shades over room windows. (p96)

Vintage Ford Thunderbird outside the Avalon Hotel

# Quirky Deco Delights

Tropical deco is mainly concerned with stimulating the imagination. Painted accents lifted from archaeology sites might make a passerby think of travel, maybe on a cruise ship. And hey, isn't it funny the windows resemble portholes? Almost all of the preserved buildings here still inspire this childlike sense of wonder.

## Bas-Relief & Friezes

Although art deco was inspired by stripped-down modernist aesthetics, it also rebelled against utilitarianism. Its bas-relief and frieze work is noticeable on the exterior of many South Beach hotels.

## Portholes

The deco movement came about in the early 20th century, when affordable travel became a reality for the developed world. Sea journeys were the height of luxury and many deco buildings are decorated with nautical porthole windows.

## Berkeley Shore Hotel

One of the older hotels in South Beach, the Berkeley Shore, at 1610 Collins Ave, has a striking exterior set off by a cylindrical 'prow' rising out of shade-providing 'eyebrows,' plus elegant exterior friezes.

## Avalon Hotel

The exterior of the Avalon, at 700 Ocean Dr, is a fantastic example of classical art-deco architecture – clean lines, old-school signage lit up in tropical green, with a 1950s Oldsmobile parked outside.

## 11th Street Diner

It doesn't get much more deco than dining in a classical Pullman train car. Many buildings on Miami Beach evoke planes, trains and automobiles – this diner (p99) is actually in one.

*(continued from p42)*

founders of the loopy, neo-baroque Miami Beach style, designed much of the mall, including several shady overhangs, waterfall structures and traffic barriers that look like the marbles a giant might play with. Other architectural icons of note include the Lincoln Theatre (Map p52; 541 Lincoln Rd), designed by renowned theater and cinema architect Thomas W Lamb (now an H&M), and the wonderfully deco Colony Theater (p116). There's also an excellent farmers market and the Antique & Collectible Market (www. antiquecollectiblemarket.com; ⊗8am-6pm, every 2nd Sun Oct-May), both held along Lincoln.

**1111 Lincoln Rd**                                         BUILDING
(Map p52; www.1111lincolnroad.com; P) The west side of Lincoln Rd is anchored by what may be the most impressive parking garage you'll ever lay eyes on, a geometric pastiche of sharp angles, winding corridors and incongruous corners that looks like a lucid fantasy dreamed up by Pythagoras after a long night out. In fact, the building was designed by Swiss architecture firm Herzog & de Meuron, who describe the structure as 'all muscle without cloth.' Besides parking, 1111 Lincoln is filled with retail shops and residential units.

**ArtCenter/South Florida**                          GALLERY
(Map p52; ✆305-674-8278; www.artcentersf. org; 924 Lincoln Rd) Established in 1984 by a small but forward-thinking group of artists, this compound is the creative heart of South Beach. In addition to some 52 artists' studios (many of which are open to the public), ArtCenter offers an exciting lineup of classes and lectures. The residences are reserved for artists who do not have major exposure, so this is a good place to spot up-and-coming talent. Monthly rotating exhibitions keep the presentation fresh and pretty avant-garde.

**Miami Beach Community Church**       CHURCH
(Map p52; http://miamibeachcommunitychurch.com; 1620 Drexel Ave) In rather sharp and refreshing contrast to all the ubermodern structures muscling their way into the art-deco design of South Beach, this community church puts one in mind of an old Spanish mission – humble, modest and elegantly understated in an area where overstatement is the general philosophy. Fourteen stained-glass windows line the relatively simple interior, while the exterior is built to resemble coral stone in a Spanish Revival style. The congregation is LGBT friendly and welcomes outside visitors; sermons are at 10:30am on Sunday and 6pm nightly.

**New World Center**                                   BUILDING
(Map p52; ✆305-673-3331; www.newworldcenter. com; 500 17th St; tours $5; ⊗tours 4pm Tue & Thu, noon Fri & Sat) Miami has a penchant for sumptuous performing-arts venues and the New World Center is certainly competing with the Arsht Center for most impressive concert hall in the city. Designed by Frank Gehry, the Center rises majestically out of a manicured lawn just above Lincoln Rd, looking somewhat like a tissue box from the year 3000 with a glass facade; note the 'fluttering' stone waves that pop out of the exterior. The grounds form a 2½-acre public park; performances inside the center are projected to those outside via a 7000-sq-ft projection wall (like you're in the classiest drive-in movie theater in the universe). Inside, the folded layers of white walls feel somewhere between organic and origami. Tours are led by docents; call ahead to book, as space is limited.

**Ocean Drive**                                              ROAD
(Map p56; from 1st to 11th St) This is the great cruising strip of Miami; an endless parade of classic cars, testosterone-sweating young men, peacocklike young women, street performers, vendors, those guys who yell unintelligible crap at everyone, celebrities pretending to be tourists, tourists who want to play celebrity, beautiful people, ugly people, people people and the best ribbon of art-deco preservation on the beach. Say 'Miami.' That image in your head? Probably Ocean Dr.

**South Pointe Park**                                    PARK
(Map p56; 1 Washington Ave; ⊗sunrise-10pm) The very southern tip of Miami Beach has been converted into a lovely park, replete with manicured grass for lounging; views over a remarkably teal and fresh ocean; a restaurant; a refreshment stand; warm, scrubbed-stone walkways; and lots of folks who want to enjoy the great weather and views sans the South Beach strutting. That said, we saw two model photo shoots here in under an hour, so it's not all casual relaxation.

**A1A**                                                             ROAD
'Beachfront Avenue!' The A1A causeway, coupled with the Rickenbacker Causeway in Key Biscayne, is one of the great bridges in America, linking Miami and Miami Beach via the glittering turquoise of Biscayne Bay. To drive this road in a convertible or with the windows down, with a setting sun behind you, enormous cruise ships to the side, the palms swaying in the ocean breeze, and

# South Beach (11th to 23rd Streets)

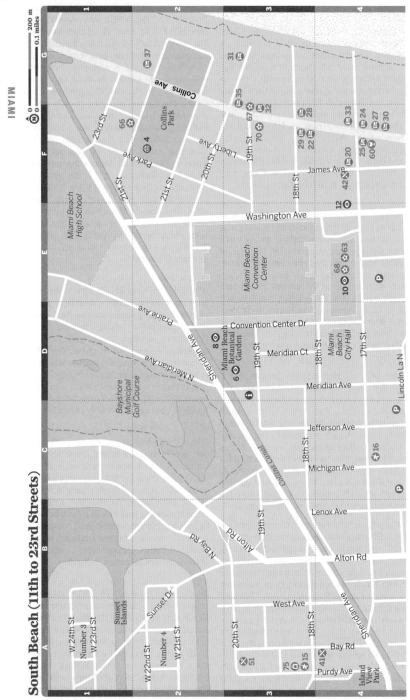

MIAMI

ATLANTIC OCEAN

South Beach

1 Art Deco Historic District

Collins Ave

The Promenade

Lummus Park

Old City Hall

Drexel Ave

Espanola Way

Euclid Ave

Pennsylvania Ave

Lincoln Rd Mall

Meridian Ave

Jefferson Ave

Flamingo Park

MIAMI BEACH

Michigan Ave

Courtyard

Lincoln La S

Lenox Ave

Sun Trust Bank

Alton Rd

Alton Ct

West Ave

Bay Rd

Lincoln Rd

See South Beach (1st to 11th Streets) Map (p56)

## South Beach (11th to 23rd Streets)

◎ **Top Sights**
1 Art Deco Historic District......................F5

◎ **Sights**
2 1111 Lincoln Rd..........................................B5
3 ArtCenter/South Florida .....................D5
4 Bass Museum of Art................................F2
5 Española Way Promenade ....................E6
6 Holocaust Memorial...............................D3
7 Lincoln Road Mall...................................C5
8 Miami Beach Botanical Garden............D2
9 Miami Beach Community Church.........E5
10 New World Center ...................................E4
11 Post Office................................................E7
12 Temple Emanu-El .....................................E4
13 World Erotic Art Museum......................E8

◎ **Activities, Courses & Tours**
14 Fritz's Skate, Bike & Surf.......................E5
15 Green Monkey Yoga ............................... A3
16 Lucky Strike..............................................C4
17 Miami Design Preservation League ......F8
Spa at the Setai............................(see 31)

◎ **Sleeping**
18 Aqua Hotel ...............................................F6

19 Betsy Hotel...............................................F7
20 Cadet Hotel ..............................................F4
21 Cardozo Hotel..........................................F7
22 Catalina Hotel ..........................................F3
Cavalier South Beach ..................(see 21)
23 Clay Hotel .................................................E6
24 Delano Hotel.............................................F4
25 Gale South Beach.....................................F4
26 James Royal Palm
Hotel......................................................F6
27 National Hotel..........................................F4
28 Raleigh Hotel............................................F3
29 Redbury South Beach...............................F3
30 Sagamore..................................................F4
31 Setai...........................................................G3
32 Shore Club.................................................F3
33 Surfcomber...............................................F4
34 Tides..........................................................F8
35 Townhouse Hotel .....................................G3
36 Tropics Hotel & Hostel............................F6
37 W Hotel......................................................G2
38 Winter Haven Hotel.................................F7

◎ **Eating**
39 A La Folie ..................................................E6
40 Balans .......................................................C5

let's just say 'Your Love' by the Outfield on the radio, is basically the essence of Miami.

**Bass Museum of Art** MUSEUM
(Map p52; ☎305-673-7530; www.bassmuseum. org; 2121 Park Ave; adult/child $8/6; ☺noon-5pm Wed, Thu, Sat, Sun, to 9pm Fri) The best art museum in Miami Beach has a playfully futuristic facade, a crisp interplay of lines and bright, white wall space – like an Orthodox church on a space-age Greek isle. All designed, by the way, in 1930 by Russell Pancoast (grandson of John A Collins, who lent his name to Collins Ave). The collection isn't shabby either: permanent highlights range from 16th-century European religious works to northern European and Renaissance paintings. The Bass forms one point of the Collins Park Cultural Center triangle, which also includes the three-story Miami City Ballet and the lovingly inviting Miami Beach Regional Library, which is a great place for free wi-fi.

**Española Way Promenade** PROMENADE
(Map p52; btwn 14th & 15th Sts) Española Way is an 'authentic' Spanish promenade...in the Florida theme-park spirit of authenticity. Oh, whatever; it's a lovely, terra-cotta and cobbled arcade of rose pink and Spanish cream architecture, perfect for browsing art

(it was an arts colony in the 1920s and today houses the studios of several local artists), window-shopping, people-watching and coffee-sipping. A craft market operates here on weekend afternoons.

**Jewish Museum of Florida** MUSEUM
(Map p56; ☎305-672-5044; http://jmof.fiu.edu; 301 Washington Ave; adult/student & senior $6/5, Sat admission free; ☺10am-5pm Tue-Sun, closed Jewish holidays) Housed in a 1936 Orthodox synagogue that served Miami's first congregation, this small museum chronicles the rather large contribution Jews have made to the state of Florida. After all, it could be said that while Cubans made Miami, Jews made Miami Beach, both physically and culturally. Yet there were times when Jews were barred from the American Riviera they carved out of the sand, and this museum tells that story, along with some amusing anecdotes (like seashell Purim dresses).

**Holocaust Memorial** MEMORIAL
(Map p52; www.holocaustmmb.org; cnr Meridian Ave & Dade Blvd) Even for a Holocaust memorial, this sculpture is particularly grim. The light from a Star of David is blotted by the racist label of *Jude* (the German word for 'Jew'); a family surrounded by a hopeful Anne Frank quote is later shown murdered,

41 Burger & Beer Joint..............................A4
42 Casa Tua .............................................F4
43 Flamingo Restaurant...........................E6
44 Front Porch Cafe.................................F6
45 Gelateria 4D........................................D5
46 Jerry's Famous Deli.............................F6
47 Jimmy'z Kitchen .................................B6
    Juvia...............................................(see 2)
    Mr Chow Chinese...........................(see 37)
    Nespresso......................................(see 2)
48 Nexxt Cafe .........................................D5
49 Osteria del Teatro ...............................F6
50 Paul.....................................................E5
51 Pubbelly .............................................A3
52 Segafredo L'Originale...........................C5
53 Van Dyke Cafe.....................................E5
54 Yardbird .............................................B5
55 Yuca....................................................E5

⊚ **Drinking & Nightlife**
56 Abbey Brewery.................................. B5
    B Bar..............................................(see 19)
57 Kill Your Idol.......................................F6
58 Lost Weekend.....................................F6
59 Mac's Club Deuce Bar ..........................F7
    Pool Bar at the Sagamore ..........(see 30)

60 Rose Bar at the Delano.........................F4

⊚ **Entertainment**
61 Cameo................................................F6
62 Colony Theater ...................................B5
    FDR................................................(see 24)
63 Fillmore Miami Beach/Jackie
    Gleason Theater...............................E4
64 Lincoln Theatre...................................E5
65 Mansion..............................................E8
66 Miami City Ballet ................................F1
67 Mynt ...................................................F3
68 New World Symphony...........................E4
69 Score...................................................D5
70 Skybar.................................................F3

⊚ **Shopping**
    Alchemist........................................(see 2)
71 Base ...................................................C5
72 Consign of the Times...........................C5
73 Española Way Art Center......................D6
74 Eyes on Lincoln...................................D5
75 Metta Boutique...................................A3
76 Ricky's NYC ........................................E5
    Taschen ..........................................(see 2)

## MIAMI IN...

### Two Days

There's more to Miami than South Beach, but we're assuming you're starting – and sleeping – here. Have breakfast at **Puerto Sagua** (p99) and, gorged, waddle to the **Wolfsonian-FIU** (p42) to get some background on the surrounding art-deco architecture. Now stroll around **Lincoln Road** (p42), hotel-spot on Collins Ave or check out South Beach's most flamboyant structures, like the **Delano Hotel** (p95), **Tides** (p95) and the **Shore Club** (p94).

Get in some beach time and as evening sets in consider an excellent deco district tour with the **Art Deco Welcome Center** (p122). For a nice Haitian dinner try **Tap Tap** (p99). Afterwards, grab a craft cocktail at **Broken Shaker** (p112).

The next day potter around either of the excellent ethnic enclaves of **Little Haiti** (p70) or **Little Havana** (p73) before dining in the trendy **Design District** (p105). End your trip rocking out in one of Midtown's excellent venues, like **Bardot** (p115) or **Wood Tavern** (p114).

### Four Days

Follow the two-day itinerary and visit whichever one of the 'Littles' (Haiti or Havana) you missed the first time round. If you can, visit Coral Gables, making sure not to miss the **Biltmore Hotel** (p77), the **Venetian Pool** (p77) and a shopping stroll down Miracle Mile. If all that isn't opulent enough for you, see what happens when Mediterranean revival, baroque stylings and a lot of money gets mashed together at the **Vizcaya Museum & Gardens** (p75). Top off a visit to these elegant manses with dinner at one of the best restaurants in Miami in, no kidding, a gas station at **El Carajo** (p109).

On day four, head downtown and take a long ride on the free **Metromover** (p64), hopping on and off to see the gorgeous **Adrienne Arsht Center for the Performing Arts** (p64). Have your last meal at **Blue Collar** (p105) on emergent N Biscayne Blvd before having a farewell drink under the stars in the courtyard of the **Blackbird Ordinary** (p113).

MIAMI

# South Beach (1st to 11th Streets)

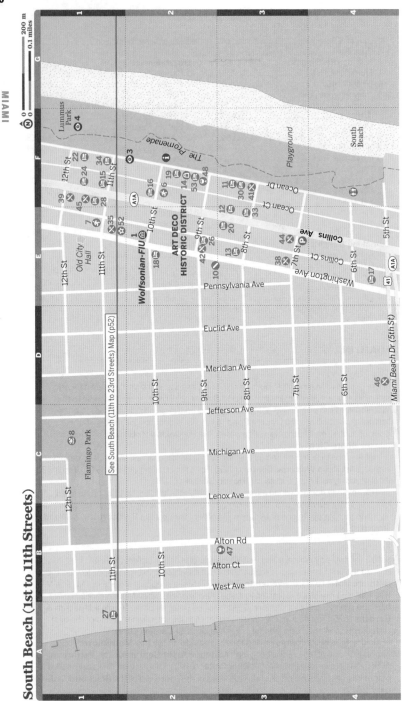

200 m
0.1 miles

Lummus Park

○4

The Promenade

○3

○1

12th St

○22
○24
○15
○34
11th St

○39
○45
○28

○16
○6 ○19
○14
○53
○48

○11
○30 ○41
○33

○7
○35
○52

Old City Hall

11th St

A1A

○18

Wolfsonian-FIU

10th St

ART DECO HISTORIC DISTRICT

9th St

○12
○20

○42
○26

○13

8th St

○44
○38
7th St

Ocean Dr

Ocean Ct

Collins Ave

Collins Ct

Washington Ave

○10

Pennsylvania Ave

12th St

11th St

See South Beach (11th to 23rd Streets) Map (p52)

10th St

9th St

8th St

7th St

6th St

Euclid Ave

Meridian Ave

Jefferson Ave

Michigan Ave

Lenox Ave

Alton Rd
○47

Alton Ct

West Ave

Flamingo Park

○8

12th St

11th St

10th St

○27

Miami Beach Dr (5th St)

○46

South Beach

Playground

5th St

○19
○17
A1A
41

6th St

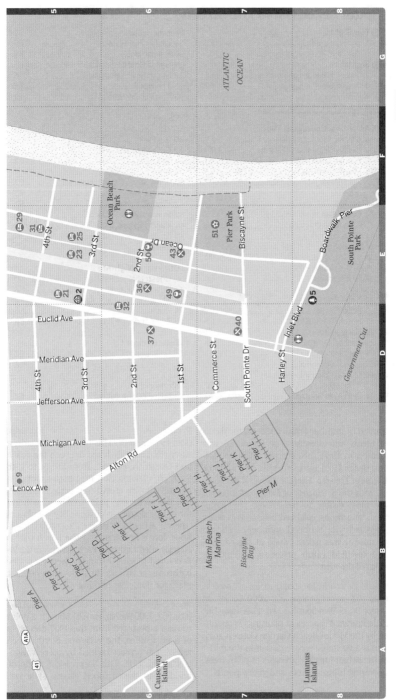

## South Beach (1st to 11th Streets)

### ⊙ Top Sights
1 Wolfsonian-FIU.................................E2

### ⊙ Sights
2 Jewish Museum of Florida.....................E5
3 Ocean Drive.....................................F2
4 Promenade.......................................F1
5 South Pointe Park............................E8

### 🚴 Activities, Courses & Tours
6 BikeAndRoll......................................F2
7 Bikram Yoga Miami Beach...................E1
8 Flamingo Park Swimming Pool.............C1
9 Miami Food Tours.............................C5
10 South Beach Divers.........................E2

### 😴 Sleeping
11 Casa Grande Hotel..........................F3
12 Chesterfield Hotel...........................E3
13 Clinton Hotel...................................E3
14 Deco Walk......................................F2
15 Dream South Beach.........................F1
16 Essex House Hotel...........................F2
17 Fashionhaus...................................E4
18 Hotel Astor.....................................E2
19 Hotel Breakwater............................F2
20 Hotel Shelley..................................E3
21 Hotel St Augustine..........................E5
22 Hotel Victor.....................................F1
23 Jazz on South Beach.......................E5
24 Kent Hotel.......................................F1
25 Lord Balfour Hotel...........................E5
26 Miami Beach International
    Hostel............................................E2
27 Mondrian South Beach.....................A1

28 Nash Hotel......................................F1
29 Ocean Five Hotel.............................E5
30 Pelican Hotel...................................F3
31 Sense South Beach..........................E5
32 South Beach Hostel.........................D6
33 The Hotel........................................E3
34 The Villa by Barton G.......................F1

### 🍴 Eating
35 11th St Diner..................................E1
36 Big Pink..........................................E6
37 Cafe Mistral....................................D6
38 Grazie............................................E3
39 Guru...............................................F1
40 Joe's Stone Crab Restaurant............D7
41 News Cafe.......................................F3
42 Pizza Rustica...................................E2
43 Prime 112........................................E6
44 Puerto Sagua...................................E3
45 Spiga..............................................F1
46 Tap Tap...........................................D4

### 🍷 Drinking & Nightlife
Chesterfield Hotel Bar...................(see 12)
47 Dewey's Tavern...............................B3
48 Mango's Tropical Café......................F2
49 Room..............................................E6
50 Ted's Hideaway...............................E6

### 🎭 Entertainment
51 Nikki Beach Club..............................E7
52 Twist...............................................E1

### 🛍 Shopping
53 U Rock Couture................................F2

framed by another Frank quote on the death of ideals and dreams. The memorial was created in 1984 through the efforts of Miami Beach Holocaust survivors and sculptor Kenneth Treister. There are several key pieces, with the *Sculpture of Love and Anguish* the most visible to passers-by. The sculpture's enormous, oxidized bronze arm bears an Auschwitz tattooed number – chosen because it was never issued at the camp – and terrified camp prisoners scaling the sides of the arm.

**Miami Beach Botanical Garden**    GARDENS
(Map p52; www.mbgarden.org; 2000 Convention Center Dr; ☺9am-5pm Tue-Sat) This lush but little-known 4½ acres of plantings is operated by the Miami Beach Garden Conservancy, and is a veritable secret garden in the midst of the urban jungle – an oasis of palm trees, flowering hibiscus trees and glassy ponds.

**Promenade**    PROMENADE
(Map p56; Ocean Dr) This beach promenade, a wavy ribbon sandwiched between the beach and Ocean Dr, extends from 5th St to 15th St. A popular location for photo shoots, especially during crowd-free early mornings, it's also a breezy, palm-tree-lined conduit for in-line skaters, cyclists, volleyball players (there's a net at 11th St), dog walkers, yahoos, locals and tourists. The beach that it edges, called Lummus Park, sports six floridly colored lifeguard stands. There's a public bathroom at 11th St; the sinks are a popular place for homeless bathing.

**Post Office**    HISTORIC BUILDING
(Map p52; 1300 Washington Ave) Make it a point to mail a postcard from this 1937 deco gem of a post office, the very first South Beach renovation project tackled by preservationists in the '70s. This Depression moderne building in the 'stripped classic' style was

constructed under President Roosevelt's reign and funded by the Works Progress Administration (WPA) initiative, which supported artists who were out of work during the Great Depression. On the exterior, note the bald eagle and the turret with iron railings, and inside, a large wall mural of Florida's Seminole Wars.

### Temple Emanu-El                    RELIGIOUS

(Map p52; www.tesobe.org; Washington Ave at 17th St) An art-deco temple? Not exactly, but the smooth, bubbly dome and sleek, almost aerodynamic profile of this Conservative synagogue, established in 1938, fits right in on SoBe's deco parade of moderne this and streamline that. Shabbat services are on Friday at 7pm and on Saturday at 10am.

### World Erotic Art Museum          MUSEUM

(Map p52; www.weam.com; 1205 Washington Ave; over 18yr $15; ☺11am-10pm Mon-Thu, to midnight Fri-Sun) In a neighborhood where no behavior is too shocking, the World Erotic Art Museum screams, 'Hey! We have a giant golden penis!' Back in 2005, then 70-year-old Naomi Wilzig turned her 5000-piece private erotica collection into a South Beach attraction. WEAM takes itself very seriously, which is part of the charm of this collection of fascinating erotica through the ages, from ancient sex manuals to Victorian peep-show photos to, yes, a big golden phallus by the exit.

---

## ⊚ Northern Miami Beach

Maps refer to the area above South Beach as Miami Beach, but locals use the jargon Mid-Beach (around the 40th streets) and North Beach (70th St and above). Communities like Surfside, Bal Harbour, Sunny Isles and Aventura are further north and can be included in spirit. Indian Creek waterway separates the luxury hotels and high-rise condos from the residential districts in the west. Keep in mind that the separate city of North Miami Beach (as opposed to the *region* of Northern Miami Beach) is not, technically, on the spit of land known as Miami Beach – it's on the mainland. Confused? So are most residents.

### Boardwalk                          BEACH

(Map p60; 21st St to 46th St) What's trendy in beachwear this season? Seventeenth-century Polish gabardine coats, apparently. There are plenty of skimpily dressed hotties on the Mid-Beach boardwalk, but there are also Orthodox Jews going about their business in

the midst of joggers, strolling tourists and sunbathers. Nearby are numerous condo buildings occupied by middle-class Latinos and Jews, who walk their dogs and play with their kids here, giving the entire place a laid-back, real-world vibe that contrasts with the nonstop glamour of South Beach.

### Little Buenos Aires            NEIGHBORHOOD

(Map p60; 71st St west of Collins Ave) The area stretching in a 10-block radius around 71st Ave and Collins Ave may be one of the best places outside Mendoza to people-watch with a *cortada* (Argentine espresso) before digging into traditional pasta and steak dishes. With that said, today the Argentines compete with their neighbors the Uruguayans, their rivals the Brazilians, and even a big crop of Colombians, for first place in the Normandy Isle ethnic-enclave stakes. Not that there's tension; this is as prosperous and pleasant as Miami gets. On Saturday mornings the small village green hosts a lovely farmers market.

### Fontainebleau                HISTORIC BUILDING

(Map p60; www.fontainebleau.com; 4441 Collins Ave) As you proceed north on Collins, the condos and apartment buildings grow in grandeur and embellishment until you enter an area nicknamed Millionaire's Row. The most fantastic jewel in this glittering crown is the Fontainebleau hotel. The hotel – mainly the pool, which has since been renovated – features in Brian de Palma's classic *Scarface*. This iconic 1954 leviathan is a brainchild of the great Miami Beach architect Morris Lapidus and has undergone many renovations; in some ways, it is utterly different from its original form, but it retains that early glamour.

---

### KEEPING IT KOSHER IN MIAMI BEACH

They're no shtetls, but Arthur Godfrey Rd (41st St) and Harding Ave between 91st and 96th Sts in Surfside are popular thoroughfares for the Jewish population of Miami Beach. Just as Jews have shaped Miami Beach, so has the beach shaped its Jews: you can eat lox y *arroz con moros* (salmon with rice and beans) and while the Orthodox men don *yarmulkes* and the women wear head-scarves, many have nice tans and drive flashy SUVs.

# Northern Miami Beach

# Northern Miami Beach

### ⊙ Sights
| | | |
|---|---|---|
| 1 | Boardwalk | D7 |
| 2 | Eden Roc Renaissance Miami Beach | D5 |
| 3 | Fontainebleau | D6 |
| 4 | Little Buenos Aires | C2 |

### ⊕ Activities, Courses & Tours
| | | |
|---|---|---|
| 5 | Canyon Ranch Hotel & Spa | D2 |
| | Lapis | (see 3) |
| 6 | Normandy Isle Park & Pool | B2 |
| 7 | Russian & Turkish Baths | D4 |

### ⊝ Sleeping
| | | |
|---|---|---|
| 8 | Circa 39 | D6 |
| 9 | Claridge Hotel | D7 |
| | Eden Roc Renaissance | (see 2) |
| | Fontainebleau | (see 3) |
| 10 | Freehand Miami | D7 |
| 11 | Mimosa | D2 |
| 12 | Palms Hotel | D7 |
| 13 | Red South Beach | D7 |

### ⊗ Eating
| | | |
|---|---|---|
| 14 | Cafe Prima Pasta | D1 |
| 15 | Chivitoteca | D1 |
| 16 | Fifi's Place | D2 |
| 17 | Indomania | D7 |
| 18 | La Perrada de Edgar | D1 |
| 19 | Roasters' n Toasters | C6 |
| 20 | Shuckers | A2 |

### ⊙ Drinking & Nightlife
| | | |
|---|---|---|
| | Broken Shaker | (see 10) |
| | Circa 39 Bar | (see 8) |
| 21 | Lou's Beer Garden | D1 |

### ⊕ Entertainment
| | | |
|---|---|---|
| 22 | Chopin Foundation of the United States | A2 |

**Eden Roc Renaissance**
**Miami Beach** HISTORIC BUILDING
(Map p60; www.edenrocmiami.com; 4525 Collins Ave) The Eden Roc Resort was the second groundbreaking resort from Morris Lapidus, and it's a fine example of the architecture known as MiMo (Miami Modern). It was the hangout for the 1960s Rat Pack – Sammy Davis Jr, Dean Martin, Frank Sinatra and crew. Extensive renovation has eclipsed some of Lapidus' style, but with that said, the building is still an iconic piece of Miami Beach architecture, and an exemplar of the brash beauty of Millionaire's Row.

**Haulover Beach Park** PARK
(www.miamidade.gov/parks/parks/haulover_park.
asp; 10800 Collins Ave; per car $4; ⊝ sunrise-sunset; P) Where are all those tanned men in gold chains and Speedos going? That would be the clothing-optional beach in this 40-acre park hidden from condos, highways and prying eyes by vegetation. There's more to do here than get in the buff, though; most of the beach is 'normal' (there's even a dog park) and is one of the nicer spots for sand in the area (also note the colorful deco-ish shower 'cones'). The park is located on Collins Ave about 4.5 miles north of 71st St.

**Oleta River State Park** PARK
(www.floridastateparks.org/oletariver; 3400 NE 163rd St; per person/car $2/6; ⊝ 8am-sunset; P) Tequesta people were boating the Oleta River estuary as early as 500 BC, so you're just following in a long tradition if you canoe or kayak in this park. At almost 1000 acres, this is the largest urban park in the state and one of the best places in Miami to escape the maddening throng. Boat out to the local mangrove island, watch the eagles fly by, or just chill on the pretension-free beach. Onsite Blue Moon Outdoor Center (p85) offers single kayaks ($18 per 1½ hours, $25 per three hours), tandem kayaks ($25.50 per 1½ hours, $40 per three hours) and bike rental ($18 per 1½ hours, $25 per three hours). The park is off 163rd St NE/FL-826 in Sunny Isles, about 8 miles north of North Miami Beach.

**Arch Creek Park** PARK
(www.miamidade.gov/parks/parks/arch_creek.
asp; 1855 NE 135th St; ⊝ 9am-5pm Wed-Sun; P) This compact-and-cute park, located near Oleta River, encompasses a cozy habitat of tropical hardwood species that surrounds a pretty, natural limestone bridge. Naturalists can lead you on kid-friendly ecotours of the area, which include a lovely butterfly garden, or visitors can peruse a small but well-stocked museum of Native American and pioneer artifacts. The excellent **Miami-Dade Eco-Adventures** (⊘ 305-365-3018; www.miamidade.gov/ecoadventures) is based here. The park is just off North Biscayne Blvd, 7 miles north of the Design District.

## ⊙ Downtown Miami

Downtown Miami, the city's international financial and banking center, is split between tatty indoor shopping arcades on the one hand, and new condos and high-rise luxury hotels in the area known as Brickell on the other. The lazy, gritty Miami River divides downtown into north and south. Miami is

MIAMI

# Downtown Miami

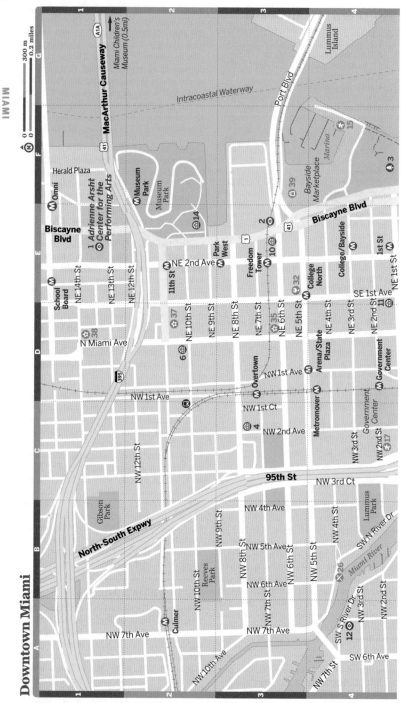

300 m
0.2 miles

Miami Children's
Museum (0.5mi)

MacArthur Causeway

Lummus
Island

Intracoastal Waterway

Port Blvd

Herald Plaza

Omni

Museum
Park

Museum
Park

Bayside
Marketplace

39

15

Marina

3

Biscayne
Blvd

1 Adrienne Arsht
Center for the
Performing Arts

14

Biscayne Blvd

NE 2nd Ave

Park
West

Freedom
Tower

2

41

College/Bayside

School
Board

NE 14th St
NE 13th St
NE 12th St

11th St

10

1st St

NE 10th St
NE 9th St
NE 8th St
NE 7th St
NE 6th St
NE 5th St

37

College
North

32

NE 4th St
NE 3rd St
NE 2nd Ave

SE 1st Ave

NE 1st St

11

38

N Miami Ave

6

35

Overtown

NW 1st Ave

Arena/State
Plaza

Government
Center

Government
Center

NW 12th St

NW 1st Ave

NW 1st Ct

Metromover

Government
Center

4

NW 2nd Ave

NW 3rd St

NW 2nd St

17

95th St

NW 3rd Ct

Gibson
Park

North-South Expwy

NW 4th Ave

NW 4th St

Lummus
Park

NW 3rd St

SW/N River Dr

Miami River

NW 9th St

NW 8th St
NW 5th Ave
NW 6th St
NW 5th St

NW 2nd St

Reeves
Park

NW 10th St

NW 7th St
NW 6th Ave

26

SW/N River Dr

Culmer

NW 10th Ave

NW 7th Ave

NW 7th Ave

SW S River Dr

12

NW 7th St

SW 6th Ave

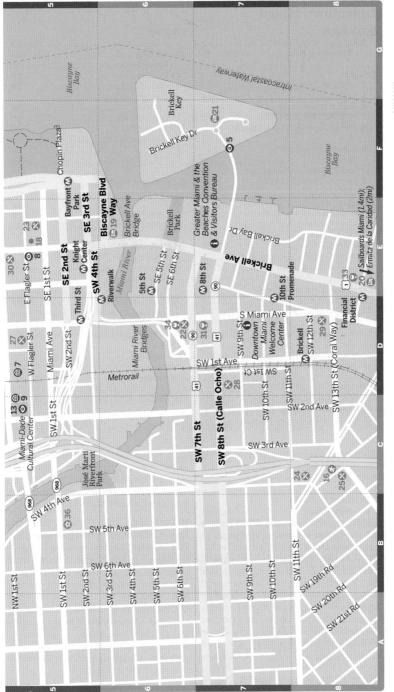

Biscayne Bay

Intracoastal Waterway

Brickell Key

📷 21

⊙ 5

Brickell Key Dr

Chopin Plaza

🚇 Bayfront Park

Biscayne Blvd

SE 3rd St

📷 19 Way

Brickell Ave Bridge

Brickell Park

Greater Miami & the Beaches Convention & Visitors Bureau

Brickell Bay Dr

Biscayne Bay

🚇 Knight Center

SE 2nd St

🚇 8

🚇 Third St

SE 1st St

SW 4th St

30 ✕

E Flagler St

Miami Ave

SW 2nd St

23
18

🚇 Riverwalk

Miami River

5th St
SE 5th St
SE 6th St

Brickell Ave

🚇 8th St

10th St Promenade

SW 1st Ave

Metrorail

Miami River Bridges

34
14 ✕
22 ✕

31 ✕
41

96

S Miami Ave

SW 9th St

Downtown Miami Welcome Center

🚇 Brickell
SW 12th St
29 ✕

Financial District

1 33
20 ➤ Ermita de la Caridad (2mi)
Sailboards Miami (1.4mi);

SW 8th St (Calle Ocho)

28 ✕

SW 10th St
SW 11th St
SW 1st Ct
SW 1st Ave

SW 13th St (Coral Way)

968

968

968

SW 4th Ave

⭐ 36

SW 5th Ave

SW 6th Ave

José Martí Riverfront Park

Miami-Dade Cultural Center

13
7
9

W Flagler St

27 ✕

Miami Ave

SW 1st St

NW 1st St
SW 1st St
SW 2nd St
SW 3rd St
SW 4th St
SW 5th St
SW 6th St

SW 3rd Ave

SW 9th St
SW 10th St

SW 2nd Ave

24 ✕

16
25 ✕

SW 11th St

SW 19th Rd
SW 20th Rd
SW 21st Rd

SW 7th St

## Downtown Miami

### ◎ Top Sights
1 Adrienne Arsht Center for the
Performing Arts .................................... E1

### ◎ Sights
2 American Airlines Arena ........................ E3
3 Bayfront Park ........................................... F4
4 Black Archives Historic Lyric
Theater Welcome Center ................ C3
5 Brickell Avenue Bridge & Brickell
Key .......................................................... F7
6 Cisneros Fontanal Arts
Foundation ........................................... D2
7 Dade County Courthouse ..................... D5
8 Gusman Center for the
Performing Arts .................................. E5
9 HistoryMiami .......................................... C5
10 MDC Museum of Art & Design ............ E3
11 Miami Center for Architecture
& Design ................................................ E4
12 Miami River .............................................. A4
13 Miami-Dade Public Library ................. C5
14 Pérez Art Museum Miami .................... E2

### ◎ Activities, Courses & Tours
15 Ace Blue Waters Charters .................... F4
16 Brickell Hot Yoga .................................. C8
Island Queen ................................. (see 39)
17 Miami-Dade County Parks &
Recreation Dept ................................. C4
Spa at Mandarin Oriental Miami .. (see 21)
18 Urban Tour Host ...................................... E5

### ◎ Sleeping
19 Epic ............................................................ E6
20 Four Seasons Miami .............................. E8
21 Mandarin Oriental Miami ..................... F7

### ◎ Eating
Azul ...................................................(see 21)
22 Bonding ..................................................... D6
23 Carol's Reasurant ................................... E5
24 Choices ..................................................... C8
25 Fresco California ................................... C8
26 Garcia's Seafood Grille & Fish
Market ................................................... B4
27 Granny Feelgoods ................................. D5
28 La Moon .................................................... D7
Mini Healthy Deli ........................... (see 39)
29 OTC ............................................................ D8
30 Soya e Pomodoro ................................... E5

### ◎ Drinking & Nightlife
31 Blackbird Ordinary ................................ D7
32 DRB ............................................................ E3
33 Level 25 .................................................... E8
34 Tobacco Road .......................................... D6

### ◎ Entertainment
Adrienne Arsht Center for the
Performing Arts .............................. (see 1)
Florida Grand Opera ...................... (see 1)
Garret .............................................. (see 35)
35 Grand Central .......................................... D3
Gusman Center for the
Performing Arts .............................. (see 8)
36 Miami Hispanic Ballet ........................... B5
37 Space ......................................................... D2
38 Vagabond .................................................. D1

### ◎ Shopping
777 International Mall ................... (see 39)
39 Bayside Marketplace ............................ F3

defined by an often frenetic pace of growth; when you visit, chances are the fruits of said growth will be visible in this area.

### ★ Adrienne Arsht Center for the Performing Arts
BUILDING

(Map p62; www.arshtcenter.com; 1300 N Biscayne Blvd) The largest performing-arts center in Florida (and second largest, by area, in the USA) is Miami's beautiful, beloved baby. It is also a major component of downtown's urban equivalent of a face-lift and several regimens of Botox. Designed by Cesar Pelli (the man who brought you Kuala Lumpur's Petronas Towers), the center has two main components: the Ziff Ballet Opera House and Knight Concert Hall, which span both sides of Biscayne Blvd. The venues are connected by a thin, elegant pedestrian bridge, while inside the theaters there's a sense of ocean and land sculpted by wind; the rounded balconies rise up in spirals that resemble a sliced-open seashell. If you have the chance, catch a show here; the interior alone is easily a highlight of any Miami trip.

### Metromover
MONORAIL

(www.miamidade.gov/transit/metromover.asp) This elevated, electric monorail is hardly big enough to serve the mass-transit needs of the city, and has become something of a tourist attraction. Whatever its virtues as a commuting tool, the Metromover is a really great (and free!) way to see central Miami from a height (which helps, given the skyscraper-canyon nature of downtown). Because it's gratis, Metromover has a reputation as a hangout for the homeless, but commuters use it as well.

## Bayfront Park
PARK

(Map p62; www.bayfrontparkmiami.com; 301 N Biscayne Blvd) Few American parks can claim to front such a lovely stretch of turquoise (Biscayne Bay), but Miamians are lucky like that. Lots of office workers catch quick naps under the palms at a little beach that does you the favor of setting out 'sit and chill' chairs. Notable park features are two performance venues: the Klipsch Amphitheater, which boasts excellent views over Biscayne Bay, is a good spot for live-music shows, while the smaller 200-seat (lawn seating can accommodate 800 more) Tina Hills Pavilion hosts free springtime performances. Look north for the JFK Torch of Friendship, and a fountain recognizing the accomplishments of longtime US congressman Claude Pepper. There's a huge variety of activities here, including yoga classes, trapeze classes and, we hear, flying-trapeze yoga classes (seriously).

Noted artist and landscape architect Isamu Noguchi redesigned much of Bayfront Park in the 1980s and dotted the grounds with three sculptures. In the southwest corner is the Challenger Memorial, a monument designed for the astronauts killed in the 1986 space-shuttle explosion, built to resemble both the twisting helix of a human DNA chain and the shuttle itself. The Light Tower is a 40ft, somewhat abstract allusion to Japanese lanterns and moonlight over Miami. Our favorite is the Mantra Slide, a twisting spiral of marble that doubles as a playground piece for the kids.

## American Airlines Arena
BUILDING

(Map p62; www.aaarena.com; 601 N Biscayne Blvd) Just north of the park, and resembling a massive spaceship that perpetually hovers at the edge of Biscayne Bay, this arena has been the home of the Miami Heat basketball team since 2000. The Waterfront Theater, Florida's largest, is housed inside; throughout the year it hosts concerts, Broadway performances and the like. A giant airplane is painted on top of the arena; you may spot it (it looks like the shadow of a plane from afar) when you fly out of the city, or if you're Superman.

## HistoryMiami
MUSEUM

(Map p62; www.historymiami.org; 101 W Flagler St; adult/child $8/5; ⊙10am-5pm Tue-Fri, from noon Sat & Sun) South Florida – a land of escaped slaves, guerilla Native Americans, gangsters, land grabbers, pirates, tourists, drug dealers and alligators – has a special history, and it takes a special kind of museum to capture that narrative. This place, located in the Miami-Dade Cultural Center, does just that, weaving together the stories of the region's successive waves of population, from Native Americans to Nicaraguans. Get off the Metromover at the Government Center stop.

## Brickell Avenue Bridge & Brickell Key
ISLAND

(Map p62) Crossing the Miami River, the lovely Brickell Avenue Bridge between SE 4th St and SE 5th St was made wider and higher several years ago, which was convenient for the speedboat-driving drug runners being chased by Drug Enforcement Administration agents on the day of the bridge's grand reopening! Note the 17ft bronze statue by Cuban-born sculptor Manuel Carbonell of a Tequesta warrior and his family, which sits atop the towering Pillar of History column. Walking here is the best way to get a sense of the sculptures and will allow you to avoid one of the most confusing traffic patterns in Miami. Brickell Key looks more like a floating porcupine, with glass towers for quills, than an island. To live the life of Miami glitterati, come here, pretend you belong, and head into a patrician hangout like the Mandarin Oriental Miami

---

### DOWNTOWN'S INTERNATIONAL BAZAARS

Downtown Miami has a reputation for being a bit rough around the edges. We think this is a bit undeserved; the area is dodgy at night but safe by day, if a little down-at-heel. Part of this ratty atmosphere is due to large amounts of cheap, knock-off electronics, fashion and jewelry shops that cluster in half-abandoned malls and shopping arcades. These stores are almost all run by immigrants, from West Africa, East Asia, South America and the Middle East (did we cover all the directions?). While we doubt you need cheap consumer goods of dubious origin, we do think it's fun to check out one of these markets, like the 777 International Mall (Map p62; 145 E Flagler St). This may be as close as you'll get to the messy, shouting, sweaty and exciting bazaars of the developing world, where folks yell at you to seal a deal and haggling is often an option. It's not as pretty as shopping in Miami Beach or the Design District, but it's a fascinating slice of this city's life.

hotel, where the lobby and intimate lounges afford sweeping views of Biscayne Bay.

### Pérez Art Museum Miami                    MUSEUM
(PAMM; Map p62; ☑ 305-375-3000; www.pamm. org; 1103 Biscayne Blvd; $12/8 adult/senior & student; ⊙10am-6pm Tue, Wed & Fri-Sun, to 9pm Thu) The Pérez can claim fine rotating exhibits that concentrate on post-WWII international art, but just as impressive are its location and exterior. This art institution inaugurated Museum Park, a patch of land that overseas the broad blue swath of Biscyane Bay. Swiss architects Herzog & de Meuron designed the structure, which integrates tropical foliage, glass and metal – a melding of tropical vitality and fresh modernism that is a nice architectural analogy for Miami itself.

### Gusman Center for
### the Performing Arts                       BUILDING
(Map p62; ☑ 305-374-2444; www.gusmancenter. org; 174 E Flagler St) Miami loves modern, but the Olympia Theater at the Gusman Center for the Performing Arts is vintage-classic beautiful. The ceiling, which features 246 twinkling stars and clouds cast over an indigo-deep night, frosted with classical Greek sculpture and Vienna Opera House–style embellishment, will melt your heart. The theater opened in 1925; today the lobby serves as the Downtown Miami Welcome Center, doling out visitor information and organizing tours of the historic district; at night you can still catch theater and music performances.

### MDC Museum of Art & Design      MUSEUM
(Freedom Tower; Map p62; ☑ 305-237-7700; www. mdcmoad.org; 600 Biscayne Blvd; free; ⊙noon-5pm Wed-Sun) Miami-Dade College operates a small but well-curated art museum downtown; the permanent collection includes works by Matisse, Picasso and Chagall and focuses on minimalism, pop art and contemporary Latin American art. The museum's home building is art itself: the Freedom Tower, an iconic slice of Miami's old skyline, is one of two surviving towers modeled after the Giralda bell tower in Spain's Cathedral of Seville. The 'Ellis Island of the South,' it served as an immigration processing center for almost half a million Cuban refugees in the 1960s. Placed on the National Register of Historic Places in 1979, it was also home to the *Miami Daily News* for 32 years.

### Miami Center for
### Architecture & Design                     MUSEUM
(Old US Post Office; Map p62; ☑ 305-448-7488; www.miamicad.org; 100 NE 1st Ave; ⊙10am-5pm Mon-Fri) It makes sense that the Miami branch of the American Institute of Architects would pick the Old US Post Office as headquarters of its Center for Architecture & Design. Constructed in 1912, this was the first federal building in Miami. It features a low-pitched roof, elaborate doors and carved entryways, and was purchased in 1937 to serve as the country's first savings and loan. Today, it houses lectures and events related to architecture, design and urban planning, and hosts a small but vibrant exhibition on all of the above subjects.

### Black Archives Historic Lyric
### Theater Welcome Center          HISTORIC BUILDING
(Lyric Theater; Map p62; ☑ 305-636-2390; www. theblackarchives.org; 819 NW 2nd Ave) Duke Ellington and Ella Fitzgerald once walked across the stage of the Lyric, a major stop on the 'Chitlin' Circuit' – the black live-entertainment trail of preintegration USA. As years passed both the theater and the neighborhood it served, Overtown, fell into disuse. Then the Black Archives History & Research Foundation of South Florida took over the building. Today the theater hosts occasional shows, while the Archives serves as an information center for those interested in Miami's African American heritage.

### Cisneros Fontanal Arts Foundation  MUSEUM
(CIFO; Map p62; ☑ 305-455-3380; www.cifo.org; 1018 N Miami Ave; ⊙10am-4pm Thu-Sun) This arts foundation displays the work of contemporary Latin American artists, and has an impressive showroom to boot. Even the exterior blends postindustrial rawness with a lurking, natural ambience, offset by the extensive use of Bisazza tiles to create an overarching tropical motif. The opening hours only apply during exhibition showings, although informal tours can be arranged if you call ahead.

### Miami-Dade Public Library          LIBRARY
(Map p62; www.mdpls.org; 101 W Flagler St; ⊙9am-6pm Mon-Wed & Fri, 9am-9pm Thu, 1-5pm Sun) To learn more about Florida (especially South Florida), take a browse through the extensive Florida Dept, or ask to see the Romer Collection, an archive of some 17,500 photos and prints that chronicles the history of the city from its early years to the 1950s.

**Miami River**                                     RIVER

(Map p62) For a taste of a seedy Old Florida, come to the lazy, sultry and still kinda spicy Miami River. Much of the shore is lined with makeshift warehouses, where you-can-only-imagine-what is loaded and unloaded onto small tugboats bound for you-can-only-imagine-where. Fisherfolk float in with their daily catch, fancy yachts 'slumming it' dock at restaurants and all in all, it just seems like a matter of time before the music from *Buena Vista Social Club* starts drifting over the scene.

**Dade County Courthouse**     HISTORIC BUILDING

(Map p62; 73 W Flagler St) If you end up on trial here, at least you'll get a free tour of one of the most imposing courthouses in the USA. Built between 1925 and 1929, this a very... appropriate building: if structures were people, the courthouse would definitely be a judge. Some trivia: back in the day, the top nine floors served as a 'secure' prison, from which more than 70 prisoners escaped.

## ◉ Wynwood, Design District & Little Haiti

Now rebranded as 'Midtown', Wynwood and the Design District are Miami's official arts neighborhoods, plus the focal points of much of the new art, food and nightlife in Greater Miami. This area still abuts some of the city's poorer 'hoods, and if you come here via city streets instead of the highway you'll see the rough edges that once characterized the vicinity. The Midtown mall is the area's natural center of gravity. Wynwood is the place for dedicated art galleries, while the small collection of posh retail outlets in the Design District are filled with things as beautiful as any canvas. Between the Italian-designed chairs, Russian Romanov-era cabinets and Dale Chihuly–esque chandeliers, the Design District tends to be expensive (we're talking thousands for a single item), although there are some relative bargains to be found if you look.

MIAMI SIGHTS

### FINDING ART IN WYNWOOD

At the time of writing, there are over 60 art galleries in Wynwood, with new spaces opening on what sometimes feels like a weekly basis. The stomping grounds of 'Wypsters' (Wynwood hipsters, those who enjoy, staff and provide content for the neighborhood's galleries) shift month by month as 'guerilla' galleries, new murals, graffiti, cafes, restaurants and studio spaces spread across Midtown. In general, art galleries can be found in a square bound by NW 20th and NW 37th Sts to the south and north, and N Miami Ave and NW 3rd Ave to the east and west. It's difficult for us to recommend one specific set of galleries given the diversity of what's on offer, but the following are some of our favorites.

**Artopia** (Map p68; ☑ 305-374-8882; www.artopiamiami.com; 1753 NE 2nd Ave; ⊙ call for hours) Proves the extents for Wynwood we mention above are flexible – Artopia is physically in Overtown, but culturally part of the gallery circuit. This was the old studio space of the late, renowned self-taught artist Purvis Young, who grew up near the studio. His folk-arty works and similar pieces are often displayed, as are pieces by up-and-coming artists, local or otherwise.

**PanAmerican Art Projects** (Map p68; ☑ 305-573-2400; www.panamericanart.com; 2450 NW 2nd Ave; ⊙ 9:30am-5:30pm Tue-Fri, noon-5:30pm Sat) Despite the name, PanAmerican also showcases work from European and Chinese artists. But much of what is on display comes from fine artists representing Latin America, the Caribbean and the USA.

**Brisky Gallery** (Map p68; ☑ 786-409-3585; www.briskygallery.com; 130 NW 24th St; ⊙ call for hours) Coming to Miami by way of its original location in Germany, Brisky boasts an enormous 4500-sq-ft warehouse that houses a museum's worth of local and international art. Need more creativity? Head outside to a 5000-sq-ft back lot filled with murals, curated graffiti, art installations and sculpture.

There are literally dozens of other galleries to check out; a nice way of seeing them and getting in some free wine and cheese is attending the famous **Wynwood Art Walks**, or if you're around at the right time, the Art Wynwood (p88) festival. Check out websites such as www.beachedmiami.com, wynwoodartwalk.com and www.miamiartguide.com for more information.

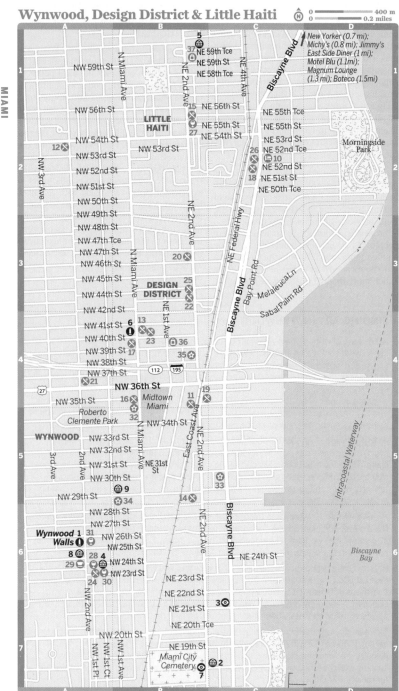

# Wynwood, Design District & Little Haiti

◎ **Top Sights**
1 Wynwood Walls........................................A6

◎ **Sights**
2 Artopia....................................................C7
3 Bacardi Building....................................C7
4 Brisky Gallery ......................................A6
5 Little Haiti Cultural Center....................B1
6 Living Room...........................................B4
7 Miami City Cemetery ...........................B7
8 PanAmerican Art Projects.....................A6
9 Rubell Family Art Collection.................B5

⊜ **Sleeping**
10 Motel Bianco.........................................C2

⊗ **Eating**
11 Cheese Course.......................................B4
12 Chef Creole ...........................................A2
13 Egg & Dart.............................................B4
14 Enriqueta's.............................................B5
15 Fiorito ....................................................B1
16 Gigi.........................................................B4
17 Harry's Pizzeria .....................................B4
18 Honey Tree ............................................C2
19 La Latina.................................................B4

20 Lemoni Café...........................................B3
21 Lost & Found Saloon..............................A4
22 Mandolin................................................B3
23 Oak Tavern.............................................B4
24 The Butcher Shop..................................A6
25 The Embassy..........................................B3
26 The Federal............................................C2

◎ **Drinking & Nightlife**
27 Churchill's..............................................B2
28 Gramps...................................................A6
29 Panther Coffee.......................................A6
30 The Social Lubricant..............................A6
31 Wood Tavern..........................................A6

◎ **Entertainment**
32 Bardot....................................................B5
33 Miami Light Project...............................C5
34 O Cinema...............................................B5
35 The Stage ..............................................B4

⊟ **Shopping**
36 Genius Jones..........................................B4
GO! Shop .........................................(see 1)
37 Libreri Mapou........................................B1
Sweat Records..............................(see 27)

Unlike Wynwood, the Design District is pretty compact and walkable. Little Haiti is not to be missed and sits above the Design District. In between the two lies the leafy, lovely residential neighborhood of Buena Vista, where restaurants, bars, gay hot spots and gentrification are rapidly spreading.

★**Wynwood Walls** PUBLIC ART
(Map p68; www.thewynwoodwalls.com; NW 2nd Ave, btwn 25th & 26th Sts; ⊙noon-8pm Wed-Sat) In the midst of rusted warehouses and concrete blah, there's a pastel-and-graffiti explosion of urban art. Wynwood Walls is a collection of murals and paintings laid out over an open courtyard that invariably bowls people over with its sheer color profile and unexpected location. What's on offer tends to change with the coming and going of major arts events such as Art Basel, but it's always interesting stuff.

**Little Haiti Cultural Center** GALLERY
(Map p68; ☎305-960-2969; www.miamigov.com/LHCulturalcenter; 212 NE 59th Tce; ⊙9am-5pm) Miami has the largest community of Ayisyens (Haitians) in the world outside Haiti, and this is the place to learn about their story. The cultural center is a study in playful island designs and motifs that houses a small but vibrant art gallery, crafts center

and activities space – dance classes, drama productions and similar events are held here year-round. The best time to visit is for the **Big Night in Little Haiti** (www.rhythmfoundation.com/series/big-night-in-little-haiti), a street party held on the third Friday of every month from 6pm to 10pm. The celebration is rife with music, mouth-watering Caribbean food and beer, and is one of the safest, easiest ways of accessing the culture of Haiti outside of that island.

**Rubell Family Art Collection** MUSEUM
(Map p68; ☎305-573-6090; www.rfc.museum; 95 NW 29th St; adult/student & under 18yr $10/5; ⊙10am-6pm Tue-Sat Dec-Aug) The Rubell family – specifically, the niece and nephew of the late Steve, better known as Ian Schrager's Studio 54 partner – operates some top-end hotels in Miami Beach, but they've also amassed an impressive contemporary-art collection that spans the last 30 years. The most admirable quality of this collection is its commitment to not just displaying one or two of its artists' pieces; the museum's aim is to showcase a contributor's entire career.

**Miami City Cemetery** CEMETERY
(Map p68; 1800 NE 2nd Ave; ⊙7am-3:30pm Mon-Fri, 8am-4:30pm Sat & Sun) This quiet graveyard, the final resting place of some of

## LITTLE HAITI

If you haven't been to Port-au-Prince, then Little Haiti (La Petite Haïti), one of the most evocative neighborhoods in Miami, is the next best thing. Young men in tank tops listen to Francophone rap, while broad-necked women wearing bright wraps gossip in front of the *botanicas* – which, by the way, are not selling plants. A *botanica* here is a *vodou* shop. The neighborhood is one of Miami's poorest and it's not advisable to walk around here alone after dark, but by day or if visiting the Little Haiti Cultural Center you'll be fine.

*Botanicas* are perhaps the most 'foreign' sight in Little Haiti. Storefronts promise to help in matters of love, work and sometimes 'immigration services,' but trust us, there are no marriage counselors or Immigration & Naturalization agents in here. As you enter you'll probably get a funny look, but be courteous, curious and respectful and you should be welcomed. Before you browse, forget stereotypes about pins and dolls. Like many traditional religions, *vodou* recognizes supernatural forces in everyday objects, and powers that are both distinct from and part of one overarching deity. Ergo, you'll see shrines to Jesus next to altars to traditional *vodou* deities. Notice the large statues of what look like people; these actually represent *loa* (pronounced lwa), intermediary spirits that form a pantheon below God in the *vodou* religious hierarchy. Drop a coin into a *loa* offering bowl before you leave, especially to Papa Legba, spirit of crossroads and, by our reckoning, travelers.

For a more cerebral taste of Haitian culture, peruse the shelves at **Libreri Mapou** (Map p68; www.librerimapou.com; 5919 NE 2nd Ave), bursting with thousands of titles (including periodicals) in English, French and Creole, as well as crafts and recorded music.

Miami-Dade's most important citizens, is a sort of narrative of the history of the city cast in bone, dirt and stone. The dichotomy of the past and modernity gets a nice visual representation in the form of looming condos shadowing the last abode of the Magic City's late, great ones. More than 9000 graves are divided into separate white, black and Jewish sections. Buried here are mayors, veterans (including about 90 Confederate soldiers) and the godmother of South Florida, Julia Tuttle, who purchased the first orange groves that attracted settlers to the area.

**Living Room**  PUBLIC ART
(Map p68; cnr NW 40th St & N Miami Ave) Just to remind you that you're entering the Design District is a big, honking public-art installation of, yep, a living room – just the sort of thing you're supposed to shop for while you're here. Actually this Living Room, by Argentine husband-and-wife team Roberto Behar and Rosario Marquardt, is an 'urban intervention' meant to be a criticism of the disappearance of public space, but we think it serves as a nice metaphor for the Design District as a whole: a contemporary interior plopped into the middle of urban decay.

**Bacardi Building**  ARCHITECTURE
(Map p68; 2100 Biscayne Blvd; ⊙9am-3:30pm or 4pm Mon-Fri) FREE You don't need to down 151 to appreciate the former Miami head-

quarters of the world's largest family-owned spirits company, Bacardi. The main event is a beautifully decorated tower that looks like the mosaic pattern of a tropical bathhouse multiplied by infinity.

## ◉ Key Biscayne

The scenic drive along the Rickenbacker Causeway leads first to small Virginia Key, then over to Key Biscayne, an island that's just 7 miles long with unrivaled views of the Miami skyline. As you drive over the causeway, note the small public beaches, picnic areas and fishing spots arranged on its margins. The road turns into Crandon Blvd, the key's only real main road, which runs to the Cape Florida Lighthouse at the island's southernmost tip.

**Crandon Park**  PARK
(Map p72; ☑305-361-5421; www.miamidade.gov/parks/parks/crandon_beach.asp; 6747 Crandon Blvd; per car $5; ⊙sunrise-sunset; P⊞☎) ✎ This 1200-acre park boasts Crandon Park Beach, a glorious but crowded beach that stretches for 3 miles. Much of the park consists of a dense coastal hammock (hardwood forest) and mangrove swamps. Pretty cabanas at the south end of the park can be rented by the day ($37.45). The 2-mile-long beach here is clean, uncluttered with tourists, faces a lovely sweep of teal goodness and is regularly named one of the best beaches in the USA.

**Miami Seaquarium** AQUARIUM
(Map p72; ☑ 305-361-5705; www.miamiseaquarium.com; 4400 Rickenbacker Causeway; adult/child $40/30; ⊙ 9:30am-6pm, last entry 4:30pm; P ⧉ ) The Seaquarium was one of the country's first facilities dedicated to marine life, and its mission remains one of protecting aquatic creatures and educating the public about its charges. There are dozens of shows and exhibits, including a tropical reef; the Shark Channel, with feeding presentations; and Discovery Bay, a natural mangrove habitat that serves as a refuge for rehabilitating rescued sea turtles. Check out the Pacific white-sided dolphins or West Indian manatees being nursed back to health; some are released into the wild.

With that said, the big attraction at the Seaquarium is also its most controversial: dolphin and whale shows, including swim-with-the-dolphin programs. While the Seaquarium says it is are protecting cetaceans (sea mammals) and educating the public about them, animal-welfare organizations claim any form of captivity and human interaction is debilitating to dolphins and whales. If you decide you want to swim with dolphins, note that people under 5ft 2in cannot participate and children under three cannot enter the observation area. Last entry is at 4:30pm.

**Marjory Stoneman Douglas Biscayne Nature Center** MUSEUM
(Map p72; ☑ 305-261-6767; www.biscaynenaturecenter.org; Crandon Park, 6767 Crandon Blvd; ⊙ 10am-4pm; P ⧉ ) ✦ FREE Marjory Stoneman Douglas was a beloved environmental crusader and worthy namesake of this child-friendly nature center. The structure is a perfect introduction and exploration of the continental USA's own subtropical ecosystem: South Florida. There are weekend hikes and nature lessons that let kids wade into the water in search of marine wildlife; check the website for a full breakdown of the many activities on offer, most of which cost $12 per person.

**Bill Baggs Cape Florida State Park** PARK
(Map p72; ☑ 305-361-5811; www.floridastateparks.org/capeflorida; 1200 S Crandon Blvd; per car/person $8/2; ⊙ 8am-sunset; P ⧉ ✿ ) ✦ If you don't make it to the Florida Keys, come to this park for a taste of their unique island ecosystems. The 494-acre space is a tangled clot of tropical fauna and dark mangroves – look for the 'snorkel' roots that provide air for half-submerged mangrove trees – all interconnected by sandy trails and wooden boardwalks, and surrounded by miles of pale ocean. A concession shack rents kayaks, bikes, in-line skates, beach chairs and umbrellas.

At the state recreation area's southernmost tip, the 1845 brick **Cape Florida Lighthouse** is the oldest structure in Florida (it replaced another lighthouse that was severely damaged in 1836 during the Second Seminole War). Free tours run at 10am and 1pm Monday to Thursday.

**Biscayne Community Center & Village Green Park** PARK
(Map p72; ☑ 305-365-8900; www.keybiscayne.fl.gov/pr; Village Green Way, off Crandon Blvd; ⊙ community center 6am-10pm Mon-Fri, 8am-8pm Sat & Sun; ⧉ ✿ ) ✦ FREE An unmissable park for

## STILTSVILLE

Head to the southern shore of Bill Baggs Cape Florida State Park and you'll see, way out in the distance, a collection of seven houses that stands on pilings in Biscayne Bay. The buildings, known as Stiltsville, have been around since the early 1930s, ever since 'Crawfish Eddie Walker' built a shack on the waves. More buildings were added over the years, and the 'village' was, at times, a gambling den, smuggling haven and, during the 1960s, a bikini club where women drank for free if they wore a two piece, and anything could famously go.

At its peak in 1960, there were 27 'homes' in Stiltsville, but as one mght guess, hurricanes and erosions took their toll. No one lives in Stiltsville today, but it is possible to take a **boat tour** (☑ 305-379-5119; www.islandqueencruises.com/stiltsville.htm; tours $49) out here with the illustrious historian Dr Paul George.

In 2003 the nonprofit Stiltsville Trust was set up by the National Parks Service to rehabilitate the buildings into as-yet-unknown facilities; proposals include a National Parks Service visitor center, artist-in-residence colony or community center. Not much work seems to have progressed toward this idea, but if you'd like more information, check out www.stiltsvilletrust.org.

# Key Biscayne

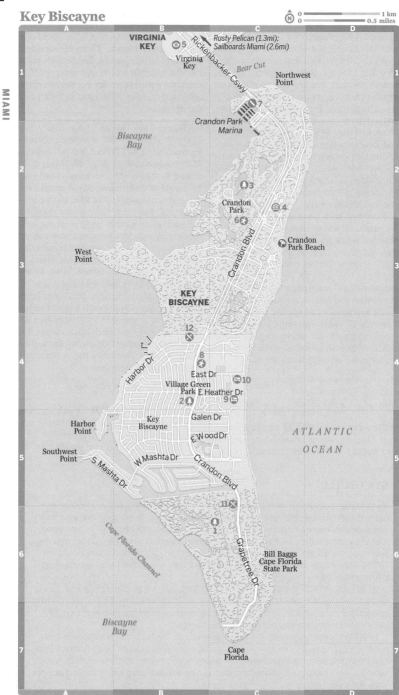

N
0 —————— 1 km
0 —————— 0.5 miles

VIRGINIA
KEY

⊙5

Virginia
Key

Rickenbacker Cswy

Bear Cut

Rusty Pelican (1.3mi);
Sailboards Miami (2.6mi)

Northwest
Point

⊙7

Crandon Park
Marina

Biscayne
Bay

3

Crandon
Park

4

6

West
Point

Crandon
Park Beach

Crandon Blvd

KEY
BISCAYNE

12

8

Harbor Dr

East Dr

10

Village Green
Park E Heather Dr

2

9

Harbor
Point

Key
Biscayne

Galen Dr

ATLANTIC

Southwest
Point

E Wood Dr

OCEAN

S. Mashta Dr

W Mashta Dr

Crandon Blvd

11

Cape Florida Channel

1

Grapetree Dr

Bill Baggs
Cape Florida
State Park

Biscayne
Bay

Cape
Florida

## Key Biscayne

**◎ Sights**
1 Bill Baggs Cape Florida State
   Park.....................................................C6
2 Biscayne Community Center &
   Village Green Park ............................B4
3 Crandon Park .......................................C2
4 Marjory Stoneman Douglas
   Biscayne Nature Center ..................C2
5 Miami Seaquarium ..............................B1

**◔ Activities, Courses & Tours**
6 Crandon Golf Course...........................C3
7 Divers Paradise ....................................C1
8 Mangrove Cycles .................................B4

**◉ Sleeping**
9 Ritz-Carlton Key Biscayne.................C4
10 Silver Sands Beach Resort................C4

**◉ Eating**
11 Boater's Grill..........................................C5
12 Oasis........................................................B4

kids: there's a swimming pool, jungle gyms, an activity room with a play set out of a child's happiest fantasies and an African baobab tree that's over a century old and teeming with tropical birdlife. Did we mention it's free?

## ◉ Little Havana

Little Havana's main thoroughfare, Calle Ocho (SW 8th St), doesn't just cut through the heart of the neighborhood; it *is* the heart of the neighborhood. In a lot of ways, this is every immigrant enclave in the USA – full of restaurants, mom-and-pop convenience shops and phonecard kiosks. Admittedly, the Cubaness of Little Havana is slightly exaggerated for visitors, and many of the Latin immigrants here are actually from Central America. With that said, this is an atmospheric place with a soul that's rooted outside the USA. Be on the lookout for the **Cuban Walk of Fame**, a series of sidewalk-implanted stars emblazoned with the names of Cuban celebrities that runs up and down much of 8th St.

The biggest event in the neighborhood's yearly calendar is the Carnaval Miami (Calle Ocho Festival, p88), a street party that showcases Miami's Latin culture over 10 frenetic days.

★**Máximo Gómez Park**    PARK
(Map p74; SW 8th St at SW 15th Ave; ⊘9am-6pm) Little Havana's most evocative reminder of Old Cuba is Máximo Gómez Park, or 'Domino Park,' where the sound of elderly men

trash-talking over games of chess is harmonized by the quick clack-clack of slapping dominoes. The jarring backtrack, plus the heavy smell of cigars and a sunrise-bright mural of the 1993 Summit of the Americas, combine to make Máximo Gómez one of the most sensory sites in Miami (although it is admittedly one of the most tourist-heavy ones as well).

**Cuban Memorials**    MONUMENT
(Map p74) The two blocks of SW 13th Ave south of Calle Ocho contain a series of monuments to Cuban and Cuban American heroes, including those that died in the Cuban War of Independence and anti-Castro conflicts. The memorials include the **Eternal Torch in Honor of the 2506th Brigade**, for the exiles who died during the Bay of Pigs Invasion; a huge **Cuba brass relief** depicting a map of Cuba, dedicated to the 'ideals of people who will never forget the pledge of making their Fatherland free'; a **José Martí memorial**; and a **Madonna statue**, which is supposedly illuminated by a shaft of holy light every afternoon. Bursting out of the island in the center of the boulevard is a massive ceiba tree, revered by followers of Santeria. The tree is an unofficial reminder of the poorer *Marielitos* (those who fled Cuba in the 1980 Mariel Boatlift) and successive waves of desperate-for-work Cubans, many of whom are *santeros* (Santeria practitioners) who have come to Miami since the 1980s.

Just away from the main drag are a fountain and monument, collectively entitled **La Plaza de la Cubanidad** (cnr W Flagler St & NW 17th Ave), which is a tribute both to the Cuban provinces and to migrants who drowned in 1994 while trying to leave Cuba on a ship, *13 de Marzo*, which was sunk by Castro's forces just off the coast.

**Cuba Ocho**    GALLERY
(Map p74; ✆305-285-5880; www.cubaocho.com; 1465 SW 8th St; ⊘11:30am-3am Tue-Sat) The jewel of the Little Havana Art District, Cuba Ocho functions as a community center, art gallery and research outpost for all things Cuban. The interior resembles a cool old Havana cigar bar, yet the walls are decked out in artwork that references both the classical past of Cuban art and its avant-garde future. Frequent live music, films, drama performances, readings and other events go off every week. The center opens during the evening for these events; check online for more information.

# Little Havana

## Little Havana

◎ **Top Sights**
1 Máximo Gómez Park ........................... D2

◎ **Sights**
2 Bay of Pigs Museum & Library ........... C2
3 Cuba Ocho ......................................... D1
4 Cuban Memorials ............................... E2
5 Little Havana Art District .................... D1
6 Tower Theater .................................... D2

✕ **Eating**
7 El Cristo ............................................. D1
8 El Rey de Las Fritas ........................... C1
9 Exquisito Restaurant .......................... D2
10 Los Pinareños Frutería ...................... E2

◎ **Drinking & Nightlife**
11 Casa Panza Bar .................................. D2

✿ **Entertainment**
12 Hoy Como Ayer ................................... A2
13 Tower Theater .................................... D2

▣ **Shopping**
14 El Crédito Cigars ................................ F1
15 M&N Variedades ................................. C1
16 Pepe Y Berta ..................................... E1

**Little Havana Art District**                    GALLERY
(Map p74; Calle Ocho, btwn SW 15th & 17th Aves)
OK, it's not Wynwood. In fact, it's more 'Art
Block' than district. But this little strip of
galleries and studios does house one of the
best concentrations of Latin American art
(particularly from Cuba) in Miami. Any one
of the studios is worth a stop and a browse.
This particular stretch of Little Havana
is the epicenter of the Viernes Culturales
(p117) celebration.

**Bay of Pigs Museum & Library**            LIBRARY
(Map p74; www.bayofpigsmuseum.org; 1821 SW
9th St; ◎9am-4pm Mon-Sat) This small museum is more of a memorial to the 2506th
Brigade, otherwise known as the crew of the
ill-fated Bay of Pigs invasion. Whatever your
thoughts on Fidel Castro and Cuban Americans, pay a visit here to flesh out one side
of this contentious story. You'll likely chat
with survivors of the Bay of Pigs, who like
to hang out here surrounded by pictures of
comrades who never made it back to the
USA.

**Tower Theater**                        HISTORIC BUILDING
(Map p74; ☏305-643-8706; www.towertheater-
miami.com; 1508 SW 8th St) This renovated
1926 landmark theater has a proud deco
facade and a newly done interior, thanks to
support from the Miami-Dade Community
College. In its heyday it was the center of
Little Havana social life, and via the films
it showed served as a bridge between immigrant society and American pop culture.
Today the space frequently shows independent and Spanish-language films (sometimes both) and hosts varied art exhibitions
in the lobby.

## ◎ Coconut Grove

Coconut Grove was once a hippie colony, but
these days its demographic is middle-class,
mall-going Miami and college students. It's
a pleasant place, especially in the evenings,
bursting with shops and restaurants. 'The
Grove' unfolds along S Bayshore Dr as it
hugs the shoreline; US Hwy 1 (S Dixie Hwy)
acts as the northern boundary.

Hwy, on the other side of the road, there's a small Buddhist temple shaded by large groves of banyan trees.

## Miami Museum of
### Science & Planetarium
MUSEUM

(☑305-646-4200; www.miamisci.org; 3280 S Miami Ave; adult/child, student & senior $15/11; ☺10am-6pm; P🖟) The Miami Museum of Science is a dedicated if small institution with exhibits ranging from weather phenomena to creepy crawlies, coral reefs and vital-microbe displays. The planetarium hosts space lessons and telescope-viewing sessions, as well as old-school laser shows with trippy flashes set to the music of the Beatles and Pink Floyd. A new facility is being built next to the Pérez Art Museum Miami (p66) in downtown's Museum Park.

## Kampong
HISTORIC SITE, GARDENS

(☑305-442-7169; www.ntbg.org/gardens/kampong.php; 4013 Douglas Rd; ☺tours by appointment only 9am-4pm Mon-Fri) David Fairchild, Indiana Jones of the botanical world and founder of Fairchild Tropical Gardens, would rest at the Kampong (Malay/Indonesian for 'village') in between journeys in search of beautiful and economically viable plant life. Today this lush garden is listed on the National Register of Historic Places and the lovely grounds serve as a classroom for the National Tropical Botanical Garden. Free self-guided tours

## ★Vizcaya Museum
### & Gardens
HISTORIC BUILDING

(☑305-250-9133; www.vizcayamuseum.org; 3251 S Miami Ave; adult/6-12yr/student & senior $18/6/10; ☺9:30am-4:30pm Wed-Mon; P) They call Miami the Magic City, and if it is, this Italian villa, the housing equivalent of a Fabergé egg, is its most fairy-tale residence. In 1916 industrialist James Deering started a long and storied Miami tradition by making a ton of money and building ridiculously grandiose digs. He employed 1000 people (then 10% of the local population) for four years to fulfill his desire for a home that looked centuries old. He was so obsessed with creating an atmosphere of old money that he had the house stuffed with 15th- to 19th-century furniture, tapestries, paintings and decorative arts; had a monogram fashioned for himself; and even had paintings of fake ancestors commissioned. The 30-acre grounds are full of splendid gardens and Florentine gazebos, and both the house and gardens are used for the display of rotating contemporary-art exhibitions.

## Barnacle Historic State Park
PARK

(Map p76; www.floridastateparks.org/thebarnacle; 3485 Main Hwy; admission $2, house tours $3; ☺park 9am-4pm Fri-Mon, house tours 10am, 11:30am, 1pm, 2:30pm Fri-Mon; 🖟) In the center of the village is the 1891, 5-acre pioneer residence of Ralph Monroe, Miami's first honorable snowbird. The house is open for guided tours, and the park it's located on is a lovely, shady oasis for strolling. Barnacle hosts frequent (and lovely) moonlight concerts, from jazz to classical. A little way down Main

# Coconut Grove

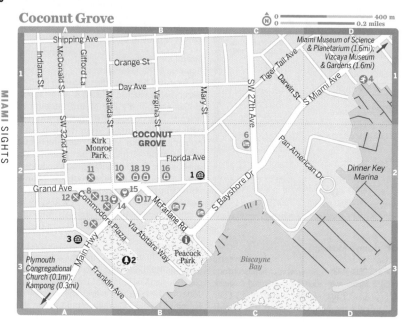

## Coconut Grove

### ⊙ Sights
**1** AC Fine Art.................................................B2
**2** Barnacle Historic State Park................B3
**3** Coconut Grove Playhouse....................A3

### ⊙ Activities, Courses & Tours
**4** Bayshore Landing Marina.....................D1

### 🛏 Sleeping
**5** Mutiny Hotel..............................................B2
**6** Ritz-Carlton Coconut Grove.................C2
**7** Sonesta Hotel & Suites Coconut
Grove.....................................................B2

### ⊗ Eating
**8** George's in the Grove............................A2

**9** Green Street Cafe...................................A3
**10** Jaguar......................................................B2
**11** Last Carrot..............................................A2
**12** LoKal........................................................A2
**13** Lulu...........................................................A2

### ⊙ Drinking & Nightlife
**14** Barracuda................................................B2
Taurus.........................................(see 3)
**15** Tavern in the Grove...............................B2

### ⊙ Shopping
**16** Bookstore in the Grove.........................B2
**17** Celestial Treasures ...............................B2
**18** CocoWalk.................................................B2
**19** Streets of Mayfair..................................B2

(allow at least an hour) are available by appointment, as are $20 two-hour guided tours.

**Coconut Grove Arts Precinct**   GALLERY
Coconut Grove, like many of Miami's neighborhoods, has been making a big deal of promoting its homegrown art galleries. You can walk among them – they're concentrated near **CocoWalk** and **Streets of Mayfair** malls (with a few exceptions) – on the first Saturday night (from 7pm) of every month;

the Coconut Grove Art Walk is decidedly the most family friendly of Miami's many neighborhood art walks.

**AC Fine Art**   GALLERY
(Map p76; ☎ 305-742-7071; www.acfineartsite.com; 2911 Grand Ave; ⊙10am-6pm) One our favorite galleries, AC Fine Art specializes in limited editions and originals (!) of masters like Dalí, Picasso, Lautrec, Warhol, Basquiat and Lichtenstein.

## EVA MUNROE'S GRAVE

Tucked into a small gated area near the Coconut Grove Library (2875 McFarlane Rd), you'll find the humble headstone of one Ms Eva Amelia Hewitt Munroe. Eva, who was born in New Jersey in 1856 and died in Miami in 1882, lies in the oldest American grave in Miami-Dade County (a sad addendum: local African American settlers died before Eva, but their deaths were never officially recorded). Eva's husband Ralph entered a deep depression, which he tried to alleviate by building the Barnacle (p75), now one of the oldest historic homes in the area.

**Plymouth Congregational Church** CHURCH
(www.plymouthmiami.com; 3400 Devon Rd; P) This 1917 coral church is striking, from its solid masonry to a hand-carved door from a Pyrenees monastery, which looks like it should be kicked in by Antonio Banderas carrying a guitar case full of explosives and Salma Hayek on his arm. Architecturally, this is one of the finest Spanish Mission–style churches in a city that does not lack for examples of the genre.

**Ermita de la Caridad** MONUMENT
(305-854-2404; www.ermitadelacaridad.org; 3609 S Miami Ave) The Catholic diocese purchased some of the bayfront land from Deering's Villa Vizcaya estate and built a shrine here for its displaced Cuban parishioners. Symbolizing a beacon, it faces the homeland, exactly 290 miles due south. There is also a mural that depicts Cuban history. After visiting Vizcaya or the science museum, consider picnicking at this quiet sanctuary on the water's edge.

## ⊙ Coral Gables

The lovely city of Coral Gables, filled with Mediterranean-style buildings, is bordered by Calle Ocho to the north, Sunset Dr to the south, Ponce de León Blvd to the east and Red Rd to the west. The main campus of the University of Miami is located just south of the enormous Biltmore Golf Course and the main pedestrian drag is Miracle Mile – heaven for the shopping obsessed.

**Venetian Pool** OUTDOORS
(Map p78; 305-460-5306; www.coralgablesvenetianpool.com; 2701 De Soto Blvd; adult/child $11.50/7.70; hours vary; ) Just imagine: it's 1923, tons of rock have been quarried for one of the most beautiful neighborhoods in Miami, but now an ugly gash sits in the middle of the village. What to do? How about pump the irregular hole full of water, mosaic and tile up the whole affair, and make it look like a Roman emperor's aquatic playground? Result: one of the few pools listed on the National Register of Historic Places, a wonderland of coral rock caves, cascading waterfalls, a palm-fringed island and Venetian-style moorings. Take a swim and follow in the footsteps (fin-steps?) of stars like Esther Williams and Johnny 'Tarzan' Weissmuller. Opening hours vary depending on the season; call or check the website for details.

**Biltmore Hotel** HISTORIC BUILDING
(Map p78; 855-311-6903; www.biltmorehotel.com; 1200 Anastasia Ave; P) In the most opulent neighborhood of one of the showiest cities in the world, the Biltmore peers down her nose and says, 'hrmph.' It's one of the greatest of the grand hotels of the American Jazz Age, and if this joint were a fictional character from a novel, it'd be, without question, Jay Gatsby. Al Capone had a speakeasy on-site, and the Capone Suite is still haunted by the spirit of Fats Walsh, who was murdered here (for more ghost details, join in the weekly storytelling in the lobby, 7pm Thursday). Back in the day, imported gondolas transported celebrity guests like Judy Garland and the Vanderbilts around because, of course, there was a private canal system out the back. It's gone now, but the largest hotel pool in the continental USA, which resembles a sultan's water garden from *One Thousand and One Nights,* is still here.

**Lowe Art Museum** MUSEUM
(www.lowemuseum.org; 1301 Stanford Dr; adult/student $10/5; 10am-4pm Tue-Sat, noon-4pm Sun) Your love of the Lowe, located on the campus of the University of Miami, depends on your taste in art. If you're into modern and contemporary works, it's good. If you're into the art and archaeology of cultures from Asia, Africa and the South Pacific, it's great. And if you're into pre-Columbian and Mesoamerican art, it's fantastic. That isn't to discount the lovely permanent collection of Renaissance and baroque art, Western sculpture from the 18th to 20th centuries, and paintings by Gauguin, Picasso and Monet.

# Coral Gables

**Merrick House**      HISTORIC BUILDING
(Map p78; 📞 305-460-5361; 907 Coral Way; adult/
child/senior $5/1/3; ⊘ tours 1pm, 2pm & 3pm Sun
& Wed) It's fun to imagine this simple homestead, with its little hints of Med style, as the
core of what would eventually become the
gaudy Gables. When George Merrick's father
purchased this plot, site unseen, for $1100, it
was all dirt, rock and guavas. The property is
now used for meetings and receptions, and
you can tour both the house and its pretty
organic garden. The modest family residence looks as it did in 1925, outfitted with
family photos, furniture and artwork.

**Entrances & Watertower**      LANDMARK
Coral Gables designer George Merrick
planned a series of elaborate entry gates to
the city, but the real-estate bust meant that
projects went unfinished. Among the completed gates worth seeing, which resemble
the entrance pavilions to grand Andalucian
estates, are the **Country Club Prado**; the

**Douglas Entrance**; the **Granada Entrance**
(Map p78; cnr Alhambra Circle & Granada Blvd);
the **Alhambra Entrance** (Map p78; cnr Alhambra Circle & Douglas Rd) and the **Coral Way Entrance** (Map p78; cnr Red Rd & Coral Way). The
**Alhambra Watertower** (Map p78; Alhambra
Circle), where Greenway Ct and Ferdinand St
meet Alhambra Circle, resembles a Moorish
lighthouse.

**Coral Gables City Hall**      HISTORIC BUILDING
(Map p78; 405 Biltmore Way) This grand building has housed boring city-commission
meetings since it opened in 1928. It's impressive from any angle, certainly befitting its
importance as a central government building. Check out Denman Fink's *Four Seasons*
ceiling painting in the tower, as well as his
framed, untitled painting of the underwater
world on the 2nd-floor landing. There's a
small farmers market on-site from 8am to
1pm, January to March.

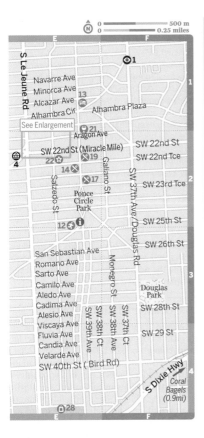

# Coral Gables

## Sights
| | |
|---|---|
| 1 Alhambra Entrance | F1 |
| 2 Alhambra Watertower | B1 |
| 3 Biltmore Hotel | C3 |
| 4 Coral Gables City Hall | E2 |
| 5 Coral Gables Congregational Church | C3 |
| 6 Coral Gables Museum | B3 |
| 7 Coral Way Entrance | A2 |
| 8 Granada Entrance | C1 |
| 9 Merrick House | C2 |
| 10 Venetian Pool | C2 |

## Activities, Courses & Tours
| | |
|---|---|
| 11 Biltmore Golf Course | B4 |
| 12 Prana Yoga Center | E2 |

## Sleeping
| | |
|---|---|
| Biltmore Hotel | (see 3) |
| 13 Hotel St Michel | E1 |

## Eating
| | |
|---|---|
| 14 Bulla | E2 |
| 15 Caffe Abbracci | A3 |
| La Palme d'Or | (see 3) |
| 16 Matsuri | A4 |
| 17 Pascal's on Ponce | E2 |
| 18 Seasons 52 | A3 |
| 19 Swine | E2 |

## Drinking & Nightlife
| | |
|---|---|
| 20 Seven Seas | A2 |
| 21 The Bar | E1 |

## Entertainment
| | |
|---|---|
| 22 Actors Playhouse | E2 |
| 23 Coral Gables Art Cinema | B3 |
| Gablestage | (see 3) |

## Shopping
| | |
|---|---|
| 24 Books and Books | B3 |
| 25 Boy Meets Girl | A3 |
| 26 Hip.e | B3 |
| 27 Olian | A3 |
| 28 Village of Merrick Park | E4 |

**Coral Gables**
**Congregational Church**            CHURCH
(Map p78; www.coralgablescongregational.org;
3010 De Soto Blvd) George Merrick's father was
a New England Congregational minister, so
perhaps that accounts for him donating the
land for the city's first church. Built in 1924
as a replica of a church in Costa Rica, the
yellow-walled, red-roofed exterior is as far
removed from New England as...well, Miami. The interior is graced with a beautiful
sanctuary and the grounds are landscaped
with stately palms.

**Coral Gables Museum**            MUSEUM
(Map p78; ☎ 305-603-8067; www.coralgablesmuseum.org; 285 Aragon Ave; adult/student/child
$7/5/3; ☺ noon-6pm Tue-Fri, 11am-5pm Sat, noon-
5pm Sun) This museum is a well-plotted introduction to the oddball narrative of the
founding and growth of the City Beautiful
(Coral Gables). The collection includes historical artifacts and mementos from suc-

ceeding generations in this tight-knit, eccentric little village. The main building is
the old Gables police and fire station, itself
a lovely architectural blend of Gables' Mediterranean revival and a more Miami Beach–
esque, muscular Depression-moderne style.

## Greater Miami – North
**Museum of Contemporary Art**
**North Miami**            MUSEUM
(MoCA; www.mocanomi.org; 770 NE 125th St; adult/
student & senior $5/3; ☺ 11am-5pm Tue-Sun; P )
The Museum of Contemporary Art has long

## HIBISCUS, PALM & STAR ISLANDS

Floating off the edge of the A1A, in the heart of Biscayne Bay (and posh exclusivity), Hibiscus Island, Palm Island and Star Island are little floating Primrose Hills. There aren't many famous people living here – just wealthy ones – although Star Island is home to Gloria Estefan and for a short time Al Capone lived (and died) on Palm Island. In the 1970s and '80s a mansion on Star Island was the headquarters of the Ethiopian Zion Coptic Church, a Rastafari sect eventually convicted of smuggling large amounts of marijuana into the US. That incident prompted a media circus that focused on both the indictments and neighborly disputes between the long-haired, bearded white Rastas and their aristocratic Star Island neighbors, who complained about the fog of cannabis smoke constantly emanating from the EZCC's compound.

Today the drives for the islands are guarded by a security booth, but the roads are public, so if you ask politely and don't look sketchy, you can get in. Star Island is little more than one elliptical road lined with royal palms, sculpted ficus hedges and fancy gates guarding houses you can't see.

been a reason to hike up to the far reaches of North Miami. Its galleries feature excellent rotating exhibitions of contemporary art by local, national and international artists.

**Ancient Spanish Monastery** CHURCH
(☎ 305-945-1461; www.spanishmonastery.com; 16711 W Dixie Hwy; adult/child $8/4; ⊙ 10am-4:30pm Mon-Sat, from 11am Sun; ℗) The Episcopal Church of St Bernard de Clairvaux is a stunning early-Gothic and Romanesque building. Constructed in 1141 in Segovia, Spain, it was converted to a granary 700 years later, and eventually bought by newspaper tycoon William Randolph Hearst. He had it dismantled and shipped to the USA in more than 10,000 crates, intending to reconstruct it at his sprawling California estate. But construction was never approved by the government, and the stones sat in boxes until 1954, when a group of Miami developers purchased the dismantled monastery from Hearst and reassembled it. Now it's a lovely, popular oasis (busy for weddings especially, so call before going) and allegedly the oldest building in the western hemisphere. Church services are held at 8am, 10:30am and noon on Sunday, and a healing service is held at 10am on Wednesday.

**Hialeah Park** PARK
(www.hialeahparkracing.com; 2200 E 4th Ave; ⊙ 9am-5pm Mon-Fri; ℗) Hialeah is more Havanan than Little Havana (more than 90% of the population speak Spanish as a first language), and the symbol and center of this working-class Cuban community is this grand former racetrack. Today a walk through the grounds is recommended, if only to gaze at the grand staircases and pastel-painted concourse, and imagine the

thunder of racing hooves. Look for the caps, boots and saddle carved into the window below the administration building, and the oft-photographed central fountain.

## ◎ Greater Miami – South

**Fairchild Tropical Garden** GARDENS
(www.fairchildgarden.org; 10901 Old Cutler Rd; adult/child/senior $25/12/18; ⊙ 7:30am-4:30pm; ℗ ✚) If you need to escape Miami's madness, consider a green day in the country's largest tropical botanical garden. A butterfly grove, jungle biospheres, and gentle vistas of marsh and keys habitats, plus frequent art installations from folks like Roy Lichtenstein, are all stunning. In addition to easy-to-follow, self-guided walking tours, a free 40-minute tram tours the entire park on the hour from 10am to 3pm. Located 5 miles south of Coral Gables.

**Deering Estate at Cutler** LANDMARK
(☎ 305-235-1668; www.deeringestate.org; 16701 SW 72nd Ave; adult/child under 14yr $12/7; ⊙ 10am-5pm; ℗ ✚) The Deering estate is sort of 'Vizcaya lite,' which makes sense as it was built by Charles, brother of James Deering (of Vizcaya fame). The 150-acre grounds are awash with tropical growth, an animal-fossil pit of bones dating back 50,000 years and the remains of Native Americans who lived here 2000 years ago. There's a free tour of the grounds included in admission, and the estate often hosts jazz evenings under the stars. Last tickets sold at 4pm.

**Zoo Miami** ZOO
(Miami Metrozoo; ☎ 305-251-0400; www.miamimetrozoo.com; 12400 SW 152nd St; adult/child

$16/12; ⊙9:30am-5:30pm, last entry 4pm; P⛔) Miami's tropical weather makes strolling around the Metrozoo almost feel like a day in the wild. Look for Asian and African elephants, rare and regal Bengal tigers prowling an evocative Hindu temple and a pair of Komodo dragons from Indonesia. For a quick overview (and because the zoo is so big), hop on the Safari Monorail; it departs every 20 minutes. There's a glut of grounds tours, and kids will love feeding the Samburu giraffes ($2). Last admission at 4pm.

**Jungle Island**                                ZOO
(⌨305-400-7000; www.jungleisland.com; 1111 Parrot Jungle Trail, off MacArthur Causeway; adult/senior/child $35/33/27; ⊙10am-5pm; P⛔) Jungle Island, packed with tropical birds, alligators, orangutans, chimps, lemurs, a (wait for it *Napoleon Dynamite* fans) liger (a cross between a lion and a tiger) and a Noah's Ark of other animals, is a ton of fun. It's one of those places kids (justifiably) beg to go, so just give up and prepare for some bright-feathered, bird-poopie-scented fun in this artificial, self-contained jungle.

**Monkey Jungle**                                ZOO
(⌨305-235-1611; www.monkeyjungle.com; 14805 SW 216th St; adult/child $30/24; ⊙9:30am-5pm, last entry 4pm; P⛔) The Monkey Jungle tag line is: 'Where humans are caged and monkeys run free.' Indeed, you'll be walking through screened-in trails, with primates swinging, screeching and chattering all around you. It's incredibly fun, and just a bit odorous. The big show of the day takes place at feeding time, when crab-eating monkeys and Southeast Asian macaques dive into the pool for fruit and other treats. There's a lovely aviary for clouds of beautiful rescued parrots.

**Pinecrest Gardens**                             PARK
(www.pinecrest-fl.gov/gardens; 11000 SW 57th Ave; adult/child $3/2; ⊙9am-5pm fall & winter, to 6pm spring & summer; P⛔) When Parrot Jungle (now Jungle Island) flew the coop for the big city, the village of Pinecrest purchased the property in order to keep it as a municipal park. It's now a quiet oasis with some of the best tropical gardens this side of the Gulf of Mexico, topped off by a gorgeous centerpiece banyan tree. Outdoor movies and jazz concerts are held here, and in all this is a total gem that is utterly off the tourism trail.

**Fruit & Spice Park**                            PARK
(⌨305-247-5727; www.fruitandspicepark.org; 24801 SW 187th Ave; adult/child/under 6 $8/2/free;

⊙9am-5pm; P) Set just on the edge of the Everglades, this 35-acre tropical public park grows all those great tropical fruits you usually have to contract dysentery to enjoy. The park is divided into 'continents' (Africa, Asia etc) and admission to the grounds includes a free tour; you can't pick the fruit, but you can eat anything that falls to the ground. If you're coming down this far, you may want to consider taking a day trip into Everglades National Park.

**Gold Coast Railroad Museum**            MUSEUM
(⌨305-253-0063; www.gcrm.org; 12450 SW 152nd St; adult/child 3-11yr $8/6; ⊙10am-4pm Mon-Fri, from 11am Sat & Sun; P) Primarily of interest to train buffs, this museum displays more than 30 antique railway cars, including the Ferdinand Magellan presidential car, where President Harry Truman famously brandished a newspaper with the erroneous headline 'Dewey Defeats Truman.' On weekends the museum offers 20-minute rides on old cabooses ($6), standard gauge cabs ($12) and, for kids, on a small 'link' train ($2.50). It's advised you call ahead to make an appointment to ride.

**Miami Children's Museum**            MUSEUM
(⌨305-373-5437; www.miamichildrensmuseum. org; 980 MacArthur Causeway; admission $16; ⊙10am-6pm; ⛔) This museum, located between South Beach and downtown Miami, isn't exactly a museum. It feels more like an uberplayhouse, with areas for kids to practice all sorts of adult activities – banking and food shopping, caring for pets, reporting scoops as a TV news anchor in a studio, and acting as a local cop or firefighter.

**Matheson Hammock Park**                 PARK
(www.miamidade.gov/parks/parks/matheson_ beach.asp; 9610 Old Cutler Rd; per car $5; ⊙sunrise-sunset; P⛔) This 100-acre county park is the city's oldest and one of its most scenic. It offers good swimming for children in an enclosed tidal pool, lots of hungry raccoons, dense mangrove swamps and (pretty rare) alligator-spotting.

**Wings Over Miami**                       MUSEUM
(⌨305-233-5197; www.wingsovermiami.com; Kendall-Tamiami Executive Airport, 14710 SW 128th St; adult/child under 12yr/senior $10/6/7; ⊙10am-5pm Wed-Sun) Plane-spotters will be delighted by this Kendall-Tamiami Executive Airport museum, which chronicles the history of aviation. Highlights include a propeller collection, J47 jet engine, a Soviet bomber from

Smolensk and the nose section of a B-29 called *Fertile Myrtle*, the same type of aircraft used to drop atomic bombs on Hiroshima and Nagasaki. An impressive exhibit on the Tuskegee Airmen features videos of the African American pilots telling their own stories.

# 🏃 Activities

Miami doesn't lack for ways to keep yourself busy. From sailing her teal waters to hiking through her tropical undergrowth, yoga in her parks and (why not?) trapeze artistry above her head, the Magic City rewards those who want an active holiday.

## Biking

**Miami-Dade County Parks & Recreation Dept**                    CYCLING
(Map p62; ☎ 305-755-7800; www.miamidade.gov/parksmasterplan/bike_trails_map.asp) 🖉 Leads frequent ecobike tours through parklands and along waterfront paths, and offers a list of traffic-free cycling paths on its website. For less strenuous rides, try the side roads of South Beach or the shady streets of Coral Gables and Coconut Grove. Some good trails include:

**Old Cutler Bike Path** Starts at the end of Sunset Dr in Coral Gables and leads through Coconut Grove to Matheson Hammock Park and Fairchild Tropical Garden.

**Rickenbacker Causeway** This route takes you up and over the bridge to Key Biscayne for an excellent workout combined with gorgeous water views.

**Oleta River State Park** (3400 NE 163rd St) Has a challenging dirt trail with hills for off-road adventures.

## Bowling

**Strike Miami**                    BOWLING
(☎ 305-594-0200; www.bowlmor.com/strike-miami; 11401 NW 12th St; ⊙ 4pm-midnight Tue-Thu, noon-3am Fri, 11am-3am Sat, 11am-midnight Sun, 4pm-1am Mon) In the Dolphin Mall, this is a good example of what happens when Miami's talent for glitz and glamor meets some humble 10-pins.

**Lucky Strike**                    BOWLING
(Map p52; ☎ 305-532-0307; www.bowlluckystrike.com; 1691 Michigan Ave; ⊙ 11:30am-1am Mon-Thu, to 2am Fri, 11am-2am Sat, 11am-1am Sun) Just off Lincoln Rd, this is Miami Beach's answer to high-end bowling, full of house and hip-hop music, electric-bright cocktails and beautiful club kids.

## Day Spas

As you may have guessed, Miami offers plenty of places to get pampered. Some of the most luxurious spas in town are found at high-end hotels, where you can expect to pay $300 to $400 for a massage and/or acupressure, and $200 for a body wrap. Notable spas are listed here.

**Spa at Mandarin Oriental Miami**                    SPA
(Map p62; ☎ 305-913-8332; www.mandarinoriental.com; 500 Brickell Key Dr, Mandarin Oriental Miami; manicures $75, spa treatments $150-400; ⊙ 8:30am-9:30pm) Calling this spa over the top is an understatement. Treatments utilize materials like bamboo and rice paper, and services include Ayurvedic herbal baths, aromatherapy, oiled massages and plenty more decadence.

---

## DOING THE DECOBIKE

Miami Beach is flat, warm, and covered in concrete. In other words, it's about perfect for cycling. Yet cycling infrastructure has been slow to develop on the beach, leading to traffic snarls, gridlock and the inevitable slow roll of a Hummer blasting electronic dance music at every stop light on Collins Ave.

Well no more (although the cars blasting dance music will probably be with us for a long time). **DecoBike** (305-532-9494; www.decobike.com) saves the day, sort of. This bike-sharing program, modeled after similar initiatives in New York, London and Paris, makes cycling from South Beach to Surfside a relative breeze. Just rock up to a solar-powered DecoBike station (a handy dandy map can be found at www.decobike.com/map-location), insert a credit card and ride away. You can return your bike at any Deco-Bike location.

Pricing varies; you'll pay $4 for 30 minutes, $6 for an hour, $10 for two hours, or $24 for a whole day's riding. If you keep your bicycle past the allotted time, you're charged $4 per half-hour. So get out there! Bike away! Get in shape so you don't feel self-conscious on South Beach while biking around South Beach. Winning all around.

# City Walk
# Art-Deco
# Miami Beach

**START** ART DECO WELCOME CENTER
**END** OCEAN'S TEN
**LENGTH** 1.2 MILES; TWO TO THREE HOURS

Start at the ① **Art Deco Welcome Center** (p122), at the corner of Ocean Dr and 10th St (named Barbara Capitman Way here after the founder of the Miami Design Preservation League). Step in for an exhibit on art-deco style, then head out and go north along Ocean Dr; between 12th St and 14th St you'll see three examples of deco hotels: the ② **Leslie**, a boxy shape with cantilevered sun shades wrapped around the side of the building; the ③ **Carlyle**, featured in the film *The Birdcage* and boasting modernistic styling; and the graceful ④ **Cardozo Hotel** (p95), built by Henry Hohauser, owned by Gloria Estefan and featuring sleek, rounded edges. At 14th St, peek inside the sun-drenched ⑤ **Winter Haven Hotel** (p96) to see its fabulous floors of terrazzo, made of stone chips set in mortar that is polished when dry. Turn left and head down 14th St to Washington Ave and the ⑥ **US Post Office** (p58), at 13th St. It's a curvy block of white deco in the stripped classic style. Step inside to admire the wall mural, domed ceiling and marble stamp tables. Stop for lunch at the ⑦ **11th St Diner** (p99), a gleaming aluminum Pullman car that was imported in 1992 from Wilkes-Barre, Pennsylvania. Get a window seat and gaze across the avenue to the corner of 10th St and the stunningly restored ⑧ **Hotel Astor** (p91), designed in 1936 by T Hunter Henderson. After your meal, walk half a block east from there to the imposing ⑨ **Wolfsonian-FIU** (p42), an excellent museum of design, formerly the Washington Storage Company. Wealthy snowbirds of the '30s stashed their pricey belongings here before heading back up north. Continue walking Washington Ave, turn left on 7th St and then continue north along Collins Ave to the ⑩ **Hotel** (p92), featuring an interior and roof deck by Todd Oldham. L Murray Dixon designed the hotel as the Tiffany Hotel, with a deco spire, in 1939. Turn right on 9th St and go two blocks to Ocean Dr and nonstop deco beauties; at 960 Ocean Dr (the middling ⑪ **Ocean's Ten** restaurant) you'll see an exterior designed in 1935 by deco legend Henry Hohauser.

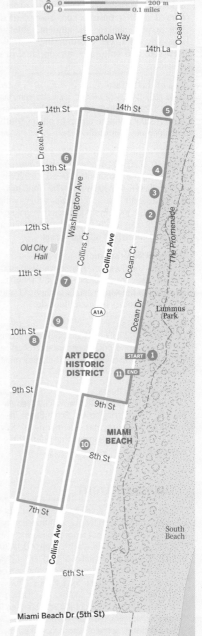

### Canyon Ranch Hotel & Spa    SPA

(Map p60; ☑305-514-7000; www.canyonranch.com/miamibeach; 6801 Collins Ave; treatments $150-350; ⊗8am-8pm) Check out the 'rituals' offered at this upscale spa: rose-scented rice scrubs, chakra realignment, shiatsu massage, reiki, chi coordinating – if it's New Age and culturally appropriated, it's on offer.

### Spa at the Setai    SPA

(Map p52; ☑305-520-6900; www.setai.com/thespa; 101 20th St; treatments $150-380; ⊗9am-9pm) A silky Balinese haven in one of South Beach's most beautiful hotels.

### Lapis    SPA

(Map p60; ☑305-674-4772; www.fontainebleau.com; 4441 Collins Ave; treatments $80-350; ⊗9:30am-6:30pm Sun-Fri, to 7:30pm Sat) The Fontainebleau's resident spa emphasizes water, with 'ritual water journeys' kicking off every spa treatment. Dip into a Turkish bath or enjoy a soak in a eucalyptus-infused spring.

## Diving & Snorkeling

Head to the Keys or Biscayne National Underwater Park (☑305-230-1100; www.nps.gov/bisc), in the southeastern corner of Dade county. Operators in Miami include:

### Divers Paradise    DIVING

(Map p72; ☑305-361-3483; www.kbdivers.com; 4000 Crandon Blvd; private open-water certification $500) In Key Biscayne, one of the area's most reliable outfits.

### South Beach Divers    DIVING

(Map p56; ☑305-531-6110; www.southbeachdivers.com; 850 Washington Ave, South Beach; dive trip $100) Runs regular excursions to Key Largo and around Miami, plus offers three-day classes.

## Fishing

Places to drop a line: South Pointe Park; Rickenbacker Causeway; Key Biscayne Beach. Fishing charters are commonplace but expensive; expect to pay at least $1000 for a day of sportfishing:

### Ace Blue Waters Charters    FISHING

(Map p62; ☑305-373-5016; www.fishingmiami.net; Bayside Marketplace, 401 Biscayne Blvd) Fish around Miami and Key Biscayne with this Bayfront Marina–based operation.

### Kelley Fleet    FISHING

(☑305-945-3801; www.miamibeachfishing.com; Haulover Beach Park, 10800 Collins Ave, Bal Harbour) Catch a group-fishing party boat with the Kelley Fleet.

## Golf

At high-end resorts expect to pay between $150 and $350 to tee off, depending on the season and time of day (it's more expensive in winter and daylight hours).

### Biltmore Golf Course    GOLF

(Map p78; ☑855-311-6903; www.biltmorehotel.com/golf; 1210 Anastasia Ave, Coral Gables) Designed by the golfer of that name and boasting the immaculate company of the Biltmore Hotel.

### Doral Golf Course    GOLF

(☑800-713-6725; www.trumphotelcollection.com/miami; 4400 NW 87th Ave) Very highly rated, which may explain why it's difficult to get in and also why it once hosted the PGA Ford Championship.

### Crandon Golf Course    GOLF

(Map p72; ☑305-361-9129; www.crandongolfclub.com; 6700 Crandon Blvd, Key Biscayne; daylight Dec-Apr $140, twilight May-Nov $30) Overlooks the bay from its perch on Key Biscayne.

---

## TURKISH DELIGHT

Just because you enjoy a good back rub doesn't mean you need to go to some glitzy spa where they constantly play soft house music on a repetitive loop. Right? Why not head to a favorite 'hot' spot among folks who want a spa experience without the glamour, the Russian & Turkish Baths (Map p60; ☑305-867-8316; www.russianandturkishbaths.com; 5445 Collins Ave; ⊗noon-midnight). Enter this little labyrinth of *banyas* (steam rooms) and there's a plethora of spa choices. You can be casually beaten with oak-leaf brooms called *venik* in a lava-hot spa (for $40; it's actually really relaxing...well, interesting anyway). There's Dead Sea salt and mud exfoliation ($50), plus, the on-site cafe serves delicious borscht, blintzes, dark bread with smoked fish and, of course, beer. The crowd is interesting too: hipsters, older Jews, model types, Europeans and folks from Russia and former Soviet states, some of whom look like, um, entirely legitimate businessmen and we're leaving it at that.

## MIAMI CRITICAL MASS

If you're in Miami at the beginning of the weekend late in any given month, you may spot hordes of cyclists and, less frequently, some skateboarders, roller skaters and other self-propelled individuals. To quote the great Marvin Gaye, 'what's going on?'

It's Miami Critical Mass. The event, put on by the **Miami Bike Scene** (www.themiamibikescene.com) is meant to raise awareness of cycling and indirectly advocate for increased bicycle infrastructure in the city. Anyone is welcome to join; the mass ride gathers at Government Center (by HistoryMiami, p65) at 6:30pm on the last Friday of each month.

The whole shebang departs on the 12-to-18-mile trek at 7:15pm. The average speed of the ride is a not-too-taxing 12mph, and you will be expected to keep up (at the same time, you're not to go faster than the pacesetters). All in all, a fun experience, and a good way to meet members of the local cycling community.

MIAMI ACTIVITIES

**Haulover Golf Course** GOLF
(305-947-3525; www.miamidade.gov/parks/haulover; 10800 Collins Ave, Bal Harbour; $21-43) A nine-hole, par-three course that's great for beginners.

### Kayaking, Paddleboarding & Windsurfing

Kayaking through mangroves, one of the coolest ecosystems on earth, is magical: all those slender roots kiss the water while the ocean breeze cools your flanks. Try these places: Haulover Beach Park (p86); Bill Baggs Cape Florida State Park (p71); Oleta River State Park (p61).

**Blue Moon Outdoor Center** WATER SPORTS
(305-957-3040; http://bluemoonoutdoor.com; 3400 NE 163rd St; 9am-sunset Mon-Fri, from 8am Sat & Sun) Offers single kayaks ($23 per 1½ hours, $41 per three hours), tandem kayaks ($33 per 1½ hours, $51 per three hours) and bike rental ($18 per 1½ hours, $26 per three hours).

**Sailboards Miami** WATER SPORTS
(305-892-8992; www.sailboardsmiami.com; 1 Rickenbacker Causeway; 10am-6pm Fri-Tue) Also rents kayaks. You can purchase 10 hours' worth of kayaking for $90. This is also a good spot to rent (and learn how to operate) windsurfing gear (lessons from $35, gear per hour $30).

**Aquatic Rental Center & Sailing School** WATER SPORTS
(305-751-7514, evening 305-279-7424; www.arcmiami.com; 1275 NE 79th St; sailboats per 2hr/3hr/4hr/day $85/125/150/225; 9am-9pm) If you're a bona fide seaworthy sailor, this place will rent you a sailboat. If you're not, it can teach you how to operate one (sailing courses $400, $500 for two people).

**Bayshore Landing Marina** SAILING
(Map p76; 305-854-7997; 2550 S Bayshore Dr) Key Biscayne sailing is a pure joy, as is gliding along the waters just about anywhere else off Miami. A good starting point is Monty's Marina, which is perfect if you have your own boat.

### Rodeo

Rodeo in South Florida? You just have to head a little way out of Miami. Check websites or call ahead for specific rodeo times. If the idea of performing animals and spurs in the same arena makes you ill at ease, you may want to avoid local rodeos.

**Bergeron Rodeo Grounds** RODEO
(954-680-3555; www.davie-fl.gov/gen/daviefl_spclprjcts/bergeronrodeo; 4271 Davie Rd, Fort Lauderdale) In Davie, about 20 miles north of downtown Miami.

**Homestead Rodeo** RODEO
(305-247-3515; http://homesteadrodeo.com; 1034 NE 8th St, Homestead) In Homestead, about an hour south of downtown.

### Running

Running is quite popular, and the beach is very good for jogging, as it's flat, wide and hard-packed (apparently with amazingly hot joggers). A great resource for races, special events and other locations is the **Miami Runners Club** (305-255-1500; www.miamirunnersclub.com).

Some good places for a run include the Flamingo Park track, located east of Alton Rd between 11th St and 12th St, for serious runners; Promenade in South Beach for its style; the boardwalk on Mid-Beach for great people-watching and scenery; and South Bayshore Dr in Coconut Grove for its shady banyan trees.

## SOUTH FLORIDA CIRCUS ARTS SCHOOL

Admit it: you always wanted to fly on the trapeze, clamber out of the clown car, tame a lion. Well, we can't really help you with those last two activities, but if you want to learn some circus-worthy acrobatics, contortion and flexibility skills, come to the **South Florida Circus Arts School** (SFCAS; ☑ 954-540-1344; www.sfcas.com; 15161 NE 21st Ave) in North Miami, off North Biscayne Blvd, about 8 miles north of the Design District. SFCAS claims to be the only institution of its kind offering all-levels accessible education in the skills of the circus. It's a ton of fun and pretty unique; classes include aerial fitness, trapeze skills and the extremely popular flying yoga course (just try it), with fees ranging from $15 to $75 for an hour of instruction. See you in the center ring...

### Skating

Serious crowds have turned promenades into obstacle courses for anyone crazy enough to strap on some blades or get on a board. Leave the crowded strips to experts and try the ocean side of Ocean Dr, or Lincoln Rd before the shoppers descend.

**Fritz's Skate, Bike & Surf** SKATING
(Map p52; ☑ 305-532-1954; www.fritzsmiami beach.com; 1620 Washington Ave; bike & skate rentals per hour/day/week $10/24/69; ⊙ 10am-9pm Mon-Sat, to 8pm Sun) Rent your wheels from Fritz's, which also offers free lessons on Sunday at 10:30am – just about the only time there's ever room on the mall anymore.

### Surfing

Miami is not a good place for surfing. The Bahamas block swells, making the water very calm; many will tell you it's best to head about 100 miles north to Jupiter or Palm Beach to catch decent waves (not big waves, just surf consistent enough to hold a board upright). Plus, Miami surfers have worse reputations than Miami drivers when it comes to aggressive, territorial behavior. If you want to ride waves here, the best surfing is just north of South Pointe Park, where you can sometimes find 2ft to 5ft waves and a nice, sandy bottom. Unfortunately it's usually closer to 2ft than 5ft, it can get a little mushy (so longboards are the way to go), and it's swamped with weekend swimmers and surfers. Conditions are better further north, near **Haulover Beach Park** (10800 Collins Ave, Bal Harbour) or anywhere north of 70th St, like **Sunny Isles Beach** (Sunny Isles Causeway). Check in with **Island Water Sports** (☑ 305-944-0104; www. iwsmiami.com; 16231 Biscayne Blvd) for gear, **SoBe Surf** (☑ 786-216-7703; www.sobesurf.com) for lessons (private instructors will meet with you somewhere on the beach) and www.dadecosurf.com for general information.

### Swimming

All of the following pools have lap lanes. Call the Venetian Pool (p77) beforehand, as its lap hours change often.

**Flamingo Park Swimming Pool** SWIMMING
(Map p56; ☑ 305-673-7750; 999 11th St, South Beach; adult/child $10/6; ⊙ laps 6:30-8:30am & 7-8:30pm) Has a swimming pool with lap lanes.

**Normandy Isle Park & Pool** SWIMMING
(Map p60; ☑ 305-673-7750; 7030 Trouville Esplanade; adult/child $10/6; ⊙ laps 6:30-8:30am & 7-8:30pm) Family-friendly pool; also offers lap swimming.

### Yoga

The beach is definitely not the only place to salute the sun in Miami. There's a lovely 'yoga by the sea' course offered at the **Barnacle Historic State Park** (per class $13; ⊙ classes 6-7:15pm Mon & Wed) in Coconut Grove. If you don't feel like breaking out your wallet, try the free yoga classes at **Bayfront Park** (⊙ classes 6-7:15pm Mon & Wed, 9-10:15am Sat), held outdoors at Tina Hills Pavilion, at the south end of the park, three times a week.

All of the following studios offer a large range of classes; bring your own mat.

**Green Monkey Yoga** YOGA
(Map p52; ☑ 305-397-8566; www.greenmonkey. net; 1827 Purdy Ave; classes from $20) Miami Beach; also has a branch in South Miami.

**Brickell Hot Yoga** YOGA
(Map p62; ☑ 305-856-1387; www.brickellyoga. com; 301 SW 17th Rd, Brickell; 1-/5-/10-class pass $22/95/180) Downtown.

**Prana Yoga Center** YOGA
(Map p78; ☑ 305-567-9812; www.pranayogamiami. com; 247 Malaga Ave, Coral Gables; 1-/5-/10-class pass $20/99/169) In Coral Gables.

**Bikram Yoga Miami Beach** YOGA
(Map p56; ☑ 305-534-2727; www.bikramyogami-ami.com; 235 11th St, Miami Beach; per day/week $25/50) South Beach.

## 👉 Tours

**Miami Design Preservation League** WALKING
(Map p52; ☑ 305-531-3484; http://www.mdpl.org; 1001 Ocean Dr, South Beach; guided tour per adult/senior & student $20/15; ⊘ tours 10:30am Fri-Wed, 6:30pm Thu) Tells the stories and history behind the art-deco buildings in South Beach, either via a lively guide from the Miami Design Preservation League, or a well-presented recording and map for self-guided walks (try the guides). Tours last 90 minutes. Also offers tours of Jewish Miami Beach, Gay & Lesbian Miami Beach and other themed walks; check website for details.

**Dr Paul George** WALKING
(☑ 305-375-1492; www.historymiami.org/tours/walking-tours; tours from $30) For great historical perspective, call the lively Dr George, a historian for HistoryMiami (p65). George leads several popular tours – including those that focus on Stiltsville, Miami crime, Little Havana and Coral Gables at twilight – between September and late June; hours vary. Dr George also offers private tours by appointment.

**Miami Food Tours** WALKING
(Map p56; ☑ 888-291-2970; www.miamifoodtours.com; 429 Lennox Ave; adult/student/child from $53/35/17.50; ⊘ tours 11am-2pm Mon-Sat) You'll be visiting five of South Beach's best restaurants, but hey, it's a walking tour – you're burning calories, right?

**Urban Tour Host** WALKING
(Map p62; ☑ 305-416-6868; www.miamicultural-tours.com; 25 SE 2nd Ave, Suite 1048; tours from $20) Has a rich program of custom tours that provides face-to-face interaction in all of Miami's neighborhoods. A deluxe city tour includes Coral Gables, South Beach, downtown Miami and Coconut Grove.

**EcoAdventure Bike Tours** CYCLING
(☑ 305-365-3018; www.miamidade.gov/ecoadventures; tours from $28) The Dade County parks system leads excellent bike tours through peaceful areas of Miami and Miami Beach, including along beaches, on Key Biscayne and into the Everglades.

**Island Queen** BOAT TOUR
(Map p62; ☑ 305-379-5119; www.islandqueencruises.com; 401 Biscayne Blvd; adult/child from $28/19) Boat tours of Millionaire's Row, the Miami River and Stiltsville, among other locations.

MIAMI TOURS

---

### MIAMI FOR CHILDREN

Well really, it's Florida, folks; your kids will be catered to. Many of the attractions run toward animal experiences, starting with the Miami Seaquarium (p71), which boasts a large collection of crocodiles, dolphins and sea lions and a killer whale, most of which perform. Next comes the Metrozoo (p80), a 740-acre zoo with plenty of natural habitats (thank you, tropical weather). Should your little ones like colorful animal shows, the outdoors and the smell of animal poo in all its myriad varieties, Miami shall not disappoint. Monkey Jungle (p81) acts as a habitat for endangered species and is everything you'd expect: screeching primates, covered pathways and a grand finale show of crab-eating monkeys diving for fruit. Jungle Island (p81), on the other hand, tends to entertain with brilliant bird shows. Next door is the new Miami Children's Museum (p81), an indoor playland where youngsters can try out the roles of TV anchor, banker and supermarket customer, among others. Coral Gables draws the water-wise to its way-fun, lagoonlike Venetian Pool (p77). For a more educational experience, let your kids explore the Marjory Stoneman Douglas Biscayne Nature Center (p71) on Key Biscayne. Coconut Grove is probably the most child-friendly neighborhood in Miami, with its malls, easy-to-digest (on every level) mainstream dining, and events put on at places such as Barnacle Historic State Park (p75).

#### Childcare

When it's time to head out for some adult time, check with your hotel, as many offer childcare services – any larger resort worth its salt should be able to provide such services. Or call the local **Nanny Poppinz** (☑ 305-607-1170; www.nannypoppinz.com). For more information, advice and anecdotes, read Lonely Planet's *Travel with Children*.

**Miami Nice Tours** BUS TOUR
(305-949-9180; www.miami-nice.com; tours from $50) Has a wide range of guided bus excursions to the Everglades, the Keys and Fort Lauderdale, as well as trips around Miami.

## ★ Festivals & Events

There's something special happening year-round in Miami, with well-touted events bringing in niche groups from serious DJs (Winter Music Conference) to obsessed foodies (Miami Spice Restaurant Month). Addresses are given where there is a fixed festival location.

### January

The beginning of the new year also happens to be the height of the tourist season in these parts. Expect fair weather, crowds of visitors, higher prices than usual and a slew of special events.

**Orange Bowl** FOOTBALL
(www.orangebowl.org; Sun Life Stadium, 2269 Dan Marino Blvd, Miami Gardens) Hordes of football fans descend on Miami for the Super Bowl of college football.

**Art Deco Weekend** CULTURE
(www.artdecoweekend.com; Ocean Dr, btwn 1st St & 23rd St) This weekend fair featuring guided tours, concerts, classic-auto shows, sidewalk cafes, arts and antiques is held in mid-January.

**Miami Jewish Film Festival** FILM
(www.miamijewishfilmfestival.com; 4200 Biscayne Blvd) A great chance to cinematically schmooze with one of the biggest Jewish communities in the USA.

### February

The last hurrah for northerners needing to escape the harsh winter, February brings arts festivals and street parties, as well as warm days and cool nights.

**Art Wynwood** ART
(www.artwynwood.com) The dozens of galleries spread throughout Wynwood strut their artistic stuff during this festival, which showcases the best of the Midtown's burgeoning arts scene. There's a palpable commercial bent to this artistic event; big wallet buyers are wooed and marketed to. Expect murals and installations to appear throughout the area. Held on the second weekend in February.

**Coconut Grove Arts Festival** CULTURE
(www.coconutgroveartsfest.com; Biscayne Blvd, btwn NE 1st St & 5th St, Coconut Grove) One of the most prestigious arts festivals in the country, this late-February fair features more than 300 artists.

**Original Miami Beach**
**Antiques Show** ANTIQUES
(www.originalmiamibeachantiqueshow.com; Miami Beach Convention Center) One of the largest events of its kind in the USA, with over 800 dealers from more than 20 countries.

**South Beach Wine & Food Festival** FOOD
(www.sobefest.com) A festival of fine dining and sipping to promote South Florida's culinary image. Expect star-studded brunches, dinners and barbecues.

### March

Spring arrives, bringing warmer weather, world-class golf and tennis, outdoor festivals and St Patrick's Day. Expect some Spring Breakers to behave badly on the beach.

**Miami International Film Festival** FILM
(www.miamifilmfestival.com) This event, sponsored by Miami-Dade College, is a two-week festival showcasing documentaries and features from all over the world.

**Calle Ocho Festival** CULTURE
(Carnaval Miami; www.carnavalmiami.com) This massive street party in March is the culmination of Carnaval Miami, a 10-day celebration of Latin culture.

**South Beach Comedy Festival** COMEDY
(www.southbeachcomedyfestival.com) Some of the best comedic talent in the world does stand-up in venues across the city.

**Miami Fashion Week** FASHION
(www.miamifashionweek.com; Miami Beach Convention Center) Models are as abundant as fish in the ocean as designers descend on the city and catwalks become ubiquitous.

**Winter Music Conference** MUSIC
(www.wmcon.com) Party promoters, DJs, producers and revelers come from around the globe to hear new artists, catch up on technology and party the nights away.

### April

Welcome to the shoulder season, bringing quieter days, lower prices, balmier temperatures and a few choice events.

**Billboard Latin Music Awards** MUSIC
(www.billboardevents.com) This prestigious awards show in late April draws top industry execs, star performers and a slew of Latin music fans.

**Miami Gay & Lesbian Film Festival** FILM
(www.mglff.com) Held in late April to early May, this annual event features shorts, feature films and documentaries screened at various South Beach theaters.

## May & June

May and June boast increased heat, fewer visitors and several cultural events.

**Sweatstock** MUSIC
(www.sweatrecordsmiami.com) Sweat Records puts on an annual music festival aimed at locals, with headline acts performing indie rock, punk and electronica.

**Goombay Festival** CULTURE
(www.goombayfestivalcoconutgrove.com) A massive festival, held in the first week of June, which celebrates Bahamian culture.

**Miami Museum Month** CULTURE
(www.miamimuseummonth.com) An excellent chance to see and hang out in some of the best museums in the city in the midst of happy hours, special exhibitions and lectures.

## July & August

The most beastly, humidity-drenched days are during these months, when locals either vacation elsewhere or spend their days melting on the beach.

**Independence Day Celebration** HOLIDAY
(Bayfront Park) July 4 is marked with excellent fireworks, a laser show and live music that draw more than 100,000 people to breezy Bayfront Park.

**Miami Spice Restaurant Month** FOOD
(www.ilovemiamispice.com) Top restaurants around Miami offer prix-fixe lunches and dinners to try to lure folks out during the heat wave.

## September & October

The days and nights are still steamy and the start of school brings back college students.

**International Ballet Festival** DANCE
(www.internationalballetfestival.org) Some of the most important ballet talent in the world performs at venues across the city.

**Great Grove Bed Race** RACE
(www.thegreatgrovebedrace.com) Between the pajama pub crawl and drag-racing beds through Coconut Grove, this is one of Miami's wackier celebrations.

## November

Tourist season kicks off at the end of the month, bringing more crowds and slightly cooler days.

**Miami Book Fair International** CULTURE
(www.miamibookfair.com; 401 NE 2nd Ave) Occurring in mid- to late November, this is among the most important and well-attended book fairs in the USA. Hundreds of nationally known writers join hundreds of publishers and hundreds of thousands of visitors.

**White Party** MUSIC
(www.whiteparty.net) If you're gay and not here, there's a problem. This weeklong extravaganza draws more than 15,000 gay men and women for nonstop partying at clubs and venues all over town.

## December

Tourist season is in full swing, with northerners booking rooms so they can bask in the sunshine and be here for holiday festivities. New Year's Eve brings fireworks and festivals to South Beach and downtown Miami's bayfront.

**Art Basel Miami Beach** ART
(www.artbaselmiamibeach.com) One of the most important international art shows in the world, with works from more than 150 galleries and a slew of trendy parties.

**Design Miami** ART
(www.designmiami.com/) Held in conjunction with Art Basel, usually in early December, Design Miami is a high-profile party hosting some of the world's top design professionals and assorted entourages. Design-inspired lectures and showcases center on the Miami Beach Convention Center.

**King Mango Strut** PARADE
(www.kingmangostrut.org; Main Ave & Grand Ave, Coconut Grove) Held each year just after Christmas since 1982, this quirky Coconut Grove parade is a politically charged, fun freak that began as a spoof on current events and the now-defunct Orange Bowl Parade.

**Art Miami** ART
(www.art-miami.com) Held in December or January, this massive fair displays modern

and contemporary works from more than 100 galleries and international artists.

## Sleeping

It's in this category, more than any other, where all the hype surrounding Miami, and particularly South Beach, is justified. What sets South Beach apart – what defines it as a travel destination – is the deco district, and the deco district's backbone is hotels. This is one of the largest concentrations of boutique hotels in the country. And the Beach's glam only grows with every new accommodation lauded by the travel glossies, which brings the designers, which brings the fashionistas, which brings the models, which brings the tourists, which brings the chefs and...well, you get the idea.

South Beach hotels are some of the most expensive in Florida. Also, if you opt for hotel parking, expect to be charged $25 to $40 a day for the privilege. It may be easier to park in the large public garages scattered all around South Beach.

Note that the following rates can vary widely based on what events are occuring around town and how far you book in advance.

### South Beach (1st to 11th Streets)

**Miami Beach International Hostel** HOSTEL $ (Map p56; ☎305-534-1740, 305-534-0268; www. hostelmiamibeach.com; 236 9th St; dm/r from $27/32; ✳@☎) An extensive makeover has turned this reliable old hostel into something like a boutique club with dorm rooms. Bright plaster, marble accents, deco-and-neon decor and hip, clean rooms all make for a hostel to remember. There's a party-friendly social vibe throughout.

**South Beach Hostel** HOSTEL $ (Map p56; ☎305-534-6669; www.sobe-hostel. com; 235 Washington Ave; dm/r from $18/60;

---

### NORTHERN CAPITAL OF THE LATIN WORLD

Miami may technically be part of the USA, but it's widely touted as the 'capital of the Americas' and the 'center of the New World.' That's a coup when it comes to marketing Miami to the rest of the world, and especially to the USA, where Latinos are now the largest minority. Miami's pan-Latin mixture makes it more ethnically diverse than any Latin American city. At the turn of the 21st century, the western suburbs of Hialeah Gardens and Hialeah were numbers one and two respectively on the list of US areas where Spanish was spoken as a first language (over 90% of the population).

How did this happen? Many of Miami's Latinos arrived in this geographically convenient city as political refugees – Cubans fleeing Castro from around the '60s, Venezuelans fleeing President Hugo Chávez (or his predecessors), Brazilians and Argentines running from economic woes, Mexicans and Guatemalans arriving to find work. And gringos, long fascinated with Latin American flavors, can now visit Miami to get a taste of the pan-Latin stew without having to leave the country.

This has all led to the growth of Latin American businesses in Miami, which has boosted the local economy. Miami is the US headquarters of many Latin companies, including Lan Chile, a Chilean airline; Televisa, a Mexican TV conglomerate; and Embraer, a Brazilian aircraft manufacturer. Miami is also home to Telemundo, one of the biggest Spanish-language broadcasters in the US, as well as MTV Networks Latin America and the Latin branch of the Universal Music Group. Miami is the host city of the annual Billboard Latin Music Conference & Awards.

Cubans have a strong influence on local and international politics in Miami. Conservative exile groups have often been characterized as extreme, many refusing to visit Cuba while the Castro family remains in power. A newer generation, however – often referred to as the 'YUCAs' (Young Urban Cuban Americans) – are more willing to see both sides of issues in Cuba.

While many of the subtleties may escape you as a visitor, one thing is obvious: the Latino influence, which you can experience by seeking it out or waiting for it to fall in your lap. Whether you're dining out, listening to live music, overhearing Spanish conversations, visiting Little Havana or Little Buenos Aires, or simply sipping a chilled *mojito* at the edge of your hotel pool, the Latin American energy is palpable, beautiful and everywhere you go.

❋@☎) On a quiet end of SoFi (the area south of 5th St, South Beach), this hostel has a happening common area and spartan rooms. It may not be too flashy, but the staff are friendly and the on-site bar (open to 5am) seems to stay busy.

**Deco Walk**  HOSTEL **$**
(Map p56; ☎ 305-531-5511; http://decowalkhostel. com; 928 Ocean Dr; dm $35; P❋☎) The Deco Walk is shooting hard for the title of hippest hostel on the beach, and it's making a good run of it. Pop-art-decorated dorms and a rooftop bar with requisite Jaccuzi and club-esque lounge area are well thought out, but as is often the case with hostels, this place is as good as the crowd staying there.

**Jazz on South Beach**  HOSTEL **$**
(Map p56; ☎ 305-672-2137; www.jazzhostels.com/ jazzlocations/jazz-on-south-beach; 321 Collins Ave; dm $13-24, d $65; ❋@☎) A nice addition to the expanding SoBe backpacker scene. The hip vibe attracts lots of scenesters and club kids.

★**Hotel St Augustine**  BOUTIQUE HOTEL **$$**
(Map p56; ☎ 305-532-0570; www.hotelstaugustine. com; 347 Washington Ave; r $155-289; P❋☎) Wood that's blonder than Barbie and a crisp-and-clean deco theme combine to create one of SoFi's most elegant yet stunningly modern sleeps. Color schemes blend beige, caramel, white and cream – the sense is the hues are flowing into one eye-smoothing palette. The familiar, warm service is the cherry on top for this hip-and-homey standout, although the soothing lighting and glass showers – that turn into personal steam rooms at the flick of a switch – are pretty appealing too.

**Kent Hotel**  BOUTIQUE HOTEL **$$**
(Map p56; ☎ 305-604-5068; www.thekentho- tel.com; 1131 Collins Ave; r from 140; P❋☎) Young party types will probably get a kick out of this lobby, filled with fuchsia- and electric-colored geometric furniture plus Lucite toy blocks, which makes for an aggressively playful welcome. Interior rooms are well appointed with earthy hardwood floors, pretty beds and bright paint palettes.

**Hotel Astor**  BOUTIQUE HOTEL **$$**
(Map p56; ☎ 305-531-8081; www.hotelastor. com; 956 Washington Ave; r/ste from $210/350; P❋☎≋) They lay the retro-punk on thick in the Astor lobby, glamorizing and exag-

gerating the Age of Transportation into a hip caricature of itself: a gigantic industrial fan blows over a ceiling studded with psychedelic 'lamp balls,' all suspended over a fanciful daydream of an old-school pilots' club. The earth-toned rooms are relaxing, and the small pool gets covered at night to make room for clubgoers who bop on the back-patio lounge.

**Fashionhaus**  BOUTIQUE HOTEL **$$**
(Map p56; ☎ 305-673-2550; www.fashionhaus hotel.com; 534 Washington Ave; r $130-250; P❋☎≋) The Fashionhaus doesn't just sound like a Berlin avant-garde theater; it kinda feels like one, with its smooth geometric furnishings, 48 individualized rooms decked out in original artwork – from abstract expressionism to washed out photography – and its general blending of comfort, technology and design. Popular with Europeans, fashionistas, artists (and European fashionista artists) and those who just want to emulate that lifestyle.

**Nash Hotel**  BOUTIQUE HOTEL **$$**
(Map p56; ☎ 305-674-7800; www.nashsouth- beach.com; 1120 Collins Ave; r $164-204, ste from $360; P❋☎≋) This used to be the Lords Hotel, an epicenter of South Beach's gay scene. Today the Nash is still a pretty cream puff of a hotel, with rooms decked out in lemony yellow and whites offset by graphic and pop art. At time of writing, it seemed less LGBT-focused than in the past, if still popular with the boys.

**Clinton Hotel**  BOUTIQUE HOTEL **$$**
(Map p56; ☎ 305-938-4040; www.clintonsouth- beach.com; 825 Washington Ave; r $150-180, ste from $205; P❋☎≋) Washington Ave is the quietest of the three main drags in SoBe, but the Clinton doesn't mind. This joint knows it would be the hottest girl in the most crowded party, with her velveteen banquettes and Zen sun porches. Balcony rooms offer a nice view onto the hip courtyard.

**Hotel Shelley**  BOUTIQUE HOTEL **$$**
(Map p56; ☎ 305-531-3341; www.hotelshelley. com; 844 Collins Ave; r from $170; ❋☎) Gossamer curtains, a lively lounge and a sublimely relaxing violet-and-blue color scheme combine with orblike lamps that look like bunched-up glass spiderwebs. The rooms are as affordably stylish as the rest of the offerings in the South Beach Group selection of hotels (see www.southbeachgroup.com).

### Lord Balfour Hotel
BOUTIQUE HOTEL $$

(Map p56; ☑ 305-673-0401; www.lordbalfourmiami.com; 350 Ocean Dr; r $196-300; P ☀ ☎) Why not name a hotel for a minor, generally ill-regarded British prime minister? Name choice aside, the Lord Balfour features the usual minimalist-plus-pop-art rooms Miami beach is famous for, along with Corinelli bed linens and an overarching Cool Britannia theme. The lobby/bar area is a gem, mixing retro accoutrements with sweeping, modernist lines.

### Hotel Breakwater
HOTEL $$

(Map p56; ☑ 305-532-2362; www.esplendorbreakwatersouthbeach.com; 940 Ocean Dr; r $190-250, ste from $360; ☀ ☎ ⇔) A towering blue marquee offset by a stylistically geometric deco facade advertises the Breakwater to all of Ocean Dr. The breezy pool is a good spot to hang before retiring to rooms splashed with citrus-tropical colors and splashes of vintage art.

### Ocean Five Hotel
BOUTIQUE HOTEL $$

(Map p56; ☑ 305-532-7093; www.oceanfive.com; 436 Ocean Dr; r/ste from $155/210; P ☀ ☎) This boutique hotel is all pumpkin-bright; deco dressed up on the outside, with cozy, quiet rooms that reveal a maritime-meets-vintage theme on the inside, with a dash of Old West ambience on top. Think mermaid murals on pale stucco walls. Good value for South Beach.

### ★ Pelican Hotel
BOUTIQUE HOTEL $$$

(Map p56; ☑ 305-673-3373; www.pelicanhotel.com; 826 Ocean Dr; r $165-425, ste $295-555; ☀ ☎) When the owners of Diesel jeans purchased the Pelican in 1999, they started scouring garage sales for just the right ingredients to fuel a mad experiment: 30 themed rooms that come off like a fantasy-suite hotel dipped in hip. From the cowboy-hipster chic of 'High Corral, OK Chaparral' to the jungly electric tiger stripes of 'Me Tarzan, You Vain,' all the rooms are completely different (although all rooms have beautiful recycled-oak floors), fun and even come with their own 'suggested soundtrack.'

### ★ Sense South Beach
BOUTIQUE HOTEL $$$

(Map p56; ☑ 305-538-5529; www.sensesobe.com; 400 Ocean Dr; r $300; P ☀ ☎ ⇔) The Sense is fantastically atmospheric – smooth white walls disappearing behind melting blue views of South Beach, wooden paneling arranged around lovely sharp angles that feel inviting, rather than imposing, and rooms that contrast whites and dark grays into straight duochromatic cool. Pop art hangings and slender furnishings round out the MacBook-esque air.

### Mondrian South Beach
RESORT $$$

(Map p56; ☑ 305-514-1500; www.mondrian-miami.com; 1100 West Ave; r/ste from $329/430; P ☀ ☎ ⇔) Morgan Hotel Group hired Dutch design star Marcel Wanders to basically crank it up to 11 at the Mondrian. The theme is inspired by *Alice in Wonderland* (if it had been penned by Crockett from *Miami Vice*) – columns carved like giant table legs, chandelier showerheads, imported Delft tiles with beach scenes instead of windmills, and magic walls with morphing celebrity faces (perhaps because the morphing nature of celebrity is what fuels South Beach's glamour?). Oh, and there's a private island (naturally).

### Hotel Victor
BOUTIQUE HOTEL $$$

(Map p56; ☑ 305-428-1234; www.hotelvictorsouthbeach.com; 1144 Ocean Dr; r/ste from $335/505; P ☀ ☎ ⇔) The Victor wins – the 'hot design' stakes, that is. And the 'fishtanks full of jellyfish' competition. And the 'damn that room is fly' pageant too. Designed by L Murray Dixon in 1938, the redone Victor was opened in 2005, marking a wave of remastered deco classics. Room interiors have a blocky, geometry-meets-minimalism sense of style.

### The Hotel
BOUTIQUE HOTEL $$$

(Map p56; ☑ 305-531-2222; www.thehotelofsouthbeach.com; 801 Collins Ave; r $260-425; P ☀ ☎ ⇔) This place is stylin' – and why shouldn't it be, when Todd Oldham designed the boldly beautiful rooms? The themed palette of 'sand, sea and sky' adds a dash of eye candy to the furnishings, as do the mosaic doorknobs and brushed-steel sinks. The Hotel boasts a fine rooftop pool, overshadowed only by a lovely deco spire (which says 'Tiffany,' because that was the name of this place before the blue-box jewelry chain threatened a lawsuit).

### Chesterfield Hotel
BOUTIQUE HOTEL $$$

(Map p56; ☑ 305-531-5831; www.thechesterfieldhotel.com; 855 Collins Ave; r $200-250, ste $300-600; P ☀ ☎) Hip-hop gets funky with zebra-stripe curtains and cushions in the small lobby, which hosts a chill happy hour when the sun goes down at the in-house Safari Bar. Rooms mix up dark wood furniture with bright-white beds and vaguely tropical colors swathed throughout. Make sure to enoy the view from the roof deck.

### Dream South Beach
BOUTIQUE HOTEL $$$

(Map p56; ☑ 305-673-4747; www.dreamsouthbeach.com; 1111 Collins Ave; r/ste from $250/527;

P ❄ 🎧) How to explain the Dream? From the outside it looks like an ice-cube box of clean white lines, but come inside and it feels like a cross between the interior of an Indian palace, an electric blue tube of toothpaste and a set piece from *Tron*. The rooftop bar is a perfect place to kick back and pretend you're some kind of film-industry mogul, before returning to your room and pretending to be a futuristic mogul. Very popular with LGBT clientele.

**Essex House Hotel**　　　BOUTIQUE HOTEL **$$$**
(Map p56; ☎ 305-534-2700; www.essexhotel.com; 1001 Collins Ave; r/ste from $220/280; ❄ 🎧 ⛵) When you gaze at this lobby, one of the best-preserved interiors in the deco district, you're getting a glimpse of South Beach's gangster heyday. Beyond that the Essex has helpful staff, rooms furnished with soft, subdued colors and a side verandah filled with rattan furnishings that's a particularly pleasant people-watching perch.

**The Villa by Barton G**　　　RESORT **$$$**
(Map p56; ☎ 305-576-8003; www.thevillabybartong.com; 1116 Ocean Dr; r from $900; P ❄ 🎧 ⛵) Formerly the Versace Mansion (see p42), it has been turned into one of South Beach's most upscale resorts by Barton G, replete with a mosaic pool plucked from ancient Rome, marble bathrooms, linen spun from angel hair and rooms that resemble the guest wing of a minor South American oligarch's personal compound.

**Casa Grande Hotel**　　　BOUTIQUE HOTEL **$$$**
(Map p56; ☎ 305-672-7003; www.casagrandesuitehotel.com; 834 Ocean Dr; r $220-380; P ❄ 🎧 ⛵) Fall colors and a splash of bright citrus start the show in the lobby, but the main event is the snow white elegance of the so-chic rooms, each one an ultramodern designer's dream – although we've got to say the big, marble Virgin Mary in the room we visited was way out of place. Pets are welcome (and pampered!) for $50 per critter.

## 🛏 South Beach (11th to 23rd Streets)

**Tropics Hotel & Hostel**　　　HOTEL **$**
(Map p52; ☎ 305-531-0361; www.tropicshotel.com; 1550 Collins Ave; dm $27, r from $65; ❄ ⛵) The Tropics looks a little ratty on the outside, but the interior is nice enough. It sports a big swimming pool and a patio area that seems consistently packed with chatting

travelers. The four-bed dorms have attached bathrooms; private rooms are basic and serviceable.

**Townhouse Hotel**　　　BOUTIQUE HOTEL **$$**
(Map p52; ☎ 305-534-3800; www.townhousehotel.com; 150 20th St at Collins Ave; r $145-195, ste from $350; ❄ 🎧 ⛵) You'd think the Townhouse was designed by the guy who styled the iPod but no, it was Jonathan Morr and India Mahdavi who fashioned a cool white lobby and igloolike rooms with random scarlet accents and a breezy, white rooftop lounge. Who needs mints on pillows when the Townhouse provides beach balls? One of the better-value hotels on South Beach.

**Aqua Hotel**　　　BOUTIQUE HOTEL **$$**
(Map p52; ☎ 305-538-4361; www.aquamiami.com; 1530 Collins Ave; r $150-180, ste from $200; P ❄ 🎧 ⛵) A front desk made of shiny surfboard sets the mellow tone at this former motel – the old, family kind where the rooms are set around a pool. That old-school vibe barely survives under the soft glare of aqua spotlights and an alfresco lounging area. The sleekness of the rooms is offset by quirky furniture and deep blue sea bathrooms.

**Catalina Hotel**　　　BOUTIQUE HOTEL **$$**
(Map p52; ☎ 877-762-3477, 305-674-1160; www.catalinahotel.com; 1732 Collins Ave; r from $200; P ❄ 🎧 ⛵) The Catalina is a lovely example of midrange deco style. Most appealing, besides the playfully minimalist rooms, is the vibe – the Catalina doesn't take itself too seriously, and staff and guests all seem to be having fun as a result. The back pool, concealed behind the main building's crisp white facade, is particularly attractive and shaded by a large grove of tropical trees.

**Clay Hotel**　　　HOTEL **$$**
(Map p52; ☎ 305-534-2988; www.clayhotel.com; 1438 Washington Ave; r $100-190; ❄ @ 🎧) Hotels are always nicer when they come packaged in a 100-year-old Spanish-style villa. The Clay has clean and comfortable rooms, not too flashy but hardly spartan, located in a medina-like maze of adjacent buildings. If you're on a budget but don't want dorm-y hostel atmosphere, head here. This is one Miami place where Al Capone got some shut-eye.

**Cavalier South Beach**　　　BOUTIQUE HOTEL **$$**
(Map p52; ☎ 305-531-3555; www.cavaliersouthbeach.com; 1320 Ocean Dr; r $129-155, ste $229;

P✳🛜) The exterior is a rare Ocean Dr example of the Mayan/Incan inspiration that graced some deco facades (look for Mesoamerican details like the step pattern on the sides of the building). Inside? The Cavalier sacrifices ultrahip for Old Florida casualness, which is refreshing.

★ **Shore Club**   BOUTIQUE HOTEL $$$
(Map p52; ☑ 305-695-3100; www.shoreclub.com; 1901 Collins Ave; r/ste from $348/455; P✳@🛜) Imagine a Zen ink-brush painting; what's beautiful isn't what's there, but what gets left out. If you could turn that sort of art into a hotel room, it might look like the stripped-down-yet-serene digs of the Shore Club. Yeah, yeah: it has the 400-thread-count Egyptian cotton sheets, Mexican sandstone floors etc, but what the Shore Club does like no other hotel is arrange these elements into a greater whole that's impressive in its understatement; the aesthetic is compelling because it comes across as an afterthought.

★ **Gale South Beach**   HOTEL $$$
(Map p52; ☑ 855-532-2212; galehotel.com; 1690 Collins Ave; r from $310; P✳🛜) The Gale's exterior is an admirable re-creation of classic boxy deco aesthetic expanded to the grand dimensions of a modern SoBe super resort. This blend of classic and haute South Beach carries on indoors, where you'll find bright rooms with clean colors and sharp lines and a retro-chic vibe inspired by the mid-Century Modern movement.

---

## MIAMI'S BEST HOTEL POOLS

Miami has some of the most beautiful hotel pools in the world, and they're more about seeing and being seen than swimming. Most of these pools double as bars, lounges or even clubs. Some hotels have a guests-only policy when it comes to hanging out at the pool, but if you buy a drink at the poolside bar you should be fine.

➡ Delano Hotel (p95)

➡ Shore Club (p94)

➡ Epic Hotel (p97)

➡ Biltmore Hotel (p99)

➡ Raleigh Hotel (p94)

➡ Fontainebleau (p96)

---

★ **The Standard**   BOUTIQUE HOTEL $$$
(☑ 305-673-1717; www.standardhotels.com/miami; 40 Island Ave; r/ste from $240/480; P✳🛜) Look for the upside-down 'Standard' sign on the old Lido building on Belle Island (between South Beach and downtown Miami) and you'll find the Standard – which is anything but. This excellent boutique blends a bevy of spa services, hipster funk and South Beach sex, and the result is a '50s motel gone glam. There are organic wooden floors, raised white beds, and gossamer curtains, which open onto a courtyard of earthly delights, including a heated hammam (Turkish bath).

★ **Raleigh Hotel**   BOUTIQUE HOTEL $$$
(Map p52; ☑ 305-534-6300; www.raleighhotel. com; 1775 Collins Ave; r/ste from $280/420; P✳🛜) While everyone else was trying to get all modern, the Raleigh painstakingly tried to restore itself to prewar glory. It succeeded in a big way. Celebrity hotelier André Balazs has managed to capture a tobacco-and-dark-wood men's club ambience and old-school elegance while sneaking in modern design and amenities. Have a swim in the stunning pool; Hollywood actress Esther Williams used to.

**National Hotel**   HOTEL $$$
(Map p52; ☑ 888-897-5959, 305-532-2311; www. nationalhotel.com; 1677 Collins Ave; r $240-420, ste from $500; P✳🛜) The National is an old-school deco icon, with its bell-tower-like cap and slim yet muscular facade. Inside the hotel itself you'll find off-white rooms fashioned to fit more traditional, as opposed to ubermodern, tastes. The lobby and halls are riots of geometric design, while outside a lovely infinity pool beckons guests and visitors. The decadent cabana suites are exercises in luxury, offering unfettered access to said pool, private terraces and on-site tropical gardens.

**Sagamore**   BOUTIQUE HOTEL $$$
(Map p52; ☑ 305-535-8088; www.sagamorehotel. com; 1671 Collins Ave; r $240-360, ste from $400; P✳@🛜) This hotel-cum-exhibition hall likes to blur the boundaries between interior decor, art and conventional hotel aesthetics. Almost every space within this hotel, from the lobbies to the rooms, doubles as an art gallery thanks to a talented curator and an impressive roster of contributing artists. Rooms? Stark whites, accented by artsy photography and sleek designer accents.

**Setai** BOUTIQUE HOTEL **$$$**
(Map p52; ☎305-520-6000; www.setai.com; 101 20th St; ste $840-6000; P ❄ ☎ ❋) There's a *linga* in the lobby – nothing says high-end luxury like a Hindu phallus. It's all part of the aesthetic at this exclusive sleep, where a well-realized theme mixes Southeast Asian temple architecture, Chinese furniture, contemporary luxury and an overarching Anywhere Asia concept. Each floor is staffed by teams of 24-hour butlers, while rooms are decked out in chocolate teak wood, clean lines, and Chinese and Khmer embellishments.

**W Hotel** RESORT **$$$**
(Map p52; ☎305-938-3000; www.wsouthbeach. com; 2201 Collins Ave; r from $470, ste $700-5700; P ❄ ☎ ❋) There's an astounding variety of rooms available at the South Beach outpost of the W chain, which brings the whole W-brand mix of luxury, hipness and overblown cool to Miami Beach in a big way. The 'spectacular studios' balance long panels of reflective glass with cool tablets of cipollino marble; the Oasis suite lets in so much light you'd think the sun had risen in your room; the Penthouse may as well be the setting of an MTV video (and given the sort of celebrities who stay here, that assessment might not be far off). The attendant bars, restaurants, clubs and pool built into this complex are some of the most well regarded on the beach.

**Cadet Hotel** BOUTIQUE HOTEL **$$$**
(Map p52; ☎305-672-6688; www.cadethotel.com; 1701 James Ave; r from $209; ❄ ☎ ❋) From paper lanterns hanging from ceilings to furry throw rugs; from clamshell designs encapsulating large mirrors to classical Asian furniture;; and, as always, a great art-deco facade, the Cadet has the aesthetics right. Check out the shaded verandah at the back, lifted from a fantasy idea of what a plantation should feel like.

**Betsy Hotel** BOUTIQUE HOTEL **$$$**
(Map p52; ☎305-531-6100; www.thebetsyhotel. com; 1440 Ocean Dr; r from $330; P ❄ ☎ ❋) The Betsy's rooms present a sort of blend of Caribbean plantation and modern IKEA store; pastel and tropical color schemes blot into the usual South Beach monochrome white, which makes for an elegant but friendly vibe. The exterior suggests much the same spirit, but given the elite set this hotel attracts, areas like the lobby and the pool feel more exclusive and self-assured. The shutter-style doors that frame the windows within the rooms are a nice touch, as are the walnut floors and bath mirrors with inbuilt LCD TVs.

**Cardozo Hotel** BOUTIQUE HOTEL **$$$**
(Map p52; ☎305-535-6500; www.cardozohotel. com; 1300 Ocean Dr; r $230-290, ste $320-460; P ❄ ☎) The Cardozo and its neighbor, the Carlyle, were the first deco hotels saved by the Miami Design Preservation League, and in the case of the Cardozo, we think they saved the best first. It's the combination of the usual contemporary sexiness (white walls, hardwood floors, high-thread-count sheets) and playful embellishments: leopard-print details, handmade furniture and a general sense that, yes, you are cool if you stay here, but you don't have to flaunt it. Oh – remember the 'hair gel' scene in *There's Something About Mary*? Filmed here.

**Delano Hotel** BOUTIQUE HOTEL **$$$**
(Map p52; ☎305-672-2000; www.delano-hotel. com; 1685 Collins Ave; r $430-650, ste from $899; P ❄ ☎ ❋) The Delano opened in the 1990s and immediately started ruling the South Beach roost. If there's a quintessential 'I'm too sexy for this song' South Beach moment, it's when you walk into the Delano's lobby, which has all the excess of an overbudgeted theater set. 'Magic mirrors' in the halls disclose weather info, tide charts and inspirational quotes. The pool area resembles the courtyard of a Disney princess's palace and includes a giant chess set; there are floor-to-ridiculously-high-ceiling curtains in the two-story waterfront rooms; and the bedouin tent cabanas are outfitted with flat-screen TVs. Rooms are almost painfully white and bright; all long, smooth lines, reflective surfaces and sexy, modern, luxurious amenities.

**Tides** BOUTIQUE HOTEL **$$$**
(Map p52; ☎305-604-5070; www.tidessouth-beach.com; 1220 Ocean Dr; r $280-625, ste $1000-4000; P ❄ ☎ ❋) The Tides' ocean-fronting rooms are icy cool, with their jumbled vintage, ocean organic and indie vibe. The pure-white bedding is overlaid by beige, tan and shell, and offset with cream accents. Rooms come with telescopes for planetary (or Hollywood) stargazing, and the lobby, bedecked with nautical embellishments, looks like a modern sea god's palace.

**Redbury South Beach** BOUTIQUE HOTEL **$$$**
(Map p52; ☎855-220-1776; http://theredbury. com/southbeach; 1776 Collins Ave; r from $260; ❄ ❋) What sets the Redbury apart is its

refusal to toe the line of identikit South Beach minimalist rooms. Rather, the interior here references art across the 20th century, 1960s psychedelia and sleek comfort. A rooftop pool makes for some chilled out lounging, while the lobby has an early-20th-century, Gatsby-era-glam vibe.

### Winter Haven Hotel
BOUTIQUE HOTEL $$$

(Map p52; ☑ 305-531-5571; www.winterhavenhotel-sobe.com; 1400 Ocean Dr; r $215-330; P ✳ 🛜 🌊) Al Capone used to stay here; maybe he liked the deco ceiling lamps in the lobby, with their sharp, retro sci-fi lines and grand-Gothic proportions, and the oddly placed oriental mirrors (which have nothing to do with art deco whatsoever). The rooms, with their dark-wood accents and ice-white bedspreads, are a bit warmer than your average South Beach digs.

### Surfcomber
HOTEL $$$

(Map p52; ☑ 305-532-7715; www.surfcomber.com; 1717 Collins Ave; r $190-350, ste from $430; P ✳ 🛜 🌊) Simply put, the Surfrcomber is one of the best deco structures in Miami. Note the movement-suggestive lines on the exterior and semicircular, shade-providing 'eyebrows' that jut out of the windows. The rounded, aeronautical feel of the lobby suggests you're entering a 1930s airline lounge but no, you're just going to your room, which replicates the classic deco and modern design marriage of the front.

### James Royal Palm Hotel
HOTEL $$$

(Map p52; ☑ 305-604-5700; www.jameshotels.com/miami; 1545 Collins Ave; r/ste from $240/500; P ✳ 🛜 🌊) Even the trolleys here have a touch of curvy deco flair, to say nothing of the chunky staircase and mezzanine, which are the best South Beach examples of the building-as-cruise-liner deco theme. The shipboard theme carries into the rooms, which are also offset by bright whites and minty color accents.

## 🛏 Northern Miami Beach

### Circa 39
BOUTIQUE HOTEL $$

(Map p60; ☑ 305-538-4900; www.circa39.com; 3900 Collins Ave; r $130-170; P ✳ @ 🌊) If you love South Beach style but loathe South Beach attitude, Circa has got your back. The lobby, with its molded furniture and wacky embellishments, is one of the funkiest in Miami. Chic rooms, bursting with tropical lime green and subtle earth tones, are hip enough for the design-obsessed scenesters.

### Freehand Miami
BOUTIQUE HOTEL $$

(Map p60; ☑ 305-531-2727; http://thefreehand.com; 2727 Indian Creek Dr; dm/r from $50/220; ✳ 🛜 🌊) The Freehand is the brilliant reimagining of the old Indian Creek Hotel, a classic of the Miami Beach scene. Rooms are comfortably minimalist, with just the right amount of local artwork and wooden tones to strike a nice balance between warm funky and cool hip. Dorms serve the hostel crowd, and the on-site Broken Shaker (p112) is one of the best bars in town.

### Red South Beach
BOUTIQUE HOTEL $$

(Map p60; ☑ 800-528-0823; www.redsouthbeach.com; 3010 Collins Ave; r $130-200; ✳ 🛜 🌊) Red is indeed the name of the game, from the cushions on the sleek chairs in the lobby to the flashes dancing around the marble pool to deep, blood crimson headboards and walls wrapping you in warm sexiness in the small but beautiful guest rooms. The Red is excellent value for money and come evening the pool-bar complex is a great place to unwind and meet fellow guests.

### Daddy O Hotel
BOUTIQUE HOTEL $$

(☑ 305-868-4141; www.daddyohotel.com; 9660 E Bay Harbor Dr; r $150-260; P ✳ 🛜 🌊) The Daddy O is a cheerful, hip option that looks, from the outside, like a large B&B that's been fashioned for MTV and Apple employees. This vibe continues in the lobby and the rooms: cool, clean lines offset by bright, bouncy colors, plus a nice list of amenities: flat-screen TVs, custom wardrobes, free wi-fi and the rest. It's located about 3 miles north of North Miami Beach.

### Mimosa
BOUTIQUE HOTEL $$

(Map p60; ☑ 305-868-4141; www.themimosa.com; 6525 Collins Ave; r $120-220; ✳ 🛜 🌊) The Mimosa is decked out in mid-20th-century modern furniture, offset by deco embellishment like portico-style mirrors, dark-and-light room color schemes and a tangerine-and-cream lobby with a citrus-bright vibe. The pool is smallish, but overlooks a lovely stretch of the Atlantic Ocean.

### Fontainebleau
RESORT $$$

(Map p60; ☑ 305-535-3283; www.fontainebleau.com; 4441 Collins Ave; r $344-461, ste from $550; P ✳ 🛜 🌊) The grand Fontainebleau opened in 1954, when it became a celeb-sunning spot. Numerous renovations have added beachside cabanas, seven tennis courts, a grand ballroom, a shopping mall and a fabulous swimming pool. The rooms are surprisingly bright and cheerful – we expected more hard-edged attempts to be cool, but the sunny disposition of these chambers is a welcome surprise.

### Eden Roc Renaissance          RESORT $$$

(Map p60; ☑ 305-531-0000, 855-433-3676; www.edenrocmiami.com; 4525 Collins Ave; r/ste from $305/440; P ⌗ ☎ ⛱) The Roc's immense inner lobby draws inspiration from the Rat Pack glory days of Miami Beach cool, and rooms in the Ocean Tower boast lovely views over the Intracoastal Waterway. All the digs here have smooth, modern embellishments and amenities ranging from MP3 players to HDTV, ergonomic furniture and turndown service, among others.

### Claridge Hotel          HOTEL $$$

(Map p60; ☑ 305-604-8485; www.claridgemiamibeach.com; 3500 Collins Ave; r from $220; ⌗ @ ⛱) This 1928 Mediterranean-style palace feels like an (Americanized) Tuscan villa, with a honey-stone courtyard enclosing a sparkling pool, framed by palms, frescoed walls and gleaming stone floors. The soothing, old-world rooms are set off by rich earth tones, and staff are eager to please.

### Palms Hotel          HOTEL $$$

(Map p60; ☑ 305-534-0505; www.thepalmshotel.com; 3025 Collins Ave; r $200-380, ste from $440; P ⌗ @ ⛱) The lobby of the Palms manages to be imposing and comfortable all at once; the soaring ceiling, cooled by slow-spinning giant rattan fans, makes for a colonial-villa-on-convention-center-steroids vibe. Upstairs the rooms are perfectly fine, a mix of pastel colors and comfortable, if slightly bland, furnishings.

## 🛏 Downtown Miami

### Epic          HOTEL $$$

(Map p62; ☑ 866-760-3742, 305-424-5226; www.epichotel.com; 270 Biscayne Blvd; r $240-510, ste from $570; P ⌗ ☎ ⛱) Epic indeed! This massive Kimpton hotel is one of the more attractive options downtown and it possesses a coolness cred that could match any spot on Miami Beach. Of particular note is the outdoor pool and sun deck, which overlooks a gorgeous sweep of Brickell and the surrounding condo canyons. The rooms are outfitted in designer-chic furnishings and some have similarly beautiful views of greater Miami-Dade. There's a youthful energy throughout that's lacking in other corporate-style downtown hotels.

---

### MIMO ON BIBO

That cute little phrase means 'Miami Modern on Biscayne Boulevard,' and refers to the architectural style of buildings on North Biscayne Blvd past 55th Street. Specifically, there are some great roadside motels here with lovely, Rat Pack–era '50s neon beckoning visitors in. This area was neglected for a long time, and some of these spots are seedy (when we asked one owner why she advertised rooms for only $25, she smiled and said, '*Por hora*' – by the hour). But north BiBo is also one of Miami's rapidly gentrifying areas, and savvy motel owners are cleaning up their act and looking to attract the hipsters, artists and gay population flocking to the area. There's already exciting food here. Now the lodgings are getting stimulating too. All these hotels provide South Beach comfort at half the price.

**New Yorker** (☑ 305-759-5823; www.hotelnewyorkermiami.com; 6500 Biscayne Blvd; r $75-130; P ⌗ ☎) This hotel has been around since the 1950s and it shows – in a good way. If you could turn a classic Cadillac into a hotel with a modern interior and hipster cred, then bam, there's the New Yorker in a nutshell. Staff are friendly and the rooms – done up with pop art, geometric designs and solid colors – would make Andy Warhol proud.

**Motel Blu** (☑ 877-784-6835; www.motelblumiami.com; 7700 Biscayne Blvd; r $52-150; P ⌗ ☎ ⛱) Situated above Miami's Little River, the Blu may not look like much from the outside, but inside you'll find freshly done-up rooms with a host of modern amenities. Rooms are comfortable and have a soothing lime-and-lemon interior.

**Motel Bianco** (Map p68; ☑ 305-751-8696; www.motelbianco.com; 5255 Biscayne Blvd; r $80-110; P ⌗ ☎) The Bianco situates several orange-and-milky-white rooms around a glittery courtyard where coffee is served and guests can get to know each other. Contemporary art designs swirl through the larger rooms and wicker furniture abounds throughout.

**Mandarin Oriental Miami**  HOTEL $$$
(Map p62; ☑866-888 6780, 305-913-8383; www.
mandarinoriental.com/miami; 500 Brickell Key
Dr; r $380-750, ste from $950; P✳🛜🏊) The
Mandarin shimmers on Brickell Key, which
is actually annoying – you're a little isolated
from the city out here. Not that it matters;
there's a luxurious world within a world in-
side this exclusive compound, from swank
restaurants to a private beach and skyline
views that look back at Miami from the far
side of Biscayne Bay. Rooms are good in a
luxury-chain kind of way, but nothing sets
them apart from other sleeps in this price
range.

**Four Seasons Miami**  HOTEL $$$
(Map p62; ☑305-358-3535; www.foursea-
sons.com/miami; 1435 Brickell Ave; r/ste from
$330/450; P✳🛜🏊) The marble common
areas double as art galleries, a massive
spa caters to corporate types and there are
sweeping, could-have-been-a-panning-shot-
from-*Miami-Vice* views over Biscayne Bay
in some rooms. The 7th-floor terrace bar, Bahia, is pure *mojito*-laced, Latin-loved swank-
iness, especially on Thursdays and Fridays
from 6pm to 8pm, when ladies drink free.

## Key Biscayne

**Silver Sands Beach Resort**  RESORT $$
(Map p72; ☑305-361-5441; www.silversands-
beachresort.com; 301 Ocean Dr; r $169-189, cottag-
es $279-349; P✳🏊) Silver Sands: aren't you
cute, with your one-story, stucco tropical
tweeness? How this little, Old Florida–style
independent resort has survived amid the
corporate competition is beyond us, but it's
definitely a warm, homey spot for those seek-
ing some intimate, individual attention –
to say nothing of the sunny courtyard,
garden area and outdoor pool.

**Ritz-Carlton Key Biscayne**  RESORT $$$
(Map p72; ☑305-365-4500; www.ritzcarlton.
com; 455 Grand Bay Dr; r/ste from $320/1200;
P✳🛜🏊) Many Ritz-Carlton outposts feel a
little cookie-cutter, but the Key Biscayne outpost of the empire is pretty unique. There's
the magnificent lobby, vaulted by four giant columns lifted from a Cecil B DeMille
set – hell, the whole hotel is lifted from a
DeMille set. Tinkling fountains, the view
of the bay and the marble grandeur speak
less of a chain hotel and more of early-20th-
century glamour. Rooms and amenities are
predictably excellent.

## Coconut Grove

**Sonesta Hotel & Suites**
**Coconut Grove**  HOTEL $$
(Map p76; ☑305-529-2828; www.sonesta.com/
coconutgrove; 2889 McFarlane Rd; r $140-400, ste
$210-660; P✳🛜🏊) The Coco Grove outpost
of this luxury chain of hotels has decked out
its rooms in almost all white with a splash
of color (South Beach style). The amenities,
from flat-screen TVs to minikitchenettes,
add a layer of luxury to this surprisingly hip
chain. Make your way to the top of the build-
ing to enjoy a wonderful outdoor deck pool.

**Mutiny Hotel**  HOTEL $$$
(Map p76; ☑888-868-8469, 305-441-2100; mu-
tinyhotel.com; 2951 S Bayshore Dr; ste $150-351;
P✳🛜🏊) This small, luxury bayfront hotel, with one- and two-bedroom suites featuring balconies, boasts an indulgent staff,
high-end bedding, gracious appointments,
fine amenities and a small heated pool. Although it's on a busy street, you won't hear
the traffic once inside. The property boasts
fine views over the water.

**Ritz-Carlton Coconut Grove**  RESORT $$$
(Map p76; ☑305-365-4500; www.ritzcarlton.com;
3300 SW 27th Ave; r & ste $270-399; P✳🛜🏊🐕)
Another member of the Ritz-Carlton organ-
ization in Miami, this one overlooks the bay,
has immaculate rooms and offers butlers for
every need, from shopping and web-surfing
to dog-walking and bathing. The massive
spa is stupendous.

**Grove Isle Club & Resort**  RESORT $$$
(☑305-858-8300; www.groveisle.com; 4 Grove Isle
Dr; r $250-529, ste $389-879; P✳🛜🏊) One
of those 'I've got my own little island' type
places, Grove Island is off the coast of Coconut Grove. This stunning boutique hotel
has colonial elegance, lush tropical gardens,
its own jogging track, decadent pool, sunset
views over Biscayne Bay, amenities galore
and the cachet of staying in your own floating temple of exclusivity.

## Coral Gables

**Hotel St Michel**  HOTEL $$
(Map p78; ☑305-444-1666; www.hotelstmichel.
com; 162 Alcazar Ave; r $120-225; P✳🛜) The
Michel is more Metropole than Miami,
and we mean that as a compliment. The
old-world wooden fixtures, refined sense
of tweedy style and dinner-jacket ambience
don't get in the way of friendly service. The

lovely restaurant and cool bar-lounge are as elegant as the hotel they occupy.

★**Biltmore Hotel**  HISTORIC HOTEL **$$$**
(Map p78; ☎855-311-6903; www.biltmorehotel. com; 1200 Anastasia Ave; r from $209; P✱🖥🎿) Though the Biltmore's standard rooms can be small, a stay here is a chance to sleep in one of the great laps of US luxury. The grounds are so palatial it would take a solid week to explore everything the Biltmore has to offer – we highly recommend reading a book in the Romanesque/Arabian Nights opulent lobby, sunning underneath enormous columns and taking a dip in the largest hotel pool in the continental USA.

## 🛏 Greater Miami

**Inn at the Fisher Island Club**  RESORT **$$$**
(☎305-535-6000; www.fisherislandclub.com; r $600-2250; ✱🎿🖥) If you're not Jeb Bush (who lives here), the only way to glimpse Fisher Island is to stay at this luxurious resort. Whether in 'simple' rooms or Vanderbilt-era cottages, your money will be well spent: one of the best-rated spas in the country is here, as well as eight restaurants (which seems like overkill given the size of the island) and enough royal perks to please a pharaoh.

## 🍴 Eating

Miami is a major immigrant entrepôt and a sucker for food trends. Thus you get a good mix of cheap ethnic eateries and high-quality top-end cuisine here. There's admittedly a lot of dross too, especially on Miami Beach, where people can overcharge tourists and get away with it. The best new spots for dining are in Wynwood and Design District (Midtown); Coral Gables is also an established foodie hot spot.

## 🍴 South Beach (1st to 11th Streets)

**Puerto Sagua**  CUBAN **$**
(Map p56; ☎305-673-1115; 700 Collins Ave; mains $6-20; ⏱7:30am-2am) There's a secret colony of older working-class Cubans and construction workers hidden among South Beach's sex-and-flash, and evidently, they eat here (next to a Benetton). Puerto Sagua challenges the US diner with this reminder: Cubans can greasy-spoon with the best of them. Portions of favorites such as *picadillo* (spiced ground beef with rice, beans and plantains) are stu-

pidly enormous. The Cuban coffee here is not for the faint of heart – strong stuff.

**11th St Diner**  DINER **$**
(Map p56; 1065 Washington Ave; mains $9-18; ⏱24hr except midnight-7am Wed) You've seen the art-deco landmarks. Now eat in one: a Pullman-car diner trucked down from Wilkes-Barre, Pennsylvania – as sure a slice of Americana as a *Leave It to Beaver* marathon. If you've been drinking all night, we'll split a three-egg omelet with you and the other drunkies at 6am – if there's a diner where you can replicate Edward Hopper's *Nighthawks,* it's here.

**Pizza Rustica**  PIZZERIA **$**
(Map p56; www.pizza-rustica.com; 863 Washington Ave; slices $5, mains $8-10; ⏱11am-6pm) South Beach's favorite pizza place has several locations to satisfy the demand for crusty Roman-style slices topped with an array of exotic offerings. A slice is a meal unto itself and goes down a treat when you need something to soak up the beer.

**News Cafe**  AMERICAN **$**
(Map p56; www.newscafe.com; 800 Ocean Dr; mains $7-17; ⏱24hr) News Cafe is an Ocean Dr landmark that attracts thousands of travelers. We find the food to be pretty uninspiring, but the people-watching is good, so take a perch, eat some over-the-average but not-too-special food and enjoy the anthropological study that is South Beach as she skates, salsas and otherwise shambles by.

★**Tap Tap**  HAITIAN **$$**
(Map p56; ☎305-672-2898; www.taptaprestaurant. com; 819 5th St; mains $9-20; ⏱noon-11:30pm) In Haiti, tap-taps are brightly colored pickup trucks turned public taxis, and their tropi-psychedelic paint schemes inspire the decor at this excellent Haitian eatery. This is no Manhattan-style South Beach lounge – here you dine under bright murals of Papa Legba, guardian of the dead, emerging from a Port-au-Prince cemetery. Meals are a happy marriage of West African, French and Caribbean: spicy pumpkin soup, snapper in a scotch-bonnet lime sauce, curried goat and charcoal-grilled Turks and Caicos conch. Make sure you try the *mayi moulen,* a signature side of cornmeal smothered in a rich bean sauce – bloody delicious! If you need some liquid courage, shoot some Barbancourt rum, available in several grades (all strong).

## BUILDING A CUBAN SANDWICH

The traditional Cuban sandwich, also known as a *sandwich mixto*, is not some slapdash creation. It's a craft best left to the experts – but here's some insight into how they do it. Correct bread is crucial – it should be Cuban white bread: fresh, soft and easy to press. The insides (both sides) should be buttered and layered (in the following order) with sliced pickles, slices of roast Cuban pork, ham (preferably sweet-cured ham) and baby Swiss cheese. Then it all gets pressed in a hot *plancha* (sandwich press) until the cheese melts. Mmmm.

### Cafe Mistral                    FRENCH $$

(Map p56; ☎305-763-8184; 110 Washington Ave; mains $11-18; ⊙9am-11pm Tue-Sat; ♠) Mistral's simple French fare makes this spot a favorite breakfast and lunch spot in SoFi. You're on Miami Beach but removed from its worst excesses, and treated instead to tasty croque monsieurs, garden salads, the 'Fruban' (which of course blends a Cuban sandwich and a baguette) and killer coffee.

### Big Pink                         DINER $$

(Map p56; ☎305-532-4700; 157 Collins Ave; mains $11-26; ⊙8am-midnight Sun-Wed, to 2am Thu, to 5am Fri & Sat) Big Pink does American comfort food with joie de vivre and a dash of whimsy. The Americana menu is consistently good throughout the day; pulled Carolina pork holds the table next to a nicely done reuben. The interior is somewhere between a '50s sock hop and a South Beach club; expect to be seated at a long communal table.

### Grazie                          ITALIAN $$$

(Map p56; ☎305-673-1312; www.grazieitalian-cuisine.com; 702 Washington Ave; mains $19-34; ⊙noon-3pm Mon-Fri, 6pm-midnight daily) Thanks indeed; Grazie is top class and comfortably old-school northern Italian. There's a distinct lack of gorgeous, clueless waitstaff and unwise menu experimentation. Instead there's attentive service, solid and delicious mains, and extremely decent prices given the quality of the dining and high-end nature of the location. The porcini risotto is simple in construction yet deeply complex in execution – one of the best Italian dishes on the beach.

### Prime 112                    STEAKHOUSE $$$

(Map p56; ☎305-532-8112; www.prime112.com; 112 Ocean Dr; mains $29-75; ⊙noon-3pm Mon-Fri, 5:30pm-midnight Sun-Thu, to 1am Sat & Sun) Sometimes, you need a steak: well aged, juicy, marbled with the right bit of fat, served in a spot where the walls sweat testosterone, the bar serves Manhattans and the hostesses are models. Chuck the above into Miami Beach's oldest inn – the beautiful 1915 Browns Hotel – and there's Prime 112. Dress up, because there's a good chance you'll be dining next to a celebrity.

### Joe's Stone Crab Restaurant    AMERICAN $$$

(Map p56; ☎305-673-0365; www.joesstonecrab.com; 11 Washington Ave; mains $11-60; ⊙11:30am-2pm Wed-Sun, except in summer, & 6-10pm Wed-Sun year-round) The wait is long, the prices high. But if those aren't deal-breakers, queue up to don a bib in Miami's most famous restaurant and enjoy deliciously fresh stone-crab claws.

## ✕ South Beach (11th to 23rd Streets)

### Burger & Beer Joint             BURGERS $

(Map p52; ☎305-672-3287; www.bnbjoint.com; 1766 Bay Rd; mains $5.50-9; ⊙11:30am-midnight Sun-Thu, to 2am Fri & Sat; ♠) Gourmet burgers. Microbrew beer. Clearly, the folks at B&B did their marketing research. Because who doesn't love both? Oh yes, vegetarians, you're catered to as well: the 'Dear Prudence', a mix of portobello, red pepper, walnut pesto and zucchini fries will keep herbivores happy. Oh, there's a turkey and stuffing burger with gravy served *between turkey patties,* an ahi tuna burger, a patty of wagyu beef with foie gras...you get the idea. Did we mention the microbrew beer?

### Flamingo Restaurant           NICARAGUAN $

(Map p52; ☎305-673-4302; 1454 Washington Ave; mains $2.50-7; ⊙7am-9pm Mon-Sat) This tiny Nicaraguan storefront-cafe serves the behind-the-scenes laborers who make South Beach function. You will very likely be the only tourist eating here. Workers devour hen soup, pepper chicken and cheap breakfasts prepared by a meticulous husband-and-wife team.

### Paul                             BAKERY $

(Map p52; 450 Lincoln Rd; mains $5.50-11; ⊙8:30am-8pm; ♠) Paul sells itself as a 'Maison de Qualite,' which in other words means you can get some very fine bread here, the sort of crusty-outside and pillow-soft-inside bread you associate with a Parisian *boulangerie*. Gourmet sandwiches and light pastries make for a refreshing Lincoln Rd lunch stop.

### Gelateria 4D                    ICE CREAM $

(Map p52; ☎ 305-538-5755; 670 Lincoln Rd; ice creams $3.85-8; ☺ 9am-midnight Sun-Thu, to 1:30am Fri & Sat) It's hot. You've been walking all day. You need ice cream, stat. Why hello, 4D! This is an excellent spot for creamy, pillowy waves of European-style frozen goodness, and based on the crowds it's the favorite ice cream on South Beach.

### ★ Pubbelly                    FUSION $$

(Map p52; ☎ 305-532-7555; 1418 20th Street; mains $11-26; ☺ 6pm-midnight Tue-Thu & Sun, to midnight Fri & Sat) Pubbelly's dining genre is hard to pinpoint, besides delicious. It skews between Asian, North American and Latin American, gleaning the best from all cuisines. Examples? Try duck and scallion dumplings, or the mouth-watering udon 'carbonara' with pork belly, poached eggs and parmesan. Hand-crafted cocktails wash down the dishes a treat.

### Jerry's Famous Deli                    DELI $$

(Map p52; ☎ 305-532-8030; www.jerrysfamousdeli.com; 1450 Collins Ave; mains $9-18; ☺ 24hr) Important: Jerry's delivers. Why? Because when you've gorged on the pastrami on rye, turkey clubs and other mile-high sandwiches at this enormous Jewish deli (housed in what used to be the Warsaw nightclub), you'll be craving more of the above 24/7.

### Spiga                    ITALIAN $$

(Map p56; ☎ 305-534-0079; www.spigarestaurant.com; Impala Hotel, 1228 Collins Ave; mains $15-28; ☺ 6pm-midnight) This romantic nook is a perfect place to bring your partner and gaze longingly at one another over candlelight, before you both snap out of it and start digging into excellent traditional Italian such as lamb in olive oil and rosemary, and baby clams over linguine.

### Jimmy'z Kitchen                    LATIN AMERICAN $$

(Map p52; ☎ 305-534-8216; 1542 Alton Rd; mains $8-18; ☺ 11am-10pm Sat-Thu, to 11pm Fri; ✍) It's hard to find Nuevo Latino cuisine that comfortably fits a midrange budget and is still tasy, but in steps Jimmy'z. Make sure to try the *mofongo*, a ridculously filling fried plantain dish from Puerto Rico. Make sure to top the evening off with some decadent guava cheesecake.

### Van Dyke Cafe                    FUSION $$

(Map p52; ☎ 305-534-3600; 846 Lincoln Rd; mains $12-28; ☺ 8am-1am) One of Lincoln Rd's most touristed spots, the Van Dyke is an institution akin to the News Cafe, serving adequate food in a primo spot for people-watching. It's usually packed and takes over half the sidewalk. Service is friendly and efficient, and you get free preening models with your burgers and eggplant parmigiana. There's excellent nightly jazz upstairs.

### Guru                    INDIAN $$

(Map p56; ☎ 305-534-3996; 232 12th St; mains $15-23; ☺ noon-11:30pm; ✍) A sexy, soft-lit interior of blood reds and black wood sets the stage for this Indian eatery, where local ingredients like lobster swim into the korma. Goan fish curry goes down a treat but the service often seems rushed and the kitchen can be inconsistent. Try coming at lunchtime for the *thali* special, an assemble-your-own meal extravaganza.

### Balans                    FUSION $$

(Map p52; ☎ 305-534-9191; 1022 Lincoln Rd; mains $13-36; ☺ 8am-midnight) Kensington, Chiswick...South Beach? Oi, give this Brit-owned fusion favorite a go. Where else do veal saltimbocca and lamb *jalfrezi* share a menu? After you down the signature lobster club, you'll agree tired stereotypes about English cooking need to be reconsidered.

### Nexxt Cafe                    FUSION $$

(Map p52; ☎ 305-532-6643; 700 Lincoln Rd; mains $7-23; ☺ 11:30am-11pm Mon-Thu, to midnight Fri & Sat, 11am-11pm Sun) There's a lot of cafes arranged around Lincoln Rd that offer good people-watching along one of Miami Beach's most fashionable stretches. Many of these spots are of questionable quality. Nexxt is the best of the bunch, with a huge menu that jumps between turkey chili, gourmet burgers and low-cal salads the size of your face. Speaking of which, the menu is simply enormous, and though nothing is really excellent, everything is pretty good.

### Front Porch Cafe                    AMERICAN $$

(Map p52; ☎ 305-531-8300; 1418 Ocean Dr; mains $10-18; ☺ 7am-11pm) A blue-and-white escape from the madness of the cruising scene, the Porch has been serving excellent salads, sandwiches and the like since 1990 (eons by South Beach standards). Weekend brunch is justifiably mobbed; the big omelets are delicious, as are the fat pancakes and strong coffees.

### ★ Osteria del Teatro
ITALIAN $$$

(Map p52; ☎ 305-538-7850; 1443 Washington Ave; mains $17-45; ⊗ 6-11pm Mon-Thu, to 1am Fri-Sun) There are few things to swear by but the specials board of Osteria, one of the oldest and best Italian restaurants in Greater Miami, ought to be one. When you get here, let the gracious Italian waiters seat you, coddle you and then basically order for you off the board. They never pick wrong.

### Yardbird
SOUTHERN $$$

(Map p52; ☎ 305-538-5220; 1600 Lenox Ave; mains $26-42; ⊗ 11:30am-11pm Mon-Thu, to midnight Fri, 10am-midnight Sat, 10am-11pm Sun) Yardbird is one of the most popular practitioners of Miami's surprisingly deep wave of haute Southern comfort food. The restaurant dishes out some nice Salisbury steak, St Louis ribs, grits and kale, but it's most famous for a signature chicken and waffles dish that strikes a nice balance of salty, savory and sweet.

### Casa Tua
ITALIAN $$$

(Map p52; ☎ 305-673-1010; www.casatualifestyle.com/miami; 1700 James Ave; mains $23-58; ⊗ 11:30am-3pm Mon-Fri, 7:30-11pm daily) Casa Tua is way too cool to have a sign out front. You'll know it by the oh-so-fabulous crowd streaming in, the hovering limos and what you can see of the beautiful building itself (much of it hidden behind a high hedge). If you manage to get a table in the magnificent, 1925 Mediterranean-style villa, you can linger over delicious prosciutto, Dover sole, risotto with lobster and veal cheeks.

### Juvia
FUSION $$$

(Map p52; ☎ 305-763-8272; 1111 Lincoln Rd; mains $23-55; ⊗ noon-3pm & 6pm-midnight daily, to 1am Fri & Sat; ☑) Juvia blends the trendsetters that have staying power in Miami's culinary world: namely, France, Latin America and Japan. Chilean seabass comes cooked in soy butter, while sea scallops are dressed with shiitakes and garlic chips. The big, bold, beautiful dining room, which sits on the high floors of 1111 Lincoln Rd (p51), is quintessential South Beach glam.

### Mr Chow Chinese
CHINESE, FUSION $$$

(Map p52; ☎ 305-695-1695; www.mrchow.com; 2201 Collins Ave; mains $30-45; ⊗ 6pm-midnight) Located in the W Hotel (p95), Mr Chow takes Chinese American comfort food to gourmet heights. The setting is almost intimidatingly cool, with dangling moderne-style chandeliers and an enormous bar plucked out of *Sex and the City,* yet service is friendly and the food lovely: velvet chicken served with diced chilies; stinky, spicy tofu; squid sautéed with asparagus.

### Yuca
LATIN AMERICAN $$$

(Map p52; ☎ 305-532-9822; 501 Lincoln Rd; mains $22-48; ⊗ noon-11:30pm) This was one of the first Nuevo Latino hot spots in Miami and it's still going strong, even if locals say it has lost a little luster over the years. The Yuca *rellena* (a mild chili stuffed with truffle-laced mushroom *picadillo*) and the tender guava ribs still make our mouth water.

## Northern Miami Beach

### Roasters' n Toasters
DELI $

(Map p60; ☎ 305-531-7691; 525 Arthur Godfrey Rd; mains $8-16; ⊗ 6:30am-3:30pm) Given the crowds and the satisfied smiles of customers, Roasters' n Toasters meets the demanding standards of Miami Beach's large Jewish demographic, thanks to juicy deli meat, fresh bread, crispy bagels and warm *latkes.* Sliders (mini-sandwiches) are served on challah bread, an innovation that's as charming as it is tasty.

### Josh's Deli
DELI $

(☎ 305-397-8494; 9517 Harding Ave; mains $6-14; ⊗ 8:30am-3:30pm) Josh's is simplicity itself. Here in the heart of Jewish Miami, it serves Jewish deli meat, and that deli meat is delicious. Corned beef, pastrami, rye bread, mustard – truly, what more do we need from life?

### Shuckers
AMERICAN $

(Map p60; ☎ 305-866-1570; 1819 79th St Causeway; mains $8-19; ⊗ 11am-late) With excellent views overlooking the waters from the 79th St Causeway, Shuckers has to be one of the best-positioned restaurants around. The food is pub grub: burgers, fried fish and the like. We come here for one reason: the chicken wings. They're basted in several mouthwatering sauces, deep-fried and grilled again. We could sit here and devour a flock of poultry if our willpower was low.

### Chivitoteca
URUGUAYAN $

(Map p60; ☎ 305-864-5252; 6987 Collins Ave; mains $5.50-16; ⊗ noon-11:30pm Mon-Thu, to 1am Fri & Sat, to midnight Sun) Heart, meet the *chivito*: a Uruguayan sandwich of steak, ham, cheese, fried eggs and mayonnaise (there may have been lettuce, peppers and tomatoes too, but the other ingredients just laughed at them). Now run, heart, run away! That's just the basics, by the way, and it comes with fries. You can also get pizza served by the meter, because honestly, at this stage you should just let yourself go.

### La Perrada de Edgar
FAST FOOD $

(Map p60; ✆305-866-4543; 6976 Collins Ave; hot dogs $4-7; ⊘noon-midnight) Back in the day, Colombia's most (in)famous export to Miami was cocaine. But seriously, what's powder got on La Perrada and its kookily delicious hot dogs that were devised by some Dr Evil of the frankfurter world? Don't believe us? Try an *especial,* topped with plums, pineapple and whipped cream. How about shrimp and potato sticks? Apparently these are normal hotdog toppings in Colombia. The homemade lemonade also goes down a treat.

### ★ Steve's Pizza
PIZZERIA $$

(✆305-891-0202; www.stevespizzas.net; 12101 Biscayne Blvd; slices $3, pizzas $10-16; ⊘11am-3am Sun-Wed, to 4am Thu & Fri, to 2am Sat) So many pizza chains compete for the attention of tourists in South Beach, but ask a Miami Beach local where to get the best pizza and they'll tell you about Steve's. This is New York–style pizza, thin crust and handmade with care and good ingredients. New branches of Steve's are opening elsewhere in Miami, all in decidedly nontouristy areas, which preserves that feeling of authenticity. Steve's flagship is in South Miami; the closer North Miami outpost listed here caters to nighthawks, and is located about 6 miles (15 minutes' drive) north of the Design District.

### Indomania
INDONESIAN $$

(Map p60; ✆305-535-6332; 131 26th St; mains $17-28; ⊘6-10:30pm Tue-Sun) There's a lot of watered-down Asian cuisine in Miami; Indomania bucks this trend with an authentic execution of dishes from Southeast Asia's largest nation. Dishes reflect Indonesia's diversity, ranging from chicken in coconut curry to snapper grilled in banana leaves to gut-busting *rijsttafel,* a sort of buffet of small, tapas-style dishes that reflects the culinary character of particular Indonesian regions.

### Cafe Prima Pasta
ARGENTINE $$

(Map p60; ✆305-867-0106; 414 71st St; mains $13-24; ⊘5pm-midnight Mon-Sat, 4-11pm Sun) We're not sure what's better at this Argentine-Italian place: the much-touted pasta, which deserves every one of the accolades heaped on it (try the gnocchi), or the atmosphere, which captures the dignified sexiness of Buenos Aires. Actually, it's no contest: you're the winner, as long as you eat here.

### Fifi's Place
SEAFOOD $$

(Map p60; ✆305-865-5665; 6976 Collins Ave; mains $13-30; ⊘noon-midnight) Latin seafood is the name of the game here – Fifi's does delicious seafood paella, a dish that mixes the supporting cast of *The Little Mermaid* with Spanish rice, and an equally good seafood *parrillada,* which draws on the same ingredients and grills them with garlic butter. Awesome.

## ✕ Downtown Miami

### La Moon
COLOMBIAN $

(Map p62; ✆305-379-5617; www.lamoonrestaurantmiami.com; 144 SW 8th St; meals $6-15; ⊘9am-midnight Mon-Wed, 9am-6am Thu-Sun) Nothing – and we're not necessarily saying this in a good way – soaks up the beer like a Colombian hot dog topped with eggs and potato sticks. Or fried pork belly and pudding. These delicacies are the preferred food and drink of Miami's party people, and the best place for this wicked fare is here, within stumbling distance of bars like Tobacco Road. To really fit in, order a *refajo:* Colombian beer (Aguila) with Colombian soda (preferably the red one).

### Soya e Pomodoro
ITALIAN $

(Map p62; ✆305-381-9511; 120 NE 1st St; lunch $9-16, dinner $13-22; ⊘11:30am-4pm Mon-Fri, 7-11:30pm Thu-Sat) Soya e Pomodoro feels like a bohemian retreat for Italian artists and filmmakers, who can dine on bowls of fresh pasta under vintage posters, rainbow paintings and wall-hangings. Think what would happen if hippies were dropped into the set of *Casablanca.* As per this vibe, readings, jazz shows and other arts events take place here on select evenings.

### Fresco California
MEDITERRANEAN $

(Map p62; ✆305-858-0608; 1744 SW 3rd Ave; mains $9-16; ⊘11:30am-3:30pm Mon-Fri, 5-10:30pm Mon-Thu, to 11pm Fri, 11am-11pm Sat) Fresco serves all kinds of West Coast takes on the Mediterranean palate. Relax in the candlelit backyard dining room, which feels like an Italian porch in summer when the weather is right (ie almost always). Pear and walnut salad and portobello sandwiches are lovely, while the pumpkin-stuffed ravioli is heaven on a platter.

### Mini Healthy Deli
DELI $

(Map p62; ✆305-523-2244; Station Mall, 48 E Flagler St; mains $6-10; ⊘11am-3pm; ✍) This excellent cafe, tucked into a half-vacant

MIAMI EATING

mini-mall, is where chef Carlos Bedoya works solo and churns out remarkably fresh and delicious specials such as grilled tilapia, fresh salad, and rice and beans. There are only two little tables, but it's worth waiting – or standing while you eat.

**Granny Feelgoods** HEALTH FOOD $
(Map p62; ☑ 305-377-9600; 25 W Flagler St; mains $9-15; ⊙ 7am-5pm Mon-Fri; ✔) If you need karmic balance (or just tasty vegetarian fare), try this neighborhood health-food staple. Located next to the courthouse, Granny's must have the highest lawyer-to-bean-sprouts ratio in the USA. Try simple, vegetarian dishes such as tofu sandwiches and spinach lasagna. Carnivores are catered for too – there's a turkey burger.

**★ Choices** VEGETARIAN $$
(Map p62; ☑ 305-400-8895; 379 SW 15th Rd; mains $10-16; ⊙ 8am-9pm Mon-Fri, to 9pm Sat; ✔ 🍴) ✔ The description everyone writes when vegan food tastes good is that you're not missing the meat. This trope actually holds true at Choices. With clever ingredient combinations like walnut 'meat' and daiya cheese, this restaurant lives up to its name, offering burgers, tacos and pizza – all 100% vegan, and all delicious.

**Bonding** FUSION $$
(Map p62; ☑ 786-409-4796; 638 S Miami Ave; mains $12-28; ⊙ noon-11pm Mon-Fri, to midnight Sat, 5pm-midnight Sun; ✔) Multiple Asian cuisines, including Thai, Japanese and Korean, come together into an excellent whole at Bonding. Chicken is expertly tossed with

chilis and basil, red curry is deliciously fiery and sushi rolls are given a South Florida splash with ingredients like mango salsa and spicy mayo. The bar here keeps some excellent sake under the counter.

**OTC** AMERICAN $$
(Map p62; ☑ 305-374-4612; 1250 S Miami Ave; mains $10-22; ⊙ 11:30am-11:30pm Mon-Wed, to midnight Thu, to 1am Fri, 10:30am-1am Sat, to 11pm Sun) Miami loves its food trends, and the movement of the moment is 'rustic' farm-to-table food served alongside craft beer. Brickell's OTC is an exemplar of these practices, serving up truffle steak frites and the like, although it's hard to feel connected to the land in Brickell's high-rise canyons. Whatever; the food is damn tasty.

**Garcia's Seafood Grille & Fish Market** SEAFOOD $$
(Map p62; ☑ 305-375-0765; 398 NW River Dr; mains $9-22; ⊙ 11am-9:30pm) Crowds of Cuban office workers lunch at Garcia's, which feels more like you're in a smugglers' seafood shack than the financial district. Expect occasionally spotty service (a bad thing), freshly caught-and-cooked fish (a good thing) and pleasantly seedy views of the Miami River.

**Carol's Resaurant** ITALIAN $$
(Map p62; ☑ 305-373-7622; 245 SE 1st St; mains $10-22; ⊙ 6-10pm Sun & Mon, to 11pm Tue-Thu, to midnight Fri & Sat, 11am-3pm Sat & Sun; ✔) Carol's is a rare bird in Miami's restaurant aviary: an affordable Italian place with quality food. Wild mushroom ravioli goes down a treat with some red wine, while the duck

---

### KEEP ON TRUCKIN'

Food trucks are a huge deal in Miami. There's far too many to list here, but if you want a taste (pun intended) of what's good on four wheels, head to the Biscayne Triangle Truck Round-Up (BTTR). Like a herd of gastronomic wildebeests, the city's food trucks gather for the BTTR every Tuesday from 5:30pm to 10pm at the Johnson & Wales University campus in North Miami (127th St & Biscayne Blvd). Otherwise, here's some of our favorite purveyors of mobile cuisine; we've included Twitter handles so you can follow their locations online:

Purple People Eatery (www.purpleppleatery.com; @purplepleatery; mains $4-8) Battered mahimahi, herb-crusted mac 'n' cheese and gourmet bison burgers.

gastroPod (www.gastropodmiami.com/food; @gastropodmiami; mains $5-11) Sliders, short ribs, corn cakes and more.

Jefe's Original Fish Tacos & Burgers (www.jefesoriginal.com; @jefesoriginal; mains $2.50-6.50) As you may guess, the fish taco is the way to go.

Slow Food Truck (www.slowfoodtruck.com; @SlowFoodTruck; mains $4-8) Seasonal, local food – a changing menu ensures variety and straight deliciousness.

confit risotto comes out practically perfect. The interior, done up in warm wooden tones offset by plenty of natural light, is as attractive as the food.

**Azul** FUSION $$$
(Map p62; ☎305-913-8288; 500 Brickell Key Dr; mains $25-40; ☺7-11pm Tue-Sat) Falling-water windows, clean metallic spaces and curving copper facades complement one of the nicest views of the city. The Scandi-tastic decor works in harmony with a menu that marries the Mediterranean to Asia; try the oysters wrapped in beef and *hamachi* carpaccio.

## ✕ Wynwood, Design District & Little Haiti

★**Chef Creole** HAITIAN $
(Map p68; ☎305-754-2223; 200 NW 54th St; mains $7-20; ☺11am-11pm Mon-Sat) When you need Caribbean food on the cheap, head to the edge of Little Haiti and this excellent takeout shack. Order up fried conch, oxtail or fish, ladle rice and beans on the side, and you'll be full for a week. Enjoy the food on nearby picnic benches while Haitian music blasts out of tinny speakers – as island an experience as they come.

**Cheese Course** CHEESE $
(Map p68; ☎786-220-6681; www.thecheese-course.com; 3451 NE 1st Ave; mains $5-15; ☺10:30am-9pm Sun-Wed, to 10pm Thu, to 11pm Fri & Sat; ✐) We love the idea at this place – pick out a few cheeses with the help of the staff and have them assemble a platter for you with fresh bread, candied walnuts, cornichons or whatever other accoutrement you so desire. There are also nice sandwiches, spreads and preserves, but for our money you can't beat a perfect lunch here of fermented dairy goodness.

**La Latina** LATIN AMERICAN $
(Map p68; ☎305-571-9655; 3509 NE 2nd Ave; mains $4-10; ☺10am-10pm Tue-Thu, to 5am Fri & Sat, to 4pm Sun; ✐) One of the best budget meals in the immediate Design District vicinity can be found at La Latina, a Venezuelan diner that's popular with Midtown locals and artsy transplants to the area. Cheese and avocado arepas are a treat for vegetarians, but there's a lot of meat, rice, beans and sweet plantains filling out the menu.

**Lemoni Café** CAFE $
(Map p68; ☎305-571-5080; www.mylemonicafe.com; 4600 NE 2nd Ave; mains $6-10; ☺11am-

10:30pm; ✐) Lemoni is as bright as its name suggests, a cute, cozy hole in the wall that serves up superlative sandwiches, wraps and salads. The salami sandwich with greens and olive oil is a simple revelation, and we'd probably rob a bank to get another slice of its key lime pie. Located in the pretty Buena Vista neighborhood, this is a perfect place to grab a sidewalk alfresco lunch or dinner.

**Enriqueta's** LATIN AMERICAN $
(Map p68; ☎305-573-4681; 186 NE 29th St; mains $5-8; ☺6:30am-3:45pm Mon-Fri, to 2pm Sat) Back in the day, Puerto Ricans, not installation artists, ruled Wynwood. Have a taste of those times in this perpetually packed roadhouse, where the Latin-diner ambience is as strong as the steaming shots of *cortadito* (Cuban-style coffee) served at the counter. Balance the local gallery fluff with a steak-and-potato-stick sandwich.

★**Blue Collar** AMERICAN $$
(☎305-756-0366; www.bluecollarmiami.com; 6730 Biscayne Blvd; mains $15-22; ☺11:30am-3:30pm Mon-Fri, 11am-3:30pm Sat & Sun, 6-10pm Sun-Thu, 6-11pm Fri & Sat; ▣✐) ✐ It's not easy striking a balance between laid back and delicious in a city like Miami, where even 'casual' eateries can feel like nightclubs, but Blue Collar has the formula nailed. Friendly staff serve All-American fare sexied the hell up, from crispy snapper to smoky ribs to a superlatively good cheeseburger. A well-curated veg board keeps noncarnivores happy.

**Oak Tavern** AMERICAN $$
(Map p68; ☎786-391-1818; 35 NE 40th St; mains $12-26; ☺noon-10:30pm Mon-Thu, to midnight Fri, 6pm-midnight Sat, 11am-9:30pm Sun; ▣✐) Oak is a fine addition to the burgeoning dining scene in leafy Buena Vista. Grilled grouper sandwiches, wood-fired pizzas, farm-fresh vegetables, mushroom-crusted strip steaks and some great burgers are ostensibly hearty, but presented with sleek Miami attitude in a dining room that successfully pulls off sexy and rustic simultaneously.

**Gigi** ASIAN $$
(Map p68; ☎305-573-1520; 3470 North Miami Ave; mains $14-28; ☺noon-midnight Sun & Mon, to 3am Tue-Thu, to 5am Fri & Sat; ▣) Gigi does Asian cuisine, but it's the sort of Asian you'd expect to find on the border of the ultrahip Design District. Ribs come glazed in hoisin and South American aji, the sweet-and-savory cornbread is an excellent complement and

the pad Thai is divine. Does sushi go with country chicken? Surprisingly well.

### The Federal
AMERICAN $$

(Map p68; ☑ 305-758-9559; 5132 Biscayne Blvd; mains $12-25; ⊙ 5-10pm Tue-Thu & Sun, to 11pm Fri & Sat; ☑) Down-home rustic Americana dining on the upper edges of Buena Vista? Sign us up. Especially when the offerings include chili laced with slow-cooked venison, beer-braised Florida clams and a host of vegetarian options such as crispy brussels sprouts. A chilled-out bar space makes for an easy, social ambience – the buzz here is friendly and easy to fall in love with.

### Egg & Dart
GREEK $$

(Map p68; ☑ 786-431-1022; 4029 N Miami Ave; small plates $4-16, mains $15-36; ⊙ 4-11:30pm Tue-Thu, to midnight Fri, 11am-11:30pm Sat & Sun; ☑☑) Miami has a habit of sexing up the presentation of most ethnic cuisines, but we have to admit, we hadn't seen Greek done with glam till Egg & Dart. The effort is marvelous. Crafted cocktails (try the orange *mojito*) loosen up the palate for small plates like grilled *halloumi* and zucchini croquettes, and big mains like lovingly grilled lamb and a delicious beet-and-cheese stack.

### The Butcher Shop
AMERICAN $$

(Map p68; ☑ 305-846-9120; 165 NW 23rd St; mains $11-32; ⊙ 11am-11pm Sun-Thu, to 2am Fri & Sat)

We suppsoe there *is* a vegetarian option here – you could order a bread and cheese plate. But this Wynwood joint is called the Butcher Shop for a reason, and that's because it's unashamedly aimed at carnivores. From bone-in rib eyes to smoked sausages to full charcuterie, meat lovers have reason to rejoice. Beer lovers too; this butcher's doubles as a beer garden.

### The Embassy
SPANISH $$

(Map p68; ☑ 305-571-8446; 4600 NE 2nd Ave; mains $17-23; ⊙ 6pm-midnight Tue-Thu, to 3am Fri & Sat, 10am-3pm Sun; ☑) Embassy is a gastropub with Miami attitude, a Midtown veneer and an emphasis on Spanish tapas. Seared chicken with olive mashed potatoes and roasted snapper with fennel make a strong showing, as do regular vegan platters. The Buena Vista setting projects understated hip, as does the clientele.

### Fiorito
ARGENTINE $$

(Map p68; ☑ 305-754-2899; 5555 NE 2nd Ave; mains $14-21; ⊙ noon-10pm) Sometimes you need simple Latin American fare that's a cut above the average fried-plantains diner. Enter Fiorito, an excellent Argentine steakhouse that will fill your stomach way before it empties your wallet. Pastas, steaks, braised pork and some gorgeous hand-cut fries had us rolling happily out the door. Grab some excellent empanadas on the way out.

## NORTH BISCAYNE BOULEVARD

As North Biscayne Blvd continues to gentrify, better and better restaurants are opening up. Here are some winners from this foodie find:

**Michy's** (☑ 305-759-2001; http://michysmiami.com; 6927 Biscayne Blvd; meals $29-38; ⊙ 6-10:30pm Tue-Thu, to 11pm Fri & Sat, to 10pm Sun; ☑) Blue-and-white pop decor. Organic, locally sourced ingredients. A stylish, fantastical bar where Alice could drink before painting Wonderland red. Welcome to Michelle 'Michy' Bernstein's culinary lovechild – one of the brightest stars in Miami's culinary constellation. The emphasis is on good food and fun. The 'half plates' concept lets you halve an order and mix up delicious gastronomic fare, such as foie gras on corn cakes, chicken pot pie with wild mushrooms, white almond gazpacho, and blue-cheese croquettes.

**Honey Tree** (Map p68; ☑ 305-756-1696; 5138 Biscayne Blvd; mains under $10; ⊙ 8am-8pm Mon-Thu, to 7pm Fri, 9am-6pm Sat; ☑) The Honey Tree is a health-food store that happens to serve excellent juices, smoothies and what many consider to be Miami's best vegan lunch. What's on offer varies day by day, but rest assured it will be cheap (it's priced by weight) and delicious. Lunch is usually served from noon to 2pm, but keep in mind that food often runs out due to high demand.

**Jimmy's East Side Diner** (☑ 305-754-3692; 7201 Biscayne Blvd; mains $5-13; ⊙ 6:30am-4pm) Come to Jimmy's, a classic greasy spoon (that happens to be very gay friendly; note the rainbow flag out front), for big cheap breakfasts of omelets, French toast or pancakes, and turkey clubs and burgers later in the day.

### Mandolin
GREEK **$$**

(Map p68; ☑ 305-576-6066; 4312 NE 2nd Ave; mains $12-26; ⊙noon-11pm Mon-Sat, to 10pm Sun; ☑) Mandolin doesn't just provide good Greek food – although that is present in the form of fresh fish grilled in lemon and olive oil, tomato and Turkish chorizo sandwiches and light mezes such as smoked eggplant and creamy yogurt. What Mandolin also provides is excellent Greek atmosphere. It's all Aegean whites and blues, colors that come to life under the strong, melting Miami sun, especially if you sit in the back courtyard, shaded by the same trees that stretch over the surrounding Buena Vista neighborhood.

### Harry's Pizzeria
PIZZERIA **$$**

(Map p68; ☑ 786-275-4963; 3918 North Miami Ave; pizzas $15; ⊙11:30am-11pm Mon-Thu, to midnight Fri & Sat, to 10pm Sun; ☑) A stripped-down yet sumptuous dining experience awaits (pizza) pie lovers in Midtown. Harry's tiny kitchen and dining room dishes out deceptively simple wood-fired pizzas that are a perfect date meal; we're big fans of the braised fennel pie. Look out for nonpizza daily specials such as Friday's oven-roasted local fish.

### Lost & Found Saloon
MEXICAN **$$**

(Map p68; ☑ 305-576-1008; www.thelostandfound-saloon-miami.com; 185 NW 36th St; mains $10-17; ⊙11am-3am; ☑) The service is as friendly as the omelets and burritos are awesome (which is to say, very) at this little Wynwood spot, the sort of saloon where microbrews are on tap and the wine list reads like a year abroad. Come the evening, this turns into a fun hipster kind of bar.

## ✕ Key Biscayne

### Oasis
CUBAN **$**

(Map p72; ☑ 305-361-9009; 19 Harbor Dr; mains $5-12; ⊙6am-9pm) This excellent Cuban cafe has a customer base that ranges from the working poor to city players, and the socioeconomic barriers come tumbling down fast as folks sip high-octane Cuban coffee. Between the superstrong coffee and *masas de puerco* – marinated pork chunks, which go great with hot sauce – we're in hole-in-the-wall heaven.

### Boater's Grill
SEAFOOD **$$**

(Map p72; ☑ 305-361-0080; 1200 S Crandon Blvd; mains $12-29; ⊙9am-9pm) Located in Crandon Park, this waterfront restaurant (actually there's water below and all around) feels like a Chesapeake Bay sea house from up

north, except the menu is packed with South Florida maritime goodness: stone crabs, mahimahi and lobster paella.

### Rusty Pelican
SEAFOOD **$$$**

(☑ 305-361-3818; 3201 Rickenbacker Causeway; mains $18-42; ⊙11am-11pm Sun-Thu, to midnight Fri & Sat) More than the fare itself, it's the panoramic skyline views – among the best in Miami – that draw the faithful and romantic to this restaurant. But if you come for a sunset drink, the fresh air could certainly seduce you into staying for some of the surf 'n' turf menu, which is packed with high-end grilled steaks and seafood.

## ✕ Little Havana

### ★ Exquisito Restaurant
CUBAN **$**

(Map p74; ☑ 305-643-0227; 1510 SW 8th St; mains $7-13; ⊙7am-11pm) For great Cuban cuisine in the heart of Little Havana, this place is exquisite (ha ha). The roast pork has a tangy citrus kick and the *ropa vieja* (pulled braised brisket) is wonderfully rich and filling. Even standard sides like beans and rice and roasted plantains are executed with a little more care and tastiness. Prices are a steal too.

### Hy Vong Vietnamese Restaurant
VIETNAMESE **$**

(☑ 305-446-3674; 3458 SW 8th; mains $7-22; ⊙6-11pm Wed-Sun, closed mid-late Aug) In a neighborhood full of exiles from a communist regime, it makes sense to find a Vietnamese restaurant. And it's telling that despite all the great Latin food around, Little Havanans wait hours for a seat here. Why? Because this spot serves great Vietnamese food with little touches of Florida, like Florida-style mango marinade.

### Islas Canarias
CUBAN **$**

(☑ 305-559-6666; 285 NW 27th Ave; mains $8-19; ⊙7am-11pm) Islas may not look like much, sitting in a strip mall, but it serves some of the best Cuban in Miami. The *ropa vieja* is delicious and there are nice Spanish touches on the menu (the owner's father is from the Canary Islands, hence the restaurant's name). Don't pass up the signature homemade chips, especially the ones cut from plantains.

### El Cristo
CUBAN **$**

(Map p74; ☑ 305-643-9992; 1543 SW 8th St; mains $6-18; ⊙7am-11pm; ☑) A popular hangout among locals, the down-to-earth El Cristo has options from all over the Spanish-speaking world. Lots of people say it's as good as Calle Ocho gets. The menu has daily specials, but the standout is fish – try it fried for a local version of fish and chips, or take away some excellent fish empanadas and *croquetas* (deep-fried in breadcrumbs).

### Yambo
LATIN AMERICAN $

(1643 SW 1st St; mains $4-11; ⊘24hr) If you're a bit drunk in the middle of the night and can find a cab or a friend willing to drive all the way out to Little Havana, direct them to Yambo. We've never actually been here during the day, although the restaurant is surely a pretty place for lunch or breakfast. At night Yambo does a roaring stock in trade selling trays and take-away boxes about to burst with juicy slices of carne asada, piles of rice and beans and sweet fried plantains. If you're going to soak up beer, this is a great sponge.

### Los Pinareños Frutería
FRUIT STAND $

(Map p74; 1334 SW 8th St; snacks & drinks $2-4; ⊘7am-7pm Mon-Sat, to 2pm Sun) Nothing says refreshment on a sweat-stained Miami afternoon like a long, cool glass of fruit smoothie at this popular juice and veggie stand – try the sugarcane juice for something particularly sweet and bracing. The produce is pretty fresh and flavorful too.

### El Rey de Las Fritas
BURGERS $

(Map p74; www.reydelasfritas.com; 1821 SW 8th St; snacks $2-3; ⊘8am-10:30pm Mon-Sat) If you've never had a *frita* (Cuban-style burger) make your peace with McDonald's and come down to El Rey with the lawyers, developers, construction workers and every other slice of Miami's Latin life. These *fritas* are big, juicy and served under a mountain of shoestring fries. Plus, the *batidos* (Latin American milkshakes) definitely bring the boys to the yard.

### Versailles
CUBAN $$

(⏺305-444-0240; 3555 SW 8th St; mains $5-26; ⊘8am-1am) Versailles (ver-*sigh*-yay) is an institution, one of the mainstays of Miami's Cuban gastronomic scene. Try the ground beef in a gratin sauce or chicken breast cooked in creamy garlic sauce. Older Cubans and Miami's Latin political elite still love coming here, so you've got a real chance to rub elbows with a who's who of Miami's most prominent Latin citizens.

---

## 🍴 Coconut Grove

### Coral Bagels
DELI $

(⏺305-854-0336; 2750 SW 26th Ave; mains $3.75-9; ⊘6:30am-3pm Mon-Fri, 7am-4pm Sat & Sun;

⏺⏺) At the risk of engaging in hyperbole, we can't imagine a better way of starting the day than a garlic bagel at this little deli. Breakfast (bagels and more traditional eggs, meat and potatoes) is the way to go; you'll be hard pressed to spend double digits, and you'll leave satisfied.

### Last Carrot
VEGETARIAN $

(Map p76; ⏺305-445-0805; 3133 Grand Ave; mains $6; ⊘10am-6pm Mon-Fri, to 4pm Sun; ⏺) Folks of all walks, corporate suits included, come here for fresh juice, delicious wraps (veggie options are great but the tuna melt is divine) and old-Grove neighborliness. The Carrot's endurance next to massive CocoWalk is testament to the quality of its good-for-your-body food served in a good-for-your-soul setting.

### LoKal
AMERICAN $

(Map p76; ⏺305-442-3377; 3190 Commodore Plaza; burgers $11-14; ⊘noon-10pm Sun-Thu, to 11pm Fri & Sat; ⏺⏺⏺) 🍴 This little Coconut Grove joint does two things very well: burgers and smart ingredient sourcing. The former come in several variations, all utilizing excellent beef (bar the oat-bran-based veggie version); we love the frita, which adds in guava sauce. The latter comes in the form of genuine farm-to-table relationships; there's a reason the avocado slices are so beautiful.

### Xixon
SPANISH $$

(⏺305-854-9350; 2101 SW 22nd St; tapas $8-15; ⊘11am-10pm Mon-Thu, to 11pm Fri & Sat; ⏺) It takes a lot to stand out in Miami's crowded tapas-spot stakes. Bread that has a crackling crust and a soft center, delicate explosions of *bacalao* (cod) fritters and the best eels cooked in garlic we've ever eaten secure Xixon's status as a top tapas contender. The *bocadillo* (sandwiches), with their blood red Serrano ham and salty Manchego cheese, are great picnic fare.

### Lulu
AMERICAN $$

(Map p76; ⏺305-447-5858; 3105 Commodore Plaza; mains $9-25; ⊘11:30am-10:45pm Sun-Thu, to 11:45pm Fri & Sat; ⏺) Lulu is the Grove's exemplar of using local, organic ingredients to provide gourmet versions of comfort food in a nice outdoor setting. Well, there is an interior dining space, and it is lovely, but the outdoor seating, shaded by the spreading boughs of Coconut Grove's many trees, is where we prefer to be. The truffle mac 'n' cheese is rich and immensely satisfying, while the Lulu burger is to die for.

**Green Street Cafe** AMERICAN **$$**

(Map p76; ☑ 305-567-0662; 3468 Main Hwy; mains $10-23; ⊙7:30am-1am) Sidewalk spots don't get more popular (and many say more delicious) than Green Street, where the Grove's young and gorgeous congregate at sunset. There's an excellent mix of lamb burgers with goat's cheese, salmon salads, occasional art shows and general indie defiance of Grove gentrification, which makes for an idiosyncratic dining experience.

**Jaguar** LATIN AMERICAN **$$**

(Map p76; ☑ 305-444-0216; www.jaguarspot.com; 3067 Grand Ave; mains $17-32; ⊙11:30am-11pm Mon-Thu, to 11:30pm Fri & Sat, 11am-11pm Sun) The menu spans the Latin world, but really, everyone's here for the ceviche 'spoon bar.' The idea: pick from six styles of ceviche (raw, marinated seafood), ranging from swordfish with cilantro to corvina in lime juice, and pull a culinary version of DIY. It's novel and fun, and the $2 ceviche varieties are pretty damn delicious. Other mains include different kinds of grilled meats and fish – endearing in their simplicity, but lacking the tasty complexity of the ceviche.

**George's in the Grove** FRENCH **$$**

(Map p76; ☑ 305-444-7878; 3145 Commodore Plaza; mains $13-29; ⊙10am-11pm Mon-Fri, 8am-11pm Sat & Sun) George's has a manically over-the-top menu that throws in everything from French to Italian to Latin plus the kitchen sink. This all comes packaged with manic, over-the-top decor that looks like a cozy attic just exploded all over Coconut Grove. Mains are rich in the best rural French culinary tradition; standbys include steak *frites*, duck confit and grilled branzino.

## ✕ Coral Gables

**Matsuri** JAPANESE **$**

(Map p78; ☑ 305-663-1615; 5759 Bird Rd; mains $7-23; ⊙11:30am-2:30pm Tue-Fri, 5:30-10:30pm Tue-Sat) Note the customers here: Matsuri, tucked into a nondescript shopping center, is consistently packed with Japanese customers. They don't want scene; they want a taste of home, although many of the diners are actually South American Japanese who order *unagi* (eels) in Spanish. Spicy *toro* (fatty tuna) and scallions, grilled mackerel with natural salt, and an ocean of raw fish are all *oishii* (delicious).

★ **El Carajo** SPANISH **$$**

(☑ 305-856-2424; www.elcarajointernationaltapasandwines.com; 2465 SW 17th Ave; tapas $4.50-17; ⊙noon-10pm Mon-Wed, to 11pm Thu-Sat, 1-9pm Sun) Pass the Penzoil please. We know it is cool to tuck restaurants into unassuming spots, but the Citgo station on SW 17th Ave? Really? Really. Walk past the motor oil into a Granadan wine cellar and try not to act too fazed. And now the food, which is absolutely incredible: chorizo in cider blends burn, smoke and juice; frittatas are comfortably filling; and *sardinas* and *boquerones*...wow. These sardines and anchovies cooked with a bit of salt and olive oil are dizzyingly delicious.

**Swine** SOUTHERN **$$**

(Map p78; ☑ 786-360-6433; 2415 Ponce De Leon Blvd; mains $16-40; ⊙11:30am-11pm Tue-Thu, to midnight Fri, 10am-midnight Sat, 10am-10pm Sun, 11:30am-10pm Mon) Rustic smoked pork and whiskey comes to chic Coral Gables courtesy of Swine. Well, to be fair, there's more than pig on the menu; confit rabbit legs, Florida shrimp and grits, country-fried bacon and burgers all make an appearance, and by heavens they're some kind of delicious. Pair with a craft cocktail from the expertly run bar.

**Bulla** SPANISH **$$**

(Map p78; ☑ 305-441-0107; 2500 Ponce de Leon Blvd; small plates $4-17; ⊙noon-10pm Sun-Thu, to late Fri & Sat; ☑) Bulla serves up tapas, which is nothing new in Miami, let alone Coral Gables. But it does so in a gastropub atmosphere, which adds a touch of debauchery to an already hedonistic gastronomic experience, and the tapas themselves are a cut above the rest. Cheeses, grilled fish and Iberico ham croquettes will keep a smile on your face.

**Seasons 52** FUSION **$$**

(Map p78; ☑ 305-442-8552; 321 Miracle Mile; mains $14-32; ⊙11:30am-11pm Mon-Thu, to midnight Fri & Sat, to 10pm Sun) 🍴 We love the concept and the execution at Seasons 52. The concept? A menu that partially rotates on a weekly basis depending on what is seasonally available (now the title makes sense). The execution? Warm flatbreads overlaid with sharp melted cheese and steak; tiger shrimp tossed in a light pasta and chili that manages elegance and heartiness all at once.

**Caffe Abbracci** ITALIAN **$$**

(Map p78; ☑ 305-441-0700; www.caffeabbracci.com; 318 Aragon Ave; mains $17-37; ⊙11:30am-3:30pm Mon-Fri, 6pm-midnight daily) Perfect moments

MIAMI EATING

in Coral Gables come easy. Here's a simple formula: you, a loved one, a muggy Miami evening, some delicious pasta and a glass of red at a sidewalk table at Abbracci – one of the finest Italian restaurants in the Gables.

**La Palme d'Or** FRENCH **$$$**
(Map p78; ☑ 305-913-3200; Biltmore Hotel, 1200 Anastasia Ave; 5-/9-course tasting menu $105/175; ⊗ 6:30-10:30pm Tue-Sat) One of the most acclaimed French restaurants in the USA, the Palme is the culinary match for the Jazz Age opulence that ensconces it. With its white-gloved, old-world class and US attention to service, unmuddled by pretensions of hipness, this place captures, in one elegant stroke, all the exclusivity a dozen South Beach restaurants could never grasp.

**Pascal's on Ponce** FRENCH **$$$**
(Map p78; ☑ 305-444-2024; www.pascalmiami.com; 2611 Ponce de Leon Blvd; mains $30-42; ⊗ 11:30am-2:30pm Mon-Fri, 6-10pm Mon-Thu, to 11pm Fri & Sat) They're fighting the good fight here: sea scallops with beef short rib, crème brûlée and other French fine-dining classics set the elegant stage at this neighborhood hangout, a favorite night out among Coral Gables foodies who appreciate time-tested standards. The menu and the atmosphere rarely changes, and frankly we think this a good thing: if it ain't broke...

## Greater Miami

**Lots of Lox** DELI **$**
(www.originallotsoflox.com; 14995 S Dixie Hwy; mains $4-13; ⊗ 8am-2:30pm) In a city with no shortage of delis, especially in mid–Miami Beach, who would have thought some of the best chopped liver on rye could be found in this unassuming place all the way down in Palmetto Bay? It is bustling, friendly and the excellent lunch meats sneer at their cousins over on Arthur Godfrey Rd, secure in their dominance of Greater Miami's deli ranks.

**Fritanga Montelimar** NICARAGUAN **$**
(☑ 305-388-8841; 15722 SW 72nd St; buffet $9-13; ⊗ 9am-11pm) A *fritanga* is a Nicaraguan cafe, and if you've never eaten at one, here's a warning: Nicaraguans are not scared of big portions. This beloved spot, located deep in Kendall, serves up grilled pork, chicken stew, meltingly soft beef and other goodies on Styrofoam plates collapsing under the weight of beans and rice. Delicious and cheaper than chips.

## 🍷 Drinking & Nightlife

Too many people assume Miami's nightlife is all about being superattractive, super-rich and supersnooty. Disavow yourself of this notion, which only describes a small slice of the scene in South Beach. Miami has an intense variety of bars to pick from that range from grotty dives to beautiful – but still laid-back – lounges and nightclubs. Not to say you can't spot celebrities if you want to...

In South Beach and the big Miami superclubs, covers range from $20 to $30 (sometimes higher!), so get your wallet ready.

Gay and lesbian nightlife used to be the province of South Beach, but today the scene is pretty integrated into straight Miami. Some clubs are still found in South Beach, while more casual gay bars are in Midcity, North Biscayne Blvd and Northern Miami Beach.

## 🍸 South Beach

★**Room** BAR
(Map p56; www.theotheroom.com; 100 Collins Ave; ⊗ 7pm-5am) The Room's a gem: a crowded, dimly lit boutique beer bar where you can guzzle the best (brew) Miami has to offer and gawk at the best (hotties) South Beach has to show off. It's hip as hell, but the attitude is as low-key as the sexy mood lighting. Just beware, it gets crowded and it can be tough to find seats as the night goes on.

**Kill Your Idol** BAR
(Map p52; ☑ 305-672-1852; 222 Española Way; ⊗ 8pm-5am) Kill Your Idol is a self-conscious dive that aims snooty condescension at South Beach's celebrity scene with one hand (see: the name of the place) while sipping a PBR with the other. Precocious? But it does have sweet postmodern art, graffiti and undeniably cute hipsters, and it's adjoined to that most unselfconscious of dives, Lost Weekend.

**Abbey Brewery** BAR
(Map p52; www.abbeybrewinginc.com; 1115 16th St; ⊗ 1pm-5am) The only brewpub in South Beach is on the untouristed end of South Beach (near Alton Rd). It's friendly and packed with folks listening to the Grateful Dead and slinging back some excellent home brew: give Father Theo's stout or the Immaculate IPA a shot.

**Ted's Hideaway** SPORTS BAR
(Map p56; 124 2nd St; ⊗ noon-5am) Somewhere in the Florida panhandle is a bumpin', fabu-

lous gay club, which clearly switched places with Ted's, a no-nonsense, pool-table and sports-showin' 'lounge' smack in the middle of SoFi's elegance.

### Rose Bar at the Delano
BAR

(Map p52; ☎ 305-672-2000; 1685 Collins Ave, Delano Hotel; ☺noon-2am) The ultrachic Rose Bar at this elegant Ian Schrager original is a watering hole for beautiful creatures (or at least those with a healthy ego). Get ready to pay up for the privilege – but also prepare to enjoy it. The tiki bar in the back of the Delano is another winner; wait for staff to set out a wrought-iron table in the shallow end of the pool and you'll start rethinking your definition of opulence.

### B Bar
BAR

(Map p52; Betsy Hotel, 1440 Ocean Dr; ☺10pm-3am Wed-Sat) This smallish basement bar, tucked under the Betsy Hotel, has two salient features. One is a crowd of the beautiful, in-the-know SoBe-tastic types you expect at South Beach nightspots. The other is an odd, low-hanging reflective ceiling, built out of a sort of wobbly material that sinks in like soft Jell-O and ripples like a stone in a pond when you touch it. It's a pretty cool thing to witness, especially when all sorts of drunk, beautiful people try to (literally) raise the roof.

### Lost Weekend
BAR

(Map p52; 218 Española Way; ☺noon-5am) The Weekend is a grimy, sweaty, slovenly dive, filled with pool tables, cheap domestics and – hell yeah – Golden Tee arcade games and Big Buck Hunter. God bless it. Popular with local waiters, kitchen staff and bartenders.

### Pool Bar at the Sagamore
BAR

(Map p52; 1671 Collins Ave) Head out to the back pool and sip a beer (or a nice cocktail) in the shadow of the artsy funk and hip geometric lines of the Sagamore hotel (p94).

### Mac's Club Deuce Bar
BAR

(Map p52; 222 14th St; ☺8am-5am) The oldest bar in Miami Beach (established in 1926), the Deuce is a real neighborhood bar and hype-free zone. It's just straight-up seediness, which, depending on your outlook, can be quite refreshing. Plan to see everyone from transgendered ladies to construction workers – some hooking up, some talking rough, all having a good time.

### Chesterfield Hotel Bar
BAR

(Map p56; Chesterfield Hotel, 855 Collins Ave; ☺usually noon-3am) Perch on some prime Collins people-watching real estate and get crunk on the hip-hop and zebra-stripe theme they've got going. You'd think this would be a start-the-night-out sort of place, but the setting's so fly, folks end up stationary, sipping on martinis until they stumble into their rooms.

### Dewey's Tavern
BAR

(Map p56; 852 Alton Rd; ☺11am-5am) Dewey's is an art-deco dive (really; the exterior is a little gem of the genre) and it's as unpretentious as the best sordid watering holes get. Come here to get wasted and menace the crowds seeking serenity on quiet Alton Rd (just kidding – behave yourself!).

### Mango's Tropical Café
BAR

(Map p56; ☎ 305-673-4422; www.mangostropical-cafe.com; 900 Ocean Dr; cover $10-20; ☺11:45am-5am Mon-Fri, 10am-5am Sat & Sun) Cuba meets

---

### SOUTH BEACH SIPPIN'

Starbucks has a pretty iron grip on the Miami coffee scene (we don't count stand-up Cuban coffee counters, as you can't sit there and read a book or work on your laptop, although if you speak Spanish, they're a good place for hearing local gossip). That said, there are some options besides Starbucks in Miami Beach.

**A La Folie** (Map p52; www.alafoliecafe.com; 516 Española Way; mains $5-15; ☺11am-8pm; ☞) A *tres* French cafe where the waiters have great accents. Why yes, we would like 'zee moka.'

**Segafredo L'Originale** (Map p52; 1040 Lincoln Rd; mains $5-15; ☺10:30am-1am; ☞) Immensely popular with Europeans and South Americans, this chic cafe always seems packed with gorgeous people. Credited with being the first Lincoln Rd business to open its trade to the outside street.

**Nespresso** (Map p52; 1111 Lincoln Rd; mains $5-15; ☺10:30am-11pm; ☞) This futuristic cafe, all done up in geometric swirls and shapes, has excellent (if overpriced) coffee.

Coyote Ugly Saloon in this tourist hot spot, where a staff of gorgeous and/or ripped bodies (take your pick) dances, gyrates and puts some serious booty on the floor. Of course, you're here for anthropological reasons: to study the nuances of Latin dance. Not to watch the bartender do that thing Shakira does with her butt.

### Skybar
CLUB

(Map p52; ☑ 305-695-3100; Shore Club, 1901 Collins Ave; 4pm-2am Mon-Wed, to 3am Thu-Sat) Skybar is one of those SoBe spots that is so impossibly full of beautiful people you wonder if you've walked into a dream – and it's not just the clientele who are gorgeous. The setting: the Moroccan garden of delights that is the courtyard of the Shore Club hotel. Chill alfresco in a sultan's pleasure garden under enormous, wrought-iron lanterns, gaze at the patricians lounging around the pool, or try (and fail, if you're an unlisted travel writer) to get into the all-crimson, all-A-list Red Room.

### Twist
CLUB

(Map p56; ☑ 305-538-9478; www.twistsobe.com; 1057 Washington Ave; 1pm-5am) Never a cover, always a groove, and right across from the police station, this two-story gay club has some serious staying power and a little bit of something for everyone: six different bars; go-go dancers; drag shows; lounging areas and a small dance floor.

### Nikki Beach Club
CLUB

(Map p56; ☑ 305-538-1111; www.nikkibeach.com; 1 Ocean Dr; cover from $25; noon-6pm Mon-Thu, noon-11pm Fri & Sat, 11am-11pm Sun) Get your groove on outdoors, wandering from immaculate gossamer beach cabana to cabana at Nikki's, which feels like an incredibly upscale full-moon party. On Sunday (Sunday?!), starting around 4pm, it's the hottest party in town, as folks clamor to get in and relive whatever it was they did the night before.

### FDR
CLUB

(Map p52; ☑ 305-924-4071; 1685 Collins Ave; 11pm-5am Fri-Mon) Indigo mood lighting, lots of models, scenester DJs and general sex in the air: this is as exclusive as clubs get in Miami Beach. Show up before 11pm, be a celebrity or be on the list to get in. Located below the Delano Hotel.

### Cameo
CLUB

(Map p52; ☑ 305-532-2667; www.cameomiami.com; 1445 Washington Ave; 11pm-5am Tue, Fri & Sat) This enormous, touristy club, where Gwen

Stefani tracks get smooshed into Oakenfold, is where the sexy times are to be had – if by sexy times you're thinking thumping music, a packed crowd and sweat to slip on. Sunday's gay night (the specific party name frequently changes) is one of the best in town.

### Mansion
CLUB

(Map p52; ☑ 305-532-1525; www.mansionmiami.com; 1235 Washington Ave; cover from $20; 11pm-5am Wed-Sat) Every night the lines stretch around the block as plebs beg, cajole and strut in a vain attempt to get past that damned red rope. Inside? Well, they don't call it 'Mansion' for nothing. Expect megaclub grandiosity, plenty of attitude, waiting in line for hours and the chance to see young celebs do something tabloid-worthy.

### Mynt
CLUB

(Map p52; ☑ 305-695-1705; www.myntlounge.com; 1921 Collins Ave; noon-5am) Join the partying stars – Justin Timberlake, Vin Diesel, Britney Spears etc – by bottle servicing yourself into the VIP section. Otherwise, make friends with the red rope until you can order a drink and then try not to spill it, which is tough in the sweaty scrum of models, Moët and *mojitos*.

### Score
GAY

(Map p52; ☑ 305-535-1111; www.scorebar.net; 727 Lincoln Rd; 9pm-5am Tue, Thu & Sun, 6pm-5am Fri & Sat) Muscle boys with mustaches, glistening six-packs gyrating on stage, and a crowd of men who've decided shirts really aren't their thing: do we need to spell out the orientation of Score's customer base? It's still the best dedicated – and decadent – gay bar on the beach.

## Northern Miami Beach

### ★ Broken Shaker
BAR

(Map p60; ☑ 305-531-2727; 2727 Indian Creek Dr; 6pm-2am Sun-Thu, 2pm-2am Fri & Sat) Craft cocktails are having their moment in Miami, and if mixology is in the spotlight, you can bet Broken Shaker is sharing the glare. Expert bartenders run this spot, located in the back of the Freehand Miami hotel (p96), which takes up one closet-sized indoor niche and a sprawling outdoor courtyard of excellent drinks and beautiful people.

### Circa 39 Bar
LOUNGE

(Map p60; 3900 Collins Ave; 4pm-midnight) Tucked off to the back of Circa 39's moody front lobby, the designer dream bar has a warm, welcoming feel to it. Definitely stop

## GETTING PAST THE RED ROPE

If you're going out in Miami, ask yourself: what do I want? Do I want to dance? Hear good tunes? Score? See celebrities? If you answered 'yes' to the first two questions, the downtown Miami and Wynwood scene might be more to your liking. If you answered 'yes' to the last two questions, you may want to stay in South Beach.

Also, ask yourself another question: What do I bring? If it's good looks, money or promoter connections, the world is your oyster. If you have none of the above you can still party, but be prepared for some ego-crushing. Best overheard conversation in the course of this research:

Guy A: [Looking at model] 'How do you approach a girl like that?'

Guy B: 'In a Mercedes.'

Here's how it breaks down: the South Beach club scene plays on the appeal of celebrity. More famous customers equal more regular customers. Eventually, a strange equilibrium works out where enough regular customers make people assume famous people are there, even if they're not. But those regular customers can't appear too regular, so a little social engineering is committed by club owners and the titans of the cultural scene (bouncers) in the form of the red rope. How do you get by it?

➡ **Be polite** Don't be skittish, but don't act like you're J Lo either. And whatever you do, don't yell at the doorman – or touch him or yank on his clothing – to try to get his attention.

➡ **Get guest-listed** Ask the concierge at your hotel to help you out, or simply call the club and leave your name; it's often that simple.

➡ **Remain confidently aloof** Don't stare at the doorman. Look elsewhere – but look hot doing it.

➡ **Be aggressive. Failing that, be rich** If there's a clamoring crowd, standing at the back of it and hoping it'll part is about as effective as being meek when you need a seat on the New York subway. Push your way through to the front. Or order bottle service (an overpriced bottle of spirits), which usually guarantees you a pass to the front.

➡ **Come correct** For women, showing a sophisticated amount of skin is effective, although 'sophisticated' depends on the wearer. We've seen chic women in barely-there tops look less trashy than folks sporting a standard miniskirt ensemble. Men, don't wear T-shirts and jeans, unless you're one of those guys who can and still look put together. Also, this is Miami – be a little more daring than a button-up shirt and slacks if you want to stand out.

➡ **Get there early** Do you want to be cool or do you want to get in? From 10:30pm to 11pm is a golden time for bouncer leniency, but you can't club-hop with this strategy.

➡ **If you're a man, bring a woman** A man alone is not worth much (unless you're at a gay club, natch); up your value by having a beautiful woman – or two or three – on your arm.

Though our listings represent the hottest parties as of press time, we urge you to do some follow-up research when you arrive: talk to friends and your concierge, and pick up a copy of the local arts weekly, *Miami New Times*.

in for a cosmopolitan if you're up this way, before sauntering across the street and checking out the nighttime ocean.

**Lou's Beer Garden** PUB
(Map p60; ☎ 305-704-7879; 7337 Harding Ave; ⏰ 5pm-2am Mon-Fri, noon-2am Sat & Sun) Miami is pretty much made for beer gardens. The weather is perfect, nothing cools you off like a breeze and a beer and, well, yeah... the weather is perfect. Gather around long tables under tropical trees, order a cheese plate or a Kobe beef burger and down pints of Belgian craft ales. What could be better?

## 🍸 Downtown Miami

★ **Blackbird Ordinary** BAR
(Map p62; ☎ 305-671-3307; 729 SW 1st Ave; ⏰ 3pm-5am Mon-Fri, 6pm-5am Sat & Sun) The Ordinary is almost that...well, no. It isn't ordinary at all – this is an excellent bar, with great cocktails (the London Sparrow, with

gin, cayenne, lemon juice and passion fruit, goes down well) and an enormous courtyard. But it is 'ordinary' in the sense that it's a come-as-you-are joint that eschews judgment for easy camaraderie.

### Tobacco Road    BAR
(Map p62; ☑305-374-1198; 626 S Miami Ave; ☺11:30am-5am) Miami's oldest bar has been on the scene since the 1920s, and boasts the first liquor license issued in the city. These days it's a little touristy, but it has stayed in business for a reason: old wood, blue lights, cigarette smoke and sassy bartenders greet you like a buddy. Film buffs may recognize it as the place where Kurt Russell has a drink in *The Mean Season* (1985).

### DRB    BAR
(Map p62; 501 NE 1st Ave; ☺noon-2am Mon-Wed, to 5am Thu & Fri, 4pm-5am Sat, 4pm-2am Sun) The acronym stands for Democratic Republic of Beer, and that's what's on offer here: a good variety of microbrews and hard-to-score imports, served in a small, understated bar area or outside on comfy couches in the heart of downtown Miami.

### Level 25    BAR
(Map p62; Conrad Miami, 1395 Brickell Ave; ☺11:30am-11pm Sun-Thu, to midnight Fri & Sat) When Neo buys Morpheus a drink, they probably meet at this Conrad Miami spot (guess which floor), where it's all long white lines, low black couches, pinstriped gorgeousity and God's-eye views over Biscayne Bay.

### Grand Central    CLUB
(Map p62; ☑305-377-2277; 697 N Miami Ave; ☺10pm-5am Fri & Sat) As enormous clubs go, Grand Central is good. Yes, the bouncers have way more attitude here than other clubs, and yes, the cost of everything, from drinks to covers, borders on criminal. But the promoters consistently book big DJs and musical acts, and when things are hopping, the energy is undeniable.

### Garret    CLUB
(Map p62; ☑305-377-2277; 697 N Miami Ave; ☺10pm-4am Tue, 8pm-1am Wed, 11pm-5am Thu-Sat) Upstairs from Grand Central, the Garret is the hipster half of the big club scene downstairs. Electro pop and synth-y sounds are pumped out on Friday nights, while Saturdays feature indie dance nights and third Thursdays are devoted to a riotous Latin funk mix.

### Vagabond    CLUB
(Map p62; ☑305-379-0508; 30 NE 14th St; ☺10pm-3am Tue, 10pm-5am Thu-Sat) The folks at Vagabond are still attractive, but they're funkier, definitely more local and the music is more experimental than what you'll find on Miami Beach. The animal-print furniture and flying, loopy lines and curves are made to be gawked at, which is possible as no one keeps the Vagabond too dimly lit.

### Space    CLUB
(Map p62; ☑305-375-0001; www.clubspace.com; 34 NE 11th St; ☺24hr) This multilevel warehouse is Miami's main megaclub. With 30,000 sq ft to fill, dancers have room to strut, and an around-the-clock liquor license redefines the concept of after-hours. DJs usually pump each floor with a different sound – hip-hop, Latin, heavy trance – while the infamous rooftop lounge is the place to be for sunrise.

## Wynwood, Design District & Little Haiti

### ★Wood Tavern    BAR
(Map p68; ☑305-748-2828; 2531 NW 2nd Ave; ☺5pm-2am Tue-Sun) So many new bars in Miami want to be casual but cool; Wood is one of the few locales achieving this Golden Mean of atmosphere and aesthetic. The crowd is local Miami kids who don't want a dive, but don't want the long lines and attitude of South Beach. Ergo: Anglo kids joking with Latinos in an outdoor space that includes picnic benches, a wooden stage complete with bleachers and giant Jenga game, and an attached art gallery with rotating exhibits. Food specials are cheap, the beer selection is excellent and the crowd is friendly – this Wood's got the right grain.

### Panther Coffee    CAFE
(Map p68; ☑305-677-3952; 2390 NW 2nd Ave; ☺7am-9pm Mon-Sat, 8am-9pm Sun) The coffee is great at Panther, but what's better are frequent poetry readings, performance-art sessions and general artsy events that fill a packed schedule of events. If there's a non-alcoholic lynchpin to the Wynwood creative scene, it can be found here.

### Gramps    BAR
(Map p68; ☑786-752-6693; 176 NW 24th St; ☺6pm-3am Sun-Thu, 5pm-3am Fri & Sat) Besides being a kick-butt bar that hosts great quiz nights, Gramps has an enormous outdoor backyard that's perfect for alfresco drinking and socializing. It helps that the cocktails

are strong and the beer menu is as extensive as a complete encyclopedia set.

### Churchill's
BAR

(Map p68; ☎305-757-1807; www.churchillspub.com; 5501 NE 2nd Ave; ⊗10pm-3am) Churchill's is a Brit-owned pub in the midst of what could be Port-au-Prince. There's a lot of live music here, mainly punk, indie and more punk. Not insipid modern punk either: think the Ramones meets the Sex Pistols. While everyone's getting their ya-yas off, Haitians are waiting outside to park your car or sidle in and enjoy the gig and a beer with you.

### Magnum Lounge
GAY & LESBIAN

(☎305-757-3368; 709 NE 79th St; ⊗5pm-2am Tue-Thu, to 3am Fri & Sat) This gay piano lounge is all dark shadows and deep reds but not to the point you're blind, and the clientele is a nice mix: gays, lesbians, straights on dates or just looking for something different – and by the way, the drinks are stiff, the prices are reasonable and the piano music is quite good.

### The Social Lubricant
LOUNGE

(Map p68; ☎786-409-2241; 167 NW 23rd St; ⊗6pm-3am) Enter The Social Lubricant and you'll feel like you've entered the backstage of some surreal caberet that blends the Middle East, the Caribbean and (of course) a Miami nightclub. Sushi is served in the back, movies are shown on a big screen and DJs spin chill music to soothe the beautiful crowds.

### Boteco
BAR

(www.botecomiami.com; 916 NE 79th St; ⊗11am-midnight) If you're missing São Paolo, come to Boteco on Friday evening to see the biggest Brazilian expat reunion in Miami. *Cariocas* (Rio natives) and their countrymen flock here to listen to samba and bossa nova, and chat each other up over the best caipirinhas in town.

### Bardot
CLUB

(Map p68; ☎305-576-5570; 3456 N Miami Ave; ⊗8pm-3am Tue & Wed, to 5am Thu-Sat) You really should see the interior of Bardot before you leave the city. It's all sexy French vintage posters and furniture seemingly plucked from a private club that serves millionaires by day, and becomes a scene of decadent excess by night. The entrance looks to be on N Miami Ave, but it's actually in a parking lot behind the building.

## Little Havana

### Casa Panza Bar
TAVERNA

(Map p74; ☎305-644-3444; 1620 SW 8th St; ⊗11am-11pm) It doesn't get cornier than this 'authentic' Spanish taverna where the live shows, flamenco dancers, Spanish guitarists and audience participation reach new heights of sangria-soaked fun. Drop your cynicism, enter and enjoy.

## Coconut Grove

Everything here closes at 3am.

### Taurus
BAR

(Map p76; ☎305-529-6523; 3540 Main Hwy; ⊗4pm-3am) The oldest bar in Coconut Grove is a cool mix of wood paneling, smoky leather chairs, about 100 beers to choose from and a convivial vibe – as neighborhood bars go in Miami, this is one of the best.

### Tavern in the Grove
BAR

(Map p76; ☎305-447-3884; 3416 Main Hwy; ⊗3pm-3am) To say this sweatbox is popular with University of Miami students is like saying it rains sometimes in England. More of a neighborhood dive on weekdays.

---

#### ART WALKS: THE NEW CLUBBING?

It's hipsters gone wild! Or to put it another way: it's free wine! And artsy types, and galleries open till late, and the eye candy of a club, and the drunken momentum of a pub crawl and – best of all – no red ropes. The Wynwood & Design District Art Walks are one of the best nightlife experiences in Miami. The experience of strolling from gallery to gallery ('That piece is *gorgeous*. Pour me another'), perusing the paintings ('No, I don't think there's a bathroom behind the performance artist') and delving into the nuances of aesthetic styles ('The wine's run out? Let's bounce') is as genuinely innovative as...well, the best contemporary art. Just be careful, as a lot of galleries in Wynwood are separated by short drives (the Design District is more walkable). Art Walks take place on the second Saturday of each month, from 7pm to 10pm (some galleries stretch to 11pm); when it's all over, lots of folks repair to Wood Tavern or Bardot. Visit artofmiami.com/maps/artwalks for information on participating galleries.

**Barracuda**  BAR
(Map p76; ☑305-918-9013; 3035 Fuller St; ⏱noon-3am) The other place in the Grove to get overloaded on backwards baseball caps and coeds in miniskirts.

## ☕ Coral Gables

**Seven Seas**  BAR
(Map p78; ☑305-266-6071; 2200 SW 57th Ave; ⏱noon-1am Sun-Thu, to late Fri & Sat) Seven Seas is a genuine Miami neighborhood dive, decorated on the inside like a nautical theme park and filled with University of Miami students, Cuban workers, gays, straights, lesbians and folks from around the way. Come for the best karaoke in Miami on Tuesday, Thursday and Saturday – there's plenty of Spanish-language music, which adds Latin spice.

**The Bar**  BAR
(Map p78; ☑305-442-2730; 172 Giralda Ave; ⏱11:30am-3am) All in a name, right? Probably the best watering hole in the Gables, The Bar is just what the title says (which is unusual in this neighborhood of extravagant embellishment). If you're in the 'hood on Friday, come here for happy hour (5pm to 8pm), when young Gables professionals take their ties off and let loose long into the night.

### MIAMI'S SMALL CINEMAS

Miami has a glut of art-house cinemas showing first-run, independent and foreign films. Here are some of our favorites:

**Cosford Cinema** (☑305-284-4861; www.cosfordcinema.com; Memorial Classroom Bldg, 5030 Brunson Dr, University of Miami) On the University of Miami campus, this renovated art house was launched in memory of the *Miami Herald* film critic Bill Cosford.

**Coral Gables Art Cinema** (Map p78; ☑786-385-9689; www.gablescinema.com; 260 Aragon Ave) Indie and foreign films in a 144-seat cinema.

**Tower Theater** (Map p74; ☑305-643-8706; www.mdc.edu/culture/tower; 1508 SW 8th St) In a gem of a deco building, managed by Miami Dade College.

**O Cinema** (Map p68; ☑305-571-9970; www.o-cinema.org; 90 NW 29th St) Indie screenings in Wynwood.

**Titanic**  BAR
(☑305-668-1742; 5813 Ponce de Leon Blvd; ⏱11:30am-1am Sun-Thu, to 2am Fri & Sat) By day, it's an all-American-type bar and grill, but at night Titanic turns into a popular University of Miami watering hole. Thursday tends to be a big night. Located by the University entrance near Dixie Hwy and Red Rd (SW 57th Ave).

## 🍷 Greater Miami

**La Covacha**  CLUB
(☑305-594-3717; www.lacovacha.com; 10730 NW 25th St, Doral; ⏱9:30pm-4am Thu-Sun, from 5pm Fri) Drive out about halfway to the Everglades (just kidding, but only just) and you'll find Covacha, the most hidden, most hip Latin scene in Miami. Actually, it's not hidden; all the young Latinos know about Covacha and love it well, and we do too. It's an excellent spot to see new bands, upcoming DJs (almost all local), an enormous crowd and few tourists. Covacha is out in Doral, a good 14 miles west of downtown Miami.

## ☆ Entertainment

Miami's artistic merits are obvious, even from a distance. Could there be a better creative base? There's Southern homegrown talent, migratory snowbirds bringing the funding and attention of northeastern galleries, and immigrants from across the Americas. These disparate cultures communicate their values via the language of expression. Creole, Spanish and English, after all, are poor languages compared to dance, music and theater.

### Performing Arts

**Adrienne Arsht Center for the Performing Arts**  PERFORMING ARTS
(Map p62; www.arshtcenter.org; 1300 Biscayne Blvd) This magnificent venue manages to both humble and enthrall visitors. Today the Arsht is where the biggest cultural acts in Miami come to perform; a show here is a must-see on any Miami trip. Get off the Metromover at the Omni stop.

**Colony Theater**  PERFORMING ARTS
(Map p52; ☑305-434-7091; www.colonytheatre miamibeach.com; 1040 Lincoln Rd) The Colony is an absolute art-deco gem, with a classic marquee and Inca-style crenellations, which looks like the sort of place gangsters would go to watch *Hamlet*. Built in 1935, this used to be the main cinema house in upper South

Beach before it fell into disrepair in the mid-20th century. It was renovated and revived in 1976 and now boasts 465 seats and great acoustics. This treasure serves as a major venue for performing arts – from comedy and occasional musicals to theatrical dramas, off-Broadway productions and ballet – as well as hosting movie screenings and small film festivals.

### Gusman Center for
### the Performing Arts    PERFORMING ARTS
(Map p62; ☎305-374-2444; www.gusmancenter.org; 174 E Flagler St) This elegantly renovated 1920s movie palace services a huge variety of performing arts including film festivals, symphonies, ballets and touring shows. The acoustics are excellent.

### Fillmore Miami Beach/
### Jackie Gleason Theater    PERFORMING ARTS
(Map p52; ☎305-673-7300; www.fillmoremb.com/index; 1700 Washington Ave) Built in 1951, South Beach's premier showcase for touring Broadway shows, orchestras and other big musical productions has 2700 seats and excellent acoustics. Jackie Gleason chose to make the theater his home for the long-running 1960s TV show, but now you'll find an eclectic line-up of shows – Elvis Costello or Albita one night, the Dutch Philharmonic or an over-the-top musical the next.

### Miami Light Project    PERFORMING ARTS
(Map p68; ☎305-576-4350; www.miamilightproject.com; 3000 Biscayne Blvd) The Miami Light Project is a nonprofit cultural foundation that represents innovative shows from theater troupes and performance artists from around the world. Shows are performed across the city, but the project is housed at Light Box Theatre.

## Theater

See www.southfloridatheatre.com for a comprehensive directory of playhouses in greater South Florida.

### Actors Playhouse    THEATER
(Map p78; ☎305-444-9293; www.actorsplayhouse.org; Miracle Theater, 280 Miracle Mile; tickets $20-50) Housed within the 1948 deco Miracle Theater in Coral Gables, this three-theater venue stages musicals and comedies, children's theater on its kids stage and more avant-garde productions in its small experimental black-box space.

MIAMI ENTERTAINMENT

### VIERNES CULTURALES
### (CULTURAL FRIDAYS)

The Little Havana Arts District may not be Wynwood, but it does constitute an energetic little strip of galleries and studios (concentrated on 8th St between SW 15th Ave & SW 17th Ave) that house some of the best Latin American art in Miami. Rather than pop into each gallery, look around and feel pressure to buy, why not visit on the last Friday of each month for **Viernes Culturales** (www.viernesculturales.org; ⏱7-11pm). No wine-sipping art walk this; Cultural Fridays in Little Havana are like little carnival seasons, with music, old men in *guayaberas* (Cuban dress shirts) crooning to the stars and more booty-shaking than brie. Although there is also brie, and plenty of time to appreciate local art as all the Little Havana galleries throw open their doors.

### Gablestage    THEATER
(Map p78; ☎305-445-1119; www.gablestage.org; 1200 Anastasia Ave; tickets $15-40) Founded as the Florida Shakespeare Theatre in 1979 and now housed on the property of the Biltmore Hotel in Coral Gables, this company still performs an occasional Shakespeare play, but mostly presents contemporary and classical pieces.

### Jerry Herman Ring Theatre    THEATER
(☎305-284-3355; www.miami.edu/ring; University of Miami, 1321 Miller Dr; tickets $8-15) This University of Miami troupe stages musicals, dramas and comedies, with recent productions including *Falsettos* and *Baby*. Alumni actors include Sylvester Stallone, Steven Bauer, Saundra Santiago and Ray Liotta.

## Dance

### Miami City Ballet    DANCE
(Map p52; ☎305-929-7000; www.miamicityballet.org; 2200 Liberty Ave) Formed in 1985, this troupe is based out of a lovely three-story headquarters designed by famed local architectural firm Arquitectonica. The facade allows passers-by to watch the dancers rehearsing through big picture windows, which makes you feel like you're in a scene from *Fame,* except the weather is better and people don't spontaneously break into song.

## THE FULL MOON DRUM CIRCLE

If there's a full moon, check out the beach between 79th and 85th Sts – a big, boisterous drum circle is held here that doubles as a full-moon party. The beat tends to start between 8:30pm and 9:30pm, and can run well into the wee hours. That said, drinking (and the consumption of other substances) is technically illegal on the beach, and police have broken up the event before. Still, it tends to be a pretty fun party that shouldn't be missed if you're in the area and want to see an incredible moonset. Check www.miamidrums.com for more information. The drum circle also goes off periodically in Coconut Grove, in the tropical overgrowth of the Barnacle (p75).

**Ifé-Ilé Afro-Cuban Dance**          DANCE
(305-476-0832; www.ife-ile.org) Ifé-Ilé is a nonprofit organization that promotes cultural understanding through dance and performs in a range of styles – traditional Afro-Cuban, mambo, rumba, conga, *chancleta*, *son* (a salsalike dance that originated in Oriente, Cuba), salsa and ritual pieces. Call for further information.

**Miami Hispanic Ballet**          DANCE
(Map p62; 305-549-7711; www.miamihispanicballet.org; 111 SW 5th Ave) Directed by Cuban-trained Pedro Pablo Peña, this troupe presents mainly classical ballets based out of the Miami Hispanic Cultural Arts Center, also known as 'The White House of Ballet.'

### Classical

**Miami Symphony Orchestra**  CLASSICAL MUSIC
(305-284-6477, 305-275-5666; www.themiso.org; venues vary; tickets $15-30) Its yearly series features world-renowned soloists at shows held around the city, including the University of Miami and the Adrienne Arsht Center for the Performing Arts. Performances run from November to May.

**New World Symphony**       CLASSICAL MUSIC
(NWS; Map p52; 305-673-3330; www.nws.edu; 500 17th St) Housed in the New World Center (a funky explosion of cubist lines and geometric curves, fresh white against the blue Miami sky), the acclaimed New World Symphony holds performances from October to May. The

deservedly heralded NWS serves as a three- to four-year preparatory program for talented musicians from prestigious music schools.

**Chopin Foundation of the United States**          CLASSICAL MUSIC
(Map p60; 305-868-0624; www.chopin.org; 1440 JFK/79th St Causeway) This national organization hosts a treasure trove of performances for Chopin fans – the Chopin Festival, a series of free monthly concerts and the less-frequent National Chopin Piano Competition, an international contest held in Miami every five years.

**Florida Grand Opera**          OPERA
(Map p62; 800-741-1010; www.fgo.org; 1300 Biscayne Blvd) Founded in the 1940s, this highly respected opera company, which stages many shows including *Madame Butterfly*, *La Boheme* and *Tosca*, performs throughout the year at the Adrienne Arsht Center for the Performing Arts and Fort Lauderdale.

### Live Music

**The Stage**          LIVE MUSIC
(Map p68; 305-576-9577; www.thestagemiami.com; 170 NE 38th St; ⊙10pm-2am Tue, 9pm-2am Wed & Sun, 9pm-5am Fri & Sat) The Stage is many things: edgy art gallery, live-music venue, arts and crafts bazaar, occasional bar, and sometimes all of these things at once. Check the website to see what shows are playing and try to catch a party here – you may see a more bohemian, creative side of Miami than you initially expected.

**Hoy Como Ayer**          LIVE MUSIC
(Map p74; 305-541-2631; www.hoycomoayer.us; 2212 SW 8th St; ⊙8:30pm-4am Thu-Sat) This Cuban hot spot – with authentic music, unstylish wood paneling and a small dance floor – is enhanced by cigar smoke and Havana transplants. Stop in nightly for *son*, *boleros* (a Spanish dance in triple meter) and modern Cuban beats.

### Sports

**Miami Heat**          BASKETBALL
(786-777-1000; www.nba.com/heat; American Airlines Arena, 601 Biscayne Blvd; tickets from $26) The city's NBA franchise plays at American Airlines Arena.

**Miami Dolphins**          FOOTBALL
(305-943-8000; www.miamidolphins.com; Sun Life Stadium, 2269 Dan Marino Blvd; tickets from $35) 'Dol-fans' are respectably crazy about their team, even if a Super Bowl showing has evaded them since 1985. Games are

wildly popular and the Dolphins are painfully successful, in that they always raise fans' hopes but never quite fulfill them. Sun Life Stadium is in Miami Gardens, 15 miles north of downtown.

**University of Miami Hurricanes** FOOTBALL
(☎800-462-2637; www.hurricanesports.com; tickets $22-60) The Hurricanes were once undisputed titans of university football, but had experienced a slow decline since 2004. They've recovered a bit as of the time of writing, and attending a game surrounded by UM's pack of fanatics is lots of fun. Their season is from August to December.

**Miami Marlins** BASEBALL
(http://miami.marlins.mlb.com; Marlins Park, 501 Marlins Way; tickets from $15) The MLB regular season runs from April to September.

**University of Miami Hurricanes** BASKETBALL
(☎800-462-2637; www.hurricanesports.com; tickets $20) From November to April you can catch the beloved college Hurricanes shooting hoops at the BankUnited Center at the University of Miami.

# 🅰 Shopping

There are two main shopping strips in South Beach – Lincoln Rd Mall, a pedestrian road lined with a great mix of indie shops and chain stores; and the southern end of Collins Ave, below 9th St. Here you'll find mostly high-end chains like A/X, Ralph Lauren and Barney's Co-op. Shooting way north of here, you'll find two extremely popular

---

## CRICKET – IT'S A PITCH

Cricket in South Florida? Really? Oh yes. There's a huge West Indian and Jamaican community in South Florida, plus a very sizable British expat population. As such cricket is actually quite popular in these parts. The **South Florida Cricket Alliance** (☎954-805-2922; www.southfloridacricket.com) is one of the largest cricket clubs in the US, the **Cricket Council of the USA** (www.cricketcouncilusa.com) is based in Boca Raton, and the first dedicated cricket pitch in the country opened in Lauderhill (where the population is 25% West Indian), north of Fort Lauderdale, in 2008. Contact any of the above if you'd like to watch a match or join a team.

---

shopping malls: the **Aventura Mall** (www.shopaventuramall.com; 19501 Biscayne Blvd, Aventura), a mainstream collection including JC Penney and Bloomingdale's, and the chichi **Bal Harbour Shops** (www.balharbourshops.com; 9700 Collins Ave), a classy scene boasting Prada, Gucci, Chanel and Saks Fifth Avenue outposts. Bal Harbour is located about 3 miles north of North Miami Beach; Aventura is 9 miles north of North Miami Beach.

Move over to the mainland and there are a few options, the hippest being the Design District where you'll find a glut of art and homewares plus clothing and accessories hawkers. You'll have an easier time at the touristy, chain-store-drenched **Bayside Marketplace** (Map p62; www.baysidemarketplace.com; 401 Biscayne Blvd), on the shores of downtown Miami. Find more outdoor malls in Coconut Grove, at the ever-popular **CocoWalk** (Map p76; 3015 Grand Ave) and **Streets of Mayfair** (Map p76; www.mayfairinthegrove.net; 2911 Grand Ave); Coral Gables meanwhile, has its Miracle Mile and the classy **Village of Merrick Park** (Map p78; www.villageofmerrickpark.com; 358 San Lorenzo Ave), located a mile south of the Miracle Mile, near the intersection of S Le Jeune Rd and Dixie Hwy.

## Art

**GO! Shop** ART
(Map p68; ☎305-576-8205; 2516 NW 2nd Ave; ⊗noon-8pm Thu-Sat) If you fancy the art at the Wynwood Walls (p69), make sure to pop into the GO! shop, located within the street-art complex. Original artwork, prints and other arts accoutrements are presented on a rotating basis; the stuff for sale is either produced by or related to the works created by the current crop of Wynwood Walls artists.

**Española Way Art Center** ART
(Map p52; ☎305-673-0946; 405 Española Way) There are three levels of studios here, plus excellent original work and prints for sale, all by local artists. Hours vary by studio.

### Clothing & Accessories

**Consign of the Times** VINTAGE
(Map p52; ☎305-535-0811; www.consignofthetimes.com; 1635 Jefferson Ave; ⊗11am-9pm) Cute vintage boutique that carries labels as lovely as Gucci (patent-leather shoes!), Von Furstenberg (leather slingbacks!) and Versace (silver bustier!).

**C Madeleine's** VINTAGE
(☎305-945-7770; 13702 Biscayne Blvd; ⊗11am-6pm Mon-Sat, noon-5pm Sun) The undisputed

queen of vintage Miami, C Madeleine's is more than your standard used-clothes write-off. This is a serious temple to classical style, selling Yves Saint Laurent couture and classic Chanel suits. Come here for the sort of timeless looks that are as beautiful now as when they first appeared on the rack.

**Base** CLOTHING
(Map p52; ☑ 305-531-4982; www.baseworld.com; 939 Lincoln Rd; ☺11am-10pm) This groovy hip-hop outlet has everything you need to be a good clubber – the latest Pumas, edgy streetwear, designer baseball caps, men's shaving and skincare products from gourmet labels, and a whole range of thumpa-thumpa and bom-chika-bom-chika CDs available for sampling at storefront listening stations.

**Hip.e** CLOTHING
(Map p78; ☑ 305-445-3693; 359 Miracle Mile; ☺11am-7pm Mon-Sat) A bit more hip than hippie, the clothes and jewelry here manage to mix up indie and hip-hop aesthetics in an admirably wearable way. Think Lucite bangles just slightly embellished by bling and you've got an idea of the vibe.

**Alchemist** CLOTHING
(Map p52; ☑ 305-531-4653; 1111 Lincoln Rd; ☺10am-10pm) This high-end boutique eschews bling and snootiness for friendly attitude, minimalism and simply beautiful clothes – standout labels include Zara and Proenza Schouler.

**Pepe Y Berta** CLOTHING
(Map p74; ☑ 305-857-3771, 305-266-1007; 1421 SW 8th St; ☺ 10am-6:30pm Mon-Fri, 9am-7pm Sat) The most gorgeous collection of *guayaberas* (Cuban dress shirts) in Miami can be found in this family-run shop, where the friendly owner will hand measure you and tailor a shirt to your tastes.

**Boy Meets Girl** CHILDREN
(Map p78; ☑ 305-445-9668; 355 Miracle Mile; ☺10am-7pm Mon-Fri, 11am-6pm Sat) Fantastically upscale and frankly expensive clothing for wee ones – if the kids are getting past puberty, look elsewhere, but otherwise they'll be fashionable far before they realize it.

**Olian** MATERNITY
(Map p78; ☑ 305-446-2306; 356 Miracle Mile; ☺9am-6pm Mon-Fri) Flagship of the Olian empire and Miami's premier maternity boutique, this is where expecting mommies can outfit themselves to look as glam as any South Beach model.

**U Rock Couture** CLOTHING
(Map p56; ☑ 305-538-7625; 928 Ocean Dr; ☺10am-1am Sun-Fri, to 2am Sat) U Rock is the quintessential Miami Beach clothing store. Loud, flashy and in your face, it resembles a mangled clash of rhinestones, tight clothes, revealing dresses, deep tans, euro accents and the cast of *Jersey Shore*. Somehow, this is all strangely appealing...rather like Lincoln Rd itself.

## Gifts

**Books and Books** BOOKS
(Map p78; ☑ 305-442-4408; 265 Aragon Ave; ☺9am-11pm Sun-Thu, 9am-midnight Fri & Sat) The best indie bookstore in South Florida is a massive emporium of all things literary. Hosts frequent readings and is generally just a fantastic place to hang out. Has other outposts on **Lincoln Road** (☑305-532-3222; 927 Lincoln Rd) and at the Bal Harbour shops.

**Metta Boutique** GIFTS
(Map p52; ☑ 305-763-8230; 1845 Purdy Ave; ☺9am-8pm Mon-Thu, to 9pm Fri & Sat, 11am-6pm Sun) ✔ A cute store that brings some sustainability to South Beach. All of the goodies – clothes, journals, accessories, gifts and tchotchkes – are decidedly green/organic/sustainable/fair trade.

**Celestial Treasures** GIFTS
(Map p76; ☑ 305-461-2341; 3444 Main Hwy; ☺noon-8pm Sun-Thu, to 10pm Fri & Sat) ✔ Your one-stop shop for spiritual and metaphysical needs, this shop has books, cards and components for those interested in Zen, Buddhism, Hinduism, Wicca, kabbalah and yoga. Also has staff psychics on hand.

**Bookstore in the Grove** BOOKS
(Map p76; ☑ 305-483-2855; 3399 Virginia St; ☺7am-10pm Mon-Fri, 8am-10pm Sat & Sun) Coconut Grove's independent bookstore is a good spot for all kinds of lit, and has a great cafe (try the empanadas) to boot.

**Taschen** BOOKS
(Map p52; ☑ 305-538-6185; 1111 Lincoln Rd; ☺11am-9pm Mon-Thu, to 10pm Fri & Sat, noon-9pm Sun) Ridiculously cool, well-stocked collection of art, photography, design and coffee-table books to make your hip home look that much smarter.

**Ricky's NYC** GIFTS
(Map p52; ☑ 305-674-8511; 536 Lincoln Rd; ☺10am-midnight Sun-Fri, to 1am Sat) This South Beach standby boasts hundreds of tacky gifts (boxing-nun puppets), pop-art paraphernalia and, well, 'adult' accoutrements

such as sex toys, games, costumes and other unmentionables.

### El Crédito Cigars
TOBACCONIST
(Map p74; ☑ 305-858-4162; 1106 SW 8th St; ☺ 8am-6pm Mon-Fri, to 4pm Sat) In one of the most popular cigar stores in Miami, and one of the oldest in Florida, you'll be treated as a venerated member of the stogie-chomping club.

### M&N Variedades
BOTANICA
(Map p74; ☑ 305-649-3040; 1753 SW 8th St; ☺ 9am-8pm) This Santeria *botanica* (see p70) offers spell components, magic candles, *consultas espirituales* (spiritual consultation) and computer repair.

### Eyes on Lincoln
EYEWEAR
(Map p52; ☑ 305-532-0070; 708 Lincoln Rd; ☺ 10am-11pm) The most sexy, impressive collection of glasses, sunglasses and optical accoutrements we've seen in South Florida.

### Genius Jones
TOYS
(Map p68; ☑ 866-436-4875; 49 NE 39th St; ☺ 10am-7pm Mon-Sat, noon-6pm Sun) High-end toys, dolls and gear for babies and toddlers and their parents. Fatboy 'beanbag' chairs, Primo Viaggio car seats and Bugaboo strollers – geek out, parents.

### Music
#### Sweat Records
MUSIC
(Map p68; ☑ 786-693-9309; 5505 NE 2nd Ave; ☺ noon-10pm Tue-Sat, to 5pm Sun) Sweat's almost a stereotypical indie record store – there's funky art and graffiti on the walls, it has big purple couches, it sells weird Japanese toys and there are skinny guys with thick glasses arguing over LPs and EPs you've never heard of, and, of course, there's coffee and vegan snacks.

## ⓘ Information

### DANGERS & ANNOYANCES
There are a few areas considered by locals to be dangerous: Liberty City, in northwest Miami; Overtown, from 14th St to 20th St; Little Haiti and stretches of the Miami riverfront. In these and other reputedly 'bad' areas you should avoid walking around alone late at night – use common sense and travel in groups. If in doubt, it's best to take a taxi and to know your address.

Deserted areas below 5th St in South Beach are more dangerous at night, but your main concerns are aggressive drunks or the occasional strung-out druggie, rather than muggers. In downtown Miami, use caution near the Greyhound station and around causeways, bridges and overpasses where homeless people and some refugees have set up shanty towns.

Natural dangers include the strong sun (use a high-SPF sunscreen), mosquitoes (use a spray-on repellent) and hurricanes (between June and November). There's a **hurricane hotline** (☑ 305-468-5400), which will give you information about approaching storms, storm tracks, warnings and estimated time to touchdown – all the things you will need to know to make a decision about if and when to leave.

### EMERGENCY
**Ambulance** (☑ 911)
**Beach Patrol** (☑ 305-673-7714)
**Hurricane Hotline** (☑ 305-468-5400)
**Poison Information Center** (☑ 305-585-5250)
**Rape Hotline** (☑ 305-585-7273)
**Suicide Intervention** (☑ 305-358-4357)

### INTERNET ACCESS
Most hotels and hostels (and increasingly, even camping grounds) offer wi-fi access. Free wi-fi is also available in libraries, Starbucks and McDonald's.

### MEDIA
**Beach Channel** (www.thebeachchannel.tv) Local 24-hour TV station on channel 19, like a quirky infomercial about goings-on in Miami Beach.
**Diario Las Americas** (www.diariolasamericas.com) Spanish-language daily.
**El Nuevo Herald** (www.elnuevoherald.com) Spanish-language daily of the *Herald*.
**Miami Herald** (www.miamiherald.com) Major daily covering local, national and international news.
**Miami New Times** (www.miaminewtimes.com) Free alternative weekly paper.
**Miami Sun Post** (www.miamisunpost.com) In-depth news and lifestyle coverage.
**Sun-Sentinel** (www.sun-sentinel.com) Daily covering South Florida.
**WLRN** (www.wlrn.org) Local National Public Radio affiliate, at 91.3FM on the dial.

### MEDICAL SERVICES
**Beach Dental Center** (☑ 877-353-8845; 333 Arthur Godfrey Rd) For dental needs.
**Coral Gables Hospital** (☑ 305-445-8461; 3100 Douglas Rd, Coral Gables) A community-based facility with many bilingual doctors.
**Eckerd Drugs** (☑ 305-538-1571; 1421 Alton Rd, South Beach; ☺ 24hr) One of many 24-hour Eckerd pharmacies.
**Miami Beach Community Health Center** (Stanley C Meyers Center; ☑ 305-538-8835; 710 Alton Rd, South Beach) Walk-in clinic with long lines.

**Mount Sinai Medical Center** (☑ 305-674-2121, emergency room 305-674-2200; 4300 Alton Rd) The area's best emergency room. Beware that you must eventually pay, and fees are high.

**Visitor's Medical Line** (☑ 305-674-2222; ⊘ 24hr) For physician referrals.

## MONEY

Bank of America has branch offices all over Miami and Miami Beach. To get currency exchanged you can go to Amex.

## POST

The following branches have hours extended until evening thanks to self-serve machines in the lobbies:

**Post office** Mid-Beach (Map p60; 445 W 40th St; ⊘ 8am-5pm Mon-Fri, 8:30am-2pm Sat); South Beach (Map p52; 1300 Washington Ave; ⊘ 8am-5pm Mon-Fri, 8:30am-2pm Sat)

## TOURIST INFORMATION

**Art Deco Welcome Center** (Map p56; ☑ 305-672-2014; www.mdpl.org; 1001 Ocean Dr, South Beach; ⊘ 9:30am-5pm Fri-Wed, to 7pm Thu) Run by the Miami Design Preservation League (MDPL); has tons of art-deco district information and organizes excellent walking tours.

**Black Archives History & Research Center of South Florida** (☑ 305-636-2390; www.theblackarchives.org; 5400 NW 22nd Ave, Suite 101, Liberty City; ⊘ 9am-5pm Mon-Fri) Information about black culture.

**Coconut Grove Chamber of Commerce** (Map p76; ☑ 305-444-7270; www.coconutgrove-chamber.com; 2820 McFarlane Rd, Coconut Grove; ⊘ 9am-5pm Mon-Fri)

**Coral Gables Chamber of Commerce** (Map p78; ☑ 305-446-1657; www.coralgables-chamber.org; 224 Catalonia Ave, Coral Gables; ⊘ 9am-5pm Mon-Fri)

**Downtown Miami Welcome Center** (Map p62; ☑ 786-472-5930; www.downtownmiami.com; 900 S Miami Ave; ⊘ 9am-5pm Mon-Fri) Provides maps, brochures and tour information for the downtown area.

**Greater Miami & the Beaches Convention & Visitors Bureau** (Map p62; ☑ 305-539-3000; www.miamiandbeaches.com; 701 Brickell Ave, 27th fl; ⊘ 8:30am-5pm Mon-Fri) Located in an oddly intimidating high-rise building.

**Miami Beach Chamber of Commerce** (Map p52; ☑ 305-674-1300; www.miamibeach-chamber.com; 1920 Meridian Ave; ⊘ 9am-5pm Mon-Fri) You can purchase a Meter Card here. Denominations come in $10, $20 and $25 (and meters cost $1 per hour).

## USEFUL WEBSITES

**Art Circuits** (www.artcircuits.com) The best insider info on art events; includes excellent neighborhood-by-neighborhood gallery maps.

**Beached Miami** (www.beachedmiami.com) The best independent arts website in Miami.

**Meatless Miami** (www.meatlessmiami.com) Vegetarians in need of an eating guide, look no further.

**Miami Beach 411** (www.miamibeach411.com) A great guide for Miami Beach visitors, covering just about all concerns.

**Miami Nights** (www.miaminights.com) Get a good, opinionated lowdown on Miami's ever-shifting after-dark scene.

**Short Order** (http://blogs.miaminewtimes.com/shortorder) The *New Times* food blog that always seems ahead of the curve on eating events in the Magic City.

**That's So Miami** (http://thatssomiami.tumblr.com/) Quirky, weird and fun Miami.

# ⓘ Getting There & Away

## AIR

Miami is served by all major carriers via two main airports: Miami International Airport (MIA) and the Fort Lauderdale-Hollywood International Airport (FLL), half an hour north of MIA. **MIA** (☑ 305-876-7000; www.miami-airport.com) is the third-busiest airport in the country. Just 6 miles west of downtown Miami, the airport is open 24 hours and is laid out in a horseshoe design. There are left-luggage facilities on two concourses at MIA, between B and C, and on G; prices vary according to bag size.

The Fort Lauderdale-Hollywood International Airport (p232), about 15 miles north of Miami just off I-95, often serves as a lower-cost alternative to MIA, especially because it's serviced by popular, cut-rate flyers including Southwest Airlines and JetBlue.

## BOAT

Though it's doubtful you'll be catching a steamer to make a trans-Atlantic journey, it is quite possible that you'll arrive in Miami via a cruise ship, as the **Port of Miami** (☑ 305-347-4800; www.miamidade.gov/portofmiami), which received nearly four million passengers in 2013, is known as the 'cruise capital of the world.' Arriving in the port will put you on the edge of downtown Miami; taxis and public buses to other local points are available from nearby Biscayne Blvd. The Key West Express ferry plies to Key West from Miami.

## BUS

**Greyhound** (Map p62; ☑ 800-231-2222; www.greyhound.com) is the major carrier in and out of town. There are four major terminals: **Airport terminal** (☑ 305-871-1810; 4111 NW 27th St); **Main Downtown terminal** (☑ 305-374-6160; 1012 NW 1st Ave); **North Miami terminal** (☑ 305-945-0801; 16560 NE 6th Ave); and the **Southern Miami terminal** (Cutler Bay; ☑ 305-296-9072; Cutler Ridge Mall, 20505 S Dixie Hwy), also known as the Cutler Bay terminal. There are several buses daily that head both up the East Coast and across the panhandle through the Gulf Coast.

### TRAIN

The main Miami terminal of **Amtrak** (☑ 305-835-1222; www.amtrak.com; 8303 NW 37th Ave) connects the city with the rest of continental USA and Canada. Travel time between New York and Miami is a severe 27 to 30 hours. The Miami Amtrak station has a left-luggage facility, which costs $2 per bag.

## ❶ Getting Around

TO/FROM THE AIRPORT
### Miami International Airport

It's a cinch to get from the airport to just about anywhere in Miami, especially Mid-Beach. If you're driving, follow Rte 112 from the airport, then head east on the Julia Tuttle Causeway or the I-195 to get to South Beach. Other options include the free shuttles offered by most hotels, or a taxi ($32 flat rate from the airport to South Beach). Alternatively, catch the Airport Owl night-only public bus, or the **SuperShuttle** (☑ 305-871-8210; www.supershuttle.com) shared-van service, which will cost about $26 to South Beach. Be sure to reserve a seat the day before. Metro buses leave from across Concourse E and run throughout the city; fares are $1.50, plus 50 cents for transfers.

### Fort Lauderdale-Hollywood International Airport

Put the money you save on flights toward getting to Miami once you land; either rent a car at one of the many Fort Lauderdale agencies, or take the free shuttle from terminals 1 and 3 to the airport's **Tri-Rail station** (☑ 800-874-7245; www.tri-rail.com; 1-way $2-5.50); you can ride this commuter train into Miami. The schedule is infrequent, though, so you may want to opt for the **GOShuttle** (☑ 877-544-4646; https://goairportshuttle.com), which will cost about $30 to South Beach.

### BICYCLE

A bike-share program on Miami Beach makes cycling around the beaches, at least, a cinch.

The Miami area may be as flat as a pancake, but it's also plagued by traffic backups and speedy thoroughfares, so judge the bikeability of your desired route carefully.

The city of Miami Beach offers the DecoBike (p82) bike-share program. Bike stations are located in dozens of spots around Miami Beach (there's a map on the website, plus a link to an iPhone app that tells you where the nearest station is).

Places that rent bicycles include the following:

**BikeAndRoll** (Map p56; ☑ 305-604-0001; www.bikeandroll.com; 210 10th St; per hour/day from $5/15; ☺9am-7pm) Also does bike tours.

**Mangrove Cycles** (Map p72; ☑ 305-361-5555; 260 Crandon Blvd, Key Biscayne; per 2hr/day/week from $20/25/75; ☺10am-6pm Tue-Sun) Rents bicycles.

### BUS

The local bus system is called **Metrobus** (☑ 305-891-3131; www.miamidade.gov/transit/routes.asp; tickets $2). An easy-to-read route map is available online. You may spend more time waiting for a bus than you will riding on one.

In South Beach, an excellent option is the **South Beach Local Circulator** (☑ 305-891-3131; 25¢) – also called the South Beach Local – a looping shuttle bus with disabled-rider access that operates along Washington between S Pointe Dr and 17th St and loops back around on Alton Rd on the west side of the beach. Rides come along every 10 to 15 minutes.

### CAR & MOTORCYCLE

If you drive around Miami there are a few things to keep in mind. Miami Beach is linked to the mainland by four causeways built over Biscayne Bay. They are, from south to north: the MacArthur (the extension of US Hwy 41 and Hwy A1A); Venetian ($1.50 toll); Julia Tuttle; and John F Kennedy. There's also a $1.75 toll over the Rickenbacker Causeway to Key Biscayne.

The most important north–south highway is I-95, which ends at US Hwy 1 south of downtown Miami. US Hwy 1, which runs from Key West all the way north to Maine, hugs the coastline. It's called Dixie Hwy south of downtown Miami and Biscayne Blvd north of downtown Miami. The Palmetto Expwy (Hwy 826) makes a rough loop around the city and spurs off below SW 40th St to the Don Shula Expwy (Hwy 874, a toll road). Florida's Turnpike Extension makes the most western outer loop around the city. Hwy A1A becomes Collins Ave in Miami Beach.

Miami has an annoying convention of giving major roads multiple names. So for example, Bird Rd is also SW 40th St and Hwy 976. Hwy 826 is the Palmetto Expwy. US 1 is the Dixie Hwy – except in downtown, when it becomes Biscayne Blvd. Hwy 836 is the Dolphin Expwy, while in Miami Beach 5th St becomes A1A. Calle Ocho is SW 8th St, as well as the Tamiami Trail, and US 41 (phew), and Hwy 959 is Red Rd, except when it's SW 57th St. Somehow, this isn't as confusing as it reads on paper – most signage indicates every name a route may have, but it can be frustrating to first-time Miami drivers.

Besides the causeways to Miami Beach, the major east–west roads are SW 8th St; Hwy 112 (also called Airport Expwy); and Hwy 836 (also called Dolphin Expwy), which slices through downtown Miami and connects with I-395 and the MacArthur Causeway, and which runs west to the Palmetto Expwy and Florida's Turnpike Extension.

Miami drivers are...how can we put this delicately?...aggressive, tailgating jerks who'd cut off their grandmother if they could figure out how to properly change lanes. We are, of course, kidding. Not all Miami drivers fit the above description, but there are enough of these maniacs about to make driving here an occasional (and sometimes not-so-occasional) nightmare.

## Parking

Parking is pretty straightforward. Regulations are well signposted and meters are plentiful (except perhaps on holiday-weekend evenings in South Beach). Downtown, near the Bayside Marketplace, parking is cheap but a bit confusing: you must find a place in the head-on parking lots (backing into the parking space not allowed), buy a ticket from a central machine and display it in your windshield.

On South Beach there's metered street parking along most streets (except Lincoln Rd and residential areas). Meters are enforced from 9am to as late as 3am in some parts of South Beach. Most allow you to pay for up to three hours, although some have increased that range to 12 hours. Most Miami Beach meter machines include a credit-card option; parking rates vary, but it rarely costs more than $1.50 per hour.

There are many municipal parking garages, which are usually the easiest and cheapest option – look for giant blue 'P' signs. You'll find several located along Collins Ave and Washington Ave. If you park illegally or if the meter runs out, parking fines are about $30, but a tow could cost much more.

TAXI

**Central Cabs** (☑ 305-532-5555)
**Flamingo Taxis** (☑ 305-759-8100)
**Metro** (☑ 305-888-8888)
**Miami Taxi Service** (☑ 305-525-2455)
**Sunshine** (☑ 305-445-3333)
**Yellow** (☑ 305-400-0000)

TRAIN

The **Metromover** (www.miamidade.gov/transit/metromover.asp), which is equal parts bus, monorail and train, is helpful for getting around downtown Miami. It offers visitors a great perspective on the city and a free orientation tour of the area.

**Metrorail** (www.miamidade.gov/transit/metrorail.asp) is a 21-mile-long heavy-rail system that has one elevated line running from Hialeah through downtown Miami and south to Kendall/Dadeland. Trains run every five to 15 minutes from 6am to midnight. The fare is $2, or $1 with a Metromover transfer.

The regional **Tri-Rail** (☑ 800-874-7245; www.tri-rail.com) double-decker commuter trains run the 71 miles between Dade, Broward and Palm Beach counties. Fares are calculated on a zone basis; the shortest distance traveled costs $4.40 round-trip; the most you'll ever pay is for the ride between MIA and West Palm Beach ($11.55 round-trip). No tickets are sold on the train, so allow time to make your purchase before boarding. All trains and stations are accessible to riders with disabilities. For a list of stations, log on to the Tri-Rail website.

# The Everglades

### Includes ➜

Everglades
National Park . . . . . . .128

Tamiami Trail . . . . . . .128

Homestead to
Flamingo Point . . . . . .135

Biscayne
National Park . . . . . . .140

## Best Places to Eat

➡ Robert is Here (p137)

➡ Joannie's Blue Crab Café (p133)

➡ JT's Island Grill & Gallery (p134)

➡ Rosita's (p137)

➡ Oyster House (p134)

## Best Places to Stay

➡ Everglades International Hostel (p137)

➡ Everglades City Motel (p134)

➡ Ivey House Bed & Breakfast (p134)

➡ Wilderness Camping (p139)

➡ Swamp Cottage (p133)

## Why Go?

There is no wilderness in America quite like the Everglades. Called the 'River of Grass' by its initial Native American inhabitants, this is not just a wetland, or a swamp, or a lake, or a river, or a prairie, or a grassland – it is all of the above, twisted together into a series of soft horizons, long vistas, sunsets that stretch across your entire field of vision and the creeping grin of a large population of dinosaur-era reptiles.

When you watch anhinga flexing their wings before breaking into a corkscrew dive, or the slow, Jurassic flap of a great blue heron gliding over its domain, or the sun kissing miles of unbroken saw grass as it sets behind humps of skeletal cypress domes, you'll have an idea of what we're speaking of. In a nation where natural beauty is measured by its capacity for drama, the Everglades subtly, contentedly flows on.

## When to Go
### Everglades City

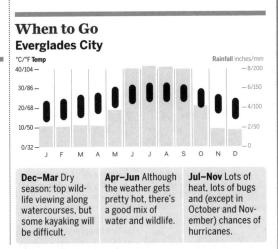

**Dec–Mar** Dry season: top wildlife viewing along watercourses, but some kayaking will be difficult.

**Apr–Jun** Although the weather gets pretty hot, there's a good mix of water and wildlife.

**Jul–Nov** Lots of heat, lots of bugs and (except in October and November) chances of hurricanes.

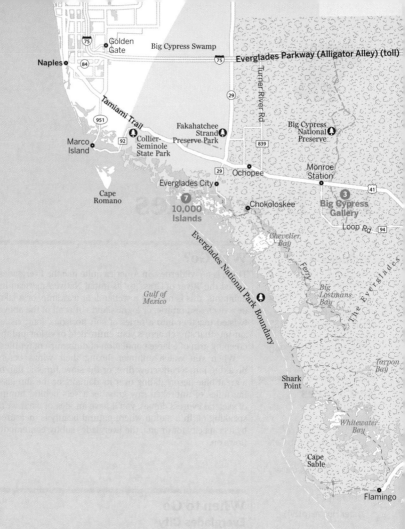

## Everglades Highlights

① Watching the sun set over the ingress road to **Pa-hay-okee Overlook** (p139) from the roof of your car.

② Canoeing or kayaking into **Hell's Bay Paddling Trail** (p139), a tangled morass of red creeks, slow blackwater and the heavy vegetative curtain of a preserved marsh.

③ Checking out some of the best photography of the surrounding swamps, forests, beaches and sea at **Big Cypress Gallery** (p129).

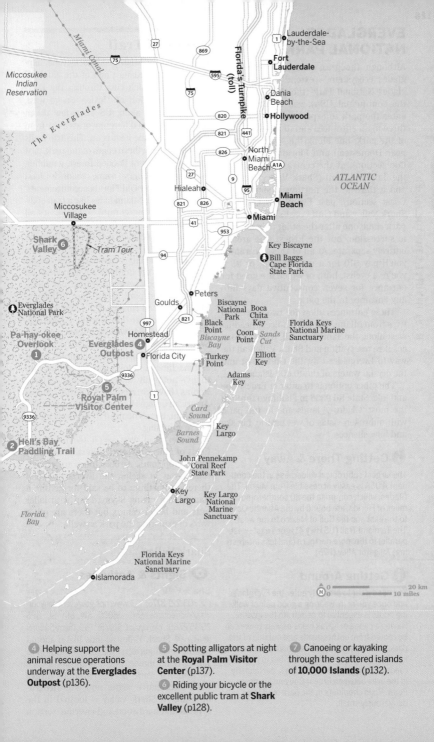

## Everglades & Around

**4** Helping support the animal rescue operations underway at the **Everglades Outpost** (p136).

**5** Spotting alligators at night at the **Royal Palm Visitor Center** (p137).

**6** Riding your bicycle or the excellent public tram at **Shark Valley** (p128).

**7** Canoeing or kayaking through the scattered islands of **10,000 Islands** (p132).

# EVERGLADES NATIONAL PARK

Although the grassy waters – the Everglades ecosystem – extend outside Everglades National Park (the third-largest in the continental USA), you really need to enter the park to experience it. There are three main entrances and three main areas of the park: one along the southeast edge near Homestead and Florida City (Ernest Coe section); at the central-north side on the Tamiami Trail (Shark Valley section); and a third at the northwest shore (Gulf Coast section), past Everglades City. The Shark Valley and Gulf Coast sections of the park come one after the other in geographic succession, but the Ernest Coe area is entirely separate. At all of these entrances you'll pay $10 for a vehicle pass, or $5 if you're a cyclist, both of which are good for entrance for seven consecutive days into any entrance in the park.

These entrances allow for two good road trips from Miami. The first choice is heading west along the Tamiami Trail, past the Miccosukee reservation and Shark Valley, all the way to Everglades City, the Gulf Coast and the crystal waters of the 10,000 Islands.

The other option is to enter at Ernest Coe and take State Rd 9336 to Flamingo through the most 'Glades-y' landscape in the park, with unbroken vistas of wet prairie, big sky and long silences.

## 🛈 Getting There & Away

The largest subtropical wilderness in the continental USA is easily accessible from Miami. The Glades, which comprise the 80 southernmost miles of Florida, are bound by the Atlantic Ocean to the east and the Gulf of Mexico to the west. The Tamiami Trail (US Hwy 41) goes east–west, parallel to the more northern (and less interesting) Alligator Alley (I-75).

## 🛈 Getting Around

You need a car to properly enter the Everglades and once you're in, wearing a good pair of walking boots is essential to penetrate the interior. Having a canoe or kayak helps as well; these can be rented from outfits inside and outside of the park, or else you can seek out guided canoe and kayak tours. Bicycles are well suited to the flat roads of Everglades National Park, particularly in the area between Ernest Coe and Flamingo Point. Road shoulders in the park tend to be dangerously small.

# Tamiami Trail

Calle Ocho, in Miami's Little Havana happens to be the eastern end of the Tamiami Trail/US 41, which cuts through the Everglades to the Gulf of Mexico. So go west, young traveler, along US 41, a few dozen miles and several different worlds away from the city where the heat is on. This trip leads you onto the northern edges of the park, past long landscapes of flooded forest, gambling halls, swamp-buggy tours, roadside food shacks and other Old Florida accoutrements.

Past Hialeah, Miami fades like a trail of diminishing Starbucks until...*whoosh*...it's all huddled forest, open fields and a big canal off to the side (evidence of US 41's diversion of the Glades' all-important sheet flow). The surest sign the city is gone and the Glades have begun is the Confederate flag decals on **Pit BBQ**, which serves decent if not memorable smoked pork and dishes of that ilk. The empty road runs past the **Miccosukee Resort & Convention Center** (☑305-222-4600, 877-242-6464; www.miccosukee.com; 500 SW 177th Ave; r Dec-Mar/Apr-Nov $150/120; ✳🛜). It's essentially a casino-hotel complex full of slot machines and folks chunking coins into them – not really an ecological wonderland. Rooms have attractive geometric Native American designs worked into the furniture, but again, there's no need to stay here unless you're gambling.

As you head west you'll see fields and fields of pine forest and billboards advertising swamp tours. Airboat tours are an old-school way of seeing the Everglades (and there is something to be said for getting a tour from a raging Skynyrd fan with killer tatts and better camo), but there are other ways of exploring the park as well.

## Shark Valley

### 🅾 Sights & Activities

**Shark Valley**                                    PARK
(☑305-221-8776; www.nps.gov/ever/planyour-visit/svdirections.htm; 36000 SW 8th St, GPS 25°45'27.60; car/cyclist $10/5; ⊙9:15am-5:15pm; 🅿🚲) 🖉 Shark Valley sounds like it should be the headquarters for the villain in a James Bond movie, but it is in fact a slice of National Park Service grounds heavy with informative signs and knowledgeable rangers. Shark Valley is located in the cypress-and-hardwood-and-riverine section

of the Everglades, a more traditionally jungly section of the park than the grassy fields and forest domes surrounding the Ernest Coe visitor center. A 15-mile/24km paved trail takes you past small creeks, tropical forest and 'borrow pits' (manmade holes that are now basking spots for gators, turtles and birdlife). The pancake-flat trail is perfect for bicycles, which can be rented at the entrance for $7.50 per hour. Bring water with you.

If you don't feel like exerting yourself, the most popular and painless way to immerse yourself in the Everglades is via the two-hour **tram tour** (☑ 305-221-8455; www.sharkvalleytramtours.com; adult/child under 12yr/senior $22/19/12.75; ⊙ departures May-Dec 9:30am, 11am, 2pm, 4pm, Jan-Apr 9am-4pm every hr on the hr) that runs along Shark Valley's entire 15-mile trail. If you only have time for one Everglades activity, this should be it, as guides are informative and witty, and you'll likely see gators sunning themselves on the road. Halfway along the trail is the 50ft-high Shark Valley Observation Tower, an ugly concrete tower that offers dramatically beautiful views of the park.

At the park entrance, the easy **Bobcat Boardwalk Trail** (800m) makes a loop through a thick copse of tropical hardwoods before emptying you out right back into the Shark Valley parking lot. A little ways past is the **Otter Cave Trail** (400m) which heads over a limestone shelf that has been Swiss-cheesed into a porous sponge by rainwater. Animals now live in the eroded holes (although it's not likely you'll spot any) and Native Americans used to live on top of the shelf.

**Miccosukee Village**                          PARK
(☑ 305-222-4600, 877-242-6464; www.miccosukee.com; Mile 70, Hwy 41; adult/child/5yr & under $10/6/free; ⊙ 9am-5pm; P ⛔) Just across the road from Shark Valley, this 'village' is an informative open-air museum that showcases the culture of the Miccosukee via guided tours of traditional homes, a crafts gift store, dance and music performances, an airboat ride into a hammock-cum-village of raised 'chickee' (wooden platforms built above the waterline) huts and (natch) gator wrestling. There's a somewhat desultory on-site restaurant if you get hungry. The art and handmade crafts from the on-site art gallery make good souvenirs.

## Big Cypress & Ochopee

The better part of the Tamiami Trail is fronted on either side by long cypress trees overhung with moss and endless vistas of soft prairie, flooded in the wet season into a boggy River of Grass.

### ◉ Sights & Activities

**Big Cypress Gallery**                          GALLERY
(☑ 941-695-2428; www.clydebutcher.com; Tamiami Trail; swamp walk 1.5hr adult/child $50/35, 45min adult/child $35/25; ⊙ 10am-5pm; P) 🖋
The highlight of many Everglades trips, this gallery showcases the work of Clyde Butcher, an American photographer who follows in the great tradition of Ansel Adams. His large-format black-and-white images elevate the swamps to a higher level. Butcher has found a quiet spirituality in the brackish waters and you might, too, with the help of his eyes. Every Labor Day (first weekend in

---

### AIRBOATS & SWAMP BUGGIES

Airboats are flat-bottomed skiffs that use powerful fans to propel themselves through the water. Their environmental impact has not been determined, but one thing is clear: airboats can't be doing much good, which is why they're not allowed in the park. Swamp buggies are enormous balloon-tired vehicles that can go through wetlands, creating ruts and damaging wildlife.

Airboat and swamp-buggy rides are offered all along US Hwy 41 (Tamiami Trail). Think twice before going on a 'nature' tour. Loud whirring fanboats and marsh jeeps really don't do the quiet serenity of the Glades justice. That said, many tourists in the Everglades are there (obviously) because of their interest in the environment, and they demand environmentally knowledgeable tours. The airboat guys are pretty good at providing these – their livelihood is also caught up in the preservation of the Glades, and they know the back country well. We recommend going with the guys at **Cooperstown** (☑ 305-226-6048; http://coopertownairboats.com; 22700 SW 8th St; adult/child $23/11; ⛔), one of the first airboat operators you encounter heading west on 41. Just expect a more touristy experience than the National Park grounds.

## THE EVERGLADES: AN OVERVIEW

It's tempting to think of the Everglades as a swamp, but 'prairie' may be a more apt description. The Glades, at the end of the day, are grasslands that happen to be flooded for most of the year: visit during the dry season (winter) and you'd be forgiven for thinking the Everglades was the Everfields.

So where's the water coming from? Look north on a map of Florida, all the way to Lake Okeechobee and the small lakes and rivers that band together around Kissimmee. Florida dips into the Gulf of Mexico at its below-sea-level tip, which happens to be the lowest part of the state geographically and topographically. Run-off water from central Florida flows down the peninsula via streams and rivers, over and through the Glades, and into Florida Bay. The glacial pace of the flood means this seemingly stillest of landscapes is actually in constant motion. Small wonder the Calusa Indians called the area Pa-hay-okee (grassy water). Famous conservationist Marjory Stoneman Douglas (1890–1998) called it the River of Grass; in her famous book of the same title, she revealed that Gerard de Brahm, a colonial cartographer, named the region the River Glades, which became Ever Glades on later English maps.

So what happens when nutrient-rich water creeps over a limestone shelf? The ecological equivalent of a sweaty orgy. Beginning at the cellular level, organic material blooms in surprising ways, clumping and forming into algal beds, nutrient blooms and the ubiquitous periphyton, which are basically clusters of algae, bacteria and detritus (ie stuff). Periphyton ain't pretty: in the water they resemble puke streaks and the dried version looks like hippo turds. But you should kiss them when you see them (well, maybe not), because in the great chain of the Everglades, this slop forms the base of a very tall organic totem pole. The smallest tilt in elevation alters the flow of water and hence the content of this nutrient soup, and thus the landscape itself: all those patches of cypress and hardwood hammock (not a bed for backpackers; in this case, hammock is a fancy Floridian way of saying a forest of broadleaf trees, mainly tropical or subtropical) are areas where a few inches of altitude create a world of difference between biosystems.

### Fight for the Green Grassy Waters

The Everglades were utter wilderness for thousands of years. Even Native Americans avoided the Glades; the 'native' Seminole and Miccosukee actually settled here as exiles escaping war and displacement from other parts of the country. But following European settlement of Florida, some pioneers saw the potential for economic development of the Grassy Waters.

Cattle ranchers and sugar growers, attracted by mucky waters and Florida's subtropical climate (paradise for sugarcane), successfully pressured the government to make land available to them. In 1905, Florida governor Napoleon Bonaparte Broward personally dug the first shovelful of a diversion that connected the Caloosahatchee River to Lake Okeechobee. Hundreds of canals were cut through the Everglades to the coastline to 'reclaim' the land, and the flow of lake water was restricted by a series of dikes. Farmland began to claim areas previously uninhabited by humans.

Unfortunately, the whole 'River of Grass' needs the river to survive. And besides being a pretty place to watch the birds, the Everglades acts as a hurricane barrier and kidney. Kidney? Yup: all those wetlands leeched out pollutants from the Florida Aquifer (the state's freshwater supply). But when farmland wasn't diverting the sheet flow, it was adding fertilizer-rich wastewater to it. Result? A very sweaty (and well-attended) biological orgy. Bacteria, and eventually plant life, bloomed at a ridiculous rate (they call it fertilizer for a reason), upsetting the fragile balance of resources vital to the Glades' survival.

Enter Marjory Stoneman Douglas, stage left. Ms Douglas gets the credit for almost single-handedly pushing the now age-old Florida issue of Everglades conservation.

Despite the tireless efforts of Douglas and other environmentalists, today the Florida Aquifer is in serious danger of being contaminated and drying up. In 2011, the water level in Okeechobee was almost 2.7 inches below normal level. The number of wading birds nesting has declined by 90% to 95% since the 1930s. Currently, there are 67 threatened and endangered plant and animal species in the park.

The diversion of water away from the Glades and run-off pollution are the main culprits behind the region's environmental degradation. This delicate ecosystem is the neighbor of one of the fastest-growing urban areas in the US. The current water-drainage system in South Florida was built to handle the needs of two million people; the local population topped six million in 2010. And while Miami can't grow north or south into Fort Lauderdale or Homestead, it can move west, directly into the Everglades. At this stage, scientists estimate the wetlands have been reduced by 50% to 75% of their original size.

Humans are not the only enemy of the Everglades. Nature has done its share of damage as well. During 2005's Hurricane Wilma, for example, six storm-water treatment areas (artificial wetlands that cleanse excess nutrients out of the water cycle) were lashed and heavily damaged by powerful winds. Without these natural filtration systems, the Glades are far more susceptible to nutrient blooms and external pollution. In 2011, wildfires caused by drought incinerated huge patches of land near the Tamiami Trail.

## Restoration of the Everglades

Efforts to save the Everglades began in the late 1920s, but were sidelined by the Great Depression. In 1926 and 1928, two major hurricanes caused Lake Okeechobee to overflow; the resulting floods killed hundreds. The Army Corps of Engineers did a really good job of damming the lake. A bit too good: the Glades were essentially cut off from their source, the Kissimmee watershed.

In the meantime, conservationists began donating land for protection, starting with 1 sq mile of land donated by a garden club. The Everglades was declared a national park in 1947, the same year Marjory Stoneman Douglas' *The Everglades: River of Grass* was published.

By draining the wetlands through the damming of the lake, the Army Corps made huge swaths of inland Florida inhabitable. But the environmental problems created by shifting water's natural flow, plus the area's ever-increasing population, now threaten to make the whole region uninhabitable. The canal system sends, on average, over 1 billion gallons of water into the ocean every day. At the same time, untreated run-off flows unfiltered into natural water supplies. Clean water is disappearing from the water cycle while South Florida's population gets bigger by the day.

Enter the Comprehensive Everglades Restoration Plan (CERP; www.evergladesplan.org). CERP is designed to address the root of all Everglades issues: water – where to get it, how to divert it and ways to keep it clean. The plan is to unblock the Kissimmee, restoring remaining Everglades lands to predevelopment conditions, while maintaining flood protection, providing freshwater for South Florida's populace and protecting earmarked regions against urban sprawl. It sounds great, but political battles have significantly slowed the implementation of CERP. The cost of the project has increased over the years, and a mix of political red tape and maneuvering courtesy of federal and state government has delayed CERP's implementation.

Not to throw another acronym at you, but a major portion of the CERP is the Central Everglades Planning Project (CEPP), the rare public works project that is supported by environmentalists and industry alike. The CEPP's aim is to clean polluted water from Florida's agricultural central heartland and redirect it towards the 'Glades. The River of Grass would be re-watered, and toxic run-off would no longer flow to the sea. But as of the time of writing, the CEPP's implementation was being delayed by the Army Corps of Engineers. Governmental gridlock may damage the Glades in the 21st century as much as government policies did in the 20th.

Bringing back the Everglades is one of the biggest, most ambitious environmental restoration projects in US history, one that combines the needs of farmers, fishers, urban residents, local governments and conservationists. The success or failure of the program will be a bellwether for the future of the US environmental movement.

## CANOE CAMPING ON 10,000 ISLANDS

One of the best ways to experience the serenity of the Everglades – somehow desolate yet lush, tropical and foreboding – is by paddling the network of waterways that skirt the northwest portion of the park. The **10,000 Islands** consist of many (but not really 10,000) tiny islands and a mangrove swamp that hugs the southwestern-most border of Florida. The **Wilderness Waterway**, a 99-mile path between Everglades City and Flamingo, is the longest canoe trail in the area, but there are shorter trails near Flamingo.

Most islands are fringed by narrow beaches with sugar-white sand, but note that the water is brackish, and very shallow most of the time. It's not Tahiti, but it's fascinating. You can camp on your own island for up to a week.

Getting around the 10,000 Islands is pretty straightforward if you religiously adhere to National Oceanic & Atmospheric Administration (NOAA) tide and nautical charts. Going against the tides is the fastest way to have a miserable trip. The Gulf Coast Visitor Center (p133) sells nautical charts and gives out free tidal charts. You can also purchase charts prior to your visit – call ☑ 305-247-1216 and ask for charts 11430, 11432 and 11433.

September), the gallery holds a gala event, which includes a fun $20 swamp walk onto his 30-acre property; the party attracts swamp-stompers from across the state.

Take a walk on the wet and wild side with a **swamp walk** behind the gallery. If you don't mind getting soggy, this is one of our favorite ways of exploring the Everglades. You'll slog under a blooming, moss-draped canopy of wispy cypress leaves and blooming flowers, squishing your way near the spidery trunks of the trees that interlace the Western Everglades. Call ahead to reserve a tour.

**Big Cypress National Preserve**    PARK
(☑ 239-695-4758; 33000 Tamiami Trail E; ⊙ 8:30am-4:30pm; P ♨) ✎ The 1139-sq-mile Big Cypress Preserve (named for the size of the park, not its trees) is the result of a compromise between environmentalists, cattle ranchers and oil-and-gas explorers. The area is integral to the Everglades' ecosystem: rains that flood the Preserve's prairies and wetlands slowly filter down through the Glades. About 45% of the cypress swamp (actually mangrove islands, hardwood hammocks, orchid flowers, slash pine, prairies and marshes) is protected. Great bald cypress trees are nearly gone, thanks to pre-Preserve lumbering, but dwarf pond cypress trees fill the area with their own understated beauty. The helpful **Oasis Visitor Center** (☑ 941-695-1201; ⊙ 8am-4:30pm Mon-Fri; ♨), about 20 miles west of Shark Valley, has great exhibits for the kids and a water-filled ditch that's popular with alligators.

**Ochopee**    VILLAGE
(GPS 25.901529, -81.306023) Drive to the hamlet of Ochopee (population about four)... no...wait...turn around, you missed it! Then pull over and break out the cameras: Ochopee's claim to fame is the country's smallest **post office**. It's housed in a former toolshed and set against big park skies; a friendly postal worker patiently poses for snapshots.

**Skunk Ape Research Headquarters**    PARK
(☑ 239-695-2275; www.skunkape.info; 40904 Tamiami Trail E; ⊙ 7am-7pm, 'zoo' closes around 4pm; P) This only-in-Florida roadside attraction is dedicated to tracking down Southeastern USA's version of Bigfoot, the eponymous Skunk Ape (a large gorilla-man who supposedly stinks to high heaven). We never saw a Skunk Ape, but you can see a corny gift shop and, in the back, a reptile-and-bird zoo run by a true Florida eccentric, the sort of guy who wraps albino pythons around his neck for fun. Donate a few bucks at the entrance.

**Florida National Scenic Trail**    HIKING
(www.fs.usda.gov/fnst) There are some 31 miles of the Florida National Scenic Trail within Big Cypress National Preserve. From the southern terminus, which can be accessed via Loop Rd, the trail runs 8.3 miles north to US 41. The way is flat, but it's hard going: you'll almost certainly be wading through water, and you'll have to pick through a series of solution holes (small sinkholes) and thick hardwood hammocks. There is often no shelter from the sun, and the bugs are... *plentiful*. There are three primitive campsites with water wells along the trail; pick up

a map at the visitor center. Most campsites are free, and you needn't register. **Monument Lake** (May-Dec 14 free, Dec 15-Apr $16) has water and toilets.

## Tours

**Everglades Adventure Tours**  TOUR
(EAT; ☑ 800-504-6554; www.evergladesadventuretours.com; tours from $69) We already like the guys at EAT for being based out of the same headquarters as the Skunk Ape people; we like them even more for offering some of the best private tours of the Everglades we've found. Swamp hikes, 'safaris,' airboats and, best of all, being poled around in a canoe or skiff by some genuinely funny guys with genuine local knowledge of the Grassy Waters; it's an absolute treat. The EAT guys have set up a campsite at Skunk Ape HQ; it costs $30 to camp here, and there's wi-fi throughout the camp.

## Sleeping & Eating

**Swamp Cottage**  COTTAGE $$
(☑ 239-695-2428; www.clydebutchersbigcypressgallery.com/swamp-cottage; cottage $275; ⓟ 🛜) 🍽 Want to get as close to the swamp as possible without giving up on the amenities? This two-bedroom cottage, which sits behind the Big Cypress Gallery (p129), may be the answer you're seeking. It's like a beach cottage, except the 'beach' is one of America's great wetlands. It's comfortably appointed, and if not luxurious, it's certainly cozy.

**Joannie's Blue Crab Café**  AMERICAN $$
(☑ 239-695-2682; Tamiami Trail; mains $9-17; ⊗ 9am-5pm) This quintessential shack, east of Ochopee, with open rafters, shellacked picnic tables and alligator kitsch, serves delicious food of the 'fried everything' variety on paper plates. There's live music most days.

## Everglades City

The end of the track is an old Florida fishing village of raised houses, turquoise water and scattershot emerald-green mangrove islands. Hwy 29 runs south through town into the peaceful residential island of Chokoloskee, past a great psychedelic mural of a gator on a shed. 'City' is an ambitious name for Everglades City, but this is a friendly fishing town where you can easily lose yourself for a day or three.

## Sights & Activities

**Museum of the Everglades**  MUSEUM
(☑ 239-695-0008; www.evergladesmuseum.org; 105 W Broadway; ⊗ 9am-5pm Tue-Fri, to 4pm Sat; ⓟ) This small museum, located in an old library, has some placards and information on the settlement of the Everglades – the focus is more concerned with the human history of the area than the natural environment. It's a decidedly community museum, with rotating local art and the feel of an attic full of everyone's interesting stuff and heirlooms, but charming for all that.

**Gulf Coast Visitor Center**  BOATING
(☑ 239-695-2591, 239-695-3311; http://evergladesnationalparkboattoursgulfcoast.com; 815 Oyster Bar Lane, off Hwy 29; per day canoe/single kayak/tandem kayak $24/45/55; ⊗ 9am-4:30pm mid-Apr–mid-Nov, 8am-4:30pm mid-Nov–mid-Apr; 🚻) 🍽 This is the northwestern-most ranger station for Everglades National Park, and provides access to the 10,000 Islands area. Boat tours depart from the downstairs marina into the mangrove flats and green islands – if you're lucky you may see dolphins springing up beside your craft. This tangled off-shore archipelago was a major smuggling point for drugs into the mainland USA during the late 1970s and early '80s; bales of marijuana were nicknamed 'square grouper' by local fishermen.

It's great fun to go kayaking and canoeing around here; boats can be rented from the marina, but make sure to take a map with you (they're available for free in the visitor center). Boaters will want to reference NOAA Charts 11430 and 11432.

## Tours

**North American Canoe Tours**  CANOEING
(NACT; ☑ 239-695-3299, 877-567-0679; www.evergladesadventures.com; Ivey House Bed & Breakfast, 107 Camellia St; tours $99, rentals from $35; ⊗ Nov–mid-Apr) 🍽 If you're up for a tour, try Everglades Adventure Tours, or the guys at North American Canoe Tours rent out camping equipment and canoes ($35 per day) and touring kayaks ($45 to $65). You get 20% off most of these services and rentals if you're staying at the Ivey House Bed & Breakfast (p134), which runs the tours. Tours shuttle you to places like Chokoloskee Island, Collier-Seminole State Park, Rabbit Key or Tiger Key for afternoon or overnight excursions (from $99).

## 🛏 Sleeping

All lodging is family-friendly, and comes with air-conditioning and parking.

⭐**Everglades City Motel** MOTEL $
(☑239-695-4224, 800-695-8353; www.evergladescitymotel.com; 310 Collier Ave; r from $80; P❄🛜) With large renovated rooms that have flat-screen TVs, arctic air-conditioning and a fantastically friendly staff that will hook you up with whatever tours your heart desires, this is an exceptionally good-value lodge for those looking to spend some time near the 10,000 Islands.

**Parkway Motel & Marina** MOTEL $
(☑239-695-3261; www.parkwaymotelandmarina.com; 1180 Chokoloskee Dr; r $99-120; P❄) An extremely friendly owner (and an even friendlier dog) runs this veritable testament to the old-school Floridian lodge: cute small rooms and one cozy apartment in a one-story motel building.

**Ivey House Bed & Breakfast** B&B $$
(☑239-695-3299, 877-567-0679; www.iveyhouse.com; 107 Camellia St; lodge $89-120, inn $99-219; P❄🛜) This family-run tropical inn serves good breakfasts in its small Ghost Orchid Grill. Plus it operates some of the best nature trips around (North American Canoe Tours (p133)). Ivey offers an entire range of package vacations (see the website), from day trips to six-day excursions including lodging, tours and some meals; trips run from $300 to $2290.

**Rod & Gun Club Lodge** B&B $$
(☑239-695-2101; www.evergladesrodandgun.com; 200 Riverside Dr; r Jul–mid-Oct $95, mid-Oct–Jun $110-140; P❄) Built in the 1920s as a hunting lodge by Barron Collier (who needed a place to chill after watching workers dig his Tamiami Trail), this masculine place, fronted by a lovely porch, has a restaurant that serves anything that moves in them thar waters.

## 🍴 Eating

**JT's Island Grill & Gallery** AMERICAN $
(238 Mamie St, Chokoloskee; mains $5-16; ⊙11am-3pm late Oct-May) Just a mile or so past the edge of town, this awesome cafe-cum-art-gallery sits in a restored 1890 general store. It's outfitted with bright retro furniture and piles of kitschy books, pottery, clothing and maps (all for sale). But the best part is the food (lunch only) – fresh crab cakes, salads, fish platters and veggie wraps, made with locally grown organic vegetables.

**Triad Seafood Cafe** SEAFOOD $
(☑239-695-0722; 401 School Dr; mains $9-16; ⊙10:30am-6pm Sun-Thu, to 7pm Fri & Sat) Triad is famous for its all-you-can-eat stone crab legs, but they serve up all kinds of seafood gleaned from the swamp and the sea (well, the Gulf of Mexico). Should you impress the friendly owners with your ability to devour arthropod legs, you get the dubious honor of having your picture hung on the Glutton Board.

**Oyster House** SEAFOOD $
(on Chokoloskee Causeway; mains $8-22; ⊙10am-11pm) Besides serving the Everglades staples of excellent fried seafood and burgers, Oyster House has a friendly bar with a screened-in porch where you can drink, slap mosquitoes and have a chat with friendly local boozehounds.

**Seafood Depot** SEAFOOD $
(102 Collier Ave; mains $6-20; ⊙10:30am-9pm) Don't totally sublimate your desire for fried

---

### DETOUR: LOOP ROAD

Loop Rd, off Tamiami Trail (Hwy 41), offers some unique sites. One: the homes of the Miccosukee, some of which have been considerably expanded by gambling revenue. You'll see some traditional chickee-style huts and some trailers with massive add-on wings that are bigger than the original trailer – all seem to have shiny new pickup trucks parked out front. Two: great pull-offs for viewing flooded forests, where egrets that look like pterodactyls perch in the trees. Three: houses with large Confederate flags and 'Stay off my property' signs; these homes are as much a part of the landscape as the swamp. And four: the short, pleasantly jungly Tree Snail Hammock Nature Trail. Be warned: the Loop is a rough, unpaved road; you'll need a 4WD vehicle (there has been talk of repaving the road, so it may have improved by the time you read this). True to its name, the road loops right back onto the Tamiami; expect a good long jaunt on the Loop to add two hours to your trip.

## AH-TAH-THI-KI MUSEUM

If you want to learn about Florida's Native Americans, come to the **Ah-Tah-Thi-Ki Seminole Indian Museum** (☎877-902-1113; www.ahtahthiki.com; Big Cypress Seminole Indian Reservation, Clewiston; adult/child/senior $9/6/6; ⊙9am-5pm), 17 miles north of I-75. All of the excellent educational exhibits on Seminole life, history and the tribe today were founded on gaming proceeds, which provide most of the tribe's multimillion-dollar operating budget.

The museum is located within a cypress dome cut through with an interpretive boardwalk, so from the start it strikes a balance between environmentalism and education. The permanent exhibit has several dioramas with life-sized figures depicting various scenes out of traditional Seminole life, while temporary exhibits have a bit more academic polish (past ones have included lengthy forays into the economic structure of the Everglades). There's an old-school 'living village' and recreated ceremonial grounds as well. The Ah-Tah-Thi-Ki is making an effort to not be a cheesy Native American theme park, and the Seminole tribe is to be commended for its effort in this regard.

food, because the gator tail and frogs legs here offer an excellent way to honor the inhabitants of the Everglades: douse them in Tabasco and devour them.

**Camellia Street Grill**　　　　SEAFOOD **$$**
(☎239-695-2003; 202 Camellia St; mains $10-20; ⊙noon-9pm Sun-Thu, to 10pm Fri & Sat) Camellia is as fancy as Everglades City gets, although even then it's easily accessible and down to earth. The food is inspired by both the American South and the Mediterranean; grouper, for example, is seared with caramelized onions but also comes with a nice bouquet of herbs. Enjoy it while watching the sun melt like honey on the water.

### ⓘ Information

**Everglades Area Chamber of Commerce**
(☎239-695-3941; cnr US Hwy 41 & Hwy 29; ⊙9am-4pm) General information about the region is available here.

### Everglades City to Naples

**Fakahatchee Strand Preserve**　　　PARK
(www.floridastateparks.org/fakahatcheestrand; Coastline Dr, Copeland; ⊙8am-sunset; P ♿) FREE
The Fakahatchee Strand, besides having a fantastic name, also houses a 20-mile by 5-mile estuarine wetland that could have emerged directly out of the *Jurassic Park* franchise. A 2000ft boardwalk traverses this wet and wild wonderland, where panthers still stalk their prey amid the black waters. While it's unlikely you'll spot any, there's a great chance you will see a large variety blooming orchids, bird life and reptiles ranging in size from tiny skinks to grinning alligators.

# Homestead to Flamingo Point

Head south of Miami to drive into the heart of the park and the best horizons of the Everglades. Plus, there are plenty of side paths and canoe creeks to detour onto. You'll see some of the most quietly exhilarating scenery the park has to offer on this route, and have better access to an interior network of trails for those wanting to push off the beaten track into the buggy, muggy solar plexus of the wetlands.

## Homestead & Florida City

Homestead is not the prettiest town in the USA. After getting battered into rubble by Hurricane Andrew in 1992 and becoming part of the expanding subdivisions of South Miami, it's been poorly planned around fast-food stops, car dealerships and gas stations. A lot of Mexicans have moved here seeking farm work (or moved here providing services for farm laborers), and as a result, if you speak Spanish, it's impossible not to notice the shift in accent as Cuban Spanish gives way to Mexican. Radio stations also shift from Cuban reggaeton and hip-hop to brass-style mariachi music.

You could pass a mildly entertaining afternoon walking around Homestead's almost quaint **Main Street** (www.homestead-mainstreet.org) which essentially comprises a couple of blocks of Krome Ave extending north and south of **Old Town Hall** (41 N Krome Ave). It's a good effort at injecting some character into 'downtown' Homestead.

## GLADES GUARDIAN

In a state known for iconoclasts, no one can hold a candle to Marjory Stoneman Douglas. Not just for her quirks, but for her drive. A persistent, unbreakable force, she fueled one of the longest conservation battles in US history.

Born in 1890, Douglas moved to Florida after her failed first marriage. She worked for the *Miami Herald* and eventually as a freelance writer, producing short stories that are notable for both the quality of the writing and their progressive themes: *Plumes* (1930) and *Wings* (1931), published in the *Saturday Evening Post*, addressed the issue of Glades bird-poaching when the business was still immensely popular (the feathers were used to decorate ladies' hats).

In the 1940s, Douglas was asked to write about the Miami River for the Rivers of America Series and promptly chucked the idea in favor of capturing the Everglades in her classic, *The Everglades: River of Grass*. Like all of Douglas' work the book is remarkable for both its exhaustive research and lyrical, rich language.

*River of Grass* immediately sold out of its first print-run, and public perception of the Everglades shifted from 'nasty swamp' to 'national treasure.' Douglas went on to be an advocate for environmental causes, women's rights and racial equality, fighting, for example, for basic infrastructure in Miami's Overtown.

Today she is remembered as Florida's favorite environmentalist. Always immaculately turned out in gloves, dress, pearls and floppy straw hat, she would bring down engineers, developers, politicians and her most hated opponents, sugar farmers by force of her oratory alone. She kept up the fight, speaking and lecturing without fail, until she died in 1998 at the age of 108.

Today it seems every environmental institution in Florida is named for Douglas, but were she around, we doubt she'd care for those honors. She'd be too busy planting herself in the CERP office, making sure everything was moving along on schedule.

With that said, let us give Homestead huge props: it houses two of the great attractions of the Florida roadside, one of its best hostels and an incredible farmers' market. Yup: four 'top picks' in one town.

## ⊙ Sights & Activities

### ★ Coral Castle
CASTLE

(☑ 305-248-6345; www.coralcastle.com; 28655 S Dixie Hwy; adult/senior/child $15/12/7; ⊗ 8am-6pm Sun-Thu, to 8pm Fri & Sat) 'You will be seeing unusual accomplishment,' reads the inscription on the rough-hewn quarried wall. That's an understatement. There is no greater temple to all that is weird and wacky about South Florida. The legend: a Latvian gets snubbed at the altar. Comes to the US. Moves to Florida. Hand carves, unseen, in the dead of night, a monument to unrequited love: a rock compound that includes a 'throne room,' a sun dial, a stone stockade (his intended's 'timeout area') and a revolving boulder gate that engineers around the world, to this day, cannot explain. Oh, and there are audio stations situated around the place that explain the site in a replicated Latvian accent, so it feels like you're getting a narrated tour by Borat.

### Everglades Outpost
WILDLIFE RESERVE

(☑ 305-247-8000; www.evergladesoutpost.org; 35601 SW 192nd Ave; recommended donation $20; ⊗ 10am-5pm Mon, Tue & Fri-Sun, by appointment Wed & Thu) The Everglades Outpost houses, feeds and cares for wild animals that have been seized from illegal traders, abused, neglected or donated by people who could not care for them. Residents of the outpost include gibbons, a lemur, wolves, cobras, alligators and a pair of majestic tigers (one of whom was bought by an exotic dancer who thought she could incorporate it into her act). Your money goes into helping the outpost's mission.

### ★ Everglades Hostel Tours
TOUR

(☑ 305-248-1122, 800-372-3874; www.evergladeshostel.com; 20 SW 2nd Ave; half-day/full-day tours from $65/120) ✎ Everglades Hostel offers fantastic tours of the Eastern Everglades. You can either paddle into the bush, or if you don't mind getting a little damp, embark on a 'wet walk' into a flowered and fecund cypress dome, stepping through black water and around the edges of an alligator wallow.

## 🛏 Sleeping

There are plenty of chains such as Best Western, Days Inn and similar hotels and motels all along Rt 1 Krome Ave.

★**Everglades**
**International Hostel**                    HOSTEL **$**
(☑ 305-248-1122, 800-372-3874; www.evergladeshostel.com; 20 SW 2nd Ave, Florida City; camping $18, dm $28, d $61-75, ste $125-225; P ✳ 🛜 🎦) Located in a cluttered, comfy 1930s boarding house, this friendly hostel has good-value dorms, private rooms and 'semi-privates' (you have an enclosed room within the dorms and share a bathroom with dorm residents). But what they've done with their backyard – wow. It's a serious garden of earthly delights. There's a tree house; a natural rock-cut pool with a waterfall; a Bedouin pavilion that doubles as a dancehall; a gazebo; an open-air tented 'bed room'; an oven built to resemble a tail-molting tadpole. It all needs to be seen to be believed, and best of all you can sleep anywhere in the back for $18. Sleep in a treehouse! We think that's an amazing deal. We should add the crowd is made up of all those funky international traveler types that made you fall in love with backpacking in the first place, and the hostel conducts some of the best tours into the Everglades around.

## 🍴 Eating

★**Robert is Here**                    MARKET **$**
(www.robertishere.com; 19200 SW 344th St, Homestead; mains $3-8; ⊘ 8am-7pm Nov-Aug) More than a farmers' stand, Robert's is an institution. This is Old Florida at its kitschy best, in love with the Glades and the agriculture that surrounds it. There's a petting zoo for the kids, live music at night, plenty of homemade preserves and sauces, and while everyone goes crazy for the milkshakes – as they should – do not leave without having the fresh orange juice. It's the best in the world.

**Rosita's**                    MEXICAN **$**
(☑ 305-246-3114; 199 W Palm Dr, Florida City; mains $6-10; ⊘ 8:30am-9pm) There's a working-class Mexican crowd here, testament to the sheer awesomeness of the tacos and burritos. Everyone is friendly, and best of all, they'll give you a takeaway plate if you're staying at the next-door Everglades International Hostel.

## ℹ Information

**Chamber of Commerce** (☑ 305-247-2332; www.chamberinaction.com; 455 N Flagler Ave, Homestead; ⊘ 9am-noon & 1-5pm Mon-Fri)

# Ernest Coe & Royal Palm to Flamingo

Drive past Florida City, through miles of paper-flat farmland and past an enormous, razor-wired jail (it seems like an escapee heads for the swamp at least once a year) and turn left when you see the signs for Robert Is Here – or stop in so the kids can pet a donkey at Robert's petting zoo.

## ⊙ Sights & Activities

**Ernest Coe Visitor Center**                    PARK
(☑ 305-242-7700; www.nps.gov/ever; State Rd 9336; ⊘ 9am-5pm) As you go past Homestead and Florida City, the farmland loses its uniformity and the flat land becomes more tangled, wild and studded with pine and cypress. After a few more miles you'll enter Everglades National Park at this friendly visitor center. Have a look at the excellent exhibits, including a diorama of 'typical' Floridians (the fisherman looks like he should join ZZ Top).

**Royal Palm Visitor Center**                    PARK
(☑ 305-242-7700; State Rd 9336; ⊘ 8am-4:15pm) Four miles past Ernest Coe Visitor Center, Royal Palm offers the easiest access to the Glades in these parts. Two trails, the Anhinga and Gumbo Limbo (the latter named for the gumbo-limbo tree, also known as the 'tourist tree' because its bark peels like a sunburned Brit), take all of an hour to walk and put you face to face with a panoply of Everglades wildlife. Gators sun on the shoreline, anhinga spear their prey and wading birds stalk haughtily through the reeds. Come at night for a ranger walk on the boardwalk and shine a flashlight into the water to see one of the coolest sights of your life: the glittering eyes of dozens of alligators prowling the waterways.

**Flamingo Visitor Center**                    PARK
(☑ 239-695-3101, 239-695-2945; ⊘ marina 7am-7pm, from 6am Sat & Sun) The most isolated portion of the park is a squat marina where you can go on a backcountry boat tour or rent boats. Due to its isolation, this area is subject to closure during bad weather. Boat tours to Florida Bay or into the swampy backcountry run for $32.25/16.13 per adult/

## PYTHONS, GATORS & CROCS, OH MY!

### Gators
Alligators are common in the park, although not so much in the 10,000 Islands, as they tend to avoid saltwater. If you do see an alligator, it probably won't bother you unless you do something overtly threatening or angle your boat between it and its young. If you hear an alligator making a loud hissing sound, get the hell out of Dodge. That's a call to other alligators when a young gator is in danger. Finally, never feed an alligator – it's stupid and illegal.

### Crocs
Crocodiles are less common in the park, as they prefer coastal and saltwater habitats. They are more aggressive than alligators, however, so the same rules apply. With perhaps only a few hundred remaining in the USA, they are also an endangered species.

### Panthers
The Florida panther is critically endangered, and although it is the state's official animal its survival in the wild is by no means assured. There are an estimated 100 panthers left in the wild, and although that number has increased from around 20 to 30 since the 1980s, it's not cause for big celebration either. As usual, humans have been the culprit behind this predator's demise. Widespread habitat reduction (ie the arrival of big subdivisions) is the major cause of concern. In the past, poor data on panther populations and the approval of developments that have been harmful to the species' survival have occurred; environmental groups contend the shoddy information was linked to financial conflicts of interest. Breeding units, which consist of one male and two to five females, require about 200 sq miles of ground to cover, and that often puts panthers in the way of one of Florida's most dangerous beasts: drivers. Fifteen panthers were killed by cars in 2013.

If you're lucky enough to see one (and you gotta be pretty damn lucky), Florida panthers are rather magnificent brown hunting cats (they are, in fact, cougars). They are extremely elusive and only inhabit 5% of their historic range. Many are relatively concentrated in Big Cypress National Preserve (p132).

### Weather
Thunderstorms and lightning are more common in summer than in winter. But in summer the insects are so bad you won't want to be outside anyway. In emergency weather, rangers will search for registered campers, but under ordinary conditions they won't unless they receive information that someone's missing. If camping, have a friend or family member ready to contact rangers if you do not report back by a certain day.

### Insects
You can't overestimate the problem of mosquito and no-see-ums (tiny biting flies) in the Everglades; they are, by far, the park's worst feature. While in most national parks there are warning signs showing the forest-fire risk, here the charts show the mosquito level (call ☎ 305-242-7700 for a report). In summer and fall, the sign almost always says 'extremely high.' You'll be set upon the second you open your car door. The only protections are 100% DEET or, even better, a pricey net suit.

### Snakes in a Glade!
There are four types of poisonous snake in the Everglades: diamondback rattlesnake (Crotalus adamanteus); pigmy rattlesnake (Sistrurus miliarius); cottonmouth or water moccasin (Agkistrodon piscivorus conanti), which swims along the surface of water; and the coral snake (Micrurus fulvius). Wear long thick socks and lace-up boots – and keep the hell away from them. Oh, and now there are Burmese pythons prowling the water too. Pet owners who couldn't handle the pythons have dumped the animals into the swamp, where they've adapted like...well, a tropical snake to a subtropical forest. The python is an invasive species that is badly mucking up the natural order of things.

child, while canoes (two hours/four hours/full day $16/22/40) and sea kayaks (half-/full day $35/45) are available for rental; if you do rent, you're largely left to explore the channels and islands of Florida Bay on your own. During rough weather be cautious, even when on land, as storm surges can turn an attractive spread of beach into a watery stretch of danger fairly quickly.

### Kayaking & Canoeing            BOATING
The real joy here in this part of the park is canoeing into the bracken heart of the swamp. There are plenty of push-off points, all with names that sound like they were read off Frodo's map to Mordor, including **Hell's Bay**, the **Nightmare**, **Snake Bight** and **Graveyard Creek**. Our favorite is Hell's Bay. 'Hell to get into and hell to get out of,' was how this sheltered launch was described by old Gladesmen, but damn if it isn't heaven inside: a capillary network of mangrove creeks, saw-grass islands and shifting mudflats, where the brambles form a green tunnel and all you can smell is sea salt and the dark organic breath of the swamp. Three chickee sites are spaced along the trail.

### Hiking Trails            HIKING
State Rd 9336 cuts through the soft heart of the park, past long fields of marsh prairie, white, skeletal forests of bald cypress and dark clumps of mahogany hammock. There are plenty of trails to detour down; all of the following are half a mile (800m) long.

**Mahogany Hammock** leads into an 'island' of hardwood forest floating on the water-logged prairie, while the **Pinelands** takes you through a copse of rare spindly swamp pine and palmetto forest. Further on, **Pahay-okee Overlook** is a raised platform that peeks over one of the prettiest bends in the River of Grass. The **West Lake Trail** runs through the largest protected mangrove forest in the Northern Hemisphere. Further down you can take a good two-hour, 1.8-mile (2.9km) hike to **Christian Point**. This dramatic walk takes you through several Glades environments: under tropical forest, past columns of white cypress and over a series of mudflats (particularly attractive on grey, cloudy days), and ends with a dramatic view of the windswept shores of Florida Bay.

## 🛏 Sleeping
**National Park Service Campsites**            CAMPGROUND $
(NPS; ☎800-365-2267; www.nps.gov/ever/planyourvisit/camping; sites May-Oct free, Nov-Apr $16) There are campgrounds run by the NPS located throughout the park. Sites are primitive and do not have hookups. Depending on the time of year, cold-water showers are either bracing or a welcome relief. The NPS information office at Royal Palm can provide a map of all campsites, as does the park website.

### WILDERNESS CAMPING
Three types of backcountry campsites are available: beach sites, on coastal shell beaches and in the 10,000 Islands; ground sites, which are basically mounds of dirt built up above the mangroves; and 'chickees,' wooden platforms built above the waterline where you can pitch a free-standing (no spikes) tent. Chickees, which have toilets, are the most civilized – there's a serenity found in sleeping on what feels like a raft levitating above the water. Ground sites tend to be the most bug-infested.

Warning: if you're paddling around and see an island that looks pleasant for camping but isn't a designated campsite, beware – you may end up submerged when the tides change.

From November to April, backcountry camping permits cost $10, plus $2 per person per night; from May to October sites are free, but you must still self-register at Flamingo and Gulf Coast Visitor Centers or call ☎239-695-2945.

Some backcountry tips:

➡ Store food in a hand-sized, raccoon-proof container (available at gear stores).

➡ Bury your waste at least 10in below ground, but keep in mind some ground sites have hard turf.

➡ Use a backcountry stove to cook. Ground fires are only permitted at beach sites, and you can only burn dead or drowned wood.

**Long Pine Key Campground** CAMPGROUND $
(☑ 305-242-7873; camp/RV site $16/30) This is a good bet for car campers, just west of Royal Palm Visitor Center.

**Flamingo Campground** CAMPGROUND $
(☑ 877-444-6777; www.recreation.gov; camp/RV site $16/30) There are 41 car-camping sites at the Flamingo Visitor Center that have electrical hookups.

# BISCAYNE NATIONAL PARK

Just to the east of the Everglades is Biscayne National Park, or the 5% of it that isn't underwater. Let us explain: a portion of the world's third-largest reef sits here off the coast of Florida, along with mangrove forests and the northernmost Florida Keys. Fortunately this unique 300-sq-mile park is easy to explore independently with a canoe, or via a glass-bottom boat tour.

A bit shadowed by the Everglades, Biscayne is unique as national parks go, requiring both a little extra planning and a lot more reward for your effort. The offshore keys, accessible only by boat, offer pristine opportunities for camping. Generally, summer and fall are the best times to visit the park; you'll want to snorkel when the water is calm. This is some of the best reef-viewing and snorkeling you'll find in the US, outside Hawaii and nearby Key Largo.

## ◉ Sights

**Biscayne National Park** PARK
(☑ 786-335-3612, 305-230-7275; www.nps.gov/bisc; 9700 SW 328th St) The park itself offers canoe rentals, transportation to the offshore keys, snorkeling and scuba-diving trips, and glass-bottom boat viewing of the exceptional

---

### MANATEES' BIGGEST THREAT

Manatees are shy, utterly peaceful mammals that are, for all intents, the poster children of Floridian environmentalism. They look like obese seals with vaguely elephantine noses. Back in the day, sailors apparently mistook them for mermaids and sirens, which suggests these guys had been at sea for entirely too long.

Jokes aside, the manatee is a major environmental concern for Florida. Pollution is a problem for these gentle giants, but their biggest killers are boaters, and of those, the worst offenders are pleasure boaters.

Manatees seek warm, shallow water and feed on vegetation. South Florida is surrounded by just such an environment, but it also has one of the highest concentrations of pleasure boats in the world. Despite pleas from environmental groups, wildlife advocates and the local, state and federal governments, which have declared many areas 'Manatee Zones,' some pleasure boaters routinely exceed speed limits and ignore simple practices that would help protect the species.

After grabbing a bite, manatees come up for air and often float just beneath the surface, chewing and hanging around. When speedboats zoom through the area, manatees are hit by the hulls and either knocked away or pushed under the boat, whose propeller then gashes the mammal as the boat passes overhead. Few manatees get through life without propeller scars, which leave slices in their bodies similar to the diagonal slices on a loaf of French bread.

There are several organizations throughout the state that rescue and rehabilitate injured manatees, but they're fighting what would appear to be a losing battle. Some of these organizations include **Save the Manatee** (www.savethemanatee.org) and the Miami Seaquarium. Divers, animal experts and veterinarians of Seaquarium's Marine Mammal Rescue Team patrol South Florida waters, responding to reports of stranded manatees, dolphins and whales. While the Seaquarium's program has been successful, pleasure boaters still threaten the manatees' survival. In 2010, the Florida Fish & Wildlife Commission reported that 83 manatees were killed by watercraft.

In February of 2011, a man was charged with killing a nursing manatee mother while speeding his boat through a slow-water area. He was put on probation for a year and had his boat seized by authorities. The ruling was welcomed by conservationists, but decisions like this are few and far between – the speeder was caught in the act of killing the manatee, but most such incidents are not reported.

reefs. All tours require a minimum of six people, so call to make reservations. Three-hour glass-bottom boat trips ($45) depart at 10am and are very popular; if you're lucky you may spot some dolphins or manatees. Canoe rentals cost $12 per hour and kayaks $16; they're rented from 9am to 3pm. Three-hour snorkeling trips ($45) depart at 1:15pm daily; you'll have about 1½ hours in the water. Scuba trips ($99) depart at 8:30am Friday to Sunday. You can also arrange a private charter boat tour around the park for $300.

### Offshore Keys                               ISLANDS

Long **Elliott Key** has picnicking, camping and hiking among mangrove forests; tiny **Adams Key** has only picnicking; and equally tiny **Boca Chita Key** has an ornamental lighthouse, picnicking and camping. These little islands were settled under the Homestead Act of 1862, which gave land freely to anyone willing to take five years at turning a scratch of the tropics into a working pineapple and Key-lime farm. No-see-ums (tiny flies) are invasive, and their bites are devastating. Make sure your tent is devoid of minuscule entry points.

### Maritime Heritage Trail                     DIVE SITE

The Maritime Heritage Trail takes 'hikers' through one of the only trails of its kind in the USA. If you've ever wanted to explore a sunken ship, this may well be the best opportunity in the country. Six are located within the park grounds; the trail experience involves taking visitors out, by boat, to the site of the wrecks where they can swim and explore among derelict vessels and clouds of fish – there are even waterproof information site cards placed among the ships. Five of the vessels are suited for scuba divers, but one, the *Mandalay,* a lovely two-masted schooner that sank in 1966, can be accessed by snorkelers.

## Activities

**Boating** and **fishing** are naturally very popular and often go hand in hand, but to do either you'll need to get some paperwork in order. Boaters will want to get tide charts from the park (or from www.nps.gov/bisc/planyourvisit/tide-predictions.htm). And make sure you comply with local slow-speed zones, designed to protect the endangered manatee.

The slow zones currently extend 1000ft out from the mainland, from Black Point south to Turkey Point, and include the marinas at Black Point and Homestead Bayfront Parks. Another slow zone extends from Sands Cut to Coon Point; maps of all of the above can be obtained from rangers, and are needed for navigation purposes in any case.

Although Biscayne is a national park, it is governed by state law when it comes to fishing, so if you want to cast a line, you'll need a state license. These come in varieties many and sundry, all of which can be looked up at http://myfwc.com/fishing, which also provides a list of places where licenses can be obtained. At the time of writing, nonresident seven-day saltwater and freshwater fishing permits cost $50 each.

For information on boat tours and rental, contact **Biscayne Underwater** (www.biscayneunderwater.com), which can help arrange logistics.

The water around Convoy Point is regarded as prime **windsurfing** territory. Windsurfers may want to contact outfits in Miami

## Sleeping

Primitive camping on Elliott and Boca Chita Keys costs $15 per tent, per night; you pay on a trust system with exact change on the harbor (rangers cruise the Keys to check your receipt). Bring all supplies, including water, and carry everything out. There's no water on Boca Chita, only saltwater toilets, and since it has a deeper port, it tends to attract bigger (and louder) boats (and boaters). Bring your own water to both islands; while there is potable water on Elliot Key, it's best to be prepared. It costs $20 to moor your boat overnight at Elliott or Boca Chita harbors, but that fee covers the use of one campsite for up to six people and two tents.

## Information

**Dante Fascell Visitor Center** (📞 305-230-7275; www.nps.gov/bisc; 9700 SW 328th St; ⏰ 8:30am-5pm) Located at Convoy Point, this center shows a great introductory film for an overview of the park, and has maps, information and excellent ranger activities. The grounds around the center are a popular picnic spot on weekends and holidays, especially for families from Homestead. Also showcases local artwork.

## Getting There & Away

To get here, you'll have to drive about 9 miles east of Homestead (the way is pretty well signposted) on SW 328th St (North Canal Dr) into a long series of green-and-gold flat fields and marsh.

# Florida Keys & Key West

## Includes ➡

Key Largo
& Tavernier ......... 146

Islamorada ......... 150

Long Key .......... 152

Grassy Key.......... 153

Marathon........... 153

Big Pine, Bahia
Honda & Looe Keys ..156

Sugarloaf
& Boca Chica Keys...158

Key West .......... 159

## Best Places to Eat

➡ Café Solé (p170)

➡ Nine One Five (p170)

➡ Midway Cafe (p152)

➡ Key Largo Conch House (p149)

## Best Places to Stay

➡ Deer Run Bed & Breakfast (p158)

➡ Lighthouse Court Inn (p168)

➡ Mermaid & the Alligator (p168)

➡ Tropical Inn (p168)

## Why Go?

If Florida is a state apart from the USA, the Keys are islands apart from Florida – in other words, it's different down here. They march to the beat of their own drum, or Alabama country band, or Bahamanian steel calypso set... This is a place where those who reject everyday life on the mainland escape. What do they find? About 113 mangrove-and-sandbar islands where the white sun melts over tight fists of deep green mangroves; long, gloriously soft mudflats and tidal bars; water as teal as Arizona turquoise; and a bunch of people often like themselves: freaks, geeks and lovable weirdoes all.

Key West is still defined by its motto, which we love – One Human Family – an ideal that equals a tolerant, accepting ethos where anything goes and life is always a party (or at least a hungover day after). The color scheme: watercolor pastels cooled by breezes on a sunset-kissed Bahamian porch. Welcome to the End of the USA.

Have a drink.

## When to Go
### Key West

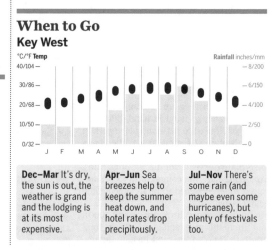

**Dec–Mar** It's dry, the sun is out, the weather is grand and the lodging is at its most expensive.

**Apr–Jun** Sea breezes help to keep the summer heat down, and hotel rates drop precipitously.

**Jul–Nov** There's some rain (and maybe even some hurricanes), but plenty of festivals too.

## History

Calusa and Tequesta peoples plied these waters for thousands of years, but that era came to a depressingly predictable end with the arrival of the Spanish, the area's first European settlers. Upon finding Native American burial sites, Spanish explorers named Key West Cayo Hueso (pronounced kah-ya way-so, meaning Bone Island), a title since anglicized into its current incarnation. From 1760 to 1763, as the Spaniards transferred control of Florida to Great Britain, all of the islands' indigenous peoples were transferred to Cuba, where they either died in exile or integrated into the local ethnic mélange.

Key West itself was purchased by John Simonton in 1821, and developed as a naval base in 1822. For a long while, the area's cycle of boom and bust was tied to the military, salt manufacturing, lime production (from coral), shipwrecks, and sponges, which were harvested, dried and turned into their namesake bath product.

In the late 1800s the area became the focus of mass immigration as Cubans fled Spanish rule and looked to form a revolutionary army. Along with them came cigar manufacturers, who turned Key West into the USA's cigar-manufacturing center. That would end when workers' demands convinced several large manufacturers, notably Vicente Martínez Ybor and Ignacio Haya, to relocate to Tampa in southwest Florida. Immigrants from the Caribbean settled in the Keys in this period, and as a result, today's local African Americans tend to be descended from Bahamian immigrants rather than Southern slaves – something of a rarity in the US.

During the Spanish-American War (1898), Key West was an important staging point for US troops, and the military presence lasted through to WWI. In the late 1910s, with Prohibition on the horizon, Key West became a bootlegging center, as people stocked up on booze. The Keys began to boom around 1938 when Henry Flagler constructed his Overseas Hwy, replacing the by-then defunct Overseas Railroad.

Key West has always been a place where people buck trends. A large society of artists and craftspeople congregated here at the end of the Great Depression because of cheap real estate, and that community continues to grow (despite today's pricey real estate). While gay men have long been welcomed, the gay community really picked up in earnest in the 1970s; today it's one of the most renowned and best organized gay communities in the country.

## Climate

Though it's warm and tropical in the Keys, it never gets higher than about 97°F. The peak in summer is usually about 89°F, with the temperature staying a few degrees cooler than Miami because the Keys are surrounded by ocean (and refreshing ocean breezes). The coldest it gets is usually in the 50s (when some people dress like a blizzard has descended), and water temperature stays in the 80s most of the time. The thunderstorm season begins by late May, and then everyone buckles down for the feared hurricanes – if they arrive, expect them in late summer and early fall.

## ℹ Information

The Monroe County Tourist Development Council's **Florida Keys & Key West Visitors Bureau** (☑ 800-352-5397; www.fla-keys.com) runs an excellent website, which is packed with information on everything the Keys has to offer.

Check www.keysnews.com for good daily online news and information about the islands.

## ℹ Getting There & Away

Getting here can be half the fun – or, if you're unlucky, a whopping dose of frustration. Imagine a tropical-island hop, from one bar-studded mangrove islet to the next, via one of the most unique roads in the world: the Overseas Hwy (US Hwy 1). On a good day, driving down the Overseas with the windows down, the wind in your face and the twin sisters of Florida Bay and the Atlantic stretching on either side, is the US road trip in tropical perfection. On a bad day, you end up sitting in gridlock behind some guy who is riding a midlife-crisis Harley.

**Greyhound** (☑ 800-229-9424; www.greyhound.com) buses serve all Keys destinations along US Hwy 1 and depart from downtown Miami and Key West; you can pick up a bus along the way by standing on the Overseas Hwy and flagging one down. If you fly into Fort Lauderdale or Miami, the **Keys Shuttle** (☑ 888-765-9997) provides door-to-door service to most of the Keys ($70/80/90 to the Upper and Middle Keys/Lower Keys/Key West). Reserve at least a day in advance.

# UPPER KEYS

No, really, you're in the islands!

It is a bit hard to tell when you first arrive, though. The huge, rooty blanket of mangrove

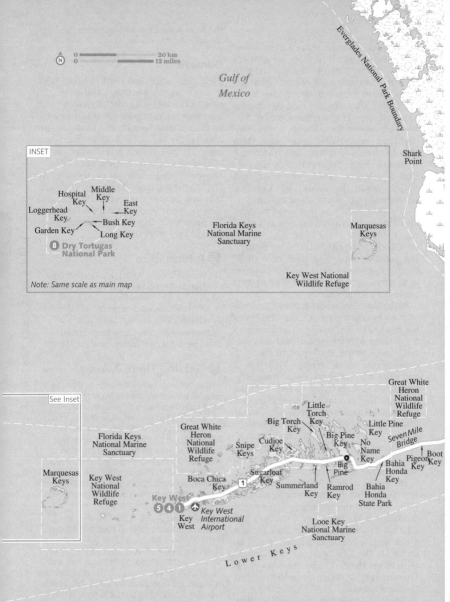

# Florida Keys & Key West Highlights

**1** Watching the sun set over the ocean as you sit and take in the raucous show at **Mallory Square** (p159).

**2** Diving around the rainbow reefs of **John Pennekamp**

**Coral Reef State Park** (p147).

**3** Paddling out to eerie, lonely, beautiful **Indian Key Historic State Park** (p150).

**4** Donning a purple-and-green crocodile costume and partying in the streets at Key West's **Fantasy Fest** (p166).

**5** Scratching Papa's six-toed cats behind their ears at the

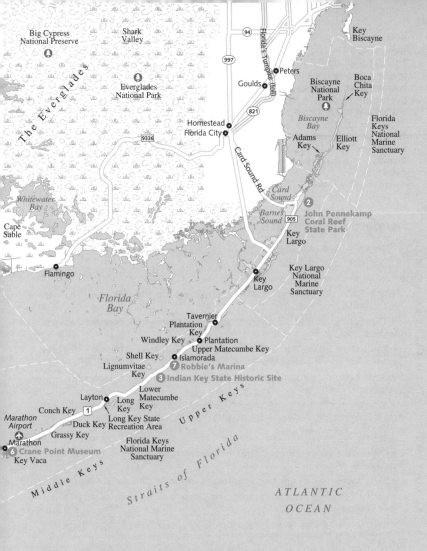

Big Cypress
National Preserve

Shark
Valley

The Everglades

Everglades
National Park

Whitewater
Bay

Cape
Sable

Flamingo

Florida
Bay

94

997

Peters

Goulds

821

Homestead
Florida City

9336

Card Sound Rd

Card
Sound

Barnes
Sound

905

Key
Largo

Key
Largo

Tavernier
Plantation
Key

Windley Key ● Plantation
Upper Matecumbe Key

Shell Key ● Islamorada
Lignumvitae
Key

Lower
Matecumbe
Key

Layton

Conch Key

Long
Key

Duck Key
Long Key State
Recreation Area

Marathon
Airport

Grassy Key

Marathon

**6** Crane Point Museum
Key Vaca

1

Middle Keys

Florida Keys
National Marine
Sanctuary

Upper Keys

Straits of Florida

Key
Biscayne

Biscayne
National
Park

Boca
Chita
Key

Biscayne
Bay

Adams
Key

Elliott
Key

Florida
Keys
National
Marine
Sanctuary

**2** John Pennekamp
Coral Reef
State Park

Key Largo
National
Marine
Sanctuary

**7** Robbie's Marina

**3** Indian Key State Historic Site

ATLANTIC
OCEAN

lovely **Hemingway House**
(p160).

**6** Strolling through the
palm-hammock and pineland
scrub at eco-educational

**Crane Point Museum**
(p154).

**7** Feeding the giant tarpon
swimming in circles at
**Robbie's Marina** (p151).

**8** Making an island-hopping
day trip and detour to **Dry
Tortugas National Park**
(p167).

forest that forms the South Florida coastline spreads like a woody morass into Key Largo; little differentiates the island from Florida proper. Keep heading south and the scenery becomes more archipelagically pleasant as the mangroves give way to wider stretches of road and ocean, until – bam – you're in Islamorada and the water is everywhere. If you want to avoid traffic on US 1, you can try the less trafficked FL 997 and Card Sound Rd to FL 905 (toll $1), which passes Alabama Jack's (p150).

# Key Largo & Tavernier

We ain't gonna lie: Key Largo (both the name of the town and the island it's on) is slightly underwhelming at a glance. 'Under' is the key word, as its main sights are under the water, rather than above. As you drive onto the islands, Key Largo resembles a long line of low-lying hammock (raised areas) and strip development. But that's just from the highway: head down a side road and duck into this warm little bar, or that converted Keys plantation house, and the island idiosyncrasies become more pronounced.

## SHOULD YOU SWIM WITH DOLPHINS?

There are five swim-with-the-dolphin (SWTD) centers in the Keys, and many more arguments for and against the practice.

### For

➡ While SWTD sites are commercial, they are also research entities devoted to learning more about their charges.

➡ The dolphins raised on-site are legally obtained and have not been not captured from the wild.

➡ The dolphins are safe from environmental hazards often found in the wild – accidental catches, run-ins with boats and pollution.

➡ Dolphin swim programs increase visitors' knowledge of dolphins and promote conservation.

➡ At places such as the Dolphin Research Center (p153), the dolphins can actually swim out of their pens into the open water, but choose not to.

### Against

➡ Dolphins are social creatures that require interaction, which is impossible to provide in captivity.

➡ SWTD tourism encourages the capture of wild dolphins in other parts of the world.

➡ Dolphin behavior is never 100% predictable. Dolphins can seriously injure a human, even while playing.

➡ SWTD centers encourage customers to think of dolphins as anthropomorphized 'friends,' rather than wild animals.

➡ Dolphins never appreciate captivity. Those that voluntarily remain in SWTD sites do so to remain close to food.

### SWTD Centers

If you decide to swim or see dolphins in the Keys, you can contact one of the following:

**Theater of the Sea** (☎305-664-2431; www.theaterofthesea.com; MM 84.7 bayside; adult/child 3-10 $30/21; ⊙9:30am-5pm) has been here since 1946. Structured dolphin swims and sea-lion programs ($135) include 30 minutes of instruction and a 30-minute supervised swim. You can also swim with stingrays ($55).

**Dolphins Plus** (☎305-451-1993, 866-860-7946; www.dolphinsplus.com; off MM 99.5 bayside; swim programs $135-220), a Key Largo center, specializes in recreational and educational unstructured swims. They expect you know a good deal before embarking upon the swim, even though a classroom session is included.

There is also dolphin swimming at Grassy Key's Dolphin Research Center (p153) and Hawk's Cay Resort (p153).

The 33-mile-long Largo, which starts at MM 106, is the longest island in the Keys, and those 33 miles have attracted a lot of marine life, all accessible from the biggest concentration of dive sites in the islands. The town of Tavernier (MM 93) is just south of the town of Key Largo.

If you approach Key Largo from FL 905, you'll be driving through **Crocodile Lake National Wildlife Refuge** (www.fws.gov/nationalkeydeer/crocodilelake; FL 905), one of the last wild sanctuaries for the threatened American crocodile, indigo snake and Key Largo woodrat – the latter is an enterprising fellow who likes to build 4ft by 6ft homes out of forest debris. That said, the wildlife areas are closed to the public, and your chances of seeing the species we've mentioned from the road are negligible.

## ◎ Sights & Activities

**Florida Keys Wild Bird Rehabilitation Center**   WILDLIFE RESERVE
(www.fkwbc.org; 93600 Overseas Hwy, MM 93.6; suggested donation $5; ☉ sunrise-sunset; P ⚿ )
🐾 This sanctuary is the first of many animal hospitals you'll come across built by critter-loving Samaritans throughout the Keys. You'll find an alfresco bird hospital that cares for birds that have swallowed fish hooks, had wings clipped in accidents, been shot by BB pellets etc. A pretty trail leads back to a nice vista of Florida Bay and a wading bird pond. Just be warned, it does smell like bird doo back here.

**Harry Harris Park**   PARK
(MM 93.5; ☉ sunrise-sunset; ⚿ ) This small park is a good place to take the kids – there's a small playground, a picnic table and other such accoutrements. Rare for the Keys, there's also a good patch of white sand fronting a warm lagoon that's excellent for swimming.

**Caribbean Club Bar**   FILM LOCATION
(☑ http://www.caribbeanclubkl.com; MM 104 bayside; ☉ 7am-4am) Here's one for the movie fans, particularly Bogie buffs: the Caribbean Club Bar is, in fact, the only place in Key Largo where *Key Largo,* starring Humphrey Bogart and Lauren Bacall, was filmed (the rest of the island was a Hollywood soundstage). If that's not enough, the original *African Queen,* of the same-titled movie, is docked in a channel at the Holiday Inn at MM 100 – just walk around the back and there she is.

**John Pennekamp
Coral Reef State Park**   PARK
(☑ 305-451-6300; www.pennekamppark.com; MM 102.6 oceanside; car/motorcycle/cyclist or pedestrian $8/4/2; ☉ 8am-sunset, aquarium to 5pm; ⚿ )
🐾 John Pennekamp has the singular distinction of being the first underwater park in the USA. There's 170 acres of dry parkland here and over 48,000 acres (ie 75 sq miles) of wet: the vast majority of the protected area is the ocean. Before you get out in that water, make sure to dig around some pleasant beaches and stroll over the nature trails.

The **Mangrove Trail** is a good boardwalk introduction to this oft-maligned, ecologically awesome arboreal species (the trees, often submerged in water, breathe via long roots that act as snorkels – neat). Stick around for nightly campfire programs and ranger discussions.

The visitor center is well run and informative and has a small, cute **aquarium** (8am to 5pm) that gives a glimpse of what's under them thar waters. To really get beneath the surface of this park (pun intended), you should take a 2½-hour **glass-bottom boat tour** (☑ 305-451-6300; adult/child $24/17; ☉ 9:15am, 12:15pm & 3:15pm). You won't be ferried around in some rinky-dink fishing boat; you're brought out in a safe, modern 38ft catamaran from which you'll ooh and aah at filigreed flaps of soft coral, technicolor schools of fish, dangerous-looking barracuda and massive, yet ballerina-graceful, sea turtles. Besides the swirl of natural coral life, interested divers can catch a glimpse of the *Christ of the Abyss*, a submerged 8.5ft, 4000lb bronze sculpture of Jesus – a copy of a similar sculpture off the coast of Genoa, Italy, in the Mediterranean Sea.

If you want to go even deeper, try straight-up **snorkeling trips** (☑ 305-451-6300; adult/child $30/25) or **diving excursions** (☑ 305-451-6322; $55). DIYers may want to take out a canoe ($20 per hour) or kayak (single/double per hour $12/$17) to journey through a 3-mile network of trails. Call ☑ 305-451-6300 for boat-rental information.

To learn more about the reef in this area, go to www.southeastfloridareefs.net.

### FLORIDA KEYS OVERSEAS HERITAGE TRAIL

One of the best ways to see the Keys is by bicycle. The flat elevation and ocean breezes are perfect for cycling, and the **Florida Keys Overseas Heritage Trail** (FKOHT; www.dep.state.fl.us/gwt/state/keystrail) will connect all the islands from Key Largo to Key West.

If you are keen to ride, it's currently possible to bike through the Keys by shoulder riding (it takes three days at a good clip). There are particularly pleasant rides around Islamorada, and if you're uncomfortable riding on the shoulder, you can contact the FKOHT through its website for recommended bike excursions.

**Jacob's Aquatics Center** WATERPARK
(☎305-453-7946; http://jacobsaquaticcenter.org; 320 Laguna Ave, MM 99.6; adult/child/student/family $10/6/8/25; ⏲11am-6pm Mon-Fri, 10am-7pm Sat & Sun; 🅼) Jacob's is a complex of all kinds of aquatic fun. There's an eight-lane pool for lap and open swimming, a therapy pool with handicapped access, courses on water aerobics. For the kids there's a small waterpark with waterslides, a playground and, of course, kiddie-sized pools.

## Sleeping

One of our favorite small hotels on the island, **Largo Lodge** (☎305-451-0424; www.largolodge.com; MM 102 bayside; cottages $150-265; P), was undergoing extensive renovations at the time of research, and was scheduled to re-open in early 2015.

Air-con is standard in virtually all Key accommodations. Lodgings have higher rates during the high season (mid-December to April). In addition, many properties add a 'shoulder' (midseason) that runs from May to June; rates may fall somewhere between low (July to November) and high during midseason. Many hotels (especially smaller properties) enforce two-night minimum stays. Expect rates to be extremely high during events such as New Year's and Fantasy Fest, when some places enforce up to seven-night minimum stays.

**John Pennekamp Coral Reef State Park** CAMPGROUND $
(☎800-326-3521; www.pennekamppark.com; camp/RV site both $36; P) You don't even have to leave Pennekamp at closing time if you opt for tent or RV camping, but be sure to make a reservation, as the sites fill up fast.

**Stone Ledge Paradise Inn** HOTEL $
(☎305-852-8114; www.stoneledgeparadiseinn.com; 95320 Overseas Hwy; r $78-118, villas $185-300; P) This is a pink palace (well, squat bunch of motel blocks) of old-school US seaside kitsch. The wooden fish hung on every door are only the tip of the nautical-kitsch iceberg, but the real joy is the sweeping view over Florida Bay at the back of the property. Rooms are pretty simple on the inside.

**Hilton Key Largo Resort** HOTEL $$
(☎305-852-5553; www.keylargoresort.com; MM 102 bayside; r from $179, ste from $315; P 📶 🏊) This Hilton has a ton of character. Folks just seem to get all laid-back when lounging in clean, designer rooms outfitted in blues, greens and (why not?) blue-green. Throw in some beiges and you've got a supremely soothing sleeping experience. The grounds are enormous and include an artificial waterfall-fed pool and frontage to a rather large stretch of private white-sand beach.

**Dove Creek Lodge** HOTEL $$
(☎800-401-0057; www.dovecreeklodge.com; 147 Seaside Ave; r $169-269, ste from $350; P 📶 🏊) This midsized hotel offers bright rooms decked out in citrus-shaded colors and a grounds that fronts the Atlantic Ocean. It's a family-friendly spot with an old-school resort feel. Can help with booking tours and excursions in the area.

**Key Largo House Boatel** HOTEL $$
(☎305-766-0871; www.keylargohouseboat.com; Shoreland Dr, MM 103.5 oceanside; houseboat small/medium/large from $75/100/150; P) There are five well-decorated houseboats available, with the largest one spacious enough to sleep six people comfortably. The boats are right on the docks (and across from a bar), so there's no possibility of being isolated from land (or booze).

**Kona Kai Resort & Gallery** HOTEL $$$
(☎305-852-7200; www.konakairesort.com; MM 97.8 bayside; r $220-439; P 📶 🏊) This hideaway is one of the only botanical gardens we can think of that integrates a hotel onto their grounds – or is that the other way around? Either way, this spot is lush. The 13 airy rooms and suites (with full kitchens) are all bright and comfortable, with good natural light and linoleum floors. Kona Kai also houses a lovely art gallery.

Guided tours of the extensive gardens are offered for nonguests Tuesday through Saturday for $25 (if you're staying, the gardens are free, because they're your backyard).

**Jules' Undersea Lodge**                    HOTEL $$$
(☑ 305-451-2353; www.jul.com; 51 Shoreland Dr, MM 103.2 oceanside; group of 3-4 per person $350, s $675) There's lots of talk about underwater hotels getting built in Dubai and Fiji, but as of this writing, Jules' Undersea Lodge is still the only place in the world outside of a submarine where you and your significant other can join the 'five-fathom club' (we're not elaborating). Once a research station, this module has been converted into a delightfully cheesy Keys motel, but wetter.

In addition to two private guest rooms, there are common rooms, a kitchen-dining room and a wet room with hot showers and gear storage. Telephones and an intercom connect guests with the surface. Guests must be at least 10 years old and you gotta dive to get here – plus, there's no smoking or alcohol. If you just want to visit, you can pop in for a three-hour visit (with pizza!) for $150.

## ✖ Eating

**Mrs Mac's Kitchen**                    AMERICAN $
(☑ 305-451-3722; www.mrsmacskitchen.com; MM 99.4 bayside; breakfast & lunch $8-12, dinner $9-22; ⊙ 7am-9:30pm Mon-Sat; P ⋔) When Applebee's stuffs its wall full of license plates, it's tacky. When Mrs Mac's does it, it's homey. Probably because the service is warm and personable, and the breakfasts are delicious. Plus, the food packs in the locals, tourists, their dogs and pretty much everyone else on the island (plus, admittedly, a fair few calories, but that's why it tastes good).

**DJ's Diner**                    AMERICAN $
(☑ 305-451-2999; 99411 Overseas Hwy; mains $6-14; ⊙ 7am-9pm to 3pm Sat & Sun; P ⋔) You're greeted by a mural of Humphrey Bogart, James Dean *and* Marilyn Monroe – that's a lot of Americana. It's all served with a heapin' helpin' of diner faves, vinyl-boothed ambience and South Florida staples like *churrasco* (skirt steak) and conch.

**Key Largo Conch House**                    FUSION $$
(☑ 305-453-4844; www.keylargoconchhouse.com; MM 100.2 oceanside; mains $8-26; ⊙ 8am-10pm; P ☎ ⋔) This wi-fi hotspot, coffeehouse and innovative kitchen likes to sex up local classics (conch in a lime and white-wine sauce, or in a vinegar sauce with capers). Set in a restored old-school Keys mansion wrapped in a *Gone With the* Wind veranda, it's hard not to love the way the period architecture blends in seamlessly with the local tropical fauna.

A justifiably popular spot with tourists and locals. The fish tacos are intensely good.

**Fish House**                    SEAFOOD $$
(☑ 305-451-4665; www.fishhouse.com; MM 102.4 oceanside; mains $9-24; ⊙ 11:30am-10pm; P ⋔) The Fish House delivers on the promise of its title – very good fish, bought whole from local fishermen and prepared fried, broiled, jerked, blackened or char-grilled. Because the Fish House only uses fresh fish, the menu changes daily based on what is available. We prefer the original Fish House over the more sushi-centered Fish House Encore next door.

---

### FLORIDA KEYS FOR CHILDREN

Check out some of the following options to entertain the kids:

**Florida Keys Eco-Discovery Center** (p160) Get an understanding of the region's environment.

**Glass-bottom boat tours at John Pennekamp Coral Reef State Park** (p147) Your own window to the underwater world.

**Key West Butterfly & Nature Conservatory** (p160) Pretty flying things.

**Turtle Hospital** (p154) Save (or watch) the turtles.

**Conch Tour Train** (p165) Kitschy, corny, enjoyable tour.

**Ghost tours** (p165) Only slightly spooky; younger kids may find this one a bit scary.

**Key-deer spotting** (p157) Kids go crazy for cute mini-deer.

**Key West Cemetery** (p160) Get Gothic with these often humorous tombs.

**Robbie's Marina** (p151) All sorts of activities, including the ever-popular tarpon (giant fish) feeding frenzy.

## KEY LIME PIE

Many places claim to serve the original Key lime pie, but no one knows who discovered the tart treat. Types of crust vary, and whether or not the pie should be topped with meringue is debated. However, the color of Key lime pie is not open to question. Beware of places serving green Key lime pie: Key limes are yellow, not green. Restaurants that add green food coloring say that tourists expect it to be green. Steer clear.

**Snook's Bayside**                    AMERICAN $$
(☑ 305-453-5004; 99470 Overseas Hwy; lunch mains $9-18, dinner mains $19-42; ☺ 11:30am-9:30pm; ℗ ☑) Floridians love their waterfront dining establishments crossed with a tiki bar, and Snook's is Key Largo's contribution to the genre. The surf-and-turf-style menu is good, but the view onto the water – and the accompanying artificial sandy beach – is better.

## 🍷 Drinking

**Alabama Jack's**                    BAR
(58000 Card Sound Rd; ☺ 11am-7pm) Welcome to your first taste of the Keys: zonked-out fishermen, exiles from the mainland and Harley heads getting drunk on a mangrove bay. This is the line where Miami-esque South Florida gives way to the country-fried American South. Wildlife-lovers: you may spot the rare mulleted version of *Jacksonvillia Redneckus*!

But seriously, everyone raves about the conch fritters, and the fact they have to close because of nightly onslaughts of mosquitoes means this place is as authentically Florida as they come. Country bands take the stage on weekends from 2pm to 5pm.

## ℹ️ Information

**Chamber of Commerce** (☑ 305-451-1414; www.keylargochamber.org; MM 106 bayside; ☺ 9am-6pm) Visit the chamber of commerce for maps and brochures.
**Mariner Hospital** (☑ 305-434-3000; www.baptisthealth.net; Tavernier, MM 91.5 bayside)

## ℹ️ Getting There & Away

The Greyhound bus stops at MM 99.6 oceanside.

# Islamorada

Islamorada (eye-luh-murr-*ah*-da) is also known as 'The Village of Islands.' Doesn't that sound pretty? Well, it really is. This little string of pearls (well, keys) – Plantation, Upper and Lower Matecumbe, Shell and Lignumvitae (lignum-*vite*-ee) – shimmers as one of the prettiest stretches of the islands. This is where the scrubby mangrove is replaced by unbroken horizons of ocean and sky, one perfect shade of blue mirroring the other. Islamorada stretches across some 20 miles, from MM 90 to MM 74.

## 👁 Sights & Activities

★**Anne's Beach**                    BEACH
(MM 73.5 oceanside) Anne's is one of the best beaches in these parts. The small ribbon of sand opens upon a sky-bright stretch of tidal flats and a green tunnel of hammock and wetland. Nearby mudflats are a joy to get stuck in, and will be much loved by the kids.

**Indian Key Historic State Park**        ISLAND
(☑ 305-664-2540; www.floridastateparks.org/indiankey; MM 78.5 oceanside; $2.50; ☺ 8am-sunset) This quiet island was once a thriving city, complete with a warehouse, docks, streets, a hotel and about 40 to 50 permanent residents. There's not much left at the historic site – just the foundation, some cisterns and jungly tangle. Robbie's Marina used to bring boats this way, and still does boat rentals (around $30 for a kayak or canoe). You can also see the island from the water on an eco-tour with Robbie's ($37.50).

By 1836, Indian Key was the first seat of Dade County, but four years later the inhabitants of the island were killed or scattered by a Native American attack during the Second Seminole War. Trails follow the old layout of the city streets, or you can walk among ruins and paddle around spotting rays and dolphins in utter isolation in a canoe or kayak.

**Lignumvitae Key**
**Botanical State Park**                ISLAND
(☑ 305-664-2540; www.floridastateparks.org/lignumvitaekey; admission/tour $2.50/2; ☺ tours 10am & 2pm Fri-Sun) This key, only accessible by boat, encompasses a 280-acre island of virgin tropical forest and is home to roughly a zillion jillion mosquitoes. The official attraction is the 1919 **Matheson House**, with its windmill and cistern; the real draw is a nice sense of shipwrecked isolation. Guided walking tours (1¼ hours) are given at 10am and 2pm Friday to Sunday. You'll have to get here via Robbie's Marina; boats depart for tours to here and Indian Key.

Strangler figs, mastic, gumbo-limbo, poisonwood and lignum vitae trees form a dark canopy that feels more South Pacific than South Florida.

## Florida Keys History of Diving Museum
MUSEUM

(📞 305-664-9737; www.divingmuseum.org; MM 83; adult/child $12/6; ⊗10am-5pm; 🅿 🚹) You can't miss the diving museum – it's the building with the enormous mural of swimming manatees on the side – and we mean that in every sense of the phrase. In other words, don't miss this museum, a collection of diving paraphernalia from around the world. This is the sort of charmingly eccentric museum that really reflects the quirks of the Keys. The hall of diving helmets from around the world, from Denmark to Japan, is particularly impressive.

We're also wowed by the exhibitions of diving 'suits' and technology from the 19th century. Folks in the museum can also provide information on diving in a vintage Mark V diving suit (the ones with the bulbous onion-heads connected to surface pumps). Hosts lectures on diving entitled (of course) 'Immerse Yourself' at 7pm on the third Wednesday of every month.

## Windley Key Fossil Reef Geological State Site
PARK

(📞 305-664-2540; www.floridastateparks.org/windleykey; MM 85.5 oceanside; admission/tour $2.50/2; ⊗8am-5pm Thu-Mon) To get his railroad built across the islands, Henry Flagler had to quarry out some sizable chunks of the Keys. The best evidence of those efforts can be found at this former quarry-cum-state-park. Besides having a mouthful of a name, Windley has leftover quarry machinery scattered along an 8ft former quarry wall. The wall offers a cool (and rare) public peek into the stratum of coral that forms the substrate of the Keys.

Ranger tours are offered at 10am and 2pm Friday to Sunday for $3.

## Rain Barrel
ARTS CENTER

(📞 305-852-3084, 305-852-8935; 86700 Overseas Hwy; ⊗9am-5pm) We want to tell you the Rain Barrel, Islamorada's local artists' village, strikes a balance between the beautiful and the tacky. But you're more likely to find souvenir-y tourist tat here than a truly striking work of art. That said, strolling around the seven studios and galleries that make up the Rain Barrel is nice, and who knows, you may find the piece of your dreams, or at least a hand-painted sign that says, 'It's always 5 o'clock somewhere.'

## ★ Robbie's Marina
MARINA

(📞 305-664-8070; www.robbies.com; MM 77.5 bayside; kayak & SUP rentals $40-75; ⊗9am-8pm; 🚹) More than a boat launch, Robbie's is a local flea market, tacky tourist shop (all the shells

you ever wanted), sea pen for tarpons (very big-ass fish) and jump-off for fishing expeditions, all wrapped into one driftwood-laced compound. Boat-rental and tour options are also available. The party boat (half-day/night trips $40/45) is just that: a chance to drink, fish and basically achieve Keys Zen.

For real Zen (ie the tranquil kind as opposed to drunken kind), take an ecotour ($35) on an electrically propelled silent boat deep into the mangroves, hammocks and lagoons. Snorkeling trips are a good deal; for $37.50 you get a few hours on a very smooth-riding Happy Cat vessel and a chance to bob amid some of the USA's only coral reefs. If you don't want to get on the water, at least feed the freakishly large tarpons from the dock ($2.79 per bucket, $1 to watch).

## 🛏 Sleeping

### Conch On Inn
MOTEL $

(📞 305-852-9309; conchoninn.com; MM 89.5, 103 Caloosa St; apt $59-129; 🅿) A simple motel popular with yearly snowbirds, Conch On Inn has basic, clean and comfortable rooms.

### Ragged Edge Resort
RESORT $$

(📞 305-852-5389; www.ragged-edge.com; 243 Treasure Harbor Rd; apt $69-259; 🅿 ✳ 🛜 🏊) This popular low-key efficiency and apartment complex, far from the maddening traffic, has friendly hosts and 10 quiet units. The larger studios have screened-in porches. There's no beach, but you can swim off the dock and at the pool.

### Casa Morada
HOTEL $$$

(📞 305-664-0044, 888-881-3030; www.casamorada.com; 136 Madeira Rd, off MM 82.2; ste incl breakfast $279-659; 🅿 ✳ 🛜 🏊) Contemporary chic comes to Islamorada, but it's not gentrifying away the village vibe. Rather, the Casa adds a welcome dab of sophistication to Conch chill: a keystone standing circle, freshwater pool, artificial lagoon, plus a *Wallpaper*-magazineworthy bar that overlooks Florida Bay – all make this boutique hotel worth a reservation. Go to the bar to catch a drink and a sunset.

### La Siesta Resort & Marina
RESORT $$$

(📞 305-664-2132; www.lasiestaresort.com; MM 80.5 oceanside; ste $190-340; 🅿 🛜 🏊) This pretty option consists of renovated suites and apartments that let in generous amounts of light and are decorated to feel modern and classy, but still refreshingly un-hip and family friendly. Service is amiable, the pool is busy and the ocean views are lovely.

**Chesapeake Resort**  RESORT $$$

(📞 305-664-4662; www.chesapeake-resort.com; 83409 Overseas Hwy; r $200-330, ste $350-550; 🅿🛜🏊) This all-inclusive resort is packed with activities and rooms that have more tropical character than the average Keys accommodation. An on-site tennis court is good for exercise, while the charter boat dock and marina keeps you linked in to the local world of recreational fishing and sea exploring. You won't lack for amenities.

## ✕ Eating

**★ Midway Cafe**  CAFE $

(📞 305-664-2622; 80499 Overseas Hwy; dishes $2-11; ⊗7am-3pm Thu-Tue, to 2pm Sun; 🅿🚼) The lovely folks who run this cafe – stuffed with every variety of heart-warming art the coffee-shop trope can muster – roast their own beans, make baked goods that we would swim across the Gulf for, and are friendly as hell. You're almost in the Middle Keys: celebrate making it this far with a cup of joe.

**Bob's Bunz**  CAFE $

(www.bobsbunz.com; MM 81.6 bayside; mains $6-12; ⊗6am-2pm; 🅿📄) The service at this cute cafe is energetic and friendly in an only-in-America kinda way, and the food is fine, filling and cheap. Key lime pie is a classic Keys dish and Key-lime anything at this bakery is highly regarded, so buy that souvenir pie here.

**Lorelei**  AMERICAN $$

(📞 305-664-2692; MM 82 bayside; mains $9-22; ⊗7am-midnight; 🅿🚼) Need a sunset and some excellent seafood? Maybe a touch of steak? Lorelei has got you covered. The sunsets really are magnificent, an experience compounded by yummy fish sandwiches, cracked conch and some frankly gorgeous ribs. Look for the big mermaid sign.

**Pierre's**  FRENCH $$$

(📞 305-664-3225; www.pierres-restaurant.com; MM 81.6 bayside; mains $28-42; ⊗5-10pm Sun-Thu, to 11pm Fri & Sat; 🅿) Why hello two-story waterfront plantation – what are you serving? A tempura-ed spiny lobster tail...good, decadent start. Hogfish meunière? Well, that's rich enough to knock out a rhino. A filet mignon with black truffle mash potatoes? Splurge, traveler, on possibly the best food between Miami and Key West.

**Beach Cafe**
**at Morada Bay**  AMERICAN $$$

(📞 305-664-0604; www.moradabay-restaurant. com; MM 81.6 bayside; mains $14-33; ⊗11:30am-10pm; 🅿) If you can ignore the service from staff who can get overwhelmed by customers and the awful bands that occasionally 'headline' the lunch rush, this is a lovely, laid-back Caribbean experience, complete with an imported, powder-white sandy beach, nighttime torches, tapas and fresh seafood.

## 🍷 Drinking & Nightlife

**Hog Heaven**  BAR

(📞 305-664-9669; MM 85 oceanside; ⊗11am-3:30am) We're tempted to place this joint in an eating section, as the seafood nachos are so good. But it deserves pride of place in any list of best places to drink in town, thanks to the huge crowds that trip all the way down from Fort Lauderdale for back-porch, alfresco imbibing.

**Morada Bay**  BAR

(📞 305-664-0604; www.moradabay.com; MM 81.6 bayside; ⊗5pm-midnight) In addition to its excellent food, the Bay holds monthly full-moon parties that attract the entire party-people population of the Keys. The whole shebang typically starts around 9pm and goes until whenever the last person passes out; check website for dates.

## ℹ Information

**Chamber of Commerce** (📞 305-664-4503; www.islamoradachamber.com; MM 83.2 bayside; ⊗9am-5pm Mon-Fri, to 4pm Sat, to 3pm Sun) Located in an old caboose.

**Post Office** (📞 305-664-4738; MM 82.9 oceanside)

## ℹ Getting There & Away

The Greyhound bus stops at the Burger King at MM 82.5 oceanside.

# Long Key

The 965-acre **Long Key State Recreation Area** (📞 305-664-4815; www.floridastateparks.org/ longkey; MM 67.5 oceanside; per car/motorcycle/cyclist $5/4/2; 🅿) 🌿 takes up much of Long Key. It's about 30 minutes south of Islamorada, and comprises a tropical clump of gumbo-limbo, crabwood and poisonwood trees; a picnic area fronting a long, lovely sweep of teal water; and lots of wading birds in the mangroves. Two short nature trails head through distinct plant communities. The park also has a 1.5-mile canoe trail through a saltwater tidal lagoon and rents out ocean-going kayaks (two hours single/double $17.50/21.50).

If you want to stay here, make reservations this minute: it's tough to get one of the 60 sites at the campground (☎800-326-3521; www.reserveamerica.com; MM 67.5 oceanside; sites $36; ℗). They're all waterfront, making this the cheapest (and probably most unspoiled) ocean view – short of squatting on a resort – you're likely to find in Florida.

# MIDDLE KEYS

As you truck down the Keys, the bodies of water get wider until you reach the big boy: Seven Mile Bridge, one of the world's longest causeways and a natural divider between the Middle and Lower Keys. In this stretch of islands you'll cross specks like Conch Key and Duck Key; green, quiet Grassy Key; and finally Key Vaca (MM 54 to MM 47), where Marathon, the second-largest town and most Key-sy community in the islands, is located.

## Grassy Key

At first blush Grassy Key seems pretty sedate. Well spotted; Grassy is very much an island of few attractions and lots of RV lots and trailer parks. These little villages were once the heart of the Keys, where retirees, escapists, fishermen and the waitstaff who served them lived, drank and dreamed (of a drink). Some of these communities remain, but development is relentless, and so, it seems, is the migration of the old Conch trailer towns.

### ◉ Sights & Activities

**Curry Hammock State Park** PARK
(☎305-289-2690; www.floridastateparks.org/curry-hammock; MM 56.2 bayside; car/motorcycle/cyclist $5/4/2; ⊙8am-sunset; ℗) 🕭 This park is small but sweet and the rangers are just lovely. Like most parks in the Keys, it's a good spot for preserved tropical hardwood and mangrove habitat – a 1.5-mile hike takes you through both environments. Rent a kayak (single/double for two hours $17.20/21.50) or, when the wind is up, join the windsurfers and kiteboarders. You can also camp at the park for $36 per night – sites have toilets and electric hookups.

Local waters are blissfully free of power boats, which is a blessing down here.

**Dolphin Research Center** WILDLIFE RESERVE
(☎305-289-0002; www.dolphins.org; MM 59 bayside; adult/under 4yr/4-12yr/senior $20/free/15/17.50, swim program $120-675; ⊙9am-4pm; 🖆) By far the most popular activity on this island is swimming with the descendants of

Flipper. Dolphins are free to leave the grounds and a lot of marine-biology research goes on behind the (still pretty commercial) tourist activities, such as getting a dolphin to paint your T-shirt or playing 'trainer for a day' ($675). Still, swimming with dolphins is an activity that raises animal rights questions (see p146).

### 🛏 Sleeping & Eating

**Grassy Key Outpost** AMERICAN $$
(☎305-743-7373; 58152 Overseas Hwy; mains $8-28; ⊙7am-10pm; ℗🍴) The Outpost is an interesting spot that skews between fine dining and Keys casualness, both in terms of atmosphere and cuisine. There's a Southern flair to the gastronomy; shrimp and grits comes rich and smoky, while the mac'n'cheese is laced with decadent slathers of rich lobster.

**Wreck Galley & Grill** AMERICAN $$
(☎305-743-8282; MM 59 bayside; mains $10-25; ⊙11am-10pm; ℗) The Wreck is a Keys classic, where fisherman types knock back brew and feast on wings. It's definitely a local haunt, where island politicos like to prattle about the issues (fishing). The food is excellent; it grills one of the best burgers in the Keys, and the aforementioned wings go down a treat with a tall beer.

**Hawk's Cay Resort** RESORT $$$
(☎305-743-7000, 888-395-5539; www.hawks-cay.com; 61 Hawk's Cay Blvd, Duck Key, off MM 61 oceanside; r & ste winter $350-1600, summer $150-500; ℗🛜🏊) The Cay is an enormous luxury compound that could well have its own zip code, and besides a series of silky-plush rooms and nicely appointed townhouses, it has a variety of island activities. The Cay has its own dolphin pool, sailing school, snorkeling tours, tennis courts and boat rentals.

**Rainbow Bend** HOTEL $$$
(☎800-929-1505; www.rainbowbend.com; MM 58 oceanside; r $165-270; ℗🏊) You'll be experiencing intensely charming Keys-kitsch in these big pink cabanas, where the apartments and suites are bright, the tiki huts are shady, the bedsheets are ghastly, the beach swing is...um, swing-y and the ocean is (splash)...right there. Half-day use of the Bend's Boston whalers (motorboats), kayaks and canoes is complimentary.

## Marathon

Marathon sits right on the halfway point between Key Largo and Key West, and it's a good place to stop on a road trip across the islands. It's perhaps the most 'developed' key outside Key West (that's really pushing the definition of the word 'developed') in the sense that it has large shopping centers and a population of a few thousand. Then again it's still a place where exiles from the mainland fish, booze it up and have a good time, so while Marathon is more family-friendly than Key West, it's hardly G-rated.

## ⊙ Sights

**Crane Point Museum** MUSEUM
(☎305-743-9100; www.cranepoint.net; MM 50.5 bayside; adult/child $12.50/8.50; ⊙9am-5pm Mon-Sat, from noon Sun; P⛟) ⨂ This is one of the nicest spots on the island to stop and smell the roses. And the pinelands. And the palm hammock – a sort of palm jungle (imagine walking under giant, organic Japanese fans) that only grows between MM 47 and MM 60. There's also Adderly House, a preserved example of a Bahamian immigrant cabin (which must have *baked* in summer) and 63 acres of green goodness to stomp through.

This is a great spot for the kids, who'll love the pirate exhibits in an on-site museum and yet another bird hospital.

**Sombrero Beach** BEACH
(Sombrero Beach Rd, off MM 50 oceanside; P) One of the few white-sand, mangrove-free beaches in the Keys. It's a good spot to lay out or swim, and it's free.

**Turtle Hospital** WILDLIFE RESERVE
(☎305-743-2552; www.theturtlehospital.org; 2396 Overseas Hwy; adult/child $15/7.50; ⊙9am-6pm; P⛟) ⨂ Be it a victim of disease, boat propeller strike, flipper entanglement with fishing lines or any other danger, an injured sea turtle in the Keys will hopefully end up in this motel-cum-sanctuary. We know we shouldn't anthropomorphize animals, but these turtles just seem so sweet. It's sad to see the injured and sick ones, but heartening to see them so well looked after. Tours are educational, fun and offered on the hour from 10am-4pm.

**Pigeon Key National Historic District** ISLAND
(☎305-743-5999; www.pigeonkey.net; MM 47 oceanside; adult/child/under 5yr $12/9/free; ⊙tours 10am, noon & 2pm) For years, tiny Pigeon Key, located 2 miles west of Marathon (basically below the Old Seven Mile Bridge) housed the rail workers and maintenance men who built the infrastructure that connected the Keys. Today you can tour the

structures of this National Historic District or relax on the beach and get in some snorkeling. Ferries leave Knight's Key (to the left of the Seven Mile Bridge if you're traveling south) to Pigeon; the last one returns at 4pm.

The Old Seven Mile Bridge, meanwhile, is closed to traffic and now serves as 'the World's Longest Fishing Bridge'; park at the northeastern foot of the bridge and have a wander.

## 🏃 Activities

**Marathon Community Park & Marina** MARINA
(12222 Overseas Hwy) Has athletic fields and a skate park for disaffected adolescents. The marina, better known as **Boot Key Harbor** (☎305-289-8877; www.bootkeyharbor.com; VHF 16), is one of the best maintained working waterfronts in the Keys, and an excellent spot to book charter-fishing and diving trips. Come during Christmas to see a 'boat parade' of boats decked out with Christmas lights.

**Marathon Kayak** KAYAKING
(☎305-395-0355; www.marathonkayak.com; 3hr tours $60) Does guided mangrove ecotours, sunset tours and boat rentals. The three-hour paddle through a canopy of red mangroves is highly recommended.

**Wheels-2-Go** RENTAL
(☎305-289-4279; http://wheels-2-go.com; 5994 Overseas Hwy; see-through kayaks/bicycles per day $40/10; ⊙9am-5pm) Friendly kayak and bicycle rental services.

**Tilden's Scuba Center** DIVING
(☎305-743-7255; www.tildensscubacenter.com; 4650 Overseas Hwy) Offers snorkeling and diving expeditions through nearby sections of the coral reef.

**Sombrero Reef Explorers** DIVING
(☎305-743-0536; www.marathoncharters.com; 19 Sombrero Rd, off MM 50 oceanside) Offers snorkeling and diving expeditions through nearby sections of the coral reef.

## 🛌 Sleeping

**Siesta Motel** MOTEL $
(☎305-743-5671; www.siestamotel.net; MM 51 oceanside; r $85-115; P🕸) Head here for one of the cheapest, cleanest spots in the Keys, located in a friendly cluster of cute Marathon homes – and it's got great service, to boot.

**Seascape Motel & Marina** MOTEL $$
(☎305-743-6212; www.seascapemotelandmarina. com; 1275 76th St Ocean E, btwn MM 51 & 52; r $99-

250; P✳🛜🚭) The classy, understated luxury in this B&B manifests in its nine rooms, all of which have a different feel – from old-fashioned cottage to sleek boutique. Seascape also has a waterfront pool, kayaks for guests to use and a lovely lobby-lounge where you'll find breakfast and afternoon wine and snacks (all included).

### Sea Dell Motel                    MOTEL $$
(📞305-743-5161; 5000 Overseas Hwy; r $89-209; P@) The Sea Dell is a Keys classic: low-slung huts containing linoleum-floored rooms and tropical bedspreads. The rooms are more or less self-sufficient small apartments, and can comfortably accommodate small families.

### Tranquility Bay                   RESORT $$$
(📞888-755-7486; www.tranquilitybay.com; MM 48.5 bayside; r $280-650; P🛜🚭) If you're serious about going upscale, you should be going here. Tranquility Bay is a massive condo-hotel resort with plush townhouses, high-thread-count sheets and all-in-white chic. The grounds are enormous and activity-filled; the owners really don't want you to leave.

### Tropical Cottages               COTTAGES $$
(📞305-743-6048; www.tropicalcottages.net; 243 61st St; cottages from $130; P🚭) These pretty pastel cottages are a good option, especially if you're traveling in a larger group. The individual cottages aren't particularly plush, but they're cozy, comfortable and offer a nice

bit of privacy, along with some Old Florida atmosphere. There's a daily $10 fee per pet.

## 🍴 Eating

### ★Keys Fisheries              SEAFOOD $
(📞305-743-4353; www.keysfisheries.com; 3502 Louisa St; mains $7-16; ⊗8am-9pm; P🚗) The lobster Reuben is the stuff of legend here. Sweet, chunky, creamy, so good it'll make you leave unsightly drool all over the place mat. But you can't go wrong with any of the excellent seafood here, all served with sass. Expect pleasant levels of seagull harassment as you dine on a working waterfront.

As an odd bonus, to order you have to identify your favorite car, color, etc; a question that depends on the mood of the guy behind the counter.

### Wooden Spoon                 AMERICAN $
(7007 Overseas Hwy; dishes $2-10; ⊗5:30am-1:30pm; P) It's the best breakfast around, served by sweet Southern women who know their way around a diner. The biscuits are fluffy, and they drown so well in that thick, delicious sausage gravy, and the grits are the most buttery soft starch you'll ever have the pleasure of seeing beside your eggs.

### Hurricane                    AMERICAN $$
(📞305-743-2200; 4650 Overseas Hwy; mains $9-19; ⊗11am-midnight; P🍴) Besides being our favorite bar in Marathon, the Hurricane also

---

## GROOVY GROVES

It's easy to think of the Keys, environmentally speaking, as a little boring. The landscape isn't particularly dramatic (with the exception of those sweet sweeps of ocean visible from the Overseas Hwy); it tends toward low brush and...well, more low brush.

Hey, don't judge a book by its cover. The Keys have one of the most unique, sensitive environments in the US. The difference between ecosystems here is measured in inches, but once you learn to recognize the contrast between a hammock and a wetland, you'll see the islands in a whole new tropical light. Some of the best introductions to the natural Keys can be found at Crane Point Museum and the Florida Keys Eco-Discovery Center (p160).

But we want to focus on the mangroves – the coolest, if not most visually arresting, habitat in the islands. They rise from the shallow shelf that surrounds the Keys (which also provides that lovely shade of Florida teal), looking like masses of spidery fingers constantly stroking the waters. Each mangrove traps the sediment that has accrued into the land your tiki barstool is perched on. That's right, no mangroves = no Jimmy Buffett.

The three different types of mangrove trees are all little miracles of adaptation. Red mangroves, which reside on the water's edge, have aerial roots, called propagules, allowing them to 'breathe' even as they grow into the ocean. Black mangroves, which grow further inland, survive via 'snorkel' roots called pneumatophores. Resembling spongy sticks, these roots grow out from the muddy ground and consume fresh air. White mangroves grow furthest inland and actually sweat out the salt they absorb through air and water to keep healthy.

The other tree worth a mention here isn't a mangrove. The lignum vitae, which is limited to the Keys in the US, is just as cool. Its sap has long been used to treat syphilis, hence the tree's Latin name, which translates to 'tree of life.'

serves a menu of creative South Florida–inspired goodness. Snapper stuffed with crabmeat comes after an appetizer of conch sliders (miniburgers) jerked in Caribbean seasoning. Save room for the chicken wings, an amazing blend of hot, sweet and plain delicious. The $5 lunch specials are great deal.

## 🍸 Drinking & Nightlife

★Hurricane                                    BAR

(📞305-743-2200; MM 49.5 bayside; ⊗11am-12am) The staff is sassy and warm. The drinks will kick your ass out the door and have you back begging for more. Locals, tourists, mad fishermen, rednecks and the odd journalist saddle up for endless Jägerbombs before dancing the night away to any number of consistently good live acts. It's the best bar before Key West, and it deserves a visit.

Island Fish Company                          BAR

(📞305-743-4191; MM 54 bayside; ⊗11:30am-10pm) The Island has a friendly staff pouring strong cocktails on a sea-breeze-kissed tiki island overlooking Florida Bay. Chat with your friendly Czech or Georgian bartender – tip well, and they'll top up your drinks without you realizing it. The laid-back, by-the-water atmosphere is quintessentially Keys.

Brass Monkey                                 BAR

(📞305-743-4028; Marathon, MM 52; ⊗10am-4am) When Colonel Kurtz whispered, 'The horror, the horror,' in *Apocalypse Now* he was probably thinking about the night he got trashed in this scuzziest of dives, frequented by off-the-clock bar- and waitstaff in Marathon.

Marathon Cinema
& Community Theater                          CINEMA

(📞305-743-0288; www.marathontheater.org; 5101 Overseas Hwy) A good, old-school, single-stage theater that shows movies and plays in big reclining seats (with even bigger cup-holders).

## ℹ Information

Fisherman's Hospital (📞305-743-5533; www.fishermanshospital.com; 3301 Overseas Hwy) Has a major emergency room.

Marathon Visitors Center Chamber of Commerce (📞305-743-5417, 800-262-7284; www.floridakeysmarathon.com; MM 53.5 bayside; ⊗9am-5pm) Sells Greyhound tickets.

## ℹ Getting There & Away

You can fly into the **Marathon Airport** (📞305-289-6060; MM 50.5 bayside) or go Greyhound, which stops at the airport.

# LOWER KEYS

The people of the Lower Keys vary between winter escapees and native Conchs. Some local families have been Keys castaways for generations, and there are bits of Big Pine that feel more Florida Panhandle than Overseas Hwy. It's an odd contrast, the islands get at their most isolated, rural and quintessentially 'Keez-y' before opening onto (relatively) cosmopolitan, heterogeneous (yet strongly homosexual) Key West.

# Big Pine, Bahia Honda & Looe Keys

Big Pine is home to endless stretches of quiet roads, Key West employees who found a way around astronomical real-estate rates, and packs of wandering Key deer. Bahia Honda has everyone's favorite sandy beach, while the coral-reef system of Looe offers amazing reef-diving opportunities.

## ◉ Sights & Activities

Bahia Honda State Park                       PARK

(📞305-872-3210; www.bahiahondapark.com; MM 36.8; car/motorcycle/cyclist $5/4/2; ⊗8am-sunset; ♿) This park, with its long, white-sand (and seaweed-strewn) beach, named Sandspur Beach by locals, is the big attraction in these parts. As Keys beaches go, this one is probably the best natural stretch of sand in the island chain, but we wouldn't vote it best beach in the continental USA (although Condé Nast did...in 1992). As a tourist, the more novel experience is walking on the **old Bahia Honda Rail Bridge**, which offers nice views of the surrounding islands.

You can also check out the nature trails (ooh, butterflies!) and science center, where helpful park employees help you identify stone crabs, fireworms, horseshoe crabs and comb jellies. The park concession offers daily 1½-hour snorkeling trips at 9:30am and 1:30pm (adult/child $30/25). Reservations are a good idea in high season.

Looe Key National
Marine Sanctuary                             MARINE PARK

(📞305-809-4700; floridakeys.noaa.gov) Looe (pronounced 'loo') Key, located five nautical miles off Big Pine, isn't a key at all but a reef, part of the Florida Keys National Marine Sanctuary. This is an area of some 2800 sq nautical miles of 'land' managed by the National Oceanic & Atmospheric Administration. The reef here can only be visited

## KEY DEER

While we can't guarantee you'll see one, if you head down the side roads of Big Pine Key, there's a pretty good chance you'll spot the Key deer, a local species roughly the size of a large dog. Once mainland dwellers, the Key deer were stranded on the Keys during the formation of the islands. Successive generations grew smaller and had single births, as opposed to large litters, to deal with the reduced food resources in the archipelago. While you won't see thundering herds of dwarfish deer, the little cuteballs are pretty easy to spot if you're persistent and patient. In fact, they're so common you need to pay careful attention to the reduced speed limits. Note: speed limits drop further at night, because cars are still the biggest killer of Key deer.

To visit the official Key deer refuge (although the deer can be spotted almost anywhere on Big Pine) take Key Deer Blvd (it's a right at the lights off the Overseas Hwy at the southern end of Big Pine) north for 3.5 miles from MM 30.5.

through a specially arranged charter-boat trip, best arranged through any Keys diving outfit, the most natural one being **Looe Key Dive Center** (☑ 305-872-2215; www.diveflakeys.com; snorkel/dive $40/70).

The marine sanctuary is named for an English frigate that sank here in 1744, and the Looe Key reef contains the 210ft MV *Adolphus Busch,* used in the 1957 film *Fire Down Below* and then sunk (110ft deep) in these waters in 1998.

### National Key Deer
### Refuge Headquarters    WILDLIFE RESERVE
(☑ 305-872-2239; www.fws.gov/nationalkeydeer; Big Pine Shopping Center, MM 30.5 bayside; ⊙ 8am-5pm Mon-Fri; ♿) What would make Bambi cuter? Mini Bambi. Introducing: the Key deer, an endangered subspecies of white-tailed deer that prance about primarily on Big Pine and No Name Keys. The folks here are an incredibly helpful source of information on the deer and all things Keys. The refuge sprawls over several islands, but the sections open to the public are on Big Pine and No Name.

The headquarters also administers the **Great White Heron National Wildlife Refuge** – 200,000 acres of open water and mangrove islands north of the main Keys that is only accessible by boat. There's no tourism infrastructure in place to get out here, but you can inquire about nautical charts and the heron themselves at the office.

### Blue Hole    POND
(off MM 30.5; ⊙ 24hr) This little pond (and former quarry) is now the largest freshwater body in the Keys. That's not saying much, but the hole is a pretty little dollop of blue (well, algal green) surrounded by a small path and information signs. The water is home to turtles, fish and wading birds. A

quarter mile further along the same road is **Watson's Nature Trail** (less than 1 mile long) and **Watson's Hammock**, a small Keys forest habitat.

Apparently people have taken to (illegally) feeding the wildlife here; please don't follow in their footsteps.

### No Name Key    ISLAND
Perhaps the best-named island in the Keys, No Name gets few visitors, as it's basically a residential island. It's one of the most reliable spots for Key deer watching. From Overseas Hwy, go on to Watson Blvd, turn right, then left onto Wilder Blvd. Cross Bogie Bridge and you'll be on No Name.

### Veterans Memorial Park & Beach    PARK
(MM 39 oceanside; ⊙ sunrise-sunset; ♿) This small park has covered picnic tables and good access to the mudflat and mangrove habitat that makes up most of the Keys' coastline. The views onto the ocean are pristine.

### Big Pine Flea Market    MARKET
(MM 30.5 oceanside; ⊙ 8am-sunset Sat & Sun) This market, which attracts folks from across the Keys, rivals local churches for weekly attendance. You know how we keep harping on about how weird Keys residents are? Well, imagine rummaging through their closets and seeing their deepest, darkest secrets – on sale for 50¢?!

### Strike Zone Charters    SNORKELING, DIVING
(☑ 305-872-9863; www.strikezonecharter.com; MM 29.5 bayside) Runs snorkeling ($38) and diving trips ($48) aboard glass-bottom boats, in which you can explore the thousands of varieties of colorful tropical fish, coral and sea life in the Looe Key sanctuary. Get open water PADI certification for $395.

## 🛏 Sleeping

### ★ Bahia Honda State Park Campground
CAMPGROUND $

(☑ 305-872-2353; www.reserveamerica.com; MM 37, Bahia Honda Key; sites/cabins $38.50/122.50; ℗) ⚲ Bahia Honda has the best camping in the Keys. There's nothing quite like waking up to the sky as your ceiling and the ocean as your shower (Ow! Damned sand flies). OK, it's not paradise...). The park has six cabins, each sleeping six people, and 200 sites a short distance from the beach. Reserve well in advance.

### Barnacle Bed & Breakfast
B&B $$

(☑ 305-872-3298; www.thebarnacle.net; 1557 Long Beach Dr, Big Pine Key; r $165-235; ℗ ⓢ) The Barnacle welcomes you into its atrium with the promise of fresh ocean breezes. Wander around the pool and Jacuzzi, past the swinging hammocks, and into highly individualized rooms that all share a lovingly mad design sense. Tropical knickknacks and big windows that let in lots of Keys sunlight are standard. Meals should be enjoyed on the deck, which overlooks the sea.

### Parmer's Resort
HOTEL $$

(☑ 305-872-2157; www.parmersresort.com; 565 Barry Ave, Little Torch Key, off MM 28.5 bayside; r winter $159-304, summer $99-209; ℗ ⓢ ⓢ) Appearing deceptively small from the outside, this 5-acre property takes up a nice chunk of Little Torch Key and fills it with inviting rooms that overlook local waterways and channels. The rooms are spacious, although you'd be mad not to step outside them and enjoy a view of the islands from your balcony.

### ★ Deer Run Bed & Breakfast
B&B $$$

(☑ 305-872-2015; www.deerrunfloridabb.com; 1997 Long Beach Dr, Big Pine Key, off MM 33 oceanside; r $255-375; ℗ ⓢ ⓢ) ⚲ This state-certified green lodge and vegetarian B&B is isolated on a lovely stretch of Long Beach Dr. It's a garden of quirky delights, complemented by love-the-earth paraphernalia, street signs and four simple but cozy rooms. The helpful owners will get you out on a boat or into the heated pool for relaxation while they whip up delicious vegetarian meals.

### Little Palm Island Resort & Spa
RESORT $$$

(☑ 305-515-3019, 800-343-8567; www.littlepalmisland.com; packages from $890; @ ⓢ ⓢ) How do you get here? By boat or by plane, accompanied by a big wad of money. If you can afford to get here you can afford to spoil yourself, and this exclusive island, with its Zen gardens, blue lagoons and general Persian Empire air of decadent luxury, is very good at spoiling you.

## ✖ Eating

### No Name Pub
PIZZERIA $

(☑ 305-872-9115; N Watson Blvd, Big Pine Key, off MM 30.5 bayside; mains $7-18; ⊙ 11am-11pm; ℗) The No Name's one of those off-the-track places that everyone seems to know about. It feels isolated, it looks isolated, yet somehow, the tourists are all here – and this doesn't detract in the slightest from the kooky ambience, friendly service, excellent locally brewed beer and primo pizzas served up at this colorful semidive.

Note: the name of this place implies that it is located on No Name Key, but it is on Big Pine Key, just over the causeway.

### Coco's Kitchen
DINER $

(Big Pine Key Shopping Center, MM 30.5 bayside; mains & sandwiches $10.50; ⊙ 7am-2pm & 4-7pm Tue-Sat; ℗ ⓐ) Enter through the oddly mirrored storefront into this tiny luncheonette, where local fishers join shoppers from the Winn Dixie next door for diner fare and local gossip. Serves a good mix of American standards and Cuban diner fare such as picadillo (ground beef cooked in Cuban spices).

### Good Food Conspiracy
VEGETARIAN $

(☑ 305-872-3945; Big Pine Key, MM 30 oceanside; mains under $10; ⊙ 9:30am-7pm Mon-Sat, 11am-5pm Sun; ℗ ⚲) ⚲ Rejoice, health-food nuts: all the greens, sprouts, herbs and tofu you've been dreaming about during that long, fried-food-studded drive down the Overseas are for sale in this friendly little macrobiotic organic shop. There is a good smoothie and fresh-juice bar on site. Note the big pink shrimp out front – Keezy kitsch as its best.

## ⓘ Information

**Lower Keys Chamber of Commerce** (☑ 305-872-2411; www.lowerkeyschamber.com; MM 31 oceanside; ⊙ 9am-5pm Mon-Fri, to 3pm Sat) Stocked with brochures and tourist information.

# Sugarloaf & Boca Chica Keys

This is the final stretch before the holy grail of Key West. There's not much going on – just bridges over lovely swathes of teal and turquoise, a few good eats and a thoroughly batty roadside attraction.

This lowest section of the Keys goes from about MM 20 to the start of Key West.

## ◎ Sights

### Perky's Bat Tower                                    TOWER
(Sugarloaf Key, MM17) It resembles an Aztec-inspired fire lookout, but this wooden tower is actually one real-estate developer's vision gone utterly awry. In the 1920s Richter C Perky had the bright idea to transform this area into a vacation resort. There was just one problem: mosquitoes. His solution? Build a 35ft tower and move in a colony of bats (he'd heard they eat mosquitoes). He imported the flying mammals, but they promptly took off, leaving the tower empty.

### Sheriff's Animal Farm                                    ZOO
(☑305-293-7300; 5501 College Rd, Stock Island; ☺1-3pm second & fourth Sun of the month or by appt; ℗🏛) 🐾 Just before you hit Key West, you may be tempted to stop at this farm, located near the Monroe County Sheriff's Office and Detention Center (no, really). This shelter for Monroe County animals that have been abandoned or given up is a lovely place to take the kids (call ahead to visit and farmer Jeanne Selander will be happy to show you around). There are tortoises, South American cavvies (a kind of rodent), birds, llamas and an albino python.

## 🛏 Sleeping

### Sugarloaf Lodge                              HOTEL $$
(☑305-745-3211, 800-553-6097; www.sugarloaflodge.net; Sugarloaf Key, MM 17; r $120-170; ℗🏊) The 55 motel-like rooms are nothing special, though every single one has a killer bay view. There is also an on-site restaurant, a tiki bar, a marina and an airstrip, from which you can charter a seaplane tour or go skydiving.

## 🍽 Eating

### Baby's Coffee                                    CAFE $
(☑305-744-9866; MM 15 oceanside; ☺7am to 6pm Mon-Fri, 7am to 5pm Sat & Sun) This very cool coffeehouse has an on-site bean-roasting plant and sells bags of the aromatic stuff along with excellent hot and cold java brews – many locals consider this to be some of the best coffee in the islands. Other essentials are sold, from yummy baked goods to Dr Bronner's liquid soap.

### Mangrove Mama's                        CARIBBEAN $$
(☑305-745-3030; MM 20 oceanside; lunch $10-15, dinner $15-29; ☺11:30am-3:30pm & 5:30-10pm; ℗🏛) This groovy roadside eatery serves Caribbean-inspired seafood – coconut shrimp, spicy conch stew, lobster – best enjoyed on the backyard patio and accompanied by a little live reggae.

# KEY WEST

The Keys, like any frontier, have always been defined by two 'E's: edge and eccentric. And when it came to the far frontier, the very edge, the last outpost of America – out here, only the most eccentric would dare venture. And thus, Key West: the most beautifully strange (or is it strangely beautiful?) island in the US. This place is seriously screwy, in a (mostly) good way. There's no middle separating the high and low brow, that's for sure. On one side of the road, literary festivals, Caribbean villas, tropical noir and expensive art galleries. On the other, an S&M fetishist parade, frat boys vomiting on their sorority girlfriends and 'I Love to Fart' T-shirts (seriously).

Where the other Keys are a bit more country-fried, Key West, a historical haven for homosexuals and artists, remains a little more left of center. The locals revel in their funky nonconformity here, probably because weirdness is still integral to the Key West brand. But past these idiosyncrasies is simply a beautiful tropical island, where the moonflowers bloom at night and the classical Caribbean homes are so sad and romantic it's hard not to sigh at them.

## ◎ Sights

### ★ Mallory Square                                    SQUARE
(🏛) Take all those energies, subcultures and oddities of Keys life and focus them into one torchlit, family-friendly (but playfully edgy), sunset-enriched street party. The child of all these raucous forces is Mallory Sq, one of the greatest shows on Earth. It all begins as the sun starts to set, a sign for the madness that it's OK to break out. Watch a dog walk a tightrope, a man swallow fire, British acrobats tumble and sass each other.

Have a beer. And a conch fritter. And wait for the sun to dip behind the ocean and for the carnival to really get going.

### Duval Street                                    STREET
Key West locals have a love-hate relationship with the most famous road in Key West (if not the Keys). Duval, Old Town Key West's main drag, is a miracle mile of booze, tacky everything and awful behavior. But it's fun. The 'Duval Crawl' is one of the wildest pub

crawls in the country. The mix of neon drink, drag shows, T-shirt kitsch, local theaters, art studios and boutiques is more charming than jarring.

### Hemingway House
HOUSE

(☑ 305-294-1136; www.hemingwayhome.com; 907 Whitehead St; adult/child $13/6; ☉ 9am-5pm) Key West's biggest darling, Ernest Hemingway, lived in this gorgeous Spanish colonial house from 1931 to 1940. Papa moved here in his early 30s with wife No 2, a Vogue fashion editor and (former) friend of wife No 1 (he left the house when he ran off with wife No 3). *The Short Happy Life of Francis Macomber* and *The Green Hills of Africa* were produced here, as well as many six-toed cats, whose descendants basically run the grounds.

### Florida Keys Eco-Discovery Center
MUSEUM

(☑ 305-809-4750; http://eco-discovery.com/ecokw.html; 35 East Quay Rd; ☉ 9am-4pm Tue-Sat; P 🖩) 🖉 FREE So, you've been making your way down the Keys, thinking, Gosh, could there be a place that ties all the knowledge of this unique ecological phenomenon into one fun, well-put-together educational exhibit? OK, maybe those weren't your exact thoughts, but this is exactly what you get at this excellent center. This place does a marvelous job of filling in all the wild details of the natural Keys. The kids love it.

### Fort Zachary Taylor Historic State Park
PARK

(☑ 305-292-6713; www.floridastateparks.org/fort-taylor; Truman Annex; per car/motorcycle/pedestrian & cyclist $6/4/2; ☉ 8am-sunset) 'America's Southernmost State Park,' this park is oft-neglected by authorities and visitors, which is a shame. The actual fort walls are still standing, and within the compound those most-blessed of nerds – historical re-enactors – sometimes act out scenes of pirate and Civil War battles. The beach here is the best one Key West has to offer – it's got white sand to lounge on, water deep enough to swim in and tropical fish under the waves.

### Key West Cemetery
CEMETERY

(cnr Margaret & Angela Sts; ☉ 7am - 6pm; 🖩) A darkly alluring Gothic labyrinth beckons at the center of this pastel town. Built in 1847, the cemetery crowns Solares Hill, the highest point on the island (with an elevation of 16ft). Some of the oldest families in the Keys rest in peace – and close proximity – here. With body space at a premium, mausoleums stand practically shoulder to shoulder. Island quirkiness penetrates the gloom: seashells and macramé adorn headstones with inscriptions like, 'I told you I was sick.'

Get chaperoned by a guide from the Historic Florida Keys Foundation, with guided tours for $10 per person at 9:30am on Tuesday and Thursday; departs from the main gate at Margaret and Angela Sts.

### Key West Butterfly & Nature Conservatory
ANIMAL SANCTUARY

(☑ 305-296-2988; www.keywestbutterfly.com; 1316 Duval St; adult/4-12yr $12/8.50; ☉ 9am-5pm; 🖩) This vast domed conservatory lets you stroll through a magic garden of flowering plants, colorful birds and up to 1800 fluttering butterflies, all live imports from around the globe.

---

## THE CONCH REPUBLIC: ONE HUMAN FAMILY

Conchs (pronounced 'conk' as in 'bonk,' not 'contsh' as in 'bunch') are people who were born and raised in the Keys. It's a rare title to achieve. Even transplants can only rise to the rank of 'freshwater Conch.' You will hear reference to, and see the flag of, the Conch Republic everywhere in the islands, which brings us to an interesting tale.

In 1982 US border patrol and customs agents erected a roadblock at Key Largo to catch drug smugglers and illegal aliens. As traffic jams and anger mounted, many tourists disappeared. They decided they'd rather take the Shark Valley Tram in the Everglades, thank you very much. To voice their outrage, a bunch of fiery Conchs decided to secede from the USA. After forming the Conch Republic, they made three declarations (in this order): secede from the USA; declare war on the USA and surrender; and request $1 million in foreign aid. The roadblock was eventually lifted, and every February, Conchs celebrate the anniversary of those heady days with nonstop parties, and the slogan 'We Seceded Where Others Failed.'

Today the whole Conch Republic thing is largely a marketing gimmick, but that doesn't detract from its official motto: 'One Human Family.' This emphasis on tolerance and mutual respect has kept the Keys' head and heart in the right place, accepting gays, straights, and peoples of all colors and religions.

**Nancy Forrester's Secret Garden** GARDEN
(www.nfsgarden.com; 518 Elizabeth St; admission adult/child $10/5; ⊙10am-3pm; ⓖ) Nancy, a local artist and fixture of the Keys community, invites you to bring lunch (but no cell phones!) into her oasis of lush palms, orchids and chatty rescued parrots and macaws. Although the place is called a secret garden, Nancy considers it to be a piece of art in and of itself – the last acre of undeveloped (although tended and cared for by human hands) natural space within the heart of Key West. Children are welcome and seem to love the local bird life.

**Museum of Art & History
at the Custom House** MUSEUM
(☑305-295-6616; www.kwahs.com/customhouse; 281 Front St; adult/child $9/5; ⊙9:30am-4:30pm) There is art at the end of the road, and you'll find the best at this museum, which is worth a look-see if only for its gorgeous home – the grand Customs House, long abandoned until its impressive renovation in the '90s. The permanent display includes massive portraits and some of the best showcases of international (particularly Caribbean) art in the region.

**Fort East Martello
Museum & Gardens** MUSEUM
(☑305-296-3913; www.kwahs.com/martello.htm; 3501 S Roosevelt Blvd; adult/child $9/5; ⊙9:30am-4:30pm) This old fortress was built to resemble an old Italian Martello-style coastal watchtower (hence the name), a design that quickly became obsolete with the advent of the explosive shell. Now the fort serves a new purpose: preserving the old. There's historical memorabilia, artifacts, the folk art of Mario Sanchez, and 'junk' sculptor Stanley Papio, who worked with scrap metal and a genuinely creepy haunted doll.

Perhaps the most haunted thing in Key West, 'Robert the doll' is a terrifying child's toy from the 19th century who reportedly causes much misfortune to those who question his powers. Honest, he looks like something out of a Stephen King novel; see www.robertthedoll.org for more information.

**Studios of Key West** GALLERY
(TSKW; ☑305-296-0458; www.tskw.org; 600 White St; ⊙10am-6pm) This nonprofit showcases about a dozen artists' studios in a gallery space located in the old Armory building, which includes a lovely sculpture garden. Besides its public visual-arts displays, TSKW hosts readings, literary and visual workshops, concerts, lectures and community discussion groups.

Essentially, it has become the accessible heart of this city's enormous arts movement, and offers a good point-of-entry for visitors who want to engage in Key West's creative scene but don't have a clue where to start.

**Little White House** HISTORIC BUILDING
(☑305-294-9911; www.trumanlittlewhitehouse.com; 111 Front St; adult/child 5-12yr/senior $16/5/14; ⊙9am-4:30pm, gardens 7am-6pm) While we were first tempted here by the prospect of a Lego-sized model of the presidential digs, this is in fact the spot where ex-president Harry S Truman used to vacation when he wasn't molding post-WWII geopolitics. It's lushly luxurious and open only for guided tours, although you are welcome to walk around the surrounding botanical gardens for free. Plenty of Truman's possessions are scattered about, but the real draw is the guides, who are intensely intelligent, quirky and helpful.

**San Carlos Institute** HISTORIC BUILDING
(☑305-294-3887; www.institutosancarlos.org; 516 Duval St) Founded in 1871 by Cuban exiles, the San Carlos is a gorgeous building constructed in classical Spanish mission style. The current structure dates from 1924. The interior is spackled with Cuban tile work, Italian marble and statues of Cuban luminaries, including Jose Marti, who spoke here and dubbed the building 'La Casa Cuba.' Today the building serves as library, art gallery, lecture hall and theater; it is only open during events, but these occur often.

**Bahama Village** NEIGHBORHOOD
Bahama Village was the old Bahamian district of the island, and in days past had a colorful Caribbean feel about it, which is resurrected a bit during the Goombay Festival (p166). But today the village is pretty gentrified; many areas have been swallowed into a sort of pseudo-Duval periphery zone, but some retain Caribbean charm. At the Office of the Secretary General of the Conch Republic (☑305-296-0213; www.conchrepublic.com; 613 Simonton St) you can see all manner of Conch Republic tat – flags, souvenirs and such.

**Casa Antigua** HISTORIC BUILDING
(314 Simonton St; ⊙10am-6pm) This was technically Hemingway's first house in Key West and where he wrote *A Farewell to Arms,* but it isn't all that notable, except for a lush garden in the back and a very kitschy 'guided tour'. For $2, they'll let you into a peaceful green area out the back, where a recorded

# Key West

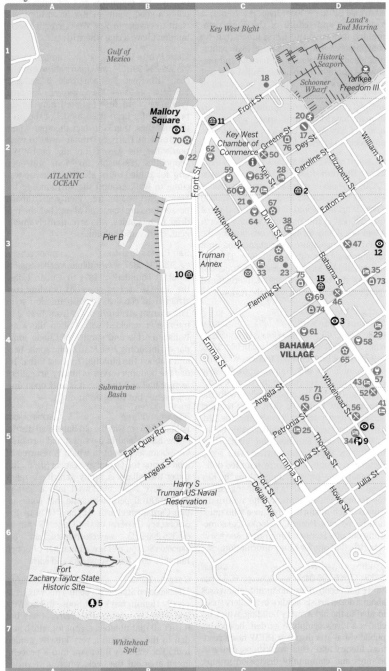

Key West Bight

Land's End Marina

Gulf of Mexico

Historic Seaport

Schooner Wharf

Yankee Freedom III

18

Front St

Mallory Square

11

20

Key West Chamber of Commerce

Greene St

17

Dey St

76

50

William St

62

59

63

28

Ann St

Caroline St

Elizabeth St

ATLANTIC OCEAN

70

1

22

60

27

21

67

64

Duval St

Whitehead St

Front St

2

Eaton St

38

Pier B

Truman Annex

12

47

10

68

33

23

35

73

Bahama St

Fleming St

75

15

69

46

74

3

61

29

58

BAHAMA VILLAGE

Emma St

65

Submarine Basin

71

45

Whitehead St

43

52

57

56

41

Petronia St

25

Thomas St

34

6

9

East Quay Rd

4

Angela St

Olivia St

Emma St

Fort St

Dekalb Ave

Howe St

Julia St

Harry S Truman US Naval Reservation

Fort Zachary Taylor State Historic Site

5

Whitehead Spit

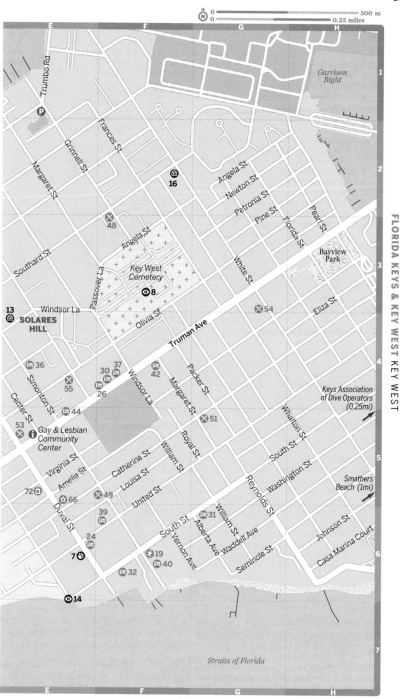

# Key West

◎ **Top Sights**
1 Mallory Square ........................................ B2

◎ **Sights**
2 Casa Antigua ......................................... D2
3 Duval Street ............................................ D4
4 Florida Keys Eco-Discovery
   Center ..................................................... B5
5 Fort Zachary Taylor Historic
   State Park ............................................. A7
6 Hemingway House .................................. D5
7 Key West Butterfly & Nature
   Conservatory ......................................... E6
8 Key West Cemetery ................................ F3
9 Key West Lighthouse ............................. D5
10 Little White House .................................. B3
11 Museum of Art & History at
   the Custom House ................................. C2
12 Nancy Forrester's Secret
   Garden .................................................... D3
13 Office of the Secretary
   General of the Conch
   Republic ................................................. E4
   San Carlos Institute ..................... (see 75)
14 Southernmost Point ............................... E6
15 Strand Building ...................................... D3
16 Studios of Key West .............................. F2

◎ **Activities, Courses & Tours**
17 Captain's Corner .................................... D2
18 Conch Tour Train .................................... C1
19 Gay & Lesbian Trolley Tour of
   Key West ................................................ F6
   Historic Key West Walking Tour .. (see 22)
20 Jolly Rover ............................................. D2
21 Key West Ghost & Mysteries
   Tour ........................................................ C3
22 Old Town Trolley Tours ......................... B2
23 Original Ghost Tours .............................. C3

◎ **Sleeping**
24 Avalon Bed & Breakfast ........................ E6
25 Caribbean House .................................... D5
26 Chelsea House ....................................... F4
27 Curry Mansion Inn ................................. C2
28 Cypress House ........................................ C2
29 Gardens Hotel ........................................ D4
30 Key Lime Inn ........................................... F4
31 Key West Youth Hostel &
   Seashell Motel ...................................... G6
32 La Mer & Dewey Hotel ........................... F6
33 L'Habitation ........................................... C3
34 Lighthouse Court Inn .............................. D5

35 Mango Tree Inn ...................................... D3
36 Merlin Inn ............................................... E4
37 Mermaid & the Alligator ........................ F4
38 Old Town Manor ..................................... C3
39 Pearl's Rainbow ..................................... F6
40 Santa Maria ........................................... F6
41 Seascape Tropical Inn ........................... D5
42 Silver Palms Inn ..................................... F4
43 Tropical Inn ............................................ D4
44 Truman Hotel .......................................... E5

◎ **Eating**
45 Blue Heaven ........................................... D5
46 Café ........................................................ D4
47 Cafe Marquesa ....................................... D3
48 Café Solé ................................................ F3
49 Camille's ................................................ F5
50 Duetto Pizza & Gelato ........................... C2
51 El Siboney .............................................. G5
   Glazed Donuts ............................. (see 68)
52 Le Bistro/Croissants de France .......... D5
53 Nine One Five ......................................... E5
54 Pierogi Polish Market ............................ G3
   Point5 Lounge .............................. (see 53)
55 Seven Fish .............................................. E4
56 Six Toed Cat ........................................... D5

◎ **Drinking & Nightlife**
57 801 Bourbon Bar .................................... D4
58 Aqua ....................................................... D4
59 Captain Tony's Saloon ........................... C2
60 Garden of Eden ...................................... C2
61 Green Parrot ........................................... D4
62 Hog's Breath .......................................... C2
63 Irish Kevin's ........................................... C2
64 Porch ...................................................... C3

◎ **Entertainment**
65 Bourbon St Pub ...................................... D4
66 La Te Da ................................................. E5
67 Red Barn Theatre ................................... C3
68 Tropic Cinema ........................................ C3
69 Virgilio's ................................................. D4
70 Waterfront Playhouse ........................... B2

◎ **Shopping**
71 Bésame Mucho ....................................... D5
72 Frangipani Gallery .................................. E5
73 Haitian Art Co ......................................... D3
74 Leather Master ....................................... D4
75 Montage .................................................. D3
76 Peppers of Key West .............................. C2

tape lays down the history of the Casa at the volume God uses whenever he says anything that begins with 'Let there be...'

**Strand Building** HISTORIC BUILDING
(527 Duval St) The historic Strand Theater was one of Key West's great old-time movie hous-

es, and it was used as a theater in the 1993 film *Matinee*. Today it's a Walgreens pharmacy, but the exterior is as romantic as ever.

**Key West Lighthouse** LIGHTHOUSE
(☎305-294-0012; www.kwahs.org/visit/lighthouse-keepers-quarters/; 938 Whitehead St; adult/

student over 7yr/senior $10/5/9; ⊘9:30am-4:30pm) You can climb up 88 steps to the top of this lighthouse, built in 1846, for a decent view. But honestly, it's just as enjoyable to gaze up at the tower from the leafy street below.

**Southernmost Point**                    LANDMARK
(cnr South & Whitehead Sts) The most photographed spot on the island, this red-and-black buoy isn't even the southernmost point in the USA (that's in the off-limits naval base around the corner). This is the most overrated attraction in Key West.

# 🏃 Activities
## Beaches
Key West is *not* about beach going. In fact, for true sun 'n' surf, locals go to Bahia Honda whenever possible. Still, the three city beaches on the southern side of the island are lovely and narrow, with calm and clear water. South Beach is at the end of Simonton St. Higgs Beach, at the end of Reynolds St and Casa Marina Ct, has barbecue grills, picnic tables and a big crowd of gay sunbathers. Smathers Beach, further east off S Roosevelt Blvd, is more popular with jetskiers, parasailers, teens and college students. The best local beach, though, is at Fort Zachary Taylor; it's worth the admission to enjoy the white sand and relative calm.

## Boating
Check www.charterboatkeywest.com for a directory of the many fishing and cruising charters offered in Key West.

**★ Jolly Rover**                    CRUISE
(☑305-304-2235; www.schoonerjollyrover.com; cnr Greene & Elizabeth Sts, Schooner Wharf; cruise $45) This outfit has a gorgeous, tanbark (reddish-brown) 80ft schooner that embarks on daily sunset cruises under sail. It looks like a pirate ship and has the cannons to back the image up.

**Reelax Charters**                    KAYAKING
(☑305-304-1392; www.keyskayaking.com; MM 17 Sugarloaf Key Marina; all inclusive kayak trips $240) Get your paddle on and slip silently into the surrounding mangroves and mudflats of the Lower Keys with Andrea Paulson. Based on Sugarloaf Key.

## Diving & Snorkeling
The diving is better in Key Largo and Biscayne National Park, but there is some decent wreck diving near Key West.

The website of the Keys Association of Dive Operators (www.divekeys.com; 3128 N Roosevelt Blvd) is a clearing house for information on diving opportunities in the islands; it also works on enhancing local sustainable underwater activities by creating artificial reefs and encouraging safe boating and diving practices.

**Captain's Corner**                    DIVING
(☑305-296-8865; 631 Greene St; snorkel/scuba from $40/75) This dive outfit leads snorkeling and scuba trips to local reefs and wrecks.

**Dive Key West**                    DIVING
(☑305-296-3823; www.divekeywest.com; 3128 N Roosevelt Blvd; snorkel/scuba from $60/75) Largest dive facility on the island. Wreck-diving trips cost $135 with all equipment and air provided.

# ☞ Tours
Worth noting is *Sharon Wells' Walking & Biking Guide to Historic Key West,* a booklet of self-guided walks available free at inns and businesses around town, written by a local. See www.walkbikeguide.com.

**Old Town Trolley Tours**                    TOUR
(☑888-910-8687; www.trolleytours.com/key-west; adult/child under 13yr/senior $30/free/27; ⊘tours 9am-4:30pm; ⓹) These tours are a great introduction to the city. The 90-minute, hop-on, hop-off narrated tram tour starts at Mallory Sq and makes a loop around the whole city, with nine stops along the way. Trolleys depart every 15 to 30 minutes from 9am to 4:30pm daily. The narration is hokey, but you'll get a good overview of Key West history.

**Conch Tour Train**                    TOUR
(☑305-294-5161; www.conchtourtrain.com; adult/child under 13yr/senior $30/free/27; ⊘tours 9am-4:30pm; ⓹) Run by the same company as Trolley Tours, this one seats you in breezy linked train cars with no on/off option. Offers discounted admission to sights such as the Hemingway House.

**Historic Key West Walking Tour**    WALKING TOUR
(☑800-844-7601; www.trustedtours.com; 1 Whitehead St; adult/child $18/9) A walking tour that takes in some of the major architecture and historical sights of the island. Takes about two hours. You need to book in advance.

**Key West Ghost & Mysteries Tour**    TOUR
(☑305-292-2040; www.keywestghostandmysteriestour.com; tours depart from Duval & Caroline; adult/child $18/10; ⊘tours 9pm) A playfully

creepy ghost tour that's as family friendly as this sort of thing gets – in other words, no big chills or pop-out screaming.

**Original Ghost Tours**                                    TOUR
(☑ 305-294-9255; www.hauntedtours.com; adult/child $15/10; ⊙ 8pm & 9pm) Stories about souls who inhabit locations that include about half the bars and hotels on the island.

## ✦ Festivals & Events

Contact the **Key West Art & Historical Society** (☑ 305-295-6616; www.kwahs.com) to get the skinny on upcoming studio shows, literary readings, film festivals and the like.

**Key West Literary Seminar**                          LITERARY
(www.kwls.org) Now in its 23rd year, draws top writers from around the country each January (although it costs hundreds of dollars to attend).

**Robert Frost Poetry Festival**                       LITERARY
Held in April. Contact the Studios of Key West (p161) for details.

**Hemingway Days Festival**                            CULTURE
(www.fla-keys.com/hemingwaymedia/) Held in late July, brings parties, a 5km run and an Ernest look-alike contest.

**WomenFest**                          LESBIAN & TRANSEXUAL
(www.womenfest.com) Nothing says dignified sexiness like this festival, held in early September, which attracts thousands of lesbians who just want to party.

**Fantasy Fest**                                       CULTURE
(www.fantasyfest.net) You gotta see this festival held throughout the week leading up to Halloween. It's when all the inns get competitive about decorating their properties, and everyone gets decked out in the most outrageous costumes they can cobble together (or decked down in daring body paint).

**Goombay Festival**                                   CULTURE
(www.goombay-keywest.org) Held during the same out-of-control week as Fantasy Fest, this is a Bahamian celebration of food, crafts and culture.

**Parrot Heads in Paradise Convention**   MUSIC
(www.phip.com/motm.asp) This festival in November is for, you guessed it, Jimmy Buffett fans (rabid ones only, naturally).

## 🛏 Sleeping

There's a glut of boutique hotels, cozy B&Bs and four-star resorts here at the end of the USA, so sleepers won't want for accommodations. Although some options are more central than others, the fact is that any hotel in Old Town will put you within walking distance of all the action. Most hotels in Key West are gay friendly.

**Caribbean House**                             GUESTHOUSE $
(☑ 305-296-0999; www.caribbeanhousekw.com; 226 Petronia St; summer $89, winter $119-139; **P** ✳ @) This is a cute, canary-yellow Caribbean cottage in the heart of Bahama Village. The 10 small, brightly colored guest rooms aren't too fancy, but it's a happy, cozy bargain.

**Key West Youth Hostel & Seashell Motel**                              HOSTEL $
(☑ 305-296-5719; www.keywesthostel.com; 718 South St; dm from $54, motel r from $95; **P** ✳) This isn't our favorite hostel, but it's about the only youth-oriented budget choice on the island. That said, both dorms and motel rooms are overpriced.

**Mango Tree Inn**                                    B&B $$
(☑ 305-293-1177; www.mangotree-inn.com; 603 Southard St; $150-200; ✳ ⚡ ✈) This down-to-earth B&B offers a courtyard pool and elegant accommodation in a number of airy rooms, each decorated with swathes of tropical-chic accoutrement, from rattan furniture to flowering hibiscus. Rates are a deal for this kind of downtown proximity.

**Seascape Tropical Inn**                             B&B $$
(☑ 305-296-7776, 800-765-6438; www.seascape-tropicalinn.com; 420 Olivia St; r $184-250; ✳ ⚡ ✈) Had this B&B existed back in the day, Hemingway could have stumbled into it after one of his epic drinking binges – it's within spitting distance of his old house. Now you can crash in one of six rooms, appointed with cool, airy interiors and warm accents like floral comforters and high-thread-count sheets.

**Old Town Manor**                          BOUTIQUE HOTEL $$
(☑ 305-292-2170; www.oldtownmanor.com; 511 Eaton St; $185-275; ✳ ⚡ ✈) While it bills itself as a B&B (and breakfast is included), the Old Town feels more like a boutique operation that offers a wide variety of rooms – 14, to be exact, spread amid lush gardens. The digs come in the usual tropically inspired palette, but they're a little more subdued than the Keys norm. Service is friendly and on point.

**L'Habitation**                              GUESTHOUSE $$
(☑ 305-293-9203; www.lhabitation.com; 408 Eaton St; r $119-189; ✳ ⚡) A beautiful, classical Keys cottage with cute rooms kitted

## DRY TORTUGAS NATIONAL PARK

After all those keys, connected by all that convenient road, the nicest islands in the archipelago require a little extra effort. Ponce de León named them Las Tortugas (The Turtles) for the sea turtles that roamed here. A lack of freshwater led sailors to add a 'dry.' Today the Dry Tortugas (☎305-242-7700; www.nps.gov/drto; adult/15yr & under $5/free) are a national park under the control of the National Park Service and are accessible by boat or plane.

Originally the Tortugas were the US's naval perch into the Gulf of Mexico. But by the Civil War, Fort Jefferson, the main structure on the islands, had become a prison for Union deserters and at least four people, among them Dr Samuel Mudd, who had been arrested for complicity in the assassination of Abraham Lincoln. Hence, a new nickname: Devil's Island. The name was prophetic; in 1867 a yellow-fever outbreak killed 38 people, and after an 1873 hurricane the fort was abandoned. It reopened in 1886 as a quarantine station for smallpox and cholera victims, was declared a national monument in 1935 by President Franklin D Roosevelt, and was upped to national park status in 1992 by George Bush Sr.

The park is open for day trips and overnight camping, which provides a rare phenomenon: a quiet Florida beach. Garden Key has 13 campsites ($3 per person, per night), which are given out on a first-come, first-served basis. Reserve early by calling the National Park Service. There are toilets, but no freshwater showers or drinking water; bring everything you'll need. The sparkling waters offer excellent snorkeling and diving opportunities. A visitor center is located within fascinating Fort Jefferson.

If you're hungry, watch for Cuban American fishing boats trolling the waters. They'll happily trade for lobster, crab and shrimp; you'll have the most leverage trading beverages. Just paddle up and bargain for your supper. In March and April, there is stupendous bird-watching, including aerial fighting. Star-gazing is mind-blowing any time of the year.

### Getting There

If you have your own boat, the Dry Tortugas are covered under National Ocean Survey chart No 11438. Otherwise, the Yankee Freedom III (☎800-634-0939; www.drytortugas. com/; Historic Seaport) operates a fast ferry between Garden Key and the Historic Seaport (at the northern end of Margaret St). Round-trip fares cost $165/120 per adult/child. Reservations are recommended. Continental breakfast, a picnic lunch, snorkeling gear and a 45-minute tour of the fort are all included.

Key West Seaplanes (☎305-294-0709; www.seaplanesofkeywest.com) can take up to 10 passengers (flight time 40 minutes each way). A four-hour trip costs $295/free/$236 per adult/child under two years/child over two; an eight-hour trip costs $515/free/$412. Again, reserve at least a week in advance.

The $5 park admission fees are included in the above prices.

out in light tropical shades, with lamps that look like contemporary art pieces and Skittles-bright quilts. The friendly bilingual owner welcomes guests in English or French. The front porch, shaded by palms, is a perfect place to stop and engage in Keys people-watching.

### Avalon Bed & Breakfast
B&B $$

(☎305-294-8233, 800-848-1317; www.avalonbnb. com; 1317 Duval St; r low season $109-229, high season $189-289; ❀ ⚡ 🖳) A restored Victorian house on the quiet end of Duval blends attentive service with stately old ceiling fans, tropical lounge-room rugs and black-and-white photos of old-timey Key West. Music the cat likes to greet guests at reception.

### Pearl's Rainbow
B&B $$

(☎305-292-1450, 800-749-6696; www.pearlsrainbow.com; 525 United St; r incl breakfast $161-318; ❀ ⚡ 🖳) Pearl's is one of the best low-key lesbian resorts in the country, an intimate garden of tropical relaxation and enticing rooms scattered across a few cottages. A clothing-optional backyard pool bar is the perfect spot for alfresco happy hour, or to enjoy your breakfast.

### Chelsea House
HOTEL $$

(☎305-296-2211; www.historickeywestinns. com/the-inns/chelsea-house; 707 Truman Ave; r low season $150-210, high season from $250; 🅿 ❀ @ ⚡ 🖳) This perfect pair of Victorian mansions beckons with large, vaulted rooms and big, comfy beds, with the whole shebang done out in floral (but not dated) chic. The old-school villa ambience clashes – in a nice way – with the happy vibe of the guests and the folks at reception.

### ★ Tropical Inn
BOUTIQUE HOTEL $$$

(☑ 888-651-6510; www.tropicalinn.com; 812 Duval St; r $175-360; ✳🕸🅿) The Tropical Inn has excellent service and a host of individualized rooms spread out over a historic home property. Each room comes decked out in bright pastels and shades of mango, lime and seafoam. A delicious breakfast is included and can be enjoyed in the jungly courtyard next to a lovely sunken pool. Two attached cottages offer romance and privacy for couples.

### Curry Mansion Inn
HOTEL $$$

(☑ 305-294-5349; www.currymansion.com; 511 Caroline St; r $240-365, summer $205-310; 🅿✳🕸🅿) In a city full of stately homes, the Curry Mansion is especially handsome. It has all the elements of an aristocratic American home, from plantation-era Southern colonnades to a New England–style widow's walk and, of course, bright Floridian rooms with canopied beds. Enjoy bougainvillea and breezes on the veranda.

### Mermaid & the Alligator
GUESTHOUSE $$$

(☑ 305-294-1894; www.kwmermaid.com; 729 Truman Ave; r winter $278-348, summer $188-248; 🅿✳@🕸) It takes a real gem to stand out amid the jewels of Keys hotels, but this place, located in a 1904 mansion, more than pulls off the job. Each of the nine rooms is individually designed with a mix of modern comfort, Keys Colonial ambience and playful laughs.

The treetop suite, with its exposed beams and alcoved bed and bathroom, is our pick of this idiosyncratic litter.

### La Mer & Dewey Hotel
BOUTIQUE HOTEL $$$

(☑ 305-296-6577, 800-354-4455; www.southermostresorts.com/lamer; 504 South St; r from $400; ✳🕸) Nineteen rooms are spread across two historic homes, one Victorian, the other fashioned like an old-school Keys cottage. Inside, rooms come equipped with a mix of European twee antiques and sleek, modern amenities. Your porch looks out onto the Atlantic Ocean, whose breezes make for nice natural air-conditioning (not that you can't crank up the air-con in your room).

### Santa Maria
BOUTIQUE HOTEL $$$

(☑ 305-600-5165; www.santamariasuites.com; 1401 Simonton St; r $300-450; 🅿✳🕸🅿) The Santa Maria looks like it took a wrong turn on South Beach, Miami, and ended up in Key West. It's an incredible deco edifice – the exterior should be studied by architecture students looking to identify the best of deco design, and the interior rooms call to mind a 1950s leisure lounge. The courtyard holds one of the finest hotel pools in Key West.

### Gardens Hotel
HOTEL $$$

(☑ 305-294-2661, 800-526-2664; www.gardenshotel.com; 526 Angela St; r & ste low season $165-425, high season $325-665; 🅿✳@🕸) Would we be stating the obvious if we mentioned this place has really nice gardens? In fact, the 17 rooms are located in the Peggy Mills Botanical Gardens, which is a longish way of saying 'tropical paradise.' Inside, Caribbean accents mesh with the fine design to create a sense of green-and-white-and-wood space that never stops massaging your eyes.

### Lighthouse Court Inn
BOUTIQUE HOTEL $$$

(☑ 305-294-5229, 800-549-4430; www.historickeywestinns.com/the-inns/lighthouse-court; 902 Whitehead St; r from $250; ✳🕸🅿) The rooms at the Lighthouse Court, which sits near the Hemingway House, may be the most handsomely appointed in town. They're elegant in their simplicity, with the warm earth tones of hardwood floors set off by just the right amount of tropical breeziness and cool colors. Affiliated with Historic Key West Inns.

### Silver Palms Inn
BOUTIQUE HOTEL $$$

(☑ 800-294-8783; www.silverpalmsinn.com; 830 Truman Ave; r from $319; 🅿✳🕸🅿) 🏊 Royal blues, sweet teals, bright limes and lemon-yellow color schemes douse the interior of this boutique property, which also boasts bicycle rentals, a saltwater swimming pool and a green certification from the Florida Department of Environmental Protection. Overall, the Silver Palms offers more of a modern, large-hotel vibe with a candy-colored dose of Keys tropics attitude.

### Cypress House
HOTEL $$$

(☑ 305-294-5229, 800-549-4430; www.cypresshousekw.com; 601 Caroline St; r $219-329; 🅿✳🕸🅿) This plantation-like getaway has wraparound porches, leafy grounds, a secluded swimming pool and spacious, individually designed bedrooms with four-poster beds. It's lazy, lovely luxury in the heart of Old Town, and one of the most extensively renovated and converted mansions we've seen anywhere. We recommend rooms in the Main House and Simonton House over the blander guest studios.

**Truman Hotel** HOTEL $$$
(☑ 866-487-8626; www.trumanhotel.com; 611 Truman Ave; r low season $195-285, high season $240-365; P ❄ ⚗ ☰) Close to the main downtown drag, these playful rooms have huge flat-screen TVs, kitchenettes, zebra-print throw rugs and mid-century modern furniture. The bouncy, fluff-errific beds will serve you well after the inevitable Duval Crawl (which is only steps from your door). Make sure to grab a drink by the courtyard pool at the bar, which looks as if it's carved from a single stone.

**Merlin Inn** GUESTHOUSE $$$
(☑ 800-549-4430; www.historickeywestinns.com/the-inns/merlin-guesthouse; 811 Simonton St; r from $240; P ❄ @ ☰) Set in a secluded garden with a pool and elevated walkways, everything here is made from bamboo, rattan and wood. Throw in the rooms' high ceilings and exposed rafters, and this hotel oozes Colonial-tropical atmosphere.

**Key Lime Inn** HOTEL $$$
(☑ 800-549-4430; www.historickeywestinns.com; 725 Truman Ave; r from $240; P ⚗ ☰) These cozy cottages are all scattered around a tropical hardwood backdrop. Inside, the blissfully cool rooms are greener than a jade mine, with wicker furniture and tiny flat-screens on hand to keep you from ever leaving.

# ✖ Eating

For such a small island, Key West has a superlative range of places to eat, from delicious neighborhood holes in the wall to top-end purveyors of haute cuisine that could easily compete with the best restaurants in Miami.

For a night in, head to **Key West Food to Go** (www.keywestfoodtogo.com), which connects you to over two dozen restaurants that offer delivery service across the island.

**Duetto Pizza & Gelato** ITALIAN $
(☑ 305-848-4981; 540 Greene St; mains under $10; ⊙ 8am-11pm; ✎ ♿) This little pizza and gelato stand is a good-value stop for a quick slice or scoop, especially compared to the greasy cardboard pie served elsewhere in town.

**Café** VEGETARIAN $
(509 Southard St; mains $7-17; ⊙ 11am-10pm Mon-Sat; ✎) The Café is the only place in Key West that exclusively caters to herbivores (OK, they have one fish dish). By day, it's a

cute, sunny, earthy-crunchy luncheonette; by night, with flickering votive candles and a classy main dish (grilled, blackened tofu and polenta cakes), it's a sultry-but-healthy dining destination.

**Six Toed Cat** AMERICAN $
(☑ 305-294-3318; 823 Whitehead St; mains $8-16; ⊙ 8:30am-5pm) Simple, fresh and filling breakfast and lunch fare is served here within spitting distance of the Hemingway House (p160) and the restaurant is indeed named for the author's six-toed felines. A lobster Benedict with avocado should satisfy the day's protein needs, but if you're here for lunch, don't miss the lovely fried shrimp sandwich.

**Pierogi Polish Market** EASTERN EUROPEAN $
(☑ 305-292-0464; 1008 White St; mains $5-10; ⊙ 10am-8pm Mon-Sat, 11am-6pm Sun; P ✎) The Keys have an enormous seasonal population of temporary workers largely drawn from Central and Eastern Europe. This is where those workers can revisit the motherland, via pierogis, dumplings, blinis (pancakes) and a great sandwich selection. Although it's called a Polish market, there's food here that caters to Hungarians, Czechs and Russians (among others).

**Glazed Donuts** BAKERY $
(☑ 305-294-9142; 420 Eaton St; under $4; ⊙ 7am-3pm; ✎ ♿) Doughnuts make the world go round, and you'll find some excellent examples of the genre at this cute bakery. The flavors are as eccentric as Key West itself, and reflect seasonal ingredients; past examples include blood orange marmalade, mango hibiscus and (of course) piña colada.

**Seven Fish** SEAFOOD $$
(☑ 305-296-2777; www.7fish.com; 632 Olivia St; mains $17-20; ⊙ 6-10pm Wed-Mon) This simple yet elegant, tucked-away spot is the perfect place for a romantic feast of homemade gnocchi or sublime banana chicken. All that said, the way to go here is to order the fresh fish of the day. The dining room might be the Zen-est interior in the islands.

**Camille's** FUSION $$
(☑ 305-296-4811; www.camilleskeywest.com; 1202 Simonton St; breakfast & lunch $4-13, dinner $15-25; ⊙ 8am-3pm & 6-10pm; ✎) This healthy and tasty neighborhood joint is a locals' place where players on the high school softball team are served by friends from science class. For 20 years the homey facade of Camille's has concealed a sharp kitchen that makes a mean chicken-salad sandwich,

stone crab claws with Dijon mayo and a macadamia-crusted yellowtail.

### Point5 Lounge
FUSION $$

(☑ 305-296-0669; 915 Duval St; small plates $5-17; ⊗ 5pm-midnight, to 2am Sat; ✎) Like stylish Nine One Five (p170) (which it sits above), Point5 is a good deal more sophisticated than the typical Duval St trough or frozen drink hall. It trades in fusion-style tapas with global influence, ranging from Asia (Vietnamese chicken rolls) to Europe (a cone of Belgian-style *frites*) to local (Key West shrimp). All, consequently, delicious.

### Le Bistro/Croissants de France
FRENCH $$

(☑ 305-294-2624; 816 Duval St; mains $12-16; ⊗ 7:30am-10pm; ✎) France comes to the Caribbean at this lovely bistro, with predictably tasty results. *Galettes* (buckwheat crepes) are filled with scallops, shrimp and crab or smoked salmon and sour cream; sweet crepes come with grilled bananas, rum and almonds, or you can just enjoy a hearty cheeseburger or some brie and baguette. The setting perfectly seizes Key West's cozy-Caribbean-chic aesthetic.

### El Siboney
CUBAN $$

(900 Catherine St; mains $8-16; ⊗ 11am-9:30pm) This is a rough-and-ready Cuban joint where the portions are big and there's no screwing around with high-end embellishment or bells and whistles. It's rice, it's beans, it's shredded beef and roasted pork, it's cooked with pride, and it's good.

### Café Solé
FRENCH $$$

(☑ 305-294-0230; www.cafesole.com; 1029 Southard St; dinner $20-34; ⊗ 5:30-10pm) Conch carpaccio with capers? Yellowtail fillet and foie gras? Oh yes. This locally and critically acclaimed venue is known for its cozy back-porch ambience and innovative menus, cobbled together by a chef trained in southern French techniques who works with island ingredients. The memory of the anchovies on crostini makes us smile as we type.

### Nine One Five
FUSION $$$

(☑ 305-296-0669; www.915duval.com; 915 Duval St; mains $18-34; ⊗ 6pm-midnight; ✎) Classy Nine One Five certainly stands out from the nearby Duval detritus of alcoholic aggression and tribal band tattoos. Ignore all that and enter this immaculate, modern and elegant space, which serves a creative, New American-dips-into-Asia menu. It's all quite rich – imagine a butternut squash and

almond risotto, or local lobster accompanied by duck confit potatoes.

### Blue Heaven
AMERICAN $$$

(☑ 305-296-8666; http://blueheavenkw.homestead.com; 729 Thomas St; dinner $17-35; ⊗ 8am-4pm, until 2pm Sun & 5-10:30pm daily; ✎) Proof that location is *nearly* everything, this is one of the quirkiest venues on an island of oddities. Customers (and a local chicken) flock to dine in the spacious courtyard where Hemingway once officiated boxing matches. This place gets packed with customers who wolf down Southern-fried takes on Keys cuisine. Restrooms are in the adjacent former brothel.

### Cafe Marquesa
FUSION $$$

(☑ 305-292-1244; 600 Fleming St; mains $32-43; ⊗ 6-10pm; ✎) The Marquesa is as elegant as it gets in Key West, all white tablecloths, candle light and good food to boot. The mains are French-inspired with little Floridan and Asian twists, like ginger-and-coconut-crusted mahi-mahi and a rack of Australian lamb served over a bed of couscous.

## 🍷 Drinking & Nightlife

Basically, Key West is a floating bar. 'No, no, it's a nuanced, multilayered island with a proud nautical and multicultural histo...' *bzzzt*! Floating bar. Bars close around 3am.

### ★ Green Parrot
BAR

(www.greenparrot.com; 601 Whitehead St; ⊗ 10am-4am) The oldest bar on an island of bars, this rogues' cantina opened in the late 19th century and hasn't closed yet. The owner tells you the parachute on the ceiling is 'weighed down with termite turds,' while defunct business signs and local artwork litter the walls and the city attorney shows off her new tattoo at the pool table.

Men: check out the Hieronymus Bosch–like painting *Proverbidioms* in the restroom, surely the most entertaining urinal talk-piece on the island.

### Porch
BAR

(www.theporchkw.com; 429 Caroline St; ⊗ 10am-2am Mon-Sat, noon-2am Sun) If you're getting tired of the frat-boy bars on the Duval St strip, head to the Porch. It's a friendly little artisan beer bar that's more laid back (but hardly civilized) than your average Keys watering hole. The knowledgeable bartenders will trade jokes with you and point you in the right direction for some truly excellent brew.

**Garden of Eden**                    BAR
(224 Duval St; ⏱12pm-4am) Go to the top of this building and discover Key West's own clothing-optional drinking patio. Lest you get too excited, cameras aren't allowed, most people come clothed, and those who do elect to go *au naturel* are often...erm...older.

**Captain Tony's Saloon**              BAR
(www.capttonyssaloon.com; 428 Greene St; ⏱10am-2am) Propagandists would have you believe the nearby megabar complex of Sloppy Joe's was Hemingway's original bar, but the physical place where the old man drank was right here, the original Sloppy Joe's location (before it was moved onto Duval St and into frat-boy hell). Hemingway's third wife (a journalist sent to profile Papa) seduced him in this very bar.

**Irish Kevin's**                      BAR
(211 Duval St; ⏱10am-2:30am) One of the most popular megabars on Duval, Kevin's has a pretty good entertainment formula pinned down: nightly live acts that are a cross between a folk singer, radio shock jock and pep-rally cheerleader. The crowd consistently goes ape-poo for acoustic covers of favorites from around 1980 onward mixed with boozy, Lee Greenwood-esque patriotic exhortations.

Basically, this is a good place to see people do tequila shots, scream 'Livin' on a Prayer' at the top of their lungs and then inexplicably sob into their Michelobs. It's more fun than it sounds.

**Hog's Breath**                       BAR
(400 Front St; ⏱10am-2am) A good place to start the infamous Duval Pub Crawl, the Hog's Breath is a rockin' outdoor bar with good live bands and better cold Coronas.

## ☆ Entertainment

**La Te Da**                       CABARET
(www.lateda.com; 1125 Duval St) While the outside bar is where locals gather for mellow chats over beer, you can catch high-quality drag acts – big names come here from around the country – upstairs at the fabulous Crystal Room on weekends. More low-key cabaret acts grace the downstairs lounge.

**Virgilio's**                        JAZZ
(www.virgilioskeywest.com; 524 Duval St) This bar-stage is as un-Keys as they come, and frankly, thank God for a little variety. This town needs a dark, candlelit martini lounge where you can chill to jazz and get down with some salsa, and Virgilio's handsomely provides. Enter on Applerouth Lane.

**Red Barn Theatre**                THEATER
(☎305-296-9911; www.redbarntheatre.org; 319 Duval St) An occasionally edgy and always fun, cozy little local playhouse.

FLORIDA KEYS & KEY WEST KEY WEST

---

### GAY & LESBIAN KEY WEST

Key West's position at the edge of the USA has always attracted artists and eccentrics, and with them a refreshing dose of tolerance. The island had one of the earliest 'out' communities in the USA, and though less true than in the past, visiting Key West is still a rite of passage for many LGBT Americans. In turn, this community has had a major impact on the local culture. Just as there is a straight trolley tour, you can hop aboard the **Gay & Lesbian Trolley Tour of Key West** (☎305-294-4603; tour $25), departing from the corner of South St and Simonton St at 11am on Saturday. The tour provides commentary on local gay lore and businesses (you'll also see the site of the infamous Monster club). It's organized by the Key West Business Guild, which represents many gay-owned businesses; the guild is housed at the **Gay & Lesbian Community Center** (☎305-292-3223; www.glcckeywest.org; 513 Truman Ave), where you can access free internet on one of the few computers, plus pick up loads of information about local gay life. For details on gay parties and events, log onto www.gaykeywestfl.com.

Gay nightlife, in many cases, blends into mainstream nightlife, with everybody kind of going everywhere these days. But the backbone of the gay bar scene can be found in a pair of cruisey watering holes that sit across the street from one another, **Bourbon St Pub** (724 Duval St) and **801 Bourbon Bar** (www.801bourbon.com; 801 Duval St), and can be summed up in five words: drag-queen-led karaoke night. For a peppier scene that includes dancing and occasional drag shows, men and women should head to **Aqua** (☎305-294-0555; www.aquakeywest.com; 711 Duval St) while women will enjoy the backyard pool bar at the women's inn Pearl's Rainbow (p167).

### Tropic Cinema
CINEMA

(☑ 877-761-3456; www.tropiccinema.org; 416 Eaton St) Great art-house movie theater with deco frontage.

### Waterfront Playhouse
THEATER

(☑ 305-294-5015; www.waterfrontplayhouse. com; Waterfront Playhouse, Mallory Sq) Catch high-quality musicals and dramas from the oldest-running theater troupe in Florida. The season runs November through April.

## 🛍 Shopping

Bright and breezy art galleries, excellent cigars, leather fetish gear and offensive T-shirts – Key West, what don't you sell?

### Montage
SOUVENIRS

(512 Duval St; ☺ 9am-10pm) Had a great meal or wild night at some bar or restaurant in the Keys? Well, this store probably sells the sign of the place (along with lots of Conch Republic tat), which makes for a nice souvenir.

### Peppers of Key West
FOOD

(602 Greene St; ☺ 10am-8pm Mon-Sat) For a downright shopping party, you should bring your favorite six-pack with you into this store and settle in at the tasting bar, where the entertaining owners use double entendres to hawk seriously mouth-burning hot sauces, like their own Right Wing Sauce (use liberally).

### Bésame Mucho
GIFTS

(315 Petronia St; ☺ 10am-6pm, to 4pm Sun) This place is well stocked with high-end beauty products, eclectic jewelry, clothing and housewares.

### Leather Master
LEATHER

(415 Applerouth Lane; ☺ 11am-10pm, to 11pm Fri & Sat, noon-5pm Sun) Besides the gladiator outfits, studded jockstraps and S&M masks, they do very nice bags and shoes here. Which is what you came for, right?

### Frangipani Gallery
ARTS & CRAFTS

(1102 Duval St; ☺ 10am-6pm) One of the best galleries of local artists' work.

### Haitian Art Co
ARTS & CRAFTS

(☑ 305-296-8932; 605 Simonton St; ☺ 10am-7pm) Haitian arts and crafts.

## ℹ Information

**Bank of America** (☑ 305-296-1204; 510 Southard St)

**Citizen** (www.keysnews.com) A well-written, oft-amusing daily.

**Key West Chamber of Commerce** (☑ 305-294-2587; www.keywestchamber.org; 510 Greene St; ☺ 8:30am-6:30pm Mon-Sat, to 6pm Sun) An excellent source of information.

**Lower Keys Medical Center** (☑ 305-294-5531, 800-233-3119; www.lkmc.com; 5900 College Rd, Stock Island, MM 5) Has a 24-hour emergency room.

**Post Office** (400 Whitehead St; ☺ 8:30am-9pm Mon-Fri, 9:30am-noon Sat)

**Solares Hill** (www.solareshill.com) Weekly, slightly activist take on community interests.

**South Med** (☑ 305-295-3838; www.southmed. us; 3138 Northside Dr) Dr Scott Hall caters especially to the gay community, but serves all visitors.

## ℹ Getting There & Around

Key West International Airport (EYW) is off S Roosevelt Blvd on the east side of the island. You can fly into Key West from some major US cities such as Miami or New York. Flights from Los Angeles and San Francisco usually have to stop in Tampa, Orlando or Miami first. **American Airlines** (☑ 800-433-7300) and **US Airways** (☑ 800-428-4322) have several flights a day. From the Key West airport, a quick and easy taxi ride into Old Town will cost about $20.

**Greyhound** (☑ 305-296-9072; www.greyhound.com; 3535 S Roosevelt Blvd) has two buses daily between Key West and downtown Miami. Buses leave Miami for the 4¼-hour journey at 12:35pm and 6:50pm and Key West at 8:55am and 5:45pm going the other way (from US$33 each way).

You can boat from Miami to the Keys on the **Key West Express** (☑ 888-539-2628; www. seakeywestexpress.com; adult/child round trip $147/85, one way $86/60), which departs from Fort Myers beach daily at 8:30am and does a 3½-hour cruise to Key West. Returning boats depart the seaport at 6pm. You'll want to show up 1½ hours before your boat departs. During winter and fall the Express also leaves from Marco Island (adult/child round-trip $147/85, one-way $86/60).

Once you're in Key West, the best way to get around is by bicycle (rentals from the Duval St area, hotels and hostels are about $12 a day). Other options include the **City Transit** (☑ 305-292-8160; tickets 75¢), with color-coded buses running about every 15 minutes; mopeds, which generally rent for $35 for four hours ($50 for a six-hour day); or the ridiculous electric tourist cars, or 'Conch cruisers,' which travel at 35mph and cost about $60/220 per hour/day.

# Understand Miami & the Keys

## MIAMI & THE KEYS TODAY.................... 174

Rising sea levels and gentrification are changing the physical face and civic spirit of South Florida.

## HISTORY ..................................... 176

From conquistadors to the Cuban Revolution, we look at the past that shapes South Florida's present.

## MULTICULTURAL MIAMI ..................... 184

Beyond the South is South Florida (Miami, the Everglades and the Keys): immigrant port, marshy frontier, America's offshore island chain and cultural melting pot.

## FOOD & DRINK ............................. 193

Local palates demand both five-star ambience and home-cooked meals – although 'home' is a relative term down here...

## OUTDOOR ACTIVITIES ...................... 201

Flat, yes. Boring, no. Swim, cycle, boat, dive and discover South Florida's outdoor extravaganza.

## ENVIRONMENT.............................208

Prehistoric reptiles prowl beautiful wetlands, mangrove islets shimmer in the sunset, and we explore the local environment.

## ART-DECO ARCHITECTURE .................. 217

Art deco gives Miami a uniquely beautiful facade; we take a look beneath the pastel exterior.

# Miami & the Keys Today

**The South Florida region is one of the most populous, diverse demographic conurbations in the United States. And it doesn't neatly fit into any of the country's cultural regions – it's too Latin-Caribbean to be Southern and too tropical to be Northern. The political forces affecting life in Latin America, and the geologic trends that are shaping the future of the world's tropical coastlines, have greater impact here than anywhere else in the USA.**

## Best on Film

**Key Largo** (1948) Bogart, Bacall and a lot of neon-soaked noir.

**Scarface** (1983) Al Pacino turns the American Dream into a nightmare.

**The Birdcage** (1996) Robin Williams and Nathan Lane as gay lovers.

**There's Something About Mary** (1998) On love, Miami and hair gel.

**Adaptation** (2002) Surreal adaption of *The Orchid Thief*.

**Porky's** (1982) High-school kids want drugs and sex.

## Best in Print

**Swamplandia!** (Karen Russell) Trag-icomic saga of a family of Everglades alligator wrestlers.

**Cold Case Squad** (Edna Buchanan) Miami noir.

**Continental Drift** (Russell Banks) New Hampshire worker flees for shallow promises in Florida.

**The Everglades: River of Grass** (Marjory Stoneman Douglas) Rich tribute to the Glades, written in 1947.

**Hoot** (Carl Hiaasen) Hiaasen on kids, Coconut Grove, conservation and spotted owls.

**Shadow Country** (Peter Matthiessen) The American Western reframed in the Florida swamps.

**92 in the Shade** (Thomas McGuane) This tale of rival fishermen may be the ultimate Key West novel.

## Rainy Days Ahead?

In 2014, rains that would have only slowed traffic a decade before began flooding main thoroughfares such as Alton Road. In response, the city governments of Miami Beach and Miami – to use a technical term – flipped out.

The problem was rising sea levels. Florida is a flat, low-lying state, and South Florida is the flattest, lowest-lying part of the peninsula. It's also exceedingly developed, even in a place where real estate and commercial development are practically official sports. This low-lying plain occupies the site of a drained swamp and mangrove forest (that sits on the summer migration route of Atlantic hurricanes), and its largest source of freshwater is barred via a series of artificial canals. Yes, somehow, that conurbation of ecological and geographic red flags is home to the eighth largest metropolitan area in the country.

We're not saying Miami shouldn't be where it is. The Netherlands hasn't exactly let issues such as elevation and sea levels get in the way of building a robust state and society. Neither has the United States, which in the early 20th century had a lackadaisical attitude toward the ecological consequences of urban planning. But where the Netherlands has a long legacy of dealing with the relationship between topography, geography and population centers, the US, via Miami, is in some ways just now facing the consequences. Miami (and South Florida in general) are case studies for how American urban areas will react to changing environmental and climatic conditions.

And those conditions are definitely changing. The impact is being felt across the region. The good news is folks are smelling the coffee. Miami, Miami Beach and neighboring suburbs and cities are creating plans that address the effects of climate change on vulnerable residential spaces. In short, South Florida is starting to be more proactive than reactive. It has to be. Because who knows how much higher those rainy-day floods will rise.

## Gentrification Rolls On

Tracking the boom-and-bust cycle of the South Florida real-estate market can give you whiplash. For much of the beginning of the 21st century, Miamians couldn't build condos fast enough. Then, from 2008–11, the bubble burst in the form of enormous swathes of foreclosures and vacant housing. Now, South Florida has re-entered boom phase, and Miami is growing condos like glass-and-concrete weeds. Brickell in particular is becoming positively Hong Kong-esque with its proliferation of high rise and neon.

Something sets this particular boom cycle a little apart, though. The development, which is happening at a formerly unimagined pace in areas such as Midtown, is not as overwhelmingly driven by the champagne dreams of the jet-set tourists who reshaped so much of South Beach. Rather, this development falls along the lines of traditional (but hyper-fast) gentrification. The ones behind it are often middle-class kids who grew up in the suburbs of Greater Miami and want the bright lights of the big city.

As a result, many of the new hotspots of Midtown, Downtown and N Biscayne Blvd have been created by Miami locals and marketed to Miami locals. That's not to say tourists aren't welcome; the crowds here are happy if folks visit from Miami Beach. But they can do without them as well. The flip side of this equation is the Miami locals leading the gentrification movement are middle class. Other Miami locals – the poor and working class – are being displaced from areas now colonized by the arts-and-urban-amenities crowd.

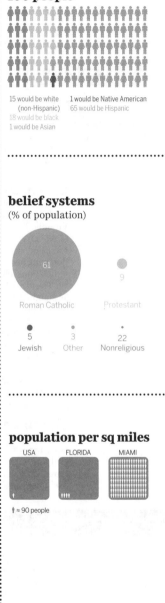

## if Miami were 100 people

15 would be white (non-Hispanic)
18 would be black
1 would be Asian
1 would be Native American
65 would be Hispanic

## belief systems
(% of population)

61 Roman Catholic
9 Protestant
5 Jewish
3 Other
22 Nonreligious

## population per sq miles

USA    FLORIDA    MIAMI

⋔ ≈ 90 people

# History

South Florida was built on boom and bust, by dreamers who took advantage of nice weather and opportunists who took advantage of natural disasters – nothing clears out old real estate like a hurricane, after all. Every chapter of the region's saga is closed by a hurricane, building boom or riot. South Florida has historically treated slow growth with contempt, and this attitude has paid with huge financial dividends on the one hand, and economic and environmental catastrophes on the other.

## Spain, Britain & Spain Again

The Spanish settled in Florida in 1565, several decades before Pilgrims landed on Plymouth Rock and English aristocrats starved in Jamestown, Virginia. The territory changed hands from Spain (until 1763) to Britain (1763–83) and back to Spain again (1783–1821). And then came American Independence. The Spanish had to deal with a big, land-hungry new nation lying just to the north.

Relations chilled when escaped American slaves made for Spanish Florida, where slavery was illegal and freed slaves were employed as standing militia members. White American Southerners saw armed black militia and started sweating the notion of slave revolts in their back plantation yard. By 1821, the USA had purchased Florida from Spain; concurrently, businessman John W Simonton bought the island of Key West from Spanish artillery officer Juan Pablo Salas.

The island was deemed the 'Gibraltar of the West' for its command of the Straits of Florida, which sit between the Atlantic Ocean and the Gulf of Mexico. In 1823, Commodore David Porter of the United States Navy took over the island, administering it as a base from which to track down illegal slave ships.

## The Unconquered People

In the late 18th century, members of the Creek Nation in Georgia and other tribes from the north migrated to Florida. These tribes intermingled and intermarried, and in the late 1700s were joined by runaway slaves. African American newcomers were generally welcomed into Native American society and were occasionally kept as slaves, although this

| TIMELINE | 10,000 BC | 2000 BC | 500 BC |
|---|---|---|---|
| | After crossing the Bering Strait from Siberia some 50,000 years earlier, humans arrive in Florida, hunting mastodon and saber-toothed tigers, at the end of the last Ice Age. | The earliest period in which archaeologists can find evidence of the creation of fired pottery in the state of Florida. | Pottery from this period is attributed to the Glades Culture, which stretches from the Keys to present-day Martin county, north of Miami. The Glades Culture does not survive European contact. |

slavery was more akin to indentured servitude (slaves, for example, had their own homes that they inhabited with their families).

At some point, these fugitive, mixed peoples occupying Florida's interior were dubbed 'Seminoles,' a corruption of the Spanish word *cimarrones,* meaning 'free people' or 'wild ones'. Defying European rule and ethnic category, they were soon considered too free for the newly independent United States, which coincidentally was growing hungrier for land.

When the majority of the Creek were forced west across the Mississippi River in 1817, Americans figured everything east of that body of water was now theirs for the settling. But the Seminoles had no intention of leaving their homes.

Bad blood and sporadic violence between Americans and Seminoles eventually gave the US the excuse it needed to make a bid for Florida, which was finally bought from Spain in 1821. Before and after that the US military embarked on several campaigns against the Seminoles and their allies, who took to the swamps, fought three guerrilla wars, and scored a respectable amount of victories against an enemy several times their size. In fact, the Second Seminole War (1835–42) was the longest in American history between the American Revolution and the Vietnam War.

Indeed, operationally the Seminole wars were a 19th-century version of Vietnam, a never-ending parade of long, pointless patrols into impenetrable swamps, always searching for an ever-invisible enemy. By 1830 Congress came up with the shocking Removal Act, a law that told Native Americans to pack up their things and move across the country to Oklahoma. Seminole Chief Osceola and his band (never exceeding more than 100 warriors) refused to sign the treaty and fled into the Everglades. After keeping thousands of soldiers jumping at the barest hint of his presence for years, Osceola was captured under a false flag of truce in 1837. Yet resistance continued, and while the Seminoles gave up fighting, the government gave up on moving them west.

By 1842 the warring had ended, but no peace treaty was ever signed, which is why the Seminoles to this day call themselves 'the unconquered

**Native American Resources**

*Ah-Tah-Thi-Ki Museum (www.ahtahthiki.com)*

*Tequesta Indians (www.floridiannature.com/tequesta.htm)*

*Heritage of the Ancient Ones (www.ancientnative.org)*

*Miccosukee Tribe (www.miccosukee.com/tribe)*

## TEQUESTA INDIANS

In 1998, 24 holes, inscribed in bedrock and arranged in the shape of a perfect circle, were found in downtown Miami. The 'Miami Circle,' as it was dubbed, is thought to be the foundations of a permanent structure and, at some 2000 years old, it's the oldest contender for that title on the US East Coast.

Archaeologists think the Circle was built by Miami's earliest known inhabitants, the Tequesta (Tekesta) Indians, who are otherwise a mystery. The tribe was mostly wiped out by Spanish first contact, which brought violence and disease, and survivors likely melted into the Miccosukee and Seminole nations.

| AD 500 | 1513 | 1702 | 1763 |
|---|---|---|---|
| The Caloosahatchee Culture develops and thrives in the area that now includes the western Everglades and 10,000 Islands. This complex society lasts till 1750. | Ponce de León arrives in Florida, landing south of Cape Canaveral, believing it an island. Since it's around Easter, he names it La Florida, 'The Flowery Land' or 'Feast of Flowers.' | In their ongoing struggle with Spain and France over New World colonies, the British burn St Augustine to the ground; two years later they destroy 13 Spanish missions in Florida. | The mixed Spanish and Native American community in Key West is resettled in Havana after the island is seized by the British. For years, the island has little real authority. |

people'. Those Seminoles who remained in Florida are now organized under a tribal government and run the Ah-Tah-Thi-Ki Museum and the Hard Rock Cafe. Not one Hard Rock Cafe: the entire chain, bought for $965 million in 2007 with money made from gambling revenue. The Seminoles were the first Native American tribe to cash in on gambling, starting with a bingo hall in 1979 that has since expanded to a multibillion-dollar empire. Not bad for a Seminole population of a little over 3000.

## A Freeze Brings Flagler – & the Railway

For decades, Florida was farming country: sugar, citrus and drained swamps. In 1875, Julia Tuttle and her tubercular husband arrived in this agricultural empire from Cleveland, Ohio. After his death she moved to South Florida to take over the land she had inherited as a widow. Proving her worth as a true Floridian, over the next 20 years she proceeded to buy more and more property.

In the meantime, Henry Morrison Flagler, a business partner of John D Rockefeller, realized Florida's tourism potential. Flagler had been busy developing the northern Florida coast in St Augustine and Palm Beach, and he also built the Florida East Coast Railroad, which extended down as far as Palm Beach. Tuttle saw a business opportunity and contacted Flagler with a proposition: if he would extend his railroad to Miami, Tuttle would split her property with him. Miami? Way down at the end of nowhere? Flagler wasn't interested.

Then, in 1895, a record freeze enveloped most of Florida (but not Miami), wiping out citrus crops and sending vacationers scurrying. Legend has it that Tuttle – who is said to have been rather quick both on the uptake and with an 'I told you so' – went into her garden at Fort Dallas on the Miami River, snipped off some orange blossoms and sent them to Flagler, who hightailed it down to Miami to see for himself.

**Historic Homes**

Merrick House (p78)

Vizcaya Museum & Gardens (p75)

Biltmore Hotel (p77)

Hemingway House (p160), Key West

### FIVE WHO SHAPED SOUTH FLORIDA

**Henry Morrison Flagler** The developer whose Florida East Coast Railroad brought scores of visitors to sunny paradise.

**Julia Tuttle** The woman behind Flagler, who (supposedly) lured the skeptical developer to Miami with a handful of orange blossoms.

**Fidel Castro** He may be reviled by local Cubans, but then again, said Cubans wouldn't be here if it wasn't for the bushy-bearded Caribbean communist leader.

**Morris Lapidus** The Fontainebleau, Eden Roc, Lincoln Rd Mall...is there anything this MiMo (Miami Modern) god didn't design?

**Pardon C Greene** One of the founding fathers of Key West; also a member of the city council and (briefly) mayor of the town.

| 1776 | Late 1700s | 1818 | 1822 |
|---|---|---|---|
| The American Revolution begins, but Florida's two colonies don't rebel. They remain loyal to the British crown, and soon English Tories flood south into Florida to escape the fighting. | Elements of the Creek Nation, supplemented by African American runaway slaves and their descendants, begin settling in South Florida, displacing local Calusa and Mayaimi Indians. | Andrew Jackson invades Western Florida after violence between settlers and a coalition of Native Americans and African Americans. The First Seminole War essentially ends when the USA buys Florida from Spain. | Commodore Matthew C Perry lands on Key West and plants the American flag, claiming the entire Keys island chain for the USA. |

## CARIBBEANS & CONFEDERATES

For most of the second half of the 19th century, Key West was the largest, wealthiest city in Florida. How did the little island do so well? Wrecking and sponges. Wrecking is the art of salvaging shipwrecks; local boosters liked to make out this was an altruistic act, and many sailors were pulled from the sea, but the cargo on their boats was sold by Keys merchants. Sponges are just that – undersea sponges that became the backbone of the actual American sponge industry for decades.

The population of the island consisted largely of Caribbean émigrés, but mainland Floridians attracted by business opportunities also made their way here. While the presence of a US Naval Base kept Key West in the Union during the American Civil War, many island residents overtly sympathized with the Confederacy.

Flagler was hooked. He and Tuttle came to terms, and all those Floridians whose livelihoods had been wiped out by the freeze followed Flagler south. Passenger-train services to Miami began on April 22, 1896, the year the city of Miami became incorporated. Incidentally, this was the same year John S Collins began selling lots out of a 5-mile strip between the Atlantic and Biscayne Bay, or what is now 14th to 67th Sts on Miami Beach (ie most of the city).

Of Miami's 502 original inhabitants, 100 of them were African American, conscripted for hard labor and relegated to the northwest neighborhood of Colored Town.

During this period, a frenzy of activity was underway to prepare South Florida for extensive settlement. In 1900, Governor Napoleon Bonaparte Broward, envisioning an 'Empire of the Everglades,' set in motion a frenzy of canal building. Over the next 70 years, some 1800 miles of canals and levees were etched across Florida's porous limestone. These earthworks drained about half the Everglades (about 1.5 million acres) below Lake Okeechobee, replacing it with farms, ranches, orange groves, sugarcane and suburbs.

## The First Big Booms

The promise of money and the expansion of Flagler's railway fueled waves of settlement. Population growth peaked during WWI, when the US military established an aviation training facility in Miami. Many of the thousands who came to work and train figured, 'Hey, the weather's nice,' and Miami's population shot from 1681 people in 1900 to almost 30,000 by 1920. The new Floridians wrote home and got relatives in on the act, and after the war came the first full-fledged Miami boom (1923–25), when Coconut Grove and Allapattah were annexed into what was dubbed, for the first time, Greater Miami.

Even then, Miami was built for good times. People wanted to drink and gamble, because although it was illegal, liquor flowed freely here throughout the entire Prohibition period.

| 1835 | 1845 | 1861 | 1868 |
|---|---|---|---|
| In attacks coordinated by Seminole leader Osceola, Seminoles destroy five sugar plantations on Christmas Day and soon after kill 100 US soldiers marching near Tampa, launching the Second Seminole War. | Florida is admitted to the Union as the 27th state. Since it is a slave state, its admission is balanced by that of Iowa, a free state. | Voting 62 to 7, Florida secedes from the US, raising its fifth flag, the stars-and-bars of the Confederacy. Florida's farms and cattle provide vital Confederate supplies during the ensuing Civil War. | Florida is re-admitted to the United States, but racial tensions between Southern whites and freed African Americans run high, resulting in discriminatory 'Jim Crow' legislation. |

## Depression, Deco & Another World War

Miami's growth was astronomical, and so was its eventual fall: the Great Miami Hurricane of 1926, which left about 220 people dead and up to 50,000 homeless; and the Great Depression. But it's in Miami's nature to weather every disaster with an even better resurgence, and in the interwar period Miami's phoenix rose in two stages. First, Franklin Roosevelt's New Deal brought the Civilian Conservation Corps, jobs and a spurt of rise-from-the-ashes building projects.

Second, in the early 1930s, a group of mostly Jewish developers began erecting small, stylish hotels along Collins Ave and Ocean Dr, jumpstarting a miniboom that resulted in the creation and development of Miami Beach's famous art-deco district. This led to a brief rise in anti-Semitism, as the Beach became segregated and 'Gentiles Only' signs began to appear. The election of a Jewish governor of Florida in 1933 led to improvement, as did airplane travel, which brought plenty of Jewish visitors and settlers from the north.

During WWII, Miami was again a major military training ground, and afterward, many of those GIs returned with their families to enjoy Florida's sandy beaches at leisure. This marked the real beginning of tourism in Florida, and large-scale settlement of South Florida in particular.

> The main (downtown) branch of the Miami-Dade Public Library has an extensive Florida collection that constitutes one of the best repositories of state history anywhere. The collection includes some 17,000 photos by Gleason Romer, who snapped South Florida as a photojournalist and amateur shooter from 1925 to the 1950s.

## Cuba Comes Over

During the 1950s progress seemed inexorable; in 1954 Leroy Collins became the first Southern governor to publicly declare racial segregation 'morally wrong,' while an entire 'Space Coast' was created around Cape Canaveral (between Daytona and Miami on the east coast) to support the development of the National Aeronautics & Space Administration (NASA).

Then, in 1959, Fidel Castro marched onto the 20th-century stage and forever changed the destiny of Cuba and Miami.

As communists swept into Havana, huge portions of the upper and middle classes of Cuba fled north and established a fiercely anti-Castro Cuban community, now 50 years old and, in some ways, as angry as ever about the dictator to the south. At the time, counter-revolutionary politics were discussed, and a group of exiles formed the 2506th Brigade, sanctioned by the US government, which provided weapons and Central Intelligence Agency (CIA) training for the purpose of launching a US attack on Cuba.

The resulting badly executed attack is remembered today as the Bay of Pigs fiasco. The first wave of counter-revolutionaries, left on the beach without reinforcements or supplies, were all captured or killed. All prisoners were released by Cuba about three months later.

In the meantime, Castro attracted Soviet missiles to his country, but couldn't keep his people. In 1965 alone some 100,000 Cubans hopped the 'freedom flight' from Havana to Miami.

| 1905 | 1912 | 1925 | 1926 |
|---|---|---|---|
| The first of many attempts to drain the Everglades begins. In coming decades, thousands of acres are destroyed as water is diverted from its natural flow from Lake Okeechobee. | 'Flagler's Folly,' Henry Flagler's 128-mile overseas railroad connecting the Florida Keys, reaches Key West. It's hailed as the 'Eighth Wonder of the World,' but is destroyed by a 1935 hurricane. | Coral Gables, one of the first planned communities in the USA, is officially founded. The 'City Beautiful' was designed by real-estate developer George Edgar Merrick. | The Great Miami Hurricane devastates South Florida, killing 220 people, leaving up to 50,000 homeless and causing some $100 million in damages. The Great Depression slows recovery. |

# Racial Tensions

Riots and skirmishes broke out between Cubans and African Americans, and African Americans and whites, in Miami. In 1968 a riot broke out after it was discovered that two white police officers had arrested a 17-year-old African American male, stripped him naked and hung him by his ankles from a bridge.

In 1970 the 'rotten meat' riot began when African American locals picketed a white-owned shop they had accused of selling spoiled meat. After three days of picketing, white officers attempted to disperse the crowds and fired on them with tear gas. During the 1970s, there were 13 other race-related violent confrontations.

Racial tensions exploded on May 17, 1980, when four white police officers, being tried on charges that they beat an African American suspect to death while he was in custody, were acquitted by an all-white jury. When the verdict was announced, race riots broke out all over Miami and lasted for three days.

# The Mariel Boatlift

In the late 1970s, Castro suddenly declared that anyone who wanted to leave Cuba had open access to the docks at Mariel Harbor. Before the ink was dry on the proclamation, the largest flotilla ever launched for non-military purposes set sail (or paddled) from Cuba in practically anything that would float the 90 miles between Cuba and the USA.

The Mariel Boatlift, as the largest of these would be called, brought 125,000 Cubans to Florida, including an estimated 25,000 prisoners and mental patients. Mariel shattered the stereotype of the wealthy Batista-exiled Cuban. The resulting strain on the economy, logistics and infrastructure of South Florida added to still-simmering racial tensions; by 1990, it was estimated that 90% of Miami's Caucasian populace was Hispanic.

The tension carried over from Hispanic-Anglo divisions to rifts between older Cubans and the new *Marielitos*. The middle- to upper-class white Cubans of the 1960s were reintroduced to that nation in the form of thousands of Afro-Cubans and *santeros,* or worshippers of Santeria, Cuba's version of *vodou* (voodoo).

# Miami Not So Nice

In the 1980s Miami became the major East Coast entry port for drug dealers and their product and earned the nickname 'Mi-Yay-Mi', 'yay' being slang for cocaine. As if to keep up with the corruption, many savings and loans (S&Ls) opened in newly built Miami headquarters. While *Newsweek* magazine called Miami 'America's Casablanca,' locals dubbed it the 'City with the S&L Skyline.'

## Miami Histories

*Miami (1987),* Joan Didion

*The Corpse Had a Familiar Face (1987), Edna Buchanan*

*Black Miami in the Twentieth Century (1997), Marvin Dunn*

*This Land Is Our Land: Immigrants and Power in Miami (2003), Alex Stepick*

*Miami, USA (2000), Helen Muir*

HISTORY RACIAL TENSIONS

| 1928 | 1933–40 | 1942 | 1947 |
|---|---|---|---|
| Ernest Hemingway pens *A Farewell to Arms* in Key West, supposedly while awaiting the delivery of a car. His wife's uncle gives the Hemingways a local house in 1931. | New Deal public-works projects employ 40,000 Floridians and help save Florida from the Depression. The most notable construction project is the Overseas Highway through the Keys. | From January to August, German U-boats sink more than two dozen tankers and ships off Florida's coast. By war's end, Florida holds nearly 3000 German POWs in 15 labor camps. | Everglades National Park is established, successfully culminating a 19-year effort, led by Ernest Coe and Marjory Stoneman Douglas, to protect the Everglades from the harm done by dredging and draining. |

A plethora of businesses – legitimate concerns as well as drug-financed fronts – and buildings sprang up all over Miami. Downtown was completely remodeled. But it was reborn in the grip of drug smugglers: shoot-outs were common, as were gangland slayings by cocaine cowboys. At one stage, up to three people per week were being killed in cocaine-related clashes.

The police, Coast Guard, Drug Enforcement Agency (DEA), Border Patrol and the Federal Bureau of Investigation (FBI) were trying to keep track of it all. Roadblocks were set up along the Overseas Hwy to Key West (prompting the quirky and headstrong residents down there to call for a secession, which eventually sent the police on their way).

*Miami Vice* was single-handedly responsible for Miami Beach rising to international fabulousness in the mid-1980s, its slick soundtrack and music-video-style montages glamorizing the rich South Florida lifestyle. Before long, people were coming down to check it out for themselves – especially photographer Bruce Weber, who began using South Beach as a gritty and fashionable backdrop for modeling shoots in the early 1980s.

Celebrities were wintering in Miami, international photographers were shooting here, and the Art Deco Historic District, having been granted federal protection, was going through renovation and renaissance. Gay men, always on the cutting edge of trends, discovered South Beach's gritty glamour. The city was becoming a showpiece of fashion and trendiness.

## The 1990s & 2000s

A combination of Hurricane Andrew and a crime wave against tourists, particularly carjackings, equaled a drop in visitors, until tourist-oriented community policing and other visible programs reversed the curse. Miami went from being the US city with the most violent crime to one with average crime statistics for a city its size. From 1992 to 1998, tourist-related crimes decreased by a whopping 80%.

The Cuban American population dominated headlines again during the Elián Gonzalez nightmare, an international custody fight that ended with federal agents storming the Little Havana house where the seven-year-old was staying to have him shipped back to Cuba while anti-Castro Cubans protested in Miami streets.

On the bright side, corruption was slightly cleaned out after the removal of Mayor Xavier Suarez in 1998, whose election was overturned following the discovery of many illegal votes. Manuel 'Manny' Diaz, who had been a lawyer for the Miami-based Gonzalez family, followed Suarez as mayor and pushed for cementing ties between Miami and the Latin American world – he was fond of saying, 'When Venezuela or Argentina sneezes, Miami catches a cold.'

During the 2000s Miami proper underwent more 'Manhattan-ization,' with more and more skyscrapers altering the city skyline. There are currently 307 high-rise buildings in Miami, 59 of which stand taller than 400

### Best Florida Histories

The New History of Florida, Michael Gannon

The Everglades: River of Grass, Marjory Stoneman Douglas

Dreamers, Schemers & Scalawags, Stuart McIver

The Enduring Seminoles, Patsy West

Miami Babylon, Gerald Posner

After WWII, the advent of effective bug spray and affordable air-conditioning did more for Florida tourism than anything else. With these two technological advancements, Florida's subtropical climate was finally safe for delicate Yankee skin.

| 1961 | May 1980 | 1980 | 1992 |
|---|---|---|---|
| Brigade 2506, a 1300-strong volunteer army, invades Cuba's Bay of Pigs on April 16. President Kennedy withholds air support, leading to Brigade 2506's immediate defeat and capture by Fidel Castro. | In the McDuffie trial, white police are acquitted of wrongdoing in the death of an African American man, igniting racial tensions and Miami's Liberty City riots; 18 people are killed. | Cuba's Castro 'opens the floodgates'. The USA's ensuing Mariel Boatlift transports 125,000 *Marielitos*, who face intense discrimination in Miami. | On August 24, Hurricane Andrew devastates Dade County, leaving 41 people dead, more than 200,000 homeless, and causing about $15.5 billion in damage. |

feet. At the same time, Diaz began using arts districts and buildings – the former represented by Wynwood and Midtown, the latter by the Adrienne Arsht Center for the Performing Arts – to revitalize blighted areas of town.

Water and a lack of it have always been nagging fears in South Florida, one of the fastest growing population areas of the country, but the issue took on new urgency in the 2000s. By the late '90s, the South Florida aquifer seemed in danger of depletion. The solution seemed to rest in the Comprehensive Everglades Restoration Plan (CERP), which was passed in 2000. Said project is aimed at restoring the flow of water to the Everglades from Lake Okeechobee, which would subsequently help replenish the South Florida aquifer and the state's most iconic wilderness space. At the time of research, the US National Research Council had determined that progress toward restoring the core of the Glades was proceeding very slowly, and quicker action was needed.

In the normally placid Keys, protests, heated town-hall meetings and various civic master plans tried to address the impact of skyrocketing costs of living on an island chain where there isn't much room to build new houses. During this period, commuter buses running from Homestead were packed full of the service industry, teachers and other backbone members of the community who could no longer afford a trailer or apartment in the Keys. Today there is high pressure on new housing projects in the islands to provide affordable units.

## The Recent Past

Journalist Tomas Regalado was elected mayor of Miami in 2009 in the wake of a financial crisis and recession. Florida led the state in foreclosures, and the evidence was visible across South Florida in the form of double-digit home vacancy rates. But for every burst bubble, there is re-inflation, and at the time of research the real estate market was in comeback mode; from Miami to Key West, condos were getting occupied, and condo rents were rising as fast as condo towers.

Miami is still, by far, the largest Cuban city outside Cuba, and most Cubans here still don't like the Castro regime. At the same time, there has been some relaxing of ultra-orthodox anti-Castroism. The original Batista refugees of the 1950s are aging, to be replaced by a new generation of 'YUCAs' – young, urban Cuban Americans. The YUCAs don't like Castro either. But they are not single-issue voters like their parents (that issue being to isolate Cuba). Many vote Democrat and, in general, they are more interested in subverting Cuba through commerce and consumer goods than by the CIA. That's an approach that was facilitated by Barack Obama, who in 2011 relaxed some elements of the US–Cuba travel ban and trade embargo.

Richard Heyman, who served two terms as mayor of Key West (1983–85 and 1987–89), was perhaps the first openly gay mayor of a sizable US town (and perhaps any US town, period). In 2010 a documentary on his life, *The Newcomer*, was released. Heyman died of AIDS-related pneumonia in 1994.

| 1999 | 2000 | 2010 | 2014 |
|---|---|---|---|
| On Thanksgiving, five-year-old Elián González is rescued at sea, his Cuban mother having died en route. Despite wild protests by Miami's Cuban exiles, the US returns the then seven-year-old Elián to his father in Cuba. | The Comprehensive Everglades Restoration Plan (CERP) is put into action. The 30-year plan aims to restore natural water flow to the Everglades and re-plenish South Florida's water reservoirs. | The Deepwater Horizon/BP oil disaster results in 11 deaths and 4.9 million barrels of oil being spilled into the Gulf of Mexico. | Flooding on Alton Rd causes the city of Miami Beach to fund both flood-relief programs and climate-change impact assessments. |

# Multicultural Miami

There's an old saw that South Florida, with its diversity and urban character, is culturally Northeastern even if it's geographically Southern, but that's reductive. Miami and surrounds aren't Manhattan with a tan. This region is an intersection of Middle America, Latin America and the Caribbean, a clash of the idiosyncratic types who decided miles of marshland, beach, mangroves and islets were a place where the American dream could be realized to subtropical perfection. In short, it's demographically interesting here.

## Greater Multicultural Miami

Contemporary South Florida is certainly more than Miami, but if the local distinct regional identity has an anchor city, Miami is that town. With that said, while Miami's energy impacts the Keys and the Glades (particularly the former), these other areas are more demographically homogenous, and in the case of Key West, have their own unique histories of settlement and demographic shift.

### Miami

It'd still be silly not to recognize Miami as the center of South Florida's cultural gravity. Which begs the question: what makes Miami, well, Miami? Basically, it's the mix: that conspicuous jumble of Cubans, Haitians, Anglos, Jews, and South and Central Americans of all stripes. Miami possesses the best and worst of its parent cultures, immigrant and migrant narratives that are embraced and rejected and spliced and diced into entirely new paradigms. How else does a Cuban American proudly show off an inherited Matanzas accent on the one hand while shrugging off the pork and rum of their island ancestors in favor of vegetarianism and yoga? As they say here, only in Miami. Of if you prefer, *sólamente en Miami.*

It can be difficult to meet someone from Miami who has more than two generations of connection to the city. At the negative end, this lack of connection can manifest as a detached sense of place and resentment toward other newcomers. Miami is not without tensions between its myriad communities. On the positive side are those Miamians concerned with building an identity for their town, the ones who patronize local sport and arts, and extend a helping hand toward newcomers from across America or the Gulf of Mexico.

It almost goes without saying, but Miami's cultural capital, even among Asian and Anglo citizens, is largely derived from the Caribbean and Latin America. There's an energy here that is cheerful, loud and colorful. It infects the place, and it will get under your skin the longer you stay.

### The Everglades

Rural Florida can still evoke America's western frontier, and the Everglades, the wildest part of the state, are still very much a hinterland populated by either frontier types, or people who self-conceptualize as frontier types. The Old West trope is exacerbated by the fact there is still a settlement pattern here of colonizers and Native Americans; the Seminole and Miccosukee tribes constitute a major part of the 'Glades' population. Their neighbors in Homestead and Everglades City are largely descended from those who came here in the 19th century, after the West was won, when Florida became one of the last places where pioneers could simply plant stakes and make a life on ostensibly unclaimed land (well, unclaimed if you weren't Native American).

These pioneers became Florida's 'Crackers,' the poor rural farmers, fisherfolk, cowhands and outlaws who traded the comforts of civilization for independence on their terms. Many Crackers came from the old Southern states, and created a culture not too far removed, geographic or otherwise, from the Confederacy. In parts of southern America, the term cracker is pejorative, but it has a specific connotation in Florida that is a badge of honor, as evidenced by the annual Cracker Storytelling Festival and *Crackers in the Glade,* a classic illustrated account of growing up in the Everglades region, among other cultural ephemera.

A bit of Southern-fried hospitality and Western independence is a feisty combination, but therein are the roots of many Glades citizens. Even the local Native Americans share these qualities; it may surprise you to see large Confederate flags and Ford F-250 pickup trucks jamming many a Seminole Nation parking lot, although many Seminole and Miccosukee also retain elements of indigenous culture. Most Everglades citizens, like rural people in much of the USA, place a high value on self-reliance and perceived freedom from government.

Finally, we'd be remiss not to mention the large number of Mexicans who now call Homestead home, the majority attracted by jobs working on nearby farms. As you drive south from Miami, the shift from Cuban Spanish to Mexican Spanish is quite distinct, even to an untrained ear.

### The Keys

The Keys constitute a fascinating combination of white Floridians, Caribbean islanders and just about anyone attracted to living an island lifestyle that's still technically in the borders of the USA. As the Keys have been settled by non–Native Americans longer than Miami, there is a distinct local culture that's a little bit country in the Outer Keys, and elegantly eccentric in Key West. Regardless of where you're from, if you're born in the Keys, you're considered a Conch – one of the members of a tribe whose bond is life amidst the islands.

There's a great deal of pride in the Keys themselves and their independence from the mainland. And while many people, especially in the Outer Keys, have conservative attitudes on gun control and the environment (ie less regulation related to both), there's also a great deal of tolerance for alternative lifestyles. Maybe because just choosing to live out here is an alternative lifestyle decision.

The search for an alternative lifestyle, plus geographic isolation, led many gay people to Key West. Richard Heyman, who was mayor of the city from 1983–85 and 1987–89, was one of the first openly gay mayors of an American city. The *Key West Citizen* has even argued that, in regards to LGBT (Lesbian, Gay, Bisexual, Transexual) politics, Key West is essentially post-sexual identity. Anything has gone for so long that nothing (between consenting adults) is off limits.

# The Arts in South Florida

Art, music and literature permeate South Florida's daily life. Because this region has a pretty face, many people think it has a correspondingly shallow mind. The stereotype isn't fair. Because what makes South Florida beautiful, from the bodies on the beach to the structure of the skyline, is diversity. The energies of the Western Hemisphere have been channeled

## EXPERIENCING MULTICULTURAL MIAMI

The following guide may help you understand some of Miami's most prominent ethnic groups.

### Cuban Miami

Cuban Miami is stereotypically associated with Little Havana, but to be fair, so much of Miami is Cuban it's more accurate to refer to Cubans as the norm, the default ethnicity. With that said, the most important cultural symbols of Cuban Miami are concentrated in Little Havana, particularly near 8th Street/Calle Ocho. Other parts of town where you can get a strong sense of Cuban identity include Hialeah, where over 90% of the population speaks Spanish as a first language.

➡ **Little Havana** (p73) The old heart of Cuban Miami.

➡ **Viernes Culturales** (p117) A regular Latin street celebration.

➡ **Versailles** (p108) The most storied standby of culinary Cuban Florida.

➡ **Cuba Ocho** (p73) Permanent art exhibit of Miami's Cuban diaspora.

➡ **Máximo Gómez Park** (p73) Watch old Cuban men trade dominoes and jibes.

### Haitian Miami

Haitian Miamians speak Kreyol (also spelled 'Creole'), which is related to French. If you speak French, you may be able to converse with local Haitians, but as Kreyol is its own language, with its own grammar and syntax, French alone may not get you far. Little Haiti is by far one of the most colorful neighborhoods in the city, but it can be rough after dark, so try and visit during the day, unless a Big Night in Little Haiti (p69) monthly street party is happening.

➡ **Tap Tap** (p99) Haitian cuisine, South Beach setting.

➡ **Libreri Mapou** (p70) A Haitian-related library.

➡ *Botanicas* (p70) Centers for *vodou* worship.

➡ **Little Haiti Cultural Center** (p69) Community center for Haitian Miami.

➡ **Chef Creole** (p105) Traditional Haitian food in Little Haiti.

### Jewish Miami

Jews were some of the first developers and residents of Miami Beach. They've maintained a strong presence here for decades, which helps explain why the Miami metro area has the nation's second-largest concentration of Jews. While many of these Jews are descended from Northeast families, many are also the children of Latin American exiles. There is a significant Cuban, Puerto Rican, Brazilian and Colombian Jewish presence in Miami. The area around 41st St in North Miami Beach, and 95th and Harding in Surfside are both streets where you'll see lots of Jewish businesses and community organizations.

➡ **Jewish Museum of Florida** (p54) Center for research on Jewish Florida.

➡ **Temple Emanu-El** (p59) One of the area's largest synagogues.

➡ **Lots of Lox** (p110) Old-school Jewish deli.

➡ **Roasters' n Toasters** (p102) Another favorite Jewish deli.

### Argentine Miami

Argentines are mainly concentrated in Northern Miami Beach. In South America, Argentines are often stereotyped as snooty compared to other South American nationalities.

Many Spanish-speaking Miamians, especially ones from South America, like to riff on this cliché with their Argentine friends, but the comments are almost always good-natured teasing and taken as such. Northern Miami Beach is also home to a good number of Uruguayans, who have cultural and geographic ties to their Argentine neighbors.

➡ **Normandy Isle & Ocean Terrace** (p59)

## Spanish Miami

When we say Miami is a capital of the Spanish-speaking world, that applies to the home of the mother tongue as well. Spaniards have been settling in Miami in large numbers for the past few decades. There is no one part of Spain that produces these new arrivals; in one part of Miami you'll find people from the Basque country who resent being called 'Spanish,' while in another you may break bread with Catalans in one restaurant, and Castillians in another. Many of the best high-end grocery stores, bakeries, cheese shops and meat shops in Miami are run by Spaniards.

➡ **El Carajo** (p109) A semi-hidden tapas joint beloved by Spanish expats.

## Japanese Miami

Miami does not have a particularly large Japanese community, but there are some Japanese here. Many are businesspeople participating in the global economy and international commerce, but there is also a large number of contemporary artists and designers who are attracted by Miami's growing cultural credibility. No one neighborhood in Miami can be said to be Japanese.

➡ **Matsuri** (p109) A popular sushi spot for expat Japanese.

## Brazilian Miami

Miami's Brazilians are mainly found in Northern Miami Beach: working, partying, eating and blending into the Miami milieu. Well, those Brazilians who live in Greater Miami proper. There is a noticeably large population of temporary Brazilians in the city, including shoppers who come here to buy electronics and clothes that lack Brazil's import duties, and a glut of designers, DJs, musicians, fashionistas, models and their respective entourages; these Brazilians tend to base themselves in South Beach with the other jet-setters.

➡ **Boteco** (p115) Popular Brazilian watering hole.

## Colombian Miami

You'll find many Colombians with their South American brethren in Northern Miami Beach, but there are also plenty of Colombians in Coral Gables (where the Colombian consulate is located). A poorer component of the Colombian population lives in parts of downtown and in the city's vast suburbs. Colombian politics are difficult to pigeonhole, as Colombian migrants have come to the USA fleeing from both left- and right-wing overthrows.

➡ **La Moon** (p103) Late night Colombian eats attract the Colombian community.

## Nicaraguan Miami

Nicaraguans make up a large percentage of the population of 'Cuban' areas such as Little Havana. It is the Nicaraguans who are leading the way, currently, to more settlement from Central America.

➡ **Yambo** (p108) An enormously good value *fritanga* (Nicaraguan diner).

into this Gateway to the Americas, and a lot of that drive is rooted in creativity and a search for self-expression.

This artistic impulse tends to derive from the immigrant experience – which this region has in spades – and the pain of exile. Living in a country where you can't be arrested for public expression helps too, as does the flush of financial success and the frustration of being shut out of the often callous American dream. Miami's greatest quality, her inborn tolerance for eccentricity, is at the root of such public innovations as the Arab fantasy-land architecture of Opa Locka, the modernistic design of the Art Deco Historic District and the condominium-lined skyscraper corridors of Brickell.

In addition, there is always a sense of the possible coupled with the fantasy of excess. Plenty of people dismiss Coral Gables and the Vizcaya as gauche and tacky, and through modern eyes they may appear as such. But they were revolutionary for their time. During the early 20th century, concepts such as a Mediterranean revival village that served as a bulwark against sprawl, or an Italianate villa carved out of the seashore, would not have flown in the aesthetically conservative Northeast, but they found legs here.

Florida's Division of Cultural Affairs (www.florida-arts.org) is a great resource for statewide arts organizations and agencies. Its Florida Artists Hall of Fame memorializes the Sunshine State's creative legacy.

## Putting Miami on the Arts Map

Miami's citizens and their memories, realities and visions have created a burgeoning art scene that truly began to be noticed with the 2002 introduction of Art Basel Miami Beach (p89), the US outpost of an annual erudite gathering that's based in Switzerland. By its second year, the event had created a buzz throughout the national art world – and had succeeded in wooing 175 exhibitors, more than 30,000 visitors and plenty of celebs to take over the galleries, clubs, and hotels of South Beach and the Design District. It has grown, in both size and strength, each year since, and its impact on the local art scene cannot be overstated; today, Art Basel Miami is the biggest contemporary arts festival in the Western Hemisphere.

### BRIGHT BRITTO

If the top public artist of a given city determines how said city sees itself, we must conclude Miami is a cartoon-like, cubist, chaotic place of bright, happy, shiny, joy.

That's the aesthetic legacy Romero Britto is leaving this town. The seemingly perpetually grinning Brazilian émigré, clad in jackets leftover from a 1980s MTV video, was the hot face of public art in the 2000s, having designed the mural of the Miami Children's Museum (p81), the 'Welcome' structure at Dadeland North Station, the central sculpture at the shops at Midtown and many others. You might need sunglasses to appreciate his work, which appeals to the islander in all of us: Saturday-morning cartoon brights, sharp geometric lines and loopy curls, inner-child character studies and, underlying everything, a scent of teal oceans on a sunny day.

Gloria Estefan loves the guy, and former governor Jeb Bush gave Tony Blair an original Britto when the ex-PM visited Miami in 2006. However, not everyone feels the Romero love; plenty of critics have dubbed Britto more commercial designer than pop artist (but, like, what is art, man?). Rather than get mired in the debate, we suggest you check out a Britto installation for yourself, or the **Britto Central** gallery at 818 Lincoln Rd. The man's work is as ubiquitous as palm trees and, hey, if you've got a spare $20,000, you can buy an original (a small one) before you go home.

## CARL HIAASEN: LOVING THE LUNACY

In Carl Hiaasen's Florida the politicians are corrupt, the rednecks are violent, the tourists are clueless, the women are fast and the ambience is smoky noir, brightened by a few buckets of loony pastel. Some would say the man knows his home state.

Hiaasen, who worked at the *Miami Herald* for decades and is now a Keys resident (he met his wife while reading in the Keys bar she managed), is both a writer gifted with crisp prose and a journalist blessed by a reporter's instinct for the offbeat. His success has rested in his ability to basically take the hyperbolic reality that is Florida and tell it to the world. Although his fiction is just that, in many ways it simply draws off the day-to-day eccentricities of the Sunshine State and novelizes them. In *Tourist Season* Hiaasen turns his pen on ecozealots with a story about a terrorist group that tries to dissuade tourists from coming to Florida and further wrecking the state – namely, by feeding them to a crocodile named Pavlov. In complete thematic contrast comes *Hoot,* a heart-warming tale (odd for Hiaasen) catering to young adults about a 12-year-old boy's fight against a corporation that threatens to pave over a Coconut Grove colony of burrowing owls. *Stormy Weather* takes on the corruption, bureaucracy and disaster tourism that fills the vacuum of the devastation trail left by a hurricane.

Hiaasen's work tends to career between satire and thriller, and betrays both an unceasingly critical eye and deep affection for all of Florida's quirks. Which ironically makes Hiaasen – enemy of almost every special-interest group in the Sunshine State – the state's biggest promoter. He is a man who loves Florida despite its warts and that, folks, is true romance.

### Public Art

This city has always been way ahead of the curve when it comes to public art. Miami and Miami Beach established the Art in Public Places program way back in 1973, when it voted to allocate 1.5% of city construction funds to the fostering of public art; since then more than 700 works – sculptures, mosaics, murals, light-based installations and more – have been created in public spots.

Barbara Neijne's *Foreverglades,* in Concourse J of Miami International Airport, uses mosaic, art-installed text from *River of Grass* (by Marjory Stoneman Douglas) and waves representing the movement of water over grass to give new arrivals a sense of the flow of Florida's most unique ecosystem. A series of handprints representing Miami's many immigrant communities link into a single community in *Reaching for Miami Skies,* by Connie Lloveras, which greets Metromover commuters at Brickell Station. In Miami-Dade Library, the floating text of *Words Without Thought Never to Heaven Go* by Edward Ruscha challenges readers to engage in thought processes that are inspired by, but go beyond, the books that surround them. The team of Roberto Behar and Rosario Marquardt, hailing from Argentina, have been among the most prolific public artists in town. Their work is deliberately meant to warp conceptions of what is or isn't public space; they created the giant red *M* at the Metromover Riverwalk Station for the city's centennial back in 1996.

You can count among Florida's snowbirds some of the USA's best writers, such as Robert Frost, Isaac Bashevis Singer and Annie Dillard, and every January, the literati of the US hold court at the Annual Key West Literary Seminar.

## Literature

Writers need to be around good stories to keep their narrative wits sharp, and no place provides stories quite like South Florida, where farmers clash with environmentalists who fight financiers, while immigrants arrive from a hundred different countries and, every summer, a hurricane hits. This proximity to real-life drama means, unsurprisingly, many of Miami's best authors cut their writing teeth in journalism. As a result, there's a breed of Miami prose that has the terse punch of the best newspaper writing. Beginning with former *Miami Herald* crime-beat reporters Edna Buchanan and Carl Hiaasen, and leading to new names such as Jeff Lindsay, the Miami crime-writing scene is alive and well.

On the other hand, local immigrant communities have lent this town's literature the poetry of exiled tongues, narratives that find a thread through the diaspora alleyways that underline Florida's identity. Look out for Carolina Garcia-Aguilera, Edwidge Danticat and Diana Abu-Jaber. And finally, the subtle beauty of South Florida has produced a certain breed of nature writer that is able to capture the nuances of the region's subdued scenery while explaining the complicated science that runs through it all – Marjory Stoneman Douglas and Ted Levin spring to mind. Pulitzer Prize–finalist Karen Russell often combines sensuous nature imagery with a sprinkling of sometimes-funny, sometimes-ominous magical realism.

## Music

As in all things, it's the mad diversity of Miami that makes its music so appealing. The southbound path of American country and Southern rock, the northbound rhythms of the Caribbean and Latin America, and the homegrown beats of Miami's African American community get mixed into a musical crossroads of the Americas. Think about the sounds the above influences produce, and you'll hear a certain thread: bouncy and percussive with a tune you can always dance to.

The above sounds, rooted in the New World, are fighting against interlopers from a far shore: Europeans and their waves of techno, house and EDM. They have brought a strong club-music scene, best evidenced by the annual Winter Music Conference in March, which brings thousands of DJs and producers to town. The gay community has traditionally been a receptive audience for club music, and many club nights have crossover with gay parties.

Miami's heart and soul is Latin, and that goes for its music as well. Producers and artists from across Latin America come here for high-quality studio facilities, the lure of global distribution and the Billboard Latin Music Conference & Awards, held here each April. The Magic City has been the cradle of stars such as Gloria Estefan, Ricky Martin and Albita, and a scan over the local airwaves always yields far more Spanish-language stations than English, playing a mix of salsa, *son* (an Afro-Cuban-Spanish mélange of musical styles), conga and reggaeton. A night out in La Covacha is a good intro to the scene.

Salsa is the most commonly heard word used to reference Latin music and dance. This makes sense as it's a generic term developed in the mid-'60s and early '70s to pull all Latin sounds under one umbrella name for gringos who couldn't recognize the subtle differences between beats. From the Spanish word for 'sauce,' salsa has its roots in Cuban culture

### MIAMI TRACKS (& WHERE TO PLAY THEM)

**'Conga'** Gloria Estefan & the Miami Sound Machine – Ocean Dr

**'Rakata'** Wisin y Yandel – Little Havana

**'Moon Over Miami'** Joe Burke and Edgar Leslie – Julia Tuttle Causeway

**'Miami'** Will Smith – I-95 past Downtown

**'Miami'** U2 – Wynwood or North Miami Beach

**'Save Hialeah Park'** Los Primeros – Hialeah

**'Swamp Music'** Lynyrd Skynyrd – Tamiami Trail to Everglades City

**'Jaspora'** Wyclef Jean – Little Haiti

**'Your Love'** the Outfield – A1A

and has a sound that's enhanced by textures of jazz. Music that lends itself to salsa dancing has four beats per bar of music.

One specific type of Cuban salsa is *son* – a sound popularized by the release of 1999's *Buena Vista Social Club*. It has roots in African and Spanish cultures and is quite melodic, usually incorporating instruments including the *tres* (a type of guitar with three sets of closely spaced strings), standard guitars and various hand drums.

Merengue originates from the Dominican Republic and can be characterized by a very fast beat, with just two beats to each bar. It's typically played on the tamboura, guiro (a ridged cylindrical percussion instrument made of metal or dried gourd) and accordion.

Hailing from the Andalusian region of Spain is the folk art of flamenco, which consists of hand clapping, finger snapping, vocals, guitar and the flamboyant dance.

Miami's Argentines love to tango, a Buenos Aires invention that draws off European classical dance and the immigrant experience of South America's French, Italian, African and indigenous enclaves.

The popular reggae sound, originating in Jamaica and having strong Rastafarian roots, is a total movement most popularly associated with Bob Marley. It's characterized by rhythm chops on a backbeat and, at least in its beginnings, a political-activist message. There are various styles within reggae, including roots (Marley's sound), dancehall (ie Yo-sexygirlwannagetboomshackalacka), raga and dub.

But it's rare to just hear one of the above. Miami is a polyglot kind of town, and it loves to blend techno with *son,* give an electronic backbeat to salsa, and overlay everything with dub, hip-hop and *bomba* (African-influenced Puerto Rican dance music). This mixed marriage produces a lot of musical children, and the most recognizable modern sound derived from the above is reggaeton, a driving mash-up that plays like Spanish rap shoved through a sexy backbeat and thumpin' dancehall speakers. Pioneers of the genre include Daddy Yankee, Don Chezina, Tito El Bambino, Wisin Y Yandel, Calle 13 and producers such as Luny Tunes and Noriega. Although it largely originated in Puerto Rico, reggaeton is one of the few musical styles that can get Latinos from across the Americas – from Nicaraguans to Mexicans to Colombians – shaking it.

Miami's hip-hop has had a bit of a circular evolution, from early '90s Miami bass (dirty-dance music, exemplified by 2 Live Crew) to more aggressive, street-style rap, which has blended and morphed into today's club-oriented tracks. These modern sounds draw off the crunk beats, Southern drawls and Atlanta overproduction of the Dirty South sound. The hit 2008 single 'Low' by Flo Rida encapsulates the genre, which sounds, in a lot of ways, like the club child of Miami bass and everything that has come since. Local hip-hop heroes work hard to keep Miami on the map and strongly rep neighborhoods such as Opa Locka, Liberty City and Overtown; artists to listen for include DJ Smallz, Rick Ross, Flo Rida and Uncle Luke. We'd be remiss not to mention Pitbull, who has successfully branded his sound as a bridge between reggaeton, hip-hop and pop.

There has been a small but strong indie-rock boom over the past decade, mainly centered on Sweat Records and Churchill's in Little Haiti. The crop of homegrown bands is growing; events such as Sweatstock are a good means of accessing the scene. Besides Churchill's, other good spots to see the cutting edge of Miami rock are Vagabond and Bardot.

## Film & TV

Crime sells this city – at least cinematically. Sam Katzman chose Miami for B-movies about gang wars, and several (lowbrow) classics – as well as the *Jackie Gleason Show* – in the 1960s. *Scarface,* Brian DePalma's over-the-top story of the excesses of capitalism, entered Miami into hip-hop's

MULTICULTURAL MIAMI FILM & TV

*Naked Came the Manatee* (1998) is a collaborative mystery novel by a constellation of famous Florida writers: Carl Hiaasen, Dave Barry, Elmore Leonard, James Hall, Edna Buchanan, and more. It's like nibbling a delectable box of cyanide-laced chocolates.

common lexicon; and *Miami Vice,* the 1980s TV series about a couple of pastel-clad vice-squad cops, put Miami on the international map. The images – of murders, rapes and drug-turf wars – were far from positive, and the powers-that-be in the city were not initially happy. But *Vice* was more about Ferraris, speedboats and booty than gang-banging, and as branding goes, it depicted Miami as more than a high-crime slum where everyone's grandparents retired. As William Cullom, a President of the Greater Miami Chamber of Commerce put it, *'[Miami Vice]* has built an awareness of Miami in young people who had never thought of visiting Miami.' A pretty mediocre Hollywood film version starring Colin Farrell and Jamie Foxx, released in 2006, capitalized on the '80s nostalgia market. There have been loads of comedies filmed here as well, but for our money, *The Birdcage* best captures the fabulosity and, yes, even community vibe, of South Beach. We're forgetting one other genre: porn. Well, what did you expect with all the silicone? There's a fair amount of homegrown adult industry going on here.

Today, Miami and Miami Beach governments love producers coming to town so much that in early 2005 they instituted the One Stop Permitting system, providing a streamlined, online way for makers of films, TV shows and commercials to apply for permits (www.filmiami.org).

Two of the best film festivals in the US are the Miami International Film Festival (www.miamifilmfestival.com), which is a showcase for Latin cinema (March), and the up-and-coming Florida Film Festival (www.floridafilmfestival.com) in Orlando (April).

## Fashion

With Miami now a hub of cool food, nightlife and arts, it makes sense that it would gain acclaim for influencing the world of fashion. And it has, with the annual Miami Fashion Week playing a large role in putting this region on the most stylish global maps.

The event is renowned globally, from Paris to Hong Kong – but it is by no means the only game in town. Miami has gained enormous cred among European designers (ironically ever since one of them, Gianni Versace, was killed here) and draws mavens from all over the Old World who find something inspiring in the combination of a Latin emphasis on appearance versus the American love of comfort and the dare-to-bare styles inspired by the sunny weather. Today Miami is the base city for Perry Ellis International, while GenArt, a national nonprofit dedicated to film, art and fashion, holds an annual Fresh Faces in Fashion showcase focusing on Miami's burgeoning designer scene.

So what defines the 'Miami look'? 'Go to a supermarket. Any supermarket. Nine out of 10 girls are wearing high heels. That's Miami,' says a local journalist. Yup, if you want to hang here, you gotta come correct. But it's a weird style – part laid back yet totally glam.

On the one hand, you'll see a desperate desire for brand-name cred, of Louis Vuitton–endowed affirmation. But on the other hand is the understated (yes, Miami can do understatement) sense of cool that comes from all that heat, exemplified by a casual dressiness the best-looking Miamians accomplish without any apparent effort. Note, for example, the older Cuban man lounging in his guayabera, an elegant but simple brocaded men's shirt; he's classy because he's looking good without seeming to try.

There is a distinctive South Beach style and there's no better place to buy it than at the source, but be warned: you must be bold, unabashed and bikini-waxed to pull off some of the more risqué outfits on display, which is to say, pretty much all of them.

# Food & Drink

**When South Florida sits at the table, who knows what language the menu is written in. This region has a rich culinary identity, which is an extension of an already rich demographic identity. As a result the local culinary scene is paradoxical, yet delicious: on the one hand a free-floating gastronomy for people unmoored from their homeland and detached from tradition, and on the other an attempt to connect to deeply felt roots and folkways via the immediacy of taste.**

## Defining Local Dining

It's hard to isolate a 'native' South Florida cuisine (actual Native American dishes such as chili and fry bread found in Everglades-area restaurants are imported from the American Southwest). The first white settlers here came from all over America, and thus the American South and its food ways, which heavily influence Northern Florida, is one of many dozens of influences in Miami, although more keenly felt in the Everglades region and the Keys.

But in general, South Florida is a region defined not by any one, but many cultures: Southern, Creole, Cuban, Caribbean, and Central and South American, but also Jewish, Japanese, Vietnamese, Nigerian, Thai, Chinese, Spanish and more. The expression 'Jack of all trades, master of none' occasionally applies in these circumstances. Local restaurants that are dedicated to a particular style of cuisine are usually a better bet than places that jumble their influences. As an example: when in Miami, you'll note dozens of 'Thai-Japanese' restaurants. These two cuisines are pretty far apart in terms of their flavor profiles, and inevitably, we've found this attempt at Asian fusion to be disappointing. Dedicated Japanese or Thai restaurants, on the other hand, are another matter entirely.

It must also be said: South Florida in general, and Miami in particular, is obsessively trendy. If barnacles are the 'it' recipe in Manhattan, you better believe barnacle sorbet will feature on at least a dozen South Beach menus within a week. This attitude is a double-edged sword, because while you're in no danger of missing culinary trends in Miami, there's a chance you'll eat at a place where the aforementioned barnacles are prepared carelessly and sold at sky-high costs.

At the time of writing, the trend of the moment was nominally rustic farm-to-table cuisine. Some great restaurants are doing culinary wonders with the genre, but there are also a lot of ridiculous eateries where elaborately coiffed scenesters are convinced a prettily distressed hardwood floor equals dining in a mountain cabin. Asian and Latin fusion are perennially popular cooking trends in Miami.

This cynical attitude most often manifests in South Beach, but is increasingly noticeable in downtown Miami, Wynwood and Coral Gables. Tourists aren't as likely to hold a bad restaurant as accountable as locals, and the fact is, most of the folks going out in South Beach are tourists. With that said, there are some fantastic restaurants in South Beach, places that are not just on top of culinary trends but redefining them, and

**South Florida's Best Cuban**

Islas Canarias (p107)

El Cristo (p107)

Exquisito Restaurant (p107)

Versailles (p108)

El Siboney (p170)

similar restaurants downtown, in Wynwood and the Design District, and even in Key West.

Few places can boast Florida's sublime fresh bounty from land and sea, and menus playfully nick influences. Gourmets can genuflect before celebrity chefs, while gourmands hunt Florida's bizarre delicacies such as boiled peanuts, frog's legs, snake and gator. Strip malls can contain gastronomic gems, while five-star hotel restaurants can be total duds. Smell, taste, enjoy and indulge – our advice to you, and a fitting motto for Floridians and food.

# Bounty of the Sea

Florida has always fed itself from the sea, which lies within arm's reach from nearly every point. If it swims or crawls in the ocean, you can bet some enterprising local has shelled or scaled it, battered it, dropped it in a fryer and put it on a menu.

## SUNSHINE STATE FOOD FESTIVALS

Many of Florida's food festivals have the tumultuous air of county fairs, with carnival rides, music, parades, beauty pageants and any number of wacky, only-in-Florida happenings.

*Food Fest!* by Joan Steinbacher is the definitive guide; her companion website (www.foodfestguide.com) lists festivals for the coming three months.

**Key West Food & Wine Festival** (www.keywestfoodandwinefestival.com; Key West; three days, late January) A weekend-long party and celebration of the finest in Key West gastronomy.

**Everglades Seafood Festival** (www.evergladesseafoodfestival.com; Everglades City; three days, early February) Not just seafood, but gator, frogs' legs and snakes, oh my!

**South Beach Food & Wine Festival** (www.sobefest.org; Miami; four days, late February) This Food Network–sponsored party is one of the largest food festivals in the country.

**Swamp Cabbage Festival** (www.swampcabbagefestival.org; La Belle; three days, late February) Armadillo races and crowning of the Miss Swamp Cabbage Queen.

**Carnaval Miami** (www.carnaval-miami.org; Miami; fortnight, early March) Negotiate drag queens and in-line skaters to reach the Cuban Calle Ocho food booths.

**Grant Seafood Festival** (www.grantseafoodfestival.com; Grant; weekend, early March) This small Space Coast town throws one of Florida's biggest seafood parties.

**Florida Strawberry Festival** (www.flstrawberryfestival.com; Plant City; 11 days, early March) Since 1930, over half a million folks come annually to pluck, eat and honor the mighty berry.

**Island Fest** (www.islamoradachamber.com; Islamorada; early April) Essentially a county fair for all things Keys.

**Taste of Key West** (www.visitkeywestonline.com/events; Key West; mid-April) Dozens of local restaurants turn their kitchens into food carts along the Truman waterfront.

**Isle of Eight Flags Shrimp Festival** (www.shrimpfestival.com; Amelia Island; three days, early May) Avast, you scurvy dog! Pirates invade for shrimp and a juried art show.

**Palatka Blue Crab Festival** (www.bluecrabfestival.com; Palatka; four-day Memorial Day weekend, which is the weekend before last Monday in May) Hosts the state championship for chowder and gumbo. Yes, it's that good.

**Florida Seafood Festival** (www.floridaseafoodfestival.com; Apalachicola; two days, early November) Stand way, way back at the signature oyster shucking and eating contests.

**Ribfest** (www.ribfest.org; St Petersburg; three days, mid-November) Three words: ribs, rock, Harleys.

Grouper is far and away the most popular fish. Grouper sandwiches are to Florida what the cheese-steak is to Philadelphia or pizza to Manhattan – a defining, iconic dish, and the standard by which many places are measured. Hunting the perfect grilled or fried grouper sandwich is an obsessive Floridian quest, as is finding the creamiest bowl of chowder (Sustain, in Midtown Miami, does excellent versions of both).

Of course, a huge range of other fish are offered. Other popular species include snapper (with dozens of varieties), mahimahi and catfish.

Florida really shines when it comes to crustaceans: try pink shrimp and rock shrimp, and don't miss soft-shell blue crab – Florida is the only place with blue-crab hatcheries, making them available fresh year-round. Winter (October to April) is the season for Florida spiny lobster and stone crab (out of season, both will be frozen). Florida lobster is all tail, without the large claws of its Maine cousin, and stone crab is heavenly sweet, served steamed with butter or the ubiquitous mustard sauce.

Finally, the Keys popularized conch (a giant sea snail); now fished out, most conch is from the Bahamas. For information on sustainable seafood, check out www.montereybayaquarium.org/cr/seafoodwatch.aspx.

## Cuban & Latin American Cuisine

Cuban food, once considered 'exotic,' is itself a mix of Caribbean, African and Latin American influences, and in Tampa and Miami it's a staple of everyday life. Sidle up to a Cuban *lonchería* (snack bar) and order a *pan cubano* (a buttered, grilled baguette stuffed with ham, roast pork, cheese, mustard and pickles).

Integral to many Cuban dishes are *mojo* (a garlicky vinaigrette, sprinkled on sandwiches), *adobo* (a meat marinade of garlic, salt, cumin, oregano and sour orange juice) and *sofrito* (a stew-starter mix of garlic, onion and chili peppers). Main-course meats are typically accompanied by rice and beans, and fried plantains.

With its large number of Central and Latin American immigrants, the Miami area offers plenty of authentic ethnic eateries. Seek out Haitian *griots* (marinated fried pork), Jamaican jerk chicken, Brazilian barbecue, Central American *gallo pinto* (red beans and rice) and Nicaraguan *tres leches* ('three milks' cake).

In the morning, try a Cuban coffee, also known as *café cubano* or *cortadito*. This hot shot of liquid gold is essentially sweetened espresso, while *café con leche* is just *café au lait* with a different accent: equal parts coffee and hot milk.

Another Cuban treat is *guarapo,* or fresh-squeezed sugarcane juice. Cuban snack bars serve the greenish liquid straight or poured over crushed ice, and it's essential to an authentic mojito (rum, sugar, mint, lemon and club soda). It also sometimes finds its way into *batidos* (a milky, refreshing Latin American fruit smoothie).

In Miami, you can find classic Cuban brands that are no longer sold in Cuba itself such as Hatuey beer, La Llave coffee and Gilda crackers.

## Eating in Miami, 'Hood by 'Hood

The Miami eating experience varies by neighborhood.

### South Beach

Restaurants open and close with the frequency of celebrity-spottings, which is to say, a lot – sometimes eating here feels like opening the pages of a British tabloid, although to be fair, usually you're surrounded by other tourists. There is no shortage of food variety, price options and presentation, but the trend is toward ostentatiousness. Even the stripped-back places are pretentiously underdone, if you know what we mean. All those restaurants with loud hostesses fronting Ocean Dr get mixed traveler reviews, so be warned that the price of pedestrian-watching might be an expensive, mediocre meal.

FOOD & DRINK CUBAN & LATIN AMERICAN CUISINE

### Northern Miami Beach

There are three good clusters of eats here: Mid-Beach, particularly 41st St, with its Jewish delis, steakhouses and sushi bars; Normandy Isle, with its expat South Americans, Brazilians, Uruguayans and their penchant for rich cuisine; and far North Beach, around Sunny Isles, home to some eclectic little gems. In general, this is an area that excels in the cheap-to-midrange-eatery category.

### Downtown

Downtown's eating options run, like Downtown itself, between extremes: from high-end corporate power lunches in glass-and-steel hotels in Brickell to down-home Latin hole-in-the-walls. The latter characterizes the center of Downtown, where you can easily find a filling Latino meal for well under $10.

If you love farmers' markets, visit www.florida-agriculture.com and click on 'Info for Consumers' and 'Community Farmers Markets' to find a state-wide list.

### Wynwood, the Design District & Little Haiti

This area, collectively known as Midtown Miami, and nearby neighborhoods including Buena Vista and North Biscayne Boulevard, is where the best food in Miami is being served. It's as trendy as South Beach but far more reliant on local clientele. Eating out here is a joy, be it in a cute cafe, fine-dining restaurant or wood-fired pizzeria-cum-craft beer house.

### Little Havana

Cuban cuisine is only a small slice of Little Havana's pan-Latin palate; there are menus from all over *el Sud,* from Ecuador to El Salvador and Mexico to Mendoza, Argentina. And while locals say you have to go further afield than Calle Ocho for the best *comida latino* (Latin food) you'll rarely go wrong when you stroll into eateries in this part of town.

### Key Biscayne

For a tiny island, Biscayne has good options that will keep you from trekking all the way over the causeway back into the city.

### Coconut Grove

The Grove may look chain heavy, but it's actually a strong spot for healthy eats, while the pedestrian-friendly nature of the neighborhood makes for pleasant culinary strolling. At night the sidewalk cafes come alive, and the nearby University of Miami means both nightlife and eating out can be fun and affordable.

### Coral Gables

The Gables is a goldmine for foodies, with an ample supply of international, eclectic and high-end dining options. Many restaurants are clustered on or near 'Restaurant Row,' on Giralda Ave between Ponce de León Blvd and Le Jeune Rd.

---

#### FLORIBBEAN CUISINE

Okay, somebody worked hard to come up with 'Floribbean' – a term for Florida's tantalizing gourmet mélange of just-caught seafood, tropical fruits and eye-watering peppers, all dressed up with some combination of Nicaraguan, Salvadoran, Caribbean, Haitian, Cajun, Cuban and even Southern influences. Some call it 'fusion,' 'Nuevo Latino,' 'New World,' 'Nouvelle Floridian' or 'Palm Tree Cuisine,' and it could refer to anything from a ceviche of lime, conch, sweet peppers and scotch bonnets to grilled grouper with mango, *adobo* and fried plantains.

## SELF-CATERING

**Epicure Market** (☑305-672-1861; 1656 Alton Rd; dishes $7-15; ☺9am-9pm), a gourmet food shop just off Lincoln Rd in South Beach, has a beautiful selection of international cheeses and wines, fresh produce, baked goods and prepared dishes. Many of the more than 25 Publix supermarkets throughout Miami are quite upscale, and the **Whole Foods Market** (1020 Alton Rd; ☺8am-11pm) is the biggest health-food store around, with an excellent produce department, pretty good deli and so-so salad bar; its biggest draw is for vegetarians (not so well catered for by markets in these parts) or health nuts who are seeking a particular brand of soy milk or wheat-free pasta.

For the freshest picnic items around, hit one of several **farmers markets** (☑305-531-0038), which are held in various areas on different days, roughly 9am to 4pm. The one on Lincoln Rd on Sundays is perhaps best known, but you'll find others on Española Way (Sunday), Normandy Village Fountain at 71st St (Saturday), the Aventura Mall (Saturday and Sunday), Downtown on Flagler St at Miami Ave (8am until 2pm Saturday), Coconut Grove on Grand Ave at Margaret St (Saturday) and Coral Gables City Hall (Saturday).

# Southern Cooking

You are technically in the South down here, but much of South Florida is so south it's *sud* as opposed to Southern if you catch our drift. Basically, we're saying Miami is too international to be classified as the American South. And as such, Southern cooking basically skips Miami as a city. That said, in the Everglades and the Keys, the Southern influence is much more keenly felt.

Southern makes up in fat and pure tastiness what it may lack in refinement. Standard Southern fare is a main meat – such as fried chicken, catfish, barbecued ribs, chicken-fried steak or even chitlins (hog's intestines) – and three sides: perhaps some combination of hushpuppies (cornbread balls), cheese grits, cornbread, coleslaw, mashed potatoes, black-eyed peas, collard greens or buttery corn. End with pecan pie, and that's living.

In the Keys, Southern-style cooking melds with Caribbean gastronomy. In truth, there's a lot of room for overlap, as black slaves developed many of the same recipes in the US and the Caribbean. Plus, Southern and Caribbean cooking are both unapologetically rich and heavy, and the latter may apply to you too if you're not careful when you eat in the Keys.

Cracker cooking is Florida's rough-and-tumble variation on Southern cuisine, but with more reptiles and amphibians. And you'll find a good deal of Cajun and Creole as well, which mix in spicy gumbos and bisques from Louisiana's neighboring swamps. Southern Floridian cooking is epitomized by writer Marjorie Kinnan Rawlings' famous cookbook *Cross Creek Cookery*.

Ice tea is ubiquitous in the Everglades and the Keys, but watch out for 'sweet tea,' which is an almost entirely different Southern drink – tea so sugary your eyes will cross.

**Florida Cookbooks**

*Cross Creek Cookery by Marjorie Kinnan Rawlings*

*New World Cuisine by Allen Susser*

*Miami Spice: The New Florida Cuisine by Steve Raichlen*

*The Florida Cookbook: From Gulf Coast Gumbo to Key Lime Pie by Jeanne Voltz and Caroline Stuart*

*Florida Bounty by Eric and Sandra Jacobs*

# South Florida Specialties

While South Florida has an international palate, some dishes have been here long enough to constitute something like a local cuisine.

## Cuban Sandwich

The traditional Cuban sandwich is a thing of some beauty, and a possible genuine native Florida dish; that Cubans invented the thing is agreed upon, but where they did so, here or Tampa or Havana, is a subject of debate. Cuban bread is buttered or oiled and hit with mustard. Layer on thin

## STONE-CRAB CLAWS

Enormous stone-crab claws are a staple of Floridian seafood menus, but some may have concerns with the way they are harvested. The crabs are legal to harvest from October 15 through May 15, although fishermen must toss back any ovigerous (egg-laying) female crabs.

The male crabs have a different fate. Their claws are broken off, and the crab, now a limb down, is tossed back into the water. After roughly three molts (periods when a crab re-grows its shell), which usually take a year, the claw will have grown back, only for the process to repeat itself.

Defenders of the harvest say that the act of tossing the crabs back, even with one arm, makes for a more sustainable fishery considering the alternative is simply keeping the whole crab. But the Department of Fish and Wildlife estimates some 28% of crabs die from the amputation; that number climbs to 47% for a double amputation. Those casualty numbers can be significantly reduced if a fisherman knows how to make a clean cut of the limb.

pickles, ham, roast pork or salami, and Swiss cheese. Press the thing in a *plancha* (a smooth panino grill) and ta-da: yumminess on warm bread.

### Colombian Hot Dog

The Colombian *perro caliente* is a work of mad genius. Colombians have...a different take on hot dogs; toppings we've seen include quail eggs, plum sauce, potato chips, pineapple and 'pink sauce' (we didn't ask). These crazy creations may not be native to South Florida, but this is about the only place you'll find them in the US outside of a few neighborhoods in New York.

### Alligator

Alligator tastes like a cross between fish and pork. The meat comes from the tail, and is usually served as deep-fried nuggets, which overwhelms the delicate flavor and can make it chewy. Try it grilled. Alligator is healthier than chicken, with as much protein but half the fat, fewer calories and less cholesterol. Most alligator is legally harvested on farms and is often sold in grocery stores. Alligator farms have their critics, but it's worth noting said farms have no worse or better a reputation than most factory farms or slaughterhouses.

### Frogs' Legs

Those who know say the 'best' legs come from the Everglades; definitely ask, since you want to avoid imported ones from India, which are smaller and disparaged as 'flavorless'.

**South Florida Food Blogs**

Jan Norris (www. jannorris.com)

Short Order (http://blogs. miaminewtimes. com/shortorder)

Meatless Miami (www.meatless miami.com)

### Stone Crabs

The first recycled crustacean: only one claw is taken from a stone crab – the rest is tossed back in the sea (the claw regrows in 12 to 18 months, and crabs plucked again are called 'retreads'). The claws are so perishable that they're always cooked before selling. October through April is less a 'season' than a stone-crab frenzy. Joe Weiss of Miami Beach is credited with starting it all. However, some have concerns with this practice. See the box text above.

### Key Lime Pie

Key limes are yellow, and that's the color of an authentic Key lime pie, which is a custard of Key lime juice, sweetened condensed milk and egg yolks in a cracker crust, then topped with meringue. Avoid any slice that is green or stands ramrod straight. The combination of extra-tart Key lime with oversweet milk nicely captures the personality of Key West Conchs.

## Conch

Speaking of conchs, the shellfish Keys natives are named for (a 'conch' is a shellfish, while a capitalized 'Conch' is a Keys native) happen to be delicious, and are difficult to find outside of South Florida (in the US). Conch meat is pleasantly springy and usually prepared according to Caribbean recipes: most of the time it's either curried or 'cracked' (fried). Either way it is seriously tasty. Café Solé (p170), in Key West, is famous for its conch carpaccio, oft-imitated but yet to be improved upon.

## Arepas

The greatness of a city can be measured by many yardsticks. The arts. Civic involvement. Infrastructure. What you eat when you're plowed at 3am. In Miami, the answer is often enough arepas, delicious South American corn cakes that can be stuffed with any manner of deliciousness; generally, you can't go wrong with cheese.

# From Farm (& Grove) to Table

Florida has worked long and hard to become an agricultural powerhouse, and has long been famous for its citrus. The state is the nation's largest producer of oranges, grapefruits, tangerines and limes, not to mention mangoes and sugarcane. Scads of bananas, strawberries, coconuts, avocados (once called 'alligator pears'), and the gamut of tropical fruits and vegetables are also grown in Florida. Homestead is a major agricultural region, with citrus groves and fields of crops extending all the way to the edge of the Everglades.

However, only relatively recently – with the advent of the USA's locavore, farm-to-table movement – has Florida started featuring vegetables in its cooking and promoting its freshness on the plate. Florida's regional highlights – its Southern and Latin American cuisines – do not usually emphasize greens or vegetarianism. But today, most restaurants with upscale or gourmet pretensions promote the local sources of their produce and offer appealing choices for vegetarians.

Inside Miami you'll find a delightful variety of vegetarian options, including a few vegan-friendly places. Funnily enough, folks here choose vegetarianism for reasons both ethical and vain; in the latter case, you'll find a lot of SUV-driving fitness nuts who don't give a fig for being green, but are obsessed with looking good. Outside Miami, dedicated vegetarian restaurants are few, and in many Keys and Everglades restaurants vegetarians can be forced to choose between iceberg-lettuce salads and pastas.

One indigenous local delicacy is heart of palm, or 'swamp cabbage,' which has a delicate, sweet crunch. The heart of the sabal palm, Florida's state tree, it was a mainstay for Florida pioneers. Try it if you can find it served fresh (don't bother if it's canned; it's not from Florida).

# Libations

Be it a lime stuffed into a Corona on a dock in the Keys, or rum served in countless permutations, South Florida really likes a drink. Or 10. There's a phrase you'll hear in the Keys that describes the islands as 'Drinking towns with a fishing problem', which more or less nails it.

Miami loves its booze too, but as with food, the focus is often on whatever happens to be the trendy drink of the moment (this rule, admittedly, does not apply to Miami's many excellent dives and neighborhood joints). And as with food, this trend-consciousness has its good and bad sides. During our research, unique cocktails created by professional 'mixologists' were all the drinking rage. You could find some incredible concoctions out there too – Blue Collar and Bonding, we're looking in your

*Edible Communities (www.edible communities. com) is a regional magazine series (print and online) that celebrates and supports local, sustainable farming, culinary artisans and seasonal produce. It publishes editions for Orlando and South Florida.*

**Vegging Out: Best Vegetarian in South Florida**

*Honey Tree (p106)*

*Choices (p104)*

*Last Carrot (p108)*

direction. But we also had far too many poorly mixed drinks that cost a rich man's price tag served in the umpteenth variation of a 'hip' Miami Beach bar.

Funnily enough, Miami's obsession with mixology represents a bit of a cocktail renaissance down here. Cuban bartenders became celebrities in the 1920s for what they did with all that sugarcane and citrus: the two classics are the *Cuba libre* (rum, lime and cola) and the mojito, traditionally served with *chicharrónes* (deep-fried pork rinds).

The beer market in Miami has definitely improved over the past few years. A demand for quality brew means you can find a gallery of international beers at some bars; on the other hand, you can go from being very international to totally local and trying a brew pub. Miami is known for its celebrity nightlife scene, but one of the first famous drinkers here was down in Key West. Old Ernest Hemingway, it was said, favored piña coladas, lots of them. In the same neighborhood, Jimmy Buffett memorialized the margarita – so that now every sweaty beach bar along the peninsula claims to make the 'best'. Welcome, good friends, to Margaritaville.

Coinciding with modern refrigeration, frozen concentrated orange juice was invented in Florida in 1946: this popularized orange juice as a year-round drink and created a generation of 'orange millionaires'.

# Outdoor Activities

**South Florida has neither elevation or topography, but it does have a gentle, user-friendly prettiness, and water. And not just bodies of water (ocean, bays, rivers, marsh, swamp) but water existing in countless permutations and evolutions thanks to its complicated relationship with the land: flooded prairies, blackwater cypress domes, mangrove coastlines, squidgy mudflats, 10,000 Islands and beach, beach, beach. Getting the most out of the outdoors here means navigating the land, the water, and the delicate balance they exist in.**

## Bikes, Boats & Beaches

Likely as not you came here for the beach. Good for you! There's a lot to do on that beach, and perhaps more pertinently, off of it: fishing, swimming, boating, snorkeling, diving – and several different types of boarding. Why not get under the water while you're at it? You will find the largest coral reef system in North America in Key Largo, and just north of there is the nation's only national park dedicated to underwater exploration.

South Florida can give the Netherlands a run for its money in the race to the bottom of the topographic map and, as such, should be traversed by ideal means for exploring areas that are either at or below sea level: via bicycle, or boat or scuba gear (ie really below sea level).

## Get in a Hammock

All across South Florida, you'll run into displays and educational signage that rambles on about the local hammocks. You may read these and think, 'Jeez, people in Florida are worryingly into relaxing. Every one of their outdoor trailheads is rife with information on deck furniture.'

While Floridians do love their hammocks, we (and all of those signs) are referring to another kind of hammock. In the southeastern United States, hammock is a term for a copse or grove of hardwood trees. What makes a hammock a hammock? In this part of the world, it comes down to elevation. Hammocks grow in wetland areas that are too sodden to support them. A few extra inches of elevation gives the trees the dryness they need to grow larger and more densely; the Pineland Trail in Everglades National Park is an excellent example of a coniferous hammock. Hammocks in the Everglades typically have a distinctive teardrop shape, formed by the flow of water around the tree 'islands.'

While there are many versions of hammocks through the American southeast, the one you will most likely encounter in South Florida is the tropical hardwood hammock. Even within this category, there are numerous subdivisions, including rockland hammocks (Big Cypress National Preserve), tree island hammocks in the Everglades and coastal berm hammocks in the Florida Keys. Also in the Keys: shell mound hammocks, which grew on top of the midden shell heaps left behind by the indigenous Calusa and Tequesta Indians. The Crane Point Museum in Marathon is an excellent introduction to the many variations of hammock in South Florida in general, and the Keys in particular.

### Wildlife-Watching Resources

Florida Fish & Wildlife Conservation Commission (http://myfwc .com)

Audubon of Florida (www.audubonof-florida.org)

Great Florida Birding Trail (http:// floridabirding trail.com)

Florida Wildlife Viewing (www. floridawildlife viewing.com)

Hammocks are particularly susceptible to fire. During the long dry season, it is not unheard of to hear about (and smell) small forest fires in the Miami area down to Homestead. But the greatest threat to hammocks is development. This flora ecosystem is rather unique to the USA, but arguments for trees often don't hold up when placed next to arguments for hotels, condo communities, and the goods and services that accompany them.

# Trails & Tents

Boardwalk paths run by still-water swamps, noodle-thin tracks lace into boonies studded with lakes and rivers, and mangrove walkways encircle white beaches. And the whole while, there are tents, cabins and pavilions for sleeping under the stars. Lace up your boots (or don some sandals; there are some very gentle trails here) and roll up your canvas.

**Great Hiking & Camping Guides**

*30 Eco-Trips in Florida (2005), Holly Ambrose*

*A Hiker's Guide to the Sunshine State (2005), Sandra Friend*

*The Best in Tent Camping: Florida (2010), John Malloy*

## Trails

One thing Florida hikers never have to worry about is elevation gain (OK, there are some artificial slopes and hills built into certain trails, if we're going to be pedantic). But if topography is easy, the weather more than balances the negative end of the trekking scales, especially in the dry season. From November through March rain, temperature, humidity and mosquitoes decrease to tolerable levels. In summer (June to September), make sure to hike first thing in the morning, or at least before noon, to avoid the midday heat and almost daily afternoon thundershowers.

South Florida swamps tend to favor 1- to 2-mile boardwalk trails; these are excellent for even out-of-shape walkers, and almost always wheelchair accessible. You'll also find lovely short trails in many state parks. The best trails in South Florida can be found in Everglades National Park and surrounds.

### Miami

It's the rare traveler who comes to Miami for the trekking. Still, there are a few nice ways of getting out into nature while you're in the Magic City. Life can't be all Latin American cuisine, flash condos and sweet nightlife. Most of Miami's green spaces can be found either in far north Miami and Miami Beach, on the island of Key Biscayne, which has large protected areas, and sprinkled amidst the miles of tract suburbia that stretch to the south of the city.

Oleta River State Park (p61) is Florida's largest urban park, and home to a decent number of trails; the same can be said of nearby Arch Creek Park (p61), with family-friendly nature trails. These North Miami parks are a nice example of the subtropical forest and stream environment that once existed across interior South Florida.

Drive over the Ricenbacker Causeway to Key Biscayne, and you'll find sandy trails leading past beaches and mangroves in Bill Baggs Cape Florida State Park (p71). Nature trails also abound in a lovely coastal ecosystem

## WILDERNESS WAY

→ When hiking, stay on the trail and pick up your trash.

→ Never pick wildflowers, especially orchids.

→ Never chase or feed wild dolphins or manatees; admire but don't touch.

→ Never feed alligators; they bite.

→ On beaches, never approach nesting sea turtles or hatchling runs. Adhere to nighttime lights-out policies when posted (usually May to October).

→ When snorkeling or diving, never touch coral reefs.

## TREAD LIGHTLY, EXPLORE SAFELY

It goes without saying that any wilderness, even a swamp, is a fragile place. Whether hiking, biking, paddling, or snorkeling, always practice 'Leave No Trace' ethics (see www.lnt.org for comprehensive advice). In short, this boils down to staying on the trail, cleaning up your own mess, and observing nature rather than plucking or feeding it.

As you enjoy Florida's natural bounty, take care of yourself, too. In particular, carry lots of water, up to a gallon per person per day, and always be prepared for rain. Line backpacks with plastic bags, and carry rain gear and extra clothes for when (not if) you get soaked. Reid Tillery's *Surviving the Wilds of Florida* will help you do just that, while Tillery's website **Florida Adventuring** (www.floridaadventuring.com) covers backcountry essentials.

at nearby Crandon Park (p70). These Key Biscayne parks give visitors a glimpse into the shrub and low-lying hammock ecosystems common to the offshore islands that ring the southern portion of the Florida peninsula.

If you just need a good walk outdoors, we'd recommend heading to the Fairchild Tropical Garden (p80). There are not many hikes, per se, but the park is so large you'll get a good walk traversing its length and breadth, and you may learn a thing or three about tropical flora while you're out there.

### The Everglades

The Everglades may largely consist of wetlands, or prairie that is liable to become waterlogged during the wet season, but it's still a magical place to walk as long as you follow the right trails. In some areas, like the trails near the southernmost **Flamingo** portion of the park (☎239-695-3101; ☺store 7am-5:30pm Mon-Fri, from 6am Sat & Sun), you'll be confronted with sandy, scrubby trails that traverse stretches of dried out mud flats and run by the lonely, windswept coast. In other areas, the vast horizons of the Everglades prairie, especially when contrasted with scattered pine hammock and cypress domes, are as humbling as any mountain range.

The Florida National Scenic Trail (p132) is one of America's 11 national scenic trails and takes in much of the geography of the Glades. The trail enters South Florida north from the swamps of Big Cypress National Preserve, and you can feasibly trek from here to Lake Okeechobee. Just expect a few mosquitoes here and there, a description we'll lovingly admit is the understatement of the year.

The Royal Palm Visitor Center (p137) and Fakahatchee Strand Preserve (p135) are great spots for more leisurely walks. These areas are both overlaid with long boardwalks that extend deep into the heart of genuine blackwater swamps and alligator wallows. On either of these walks, you'll come face to face with some local wildlife, usually of the avian, reptilian and amphibian kind. The same can be said for the asphalt path that runs through Shark Valley (p128), which also offers a tram tour.

### The Keys

Hikes in the Keys are more like short walks along nature trails that provide insight into the unique ecosystem that has developed amidst these mangrove islands. These trails are never very physically demanding, and given the plethora of teaching displays that tend to accompany them, they are usually fun (or at least, educational) if you have kids in tow. Our one caveat is that it can, of course, get pretty hot on the islands. Some of our favorite nature walks in the Keys include:

**John Pennekamp Coral Reef State Park** (p147) While this park is primarily known for its water activities, there are some small, friendly trails here for when you're finished diving.

**Windley Key Fossil Reef Geological State Park** (p151) Part of this Key has been carved out, which gives you a glimpse into the complex geology of the archipelago.
**Indian Key State Historic Site** (p150) Rotting buildings and groves of shady trees add an almost eerie touch to trekking across this island.
**Lignumvitae Key State Botanical Site** (p150) Genuine jungle has reclaimed this small, isolated island.
**Curry Hammock State Park** (p153) Narrow trails finger through the local mangrove and beachside biomes.
**Crane Point Museum** (p154) The interpretative trails attached to this museum are a great introductory lesson on the ecology of the Keys.
**Bahia Honda State Park** (p156) Probably the best park in the Keys, filled with nature, beach and boardwalk trails.
**Dry Tortugas National Park** (p167) A small series of walks stretches around this old naval fort.

## Camping

For a comprehensive list of outdoor activities in South Florida, from cycling and snorkeling to horseback riding and hunting, plus links to local outdoors organizations, check out www.florida-outdoors.com.

When you're finished hiking, take time to camp under Florida's starry skies. Camping opportunities abound. You'll be close to nature, and this is a good way to save money on accommodations. If you want to hear the heartbeat of wild Florida, nothing beats sleeping in the Everglades in a *chickee* (wooden platform above the waterline).

### Miami

Miami is not exactly a powerhouse destination for camping. Still, two options – Oleta River State Park (p61) and Bill Baggs Cape Florida State Park (p71) – are available, if you want cheap(ish) outdoor accommodation.

### The Everglades & Around

The National Park Service manages both primitive and developed campsites and can help travelers who want to pitch in the backcountry. 'Primitive' sites lack running water and electricity, while developed sites will at least possess running water and sometimes have power hookups.

Our favorite camping option in the area is finding *chickees* and isolated beaches and mangrove strands on the 10,000 Islands (p132). When you're out here amidst the stars, dolphins, birdlife, the breeze and little else, it's backcountry bliss. Off-shore islands in Biscayne National Park offer a similar experience to camping in the 10,000 Islands.

If you're into socializing with other campers and budget travelers, and aren't too interested in nights alone in the wilderness, the backyard of the Everglades International Hostel (p137) is a surreal, artsy garden, and consequently a lovely spot to pitch a tent.

### The Keys

John Pennekamp Coral Reef State Park (p147) and Bahia Honda State Park (p158) both offer excellent campsites with a good mix of hookup sites and tent areas, but these parks are very popular, so reserve in advance. If you really want to feel like you're sleeping at the end of the earth, reserve a spot at Dry Tortugas National Park (p167). It's self-service camping, although you can often barter with local fishermen for fresh fish and lobster.

For a complete listing of campgrounds operated by Miami-Dade County, see www.miamidade.gov/parks/facility-find_campground.asp.

# Canoeing & Kayaking

To really experience South Florida's swamps and rivers, its estuaries and inlets, its lagoons and barrier islands, you need watercraft, preferably the kind you paddle. The intimate quiet of dipping a paddle among mangroves – startling alligators and ibis – stirs wonder in the soul. It's not only the Everglades that are great for paddling. Don't forget the coasts. There are some choice options for coastal kayaking and canoeing in Miami and around.

As with hiking, the winter 'dry' season is best for paddling. If it's summer, canoe near cool freshwater springs and swimming beaches, 'cause you'll be dreaming about them.

## Miami

There are many waterways in the Magic City; the trick is being able to find them and then being able to find your way *on* them. We should stress that while it is easy to get into the water in Miami, a guide is crucial for getting out of it; there are strong currents in the local inlets and channels.

You'll find open waters to paddle around and mangrove tunnels to paddle through in Oleta River State Park, which sits next to the Haulover inlet. The other hot spot for kayaking and canoeing is Key Biscayne. There's a good boat launch and seawall at Bill Baggs Cape Florida State Park that fronts No Name Harbor, while offshore paddling is a popular day-tripping task at Crandon Park.

## The Everglades

You'll likely tell your grandchildren about kayaking in Everglades National Park. At times, you'll feel as if there was nothing in the world but the two mirror-flat reflections of water and sky; at other moments, that soaring sense of space is compressed into claustrophobic, capillary-esque mangrove tunnels courtesy of Hell's Bay – which, by the way, is one of the most beautiful parts of the park. Don't pass it up.

If you want a true ultimate adventure, consider boating the 99-mile long wilderness waterway along and amid the margins of the 10,000 Islands.

## The Keys

Paddling is popular in the Keys, where the water is more teal than the sky and the sun is almost always bright overhead. On Islamorada, Anne's Beach offers offshore paddling near clumps of mangrove forest, while at John Pennekamp Coral Reef State Park (p147) you can boat over the continent's largest coral-reef formations.

Still, the ultimate in Keys kayaking and canoeing is Indian Key Historic State Park and Lignumvitae Key Botanical State Park. Both sites are only boat accessible. They're not too difficult to paddle out to, but this added layer of inaccessibility, plus the combination of wilderness and the rotted ruins on Indian Key makes a trip out here pretty magical.

# Diving & Snorkeling

South Florida has, hands down, the best reef and wreck diving in the continental USA, and the snorkeling is just as magical. At times, the clarity of the water is disconcerting, as if you were floating on air; every creature and rainbow school of fish all the way to the bottom feels just out of reach, so that, as William Bartram once wrote, 'the trout swims by the very nose of the alligator and laughs in his face'. North America's largest coral-reef system is at your fingertips and wreck diving in Florida is equally epic.

How epic? Biscayne National Park (p140) has developed a wreck-centric maritime trail. Other attractions include Dry Tortugas National Park (p167), which was named for its abundant sea turtles, the fantastic Florida Keys History of Diving Museum (p151) in Islamorada, which is pretty awesome whether you dive or not, and of course, John Pennekamp Coral Reef State Park (p147), which offers the best diving in the lower 48 states. Barring Biscayne, all the aforementioned sites can be found in the Keys.

A great all-in-one paddling guide – with everything from the state's best water trails to nitty-gritty advice about weather, equipment and supplies – is *A Paddler's Guide to the Sunshine State* (2001) by Sandy Huff.

# Cycling

Florida is generally too flat for mountain biking (there are exceptions), but there are plenty of off-road opportunities, along with hundreds of miles of paved trails for those who prefer to keep their ride clean. As with hiking, avoid cycling in summer, unless you like getting hot and sweaty.

Cruiser bikes and city bikes are great here. If you're Dutch, a classic *oma* bicycle would be perfect for Miami Beach and Key West. In fact, folks from the Netherlands will find, topographically at least, the cycling conditions here are close to that of their below-sea-level home; just throw in a *lot* more sunshine and a *lot* fewer bike lanes. Miami Beach operates a bike-share program and bicycles are easy to rent in Key West, so there's really no excuse not to get on two wheels. Our favorite cycling spots in South Florida follow.

In Miami, the Promenade, which fronts Ocean Drive, is an excellent ride for those who want to take in Miami Beach and get a little exercise in while they're at it. Unfortunately, the Promenade does not extend all the way up the beach. Be careful riding on Collins Avenue as it extends further north; that road is the only major artery running north-south, and people tend to speed on it. Oleta River State Park offers four miles of novice, three miles of paved and 10 miles of mountain-biking trail.

Cycling is a very popular means of seeing the Everglades; just make sure you wear bright clothing and measure your distances so you don't accidentally find yourself on a lonely park road after the sun sets (it wouldn't be dangerous, but it'd probably be pretty unnerving). An easy ride along Shark Valley's paved asphalt track takes in plenty of wildlife.

In the Keys, cycling is perhaps the most logical way of exploring Key West. Those seeking a challenging, rewarding ride should consider the Florida Keys Overseas Heritage Trail (p148), which mirrors the Keys Highway for more than 70 noncontiguous miles.

## GET ON BOARD

South Florida is no surfing hot spot; if you want to ride waves in this state, it's generally best to head north to at least Jupiter Beach. But surfing isn't the only means of using a board to access the water. Kiteboarding and wakeboarding are growing in popularity, and are accessible to first-timers looking to try something new.

The equipment for wake- and kiteboarding is the same: the wakeboard is a smaller version of a surfboard. In either activity you're pulled along the water; by a boat with a wakeboard and, if it wasn't already blessedly obvious, by a kite while kiteboarding. Either evolution allows you to achieve some serious speed and work some magnificent tricks, although beginners aren't going to be flipping triple mad-dog overhang bazooka-busters off the bat (we made that up). The flat, shallow waters around Key Biscayne are wake- and kiteboard central. (Biscayne, by the way, is also a good place to take up windsurfing.) Check out the following:

**Miami Kiteboarding** (☎305-345-9774; www.miamikiteboarding.com; Crandon Park, Key Biscayne) Offers a range of private lessons starting from $150 for one hour of one-on-one instruction. Couples get discounted rates.

**Gator Bait Wakeboard School** (☎305-282-5706; www.gatorbaitwakeboard.com; 3301 Rickenbacker Causeway, Key Biscayne) Half-/one-hour lessons run $90/180.

**Miami Wakeboard Cable Complex** (MWCC; ☎305-476-9253; www.miamiwakeboardcablecomplex.com; Amelia Earheart Park, 401 E 65th St, Hialeah) Offers lessons in cableboarding, where the rider is pulled along by an overhead cable system. That means no boat, less pollution and less noise. Half-/one-hour lessons are $80/140.

# Fishing

The world may contain seven seas, but there's only one Fishing Capital of the World: Florida. No, this isn't typically overwrought Floridian hype. Fishing here is the best the US offers, and for variety and abundance, nowhere else on the globe can claim an indisputable advantage. The peninsula's position offers an ideal placement between Atlantic Ocean sport fishing and the calmer waters and line casting of the Gulf. There is excellent fishing infrastructure in place across the state that caters to all skill levels, from total beginners to experienced anglers.

Still, water pollution has shrunk Florida's recreational fisheries, and the quality of the angling in the state will rise and fall based on Florida's environmental conditions.

The Keys are the best place for fishing in a state that is fantastic for fishing. In the islands, Bahia Honda and Old Seven Mile Bridge offer shore-fishing par excellence. Other good sites:

**Oleta River State Park** (p61) The shores of the park front the Intracoastal Waterway; plus, there's a popular local fishing pier.

**Bill Baggs Cape Florida State Park** (p71) Off-shore fishers here pull in some truly huge hauls.

**Matheson Hammock Park** (p81) Drop a line here or just have a walk around the lovely atoll.

As 'Papa' Hemingway would tell you, the real fishing is offshore, where majestic sailfish leap and thrash. That's part of the reason the man moved to Key West, after all. Bluefish, marlin and mahimahi (known locally as dolphin fish, although it is not, in any way, the marine mammal) are other popular deep-water fish. The best strategy is to walk the harbor, talking with captains, till you find one who speaks to your experience and interests. Don't be surprised if the cost of a charter-boat hire for a day runs into four digits, depending on the size of the boat. Smaller craft should yield smaller prices.

# Sailing

If you prefer the wind in your sails, Florida is your place. Miami is a sailing sweet spot, with plenty of marinas for renting or berthing your own boat – Key Biscayne is a particular gem, and marinas in swish Coconut Grove and Brickell cater to the sailing crowd. In Key West, sail on a schooner with real cannons, though tour operators are plentiful throughout the Keys.

# Golf

Fun fact: with over 1250 courses (and counting), Florida has the most golf courses of any state. Whether or not this is related to Florida's high number of wealthy retirees isn't known, but one thing is certain: if you want to tee up, you won't have to look far. By far your best golfing options are in Miami, specifically in Coral Gables, Miami Beach and Key Biscayne. For a comprehensive list of Florida courses, see Florida Golf (www.fgolf.com).

Florida mystery writer Randy Wayne White has created an angler's delight with the *Ultimate Tarpon Book* (2010), a celebration of Florida's legendary big-game fish, with 'contributions' from Hemingway, Teddy Roosevelt, Zane Grey and more.

OUTDOOR ACTIVITIES FISHING

If you're interested in agro-tourism, check out the Redland Trail (www.redlandtrail.com). This 'trail' (more of an itinerary) is a collection of some of the weirder roadside attractions, locally sourced dining and general quirkiness of the outdoors in southern Dade County – essentially anything from the entrance to Everglades National Park to South Miami.

# Environment

Naturalist Marjory Stoneman Douglas called Florida 'a long pointed spoon' that is as 'familiar as the map of North America itself'. On that map, the shapely Floridian peninsula represents one of the most unique, ecologically diverse regions in the world. A confluence of porous rock and subtropical climate gave rise to a watery world of uncommon abundance and lush beauty, but this unique ecosystem could be undone by human hands in the geological blink of an eye.

## The Land

The Everglades once stretched over some 11,000 sq miles, but today, the wetlands are less than half the size they were a century ago.

Florida is many things, but elevated it is not. This state is as flat as a pancake, or as Douglas says, like a spoon of freshwater resting delicately in a bowl of saltwater – a spongy brick of limestone hugged by the Atlantic Ocean and the Gulf of Mexico. The highest point, the Panhandle's Britton Hill, has to stretch to reach 350ft, which isn't half as tall as the buildings of downtown Miami. This makes Florida officially the nation's flattest state, despite being 22nd in total area with 58,560 sq miles.

However, more than 4000 of those square miles is water; lakes and springs pepper the map like bullet holes in a road sign. That shotgun-sized hole in the south is Lake Okeechobee, the second-largest freshwater lake in North America. Sounds impressive, but the bottom of the lake is only a few feet above sea level, and it's so shallow you can practically wade across.

Every year, Lake Okeechobee ever so gently floods the southern tip of the peninsula. Or it wants to; canals divert much of the flow to either irrigation fields or Florida's bracketing major bodies of water – the Gulf of Mexico and the Atlantic Ocean. But were the water to follow the natural lay of the land, it would flow down: from its center, the state of Florida inclines about 6in every 6 miles until finally, the peninsula can't keep its head above water anymore. What was an unelevated plane peters out into the 10,000 Islands and the Florida Keys, which end with a flourish in the Gulf of Mexico. Key West, the last in the chain, is the southernmost point in the continental United States.

Incidentally, when the waters of Okeechobee do flood the South Florida plain, they interact with the local grasslands and limestone to create a wilderness unlike any other: the Everglades. They also fill up the freshwater aquifers that are required to maintain human existence in the ever-urbanizing Miami area. Today, numerous plans, which seem to fall prey to many private-interest and public bureaucratic roadblocks, are discussed for restoring the original flow of water from Central to South Florida, an act that would revitalize the Glades and, to some degree, address the water supply needs of Greater Miami.

What really sets Florida apart, though, is that it occupies a subtropical transition zone between northern temperate and southern tropical climates. This is key to the coast's florid coral-reef system, the largest in North America, and the key to Florida's attention-getting collection of surreal swamps, botanical oddities and monstrous critters. The

Everglades gets the most press, and as a Unesco biosphere reserve, World Heritage Site and national park, this 'river of grass' deserves it.

But the Keys are a crucially important, vital and unique treasure as well. To explore these islands is to enter genuine jungle while still technically within the 48 contiguous US states (admittedly, as low as you can get in the 'Lower 48'). The teal and blue waterways that separate the Keys are as fascinating as the islands themselves; here the water gets so shallow, you can sometimes wade from Key to Key. Couple this shallow shelf with the rich sunlight of South Florida and you get one of the world's most productive aquatic biomes.

# Wildlife

Get outside Miami's concrete jungle and you'd be forgiven for thinking you'd entered a real one. Alligators prowl the swamps, the USA's only crocodiles nest in the Keys, birds that resemble pteranodons flap over it all, and underneath rolls that gentle giant, the manatee.

## Birds

Nearly 500 avian species have been documented in Florida, including some of the world's most magnificent migratory water birds: ibis, egrets, great blue herons, white pelicans and whooping cranes. This makes Florida the ultimate birder's paradise.

Nearly 350 species spend time in the Everglades, the prime birding spot in Florida. In fact, much of the initial attention to conservation that first popped up here was related to the illegal poaching of the Everglades' wading birds; the beautiful beasts were being killed so their plumage could decorate fashionable women's hats in the early 20th century.

Songbirds and raptors fill Florida skies, too. The state has over 1000 mated pairs of bald eagles, the most in the southern US, and peregrine falcons, who can dive up to 150mph, migrate through in spring and fall.

The Everglades aren't the only place to bird-watch around here. Completed in 2006, the Great Florida Birding Trail (http://floridabirdingtrail.com) runs 2000 miles across the entire state and includes nearly 500 bird-watching sites, including many South Florida stops outside the Glades. Other good spots for birding in the region:

⇒ Oleta River State Park (p61)

⇒ Arch Creek Park (p61)

⇒ Haulover Beach Park (p61)

⇒ Bill Baggs Cape Florida State Park (p71)

⇒ Crandon Park (p70)

⇒ Indian Key Historic State Park (p150)

⇒ Lignumvitae Key State Botanical Site (p150)

⇒ Curry Hammock State Park (p153)

⇒ Crane Point Museum (p154)

⇒ Bahia Honda State Park (p156)

We'd be remiss not to mention the Florida Keys Wild Bird Rehabilitation Center (p147) in the Upper Keys, where injured birds are nursed back to health by a lovely team of volunteers. Guests are welcome to walk the paths that meander past the hurt bird life.

## Land Mammals

Florida's most endangered mammal is the Florida panther. Before European contact, perhaps 1500 roamed the state. The first panther bounty ($5 a scalp) was passed in 1832, and over the next 130 years they were

ENVIRONMENT WILDLIFE

**Green Reads**

*The Swamp,* Michael Grunwald

.........................

*Losing It All to Sprawl,* Bill Belleville

.........................

*Zoo Story,* Thomas French

.........................

*Green Empire,* Kathryn Ziewitz & June Wiaz

.........................

*Manatee Insanity,* Craig Pittman

.........................

hunted relentlessly. Though hunting was stopped in 1958, it was too late for panthers to survive on their own. Without a captive breeding program, begun in 1991, the Florida panther would now be extinct and with only some 120 known to exist, they're not out of the swamp yet.

The biggest killers of the panthers are motor vehicles. Every year, a handful – sometimes more – of panthers are killed on the road; pay particular attention to speed limits posted in area including the Tamiami Trail, which cuts through Everglades National Park and the Big Cypress Preserve.

Easy to find, white-tailed deer are a common species that troubles landscaping. Endemic to the Keys are Key deer, a Honey-I-Shrunk-the-Ungulate subspecies: less than 3ft tall and lighter than a 10-year-old boy, they live mostly on Big Pine Key.

Although they are ostensibly native to the American West, the adaptable coyote has been spotted across Florida, appearing as far south as the Florida Keys.

Shy, timid, and not to be messed with if encountered, there are several hundred specimens of the Florida black bear in Everglades National Park and the Big Cypress Preserve.

Naturalist Doug Alderson helped create the Big Bend Paddling Trail, and in *Waters Less Traveled* (2005) he describes his adventures: dodging pygmy rattlesnakes, meeting Shitty Bill, discussing Kemp's ridley sea turtles and pondering manatee farts.

## Marine Mammals

Florida's coastal waters are home to 21 species of dolphins and whales. By far the most common is the bottlenose dolphin, which is highly social, extremely intelligent and frequently encountered around the entire peninsula. Bottlenose dolphins are the species most often seen in captivity.

Winter is also the season for manatees, who seek out Florida's warm-water springs and power-plant discharge canals beginning in November. These lovable, lumbering creatures are another iconic Florida species whose conservation both galvanizes and divides state residents.

## Reptiles & Amphibians

Boasting an estimated 184 species, Florida has the nation's largest collection of reptiles and amphibians, and unfortunately, it's growing. No,

### FLORIDA'S MANATEES

It's hard to believe Florida's West Indian manatees were ever mistaken for mermaids, but it's easy to see their attraction: these gentle, curious, colossal mammals are as sweetly lovable as 10ft, 1000lb teddy bears. Solitary and playful, they have been known to 'surf' waves, and every winter, from November to March, they migrate into the warmer waters of Florida's freshwater estuaries, rivers and springs. Like humans, manatees will die if trapped in 62°F water for 24 hours, and in winter Florida's eternally 72°F springs are balmy spas.

Florida residents for over 45 million years, these shy herbivores have absolutely no defenses except their size (they can reach 13ft and 3000lb), and they don't do much, spending most of each day resting and eating the equivalent of 10% of their body weight. Rarely moving faster than a languid saunter, manatees even reproduce slowly; females birth one calf every two to five years. The exception to their docility? Mating. Males are notorious for their aggressive sex drive.

Florida's manatees have been under some form of protection since 1893, and they were included in the first federal endangered species list in 1967. Manatees were once hunted for their meat, but today collisions with boats are a leading cause of manatee death, accounting for over 20% annually. Propeller scars are so ubiquitous among the living they are the chief identifying tool of scientists.

Population counts are notoriously difficult and unreliable. In 2013, a bloom of red tide algae in southwest Florida, as well as illnesses, caused the death of more than 800 manatees – a whopping 16% of the total population of these gentle giants. As of this research, there were at least 4800 manatees in the state.

## KEEPERS OF THE EVERGLADES

Anyone who has dipped a paddle among the saw grass and hardwood hammocks of Everglades National Park wouldn't quibble with the American alligator's Florida sobriquet, 'Keeper of the Everglades.' With snout, eyeballs, and pebbled back so still they hardly ripple the water's surface, alligators have watched over the Glades for more than 200 million years.

It's impossible to count Florida's wild alligators, but estimates are that 1.5 million lumber among the state's lakes, rivers and golf courses. No longer officially endangered, they remain protected because they resemble the still-endangered American crocodile. Alligator served in restaurants typically comes from licensed alligator farms, though since 1988, Florida has conducted an annual alligator harvest, open to nonresidents, that allows two alligators per person.

Alligators are alpha predators that keep the rest of the food chain in check, and their 'gator holes' become vital water cups in the dry season and during droughts, aiding the entire wetlands ecosystem. Alligators, which live for about 30 years, can grow up to 14ft long and weigh 1000lb.

A vocal courtship begins in April, and mating takes place in May and June. By late June, females begin laying nests of 30 to 45 eggs, which incubate for two months before hatching. On average, only four alligators per nest survive to adulthood.

Alligators hunt in water, often close to shore; typically, they run on land to flee, not to chase. In Florida, an estimated 15 to 20 nonfatal attacks on humans occur each year, and there have been 22 fatal attacks since 1948.

Some estimate an alligator's top short-distance land speed at 30mph, but it's a myth that you must zigzag to avoid them. The best advice is to run in a straight line as fast as your little legs can go.

we're not antireptile, but invasive scaly species are wreaking havoc with Florida's native, delicate ecosystem. Uninvited guests add to the total regularly, many establishing themselves after being released by pet owners. Some of the more dangerous, problematic and invasive species include Burmese pythons, black and green iguanas, and Nile monitor lizards.

The American alligator is Florida's poster species, and they are ubiquitous in Central and South Florida. They don't pose much of a threat to humans unless you do something irredeemably stupid, like feed or provoke them. With that said, you may want to keep small children and pets away from unfamiliar inland bodies of water.

South Florida is also home to the only North American population of American crocodile. Florida's crocs number around 1500; they prefer saltwater, and to distinguish them from gators, check their smile – a croc's snout is more tapered and its teeth stick out.

Turtles, frogs and snakes love Florida, and nothing is cuter than watching bright skinks, lizards and anoles skittering over porches and sidewalks. Cute doesn't always describe the state's 44 species of snakes – though Floridian promoters emphasize that only six species are poisonous, and only four of those are common. Feel better? Of the baddies, three are rattlesnakes (diamondback, pygmy, canebrake), plus copperheads, cottonmouths and coral snakes. The diamondback is the biggest (up to 7ft), most aggressive and most dangerous. But rest assured, while cottonmouths live in and around water, most Florida water snakes are not cottonmouths. Whew!

If you're not daunted by the prospect of playing with some of South Florida's scaliest citizens, head to the delightful Skunk Ape Research Headquarters (p132) in the Everglades. The zoo out back has to be one of the finest amateur reptile collections anywhere, and as a bonus, you

## POISSONS DE POISON

If we have learned anything about travel and the environment, one of the more obvious lessons is: if you find a dangerously poisonous fish in the tropics, don't release it in non-native waters.

Sadly, someone in Florida did not get this memo. To be fair, experts don't believe someone intentionally released the striped, spiny, venomous lionfish into Florida waters on purpose. The theory is some aquarium lionfish were swept into the water after Hurricane Andrew in 1992. The problem? Lionfish are eating machines with no natural predators, and they are disconcertingly adept at both breeding and poisoning native fish to death faster than you can say 'Finding Nemo'. In the two decades since they've invaded these waters, they've spread like a striped plague across the Atlantic and Caribbean.

Lionfish are detrimental for several reasons. Their environmental impact is, first and foremost, enormous; they can lay *30,000* eggs at a time and spawn as frequently as every four days, according to a 2010 *New York Times* article. That's a fairly huge break in the fragile Florida food chain. Also, their stings hurt – a lot. While rarely fatal, a lionfish sting is pretty painful, and while the fish are shy, there's so many floating about these days folks are bound to feel the wrath of their fins every now and then. With that said, the victims of stings are usually fisherfolk; the few Keys beaches are shallow and swimmers are rarely at risk of coming into contact with lionfish.

The response of the fishing-crazy inhabitants of the Keys to these stinging swimmers? Sting back. With spears, bait, line and tackle. The Florida Keys National Marine Sanctuary has been holding lionfish derbies since 2010, and the response from local fisherfolk has been enthusiastic; commercial fisherfolk, after all, stand to lose their livelihood if lionfish overwhelm the Keys. The spiny critters can be cooked (and taste pretty good – they've a light, delicate flavor that's not terribly fishy) and are increasingly popping up on Keys menus. So if you're down this way, push some culinary frontiers, have a lionfish fillet – and help the local environment out all at once.

may just spot the eponymous Skunk Ape, the American South's version of Bigfoot/Yeti (actual chances: slim to none).

### Sea Turtles

Most sea-turtle nesting in the continental US occurs in Florida. Predominantly three species create over 80,000 nests annually, mostly on southern Atlantic Coast beaches but extending to all Gulf Coast beaches. Most are loggerhead, followed by far fewer green and leatherback, and historically hawksbill and Kemp's ridley as well; all five species are endangered or threatened. The leatherback is the largest, attaining 10ft and 2000lb.

During the May-to-October nesting season, sea turtles deposit 80 to 120 eggs in each nest. The eggs incubate for about two months, and then the hatchlings emerge all at once and make for the ocean. Contrary to myth, hatchlings don't need the moon to find their way to the sea. However, they can become hopelessly confused by artificial lights and noisy human audiences. For the best, least-disruptive experience, join a sanctioned turtle watch; for a list, visit www.myfwc.com/seaturtle, then click on 'Educational Information' and 'Where to View Sea Turtles.'

The Keys contain their very own Turtle Hospital (p154), a sanctuary for sick and injured gentle shelled giants. They're keen on visitors, so if you're rolling through Marathon, drop by.

## Plants

The diversity of the peninsula's flora, including more than 4000 species of plants, is unmatched in the continental US. Florida, especially South Florida, contains the southern extent of temperate ecosystems and the northern extent of tropical ones, which blend and merge in a bewildering, fluid taxonomy of environments. Interestingly, most of the world at this latitude is a desert, which Florida definitely is not.

## Wetlands & Swamps

It takes special kinds of plants to thrive in the humid, waterlogged, sometimes salty marshes, sloughs, swales, seeps, basins, marl prairies and swamps of Florida. Much of the Everglades is dominated by vast expanses of saw grass, which is actually a sedge with fine toothlike edges that can reach 10ft high. South Florida is a symphony of sedges, grasses and rushes. These hardy water-tolerant species provide abundant seeds to feed birds and animals, protect fish in shallow water, and pad wetlands for birds and alligators.

The strangest plants are the submerged and immersed species that grow in, under and out of the water. Free-floating species include bladderwort and coontail, a species that lives, flowers and is pollinated entirely underwater. Florida's swamps are abundant with rooted plants with floating leaves, such as the pretty American lotus, water lilies and spatterdock (if you love names, you'll love Florida botany). Another common immersed plant, bur marigold, can paint whole prairies yellow.

A dramatic, beautiful tree in Florida's swamps is the bald cypress, which is the most flood-tolerant tree. It can grow 150ft tall, with buttressed, wide trunks and roots with 'knees' that poke above the drenched soil.

In Florida, even the plants bite: the Panhandle has the most species of carnivorous plants in the US, the result of its nutrient-poor sandy soil.

## Forests, Scrubs & Flatwoods

The forests of the mainland, such as they are, are mainly found in the Everglades, where small changes in elevation and substrate are the difference between prairie and massive 'domes' of bald cypress and towering pine trees. Cypress domes are a particular kind of swamp when a watery depression occurs in a pine flatwood.

Scrubs are found throughout Florida; they are typically old dunes with well-drained sandy soil. Scrubs often blend into sandy pine flatwoods, which typically have a sparse longleaf or slash-pine overstory, and an understory of grasses and/or saw palmetto. Saw palmetto is a vital Florida plant: its fruit is an important food for bears and deer (and a herbal medicine that's believed to help prevent cancer), it provides shelter for

### GHOST HUNTERS

Florida has more species of orchid than any other state in the US, and orchids are themselves the largest family of flowering plants in the world, with perhaps 25,000 species. When it comes to botanical fascination, orchids rate highly, and the Florida species that inspires the most intense devotion is the extremely rare ghost orchid.

This bizarre epiphytic flower has no leaves and usually only one bloom, which is of course deathly white with two long thin drooping petals that curl like a handlebar moustache. The ghost orchid is pollinated by the giant sphinx moth in the dead of night. This moth is the only insect with a proboscis long enough to reach down the ghost orchid's 5in-long nectar spur.

The exact locations of ghost orchids are usually kept secret for fear of poachers, who, as Susan Orlean's book *The Orchid Thief* made clear, are a real threat to their survival. But the flower's general whereabouts are common knowledge: South Florida's approximately 2000 ghost orchids are almost all in Big Cypress National Preserve and Fakahatchee Strand Preserve State Park. Of course, these parks are home to a great many other wild orchids, as is Everglades National Park.

To learn more, visit Florida's Native Orchids (www.flnativeorchids.com) and Ghost Orchid (www.ghostorchid.info).

panthers and snakes, and its flower is an important source of honey. It's named for its sharp saw-toothed leaf stems.

Formed by the interplay of tides, coral and mangroves, the Florida Keys contain the best (and in many cases, only) examples of tropical and subtropical hardwood 'hammock,' or forest, in the continental USA. The Crane Point Museum is an excellent starting point for learning about this extremely niche ecosystem.

### Mangroves & Coastal Dunes

Where not shaved smooth by sand, South Florida's coastline is often covered with a three-day stubble of mangroves. Mangroves are not a single species; the name refers to all tropical trees and shrubs that have adapted to loose wet soil, saltwater and periodic root submergence. Mangroves also develop 'live birth,' germinating their seeds while they're still attached to the parent tree. Of the more than 50 species of mangroves worldwide, only three predominate in Florida: red, black and white.

Mangroves play a vital role on the peninsula, and their destruction usually sets off a domino effect of ecological damage. Mangroves 'stabilize' coastal land, trapping sand, silt and sediment. As this builds up, new land is created, which ironically strangles the mangroves themselves. Mangroves mitigate the storm surge and damaging winds of hurricanes, and they anchor tidal and estuary communities, providing vital wildlife habitats.

Coastal dunes are typically home to grasses and shrubs, saw palmetto and occasionally pines and cabbage palm (or sabal palm, the Florida state tree). Sea oats, with large plumes that trap wind-blown sand, are important for stabilizing dunes, while coastal hammocks welcome the wiggly gumbo-limbo tree, whose red peeling bark has earned it the nickname of 'tourist tree.'

Audubon of Florida (www.audubonofflorida.org) is perhaps Florida's leading conservation organization. It has tons of birding and ecological information, and it publishes *Florida Naturalist* magazine.

## National, State & Regional Parks

About 26% of Florida's land lies in public hands, which breaks down to three national forests, 11 national parks, 28 national wildlife refuges (including the first, Pelican Island), and 160 state parks. Overall, attendance is up, with more than 20 million folks visiting state parks annually. Florida's state parks have twice been voted the nation's best.

Florida's parks are easy to explore. The Florida Fish & Wildlife Commission (http://myfwc.com) manages Florida's mostly undeveloped Wildlife Management Areas (WMA). The website is an excellent resource for wildlife-viewing, as well as boating, hunting, fishing and permits. For more info on public reserves, check out the following:

**Florida State Parks** (www.floridastateparks.org)
**National Forests, Florida** (www.fs.usda.gov/florida)
**National Park Service** (NPS; www.nps.gov)
**National Wildlife Refuges, Florida** (NWR; www.fws.gov/southeast/maps/fl.html)
**Recreation.Gov** (www.recreation.gov) National lands campground reservations.

Visit the Florida Native Plant Society (www.fnps.org), a nonprofit conservation organization, for updates on preservation issues and invasive species and for a nice overview of Florida's native plants and ecosystems.

## Environmental Issues

Florida's environmental problems are the inevitable result of its century-long love affair with land development, population growth and tourism, and addressing them is especially urgent given Florida's uniquely diverse natural world. These complex, intertwined environmental impacts include erosion of wetlands, depletion of the aquifer, rampant pollution (particularly of waters), invasive species, endangered species, and widespread habitat destruction. There is nary an acre of Florida that escapes concern.

## A KINDER, GENTLER WILDERNESS ENCOUNTER

While yesterday's glass-bottom boats and alligator wrestling have evolved into today's swamp-buggy rides and manatee encounters, the question remains: just because you *can* do something, does it mean you *should?* In Florida, everyone has an obligation to consider the best ways to experience nature without harming it in the process.

For most activities, there isn't a single right answer; specific effects are often debated. However, there *are* a few clear guidelines.

**Airboats and swamp buggies** While airboats have a much lighter 'footprint' than big-wheeled buggies, both are motorized (and loud) and have far larger impacts than canoes for exploring wetlands. As a rule, nonmotorized activities are the least damaging.

**Dolphin encounters** Captive dolphins are typically already acclimated to humans. However, when encountering wild dolphins in the ocean, federal law makes it illegal to feed, pursue, or touch them. Habituating any wild animal to humans can lead to the animal's death, since approaching humans often leads to conflicts and accidents (as with boats).

**Manatee swims** When swimming near manatees, a federally protected endangered species, look but don't touch. 'Passive observation' is the standard. Harassment is a rampant problem that may lead to stricter 'no touch' legislation.

**Feeding wild animals** In a word, don't. Animals such as deer and manatees may come to rely on human food (to their detriment), while feeding bears and alligators just encourages them to hunt you.

**Sea-turtle nesting sites** It's a federal crime to approach nesting sea turtles or hatchling runs. Most nesting beaches have warning signs and a nighttime 'lights out' policy. If you encounter turtles on the beach, keep your distance and no flash photos.

**Coral-reef etiquette** Never touch the coral reef. It's that simple. Coral polyps are living organisms. Touching or breaking coral creates openings for infection and disease.

Since the turn of the century, Florida has enacted several significant conservation efforts. In 2000, the state passed the Florida Forever Act (www.supportfloridaforever.org), a 10-year, $3-billion conservation program that in 2008 was renewed for another 10 years. It also passed the multibillion-dollar Comprehensive Everglades Restoration Plan (CERP; www.evergladesplan.org).

Signs of progress can be encouraging. For instance, phosphorous levels in the Everglades have been seriously reduced, and in 2010, the state completed a purchase of 300 sq miles of Lake Okeechobee sugarcane fields from US Sugar, intending to convert them back to swamp. Along with plans to bridge 6.5 miles of the Tamiami Trail, the lake may once again water the Glades, rather than sit as a stagnant pool of contaminated algae and bacteria.

The Florida chapter of the Nature Conservancy (www.nature.org) has been instrumental in the Florida Forever legislation. Check the web for updates and conservation issues.

Studies have found that half the state's lakes and waterways are too polluted for fishing. Though industrial pollution has been curtailed, pollution from residential development (sewage, fertilizer runoff) more than compensates. This is distressing Florida's freshwater springs, which can turn murky with algae. Plus, as the groundwater gets pumped out to slake homeowners' thirsts, the springs are shrinking and the drying limestone honeycomb underfoot sometimes collapses, causing sinkholes that swallow cars and homes. In 2014, 15 Florida cities made a 'Clean Water Declaration' and began a campaign of both preventing and cleaning water pollution.

Residential development continues almost unabated. The Miami–Fort Lauderdale–West Palm Beach corridor (the USA's sixth-largest urban area) is, as developers say, 'built out'. Every day, Miami and Homestead's urban (and in the case of Homestead, agricultural) footprint grows

ENVIRONMENT ENVIRONMENTAL ISSUES

**Nature
Guides**

*The Living Gulf
Coast, Charles
Sobczak*

*Priceless Florida,
Ellie Whitney, D
Bruce Means &
Anne Rudloe*

deeper into the west, on the edge of the Everglades. While conservation laws protect the national park itself, the run-off and by-product of such a huge urban area inevitably has an impact in the incredibly fragile Glades.

Then there's the looming disaster: rising seas due to global warming. Here, the low-lying Florida Keys are a 'canary in a coalmine' that's being watched worldwide for impacts. In another century, some quip, South Florida's coastline could be a modern-day Atlantis, with its most expensive real estate underwater.

On the subject of real estate, the Keys happen to be governed by a labyrinthine set of zoning regulations. Getting permission to build on the land that remains is an arduous process, although many Keys law firms are solely dedicated to navigating this paper trail; as such, the Keys are not immune to overdevelopment, but are also better protected than much of the rest of Florida.

# Art-Deco Architecture

For years now, south Miami Beach – also known as 'South Beach' for those who may have been in a cave – has been 'hot', in the shrieking, Paris Hilton–induced awe-of-celebrity sense of the word, and it owes this cachet to two words: art deco. It was deco that first made Miami Beach distinctive, and when the celebs find a new spot to act sexy, it will (hopefully) be deco that remains: the signature, sleek face of the American Riviera.

## Deco, Design & Dreams

The early-20th-century school of design was the aesthetic backbone of old South Beach, and the driving force of its 1980s resurrection. A sustained campaign to preserve the wonderful deco hotels of Miami Beach provided what tons of tourism brochures could never create: brand. Sun, sand, surf: a lot of cities can lay claim to them, but only Miami Beach blended them with this pastel architectural heritage.

The end of WWI in 1918 ushered in an era of increased interest in the romance and glamour of travel, which lasted well into the 1930s. There was a giddy fascination with speed and cars, ocean liners, trains and planes. Not coincidentally, the US postindustrial revolution, concerned with mass production, kicked into high gear. New materials such as aluminum, polished bronze and stainless steel were utilized in new and exciting ways. Americans began looking to the future, and they wanted to be on the cutting edge.

Meanwhile, in Europe, at a 1925 Paris design fair officially called the Exposition Internationale des Arts Décoratifs et Industriels Modernes (and eventually abbreviated to Arts Deco), decorative arts were highlighted, but the US had nothing to contribute. Europeans were experimenting with repeating patterns in Cubism and were influenced by ancient cultures (King Tut's tomb was discovered in 1921), and Americans had to play catch-up.

Back in the States, a mere year later, a devastating hurricane blew through Miami Beach, leaving few buildings standing. The wealthy folks who were living here before the hurricane chose to decamp. The second blow of a one-two punch for Miami's economy was delivered by the Great Depression. But in this dark time, opportunity soon came knocking. In Miami real estate, everything was up for grabs. The clean slate of the South Florida coastline was practically begging for experimentation.

Hotel rebuilding began in Miami Beach at the rate of about 100 per year during the 1930s. Many architects had 40 to 50 buildings in production at any one time until the inception of WWII. This overlapped with a surge in middle-class tourism between 1936 and 1941, when visitors started coming for a month at a time.

The post-Depression era was an optimistic time, with hopes and dreams pinned on scientific and technological revolutions. Reverence for machines took on almost spiritual dimensions, and found its aesthetic expression in both symbolic and functional ways.

What does all this have to do with architecture? Everything. The principles of efficiency and streamlining translated into mass-produced, modest buildings without superfluous ornamentation – at least in the Northeast USA.

The deco district is bordered by Dade Blvd to the north, 6th St to the south, the Atlantic Ocean to the east and Lenox Ave to the west. The 1-sq-mile district feels like a small village, albeit one with freaks, geeks and the gorgeous. Which is pretty cool.

# Romance, Relief & Rhythms

Miami Beach, a more romantic and glamorous resort, developed what came to be known as tropical deco architecture. It organically reflected the natural world around it. For example, glass architectural blocks let bright Florida light in but kept sweltering heat out. They also served a geometric or cubist aesthetic. Floral reliefs, popular during the art nouveau period, appeared here, too. Friezes on facades or etched into glass reflected native flora and fauna such as palm trees, pelicans and flamingos. Friezes also took their cues from the uniquely American jazz movement, harmonious and lyrical. Surrounded by water, Miami Beach deco also developed a rhythmic language, with scalloped waves and fountains.

With more than 400 registered historic landmarks, you can follow the Beach boom phases through the district: in the 1930s 5th St to Mid-Beach was developed. Head toward 27th St for the late '30s to early '40s; then north into the '50s, the era of resorts, hotels and condominiums.

## Creating a Miami Look

Whereas Northeast deco buildings had industrial, socialist overtones, the clean lines of Miami Beach architecture still made room for joyful, playful, hopeful characteristics. Forward thinking and dreaming about the future took hold. Space travel was explored through design: buildings began to loosely resemble rockets, and rooflines embodied fantasies about traveling the universe. Geometric and abstract zigzag (or ziggurat) patterns not only reflected Aztec and Egyptian cultures, they also symbolized lightning bolts of electricity. Sun rays, more imagery borrowed from an ancient culture, were employed as life-affirming elements to counter the dark days of the Depression.

Since all hotels were built on the same size lots, South Beach architects began distinguishing themselves from their next-door neighbors through decorative finials and parapets. Neon signage also helped individualize buildings. Miami Beach deco relied on 'stepped-back' facades that disrupted the harsh, flat light and contributed to the rhythmic feel. Cantilevered 'eyebrows' jutted out above windows to protect interiors from unrelenting sun. Canopy porches gave hotel patrons a cool place to sit. To reflect the heat, buildings were originally painted white, with animated accent colors highlighting smaller elements. It was only later, during the 1980s, that interior designer Leonard Horowitz decreed the pastel palette that became the standard.

With the effects of the Depression lingering, ornamentation was limited to the facades; interiors were stripped down. Labor was cheap and readily available.

Miami Beach needed a large number of rooms, most of which ended up being built small. With no expectation that they remain standing this long, most hotels were built with inexpensive concrete and mortar that had too much sand in it. Stucco exteriors prevailed, but locally quarried native keystone (an indigenous limestone) was also used. Except for the keystone, none of this would withstand the test of time with grace, which is one reason the district fell into such a state of disrepair and neglect. It's also why the district remains under a constant state of renovation.

Although art deco was inspired by stripped-down modernist aesthetics, it partly rebelled against utilitarianism with fantastically embellished bas-relief and frieze work, noticeable on the exterior of many South Beach hotels.

## Restoring the Deco District

South Beach's heart is its Art Deco Historic District, one of the largest in the USA on the National Register of Historic Places. In fact, the area's rejuvenation and rebirth as a major tourist destination results directly from its protection as a historic place in 1979. The National Register designation prevents developers from razing significant portions of what was, in the 1980s, a crime-ridden collection of crumbling eyesores populated primarily by criminals and society's dispossessed – the elderly, the mentally ill and the destitute. It's a far cry from that now. Today, hotel and apartment facades are decidedly colorful, with pastel architectural details. Depending on your perspective, the bright buildings catapult you back to the Roaring Twenties or on a wacky tour of American kitsch.

The National Register listing was fought for and pushed through by the Miami Design Preservation League (MDPL), founded by Barbara

Baer Capitman in 1976. She was appalled when she heard of plans by the city of Miami to bulldoze several historic buildings in what is now the Omni Center. And she acted, forcefully.

MDPL cofounder Leonard Horowitz played a pivotal role in putting South Beach back on the map, painting the then-drab deco buildings in shocking pink, lavender and turquoise. When his restoration of Friedman's Pharmacy made the cover of *Progressive Architecture* in 1982, the would-be Hollywood producers of *Miami Vice* saw something they liked, and the rest is history.

One of the best things about the 1000 or so buildings in the deco district is their scale: most are no taller than the palm trees. And while the architecture is by no means uniform – you'll see Streamline Moderne, Mediterranean revival and tropical art-deco designs – it's all quite harmonious.

Interestingly, the value of these Miami Beach deco buildings is based more on the sheer number of structures with protected status from the National Register of Historic Places. Individually, the inexpensively constructed houses would be worth far less.

Miami Beach cross streets are determined by building number. Two zeroes after the first number means the building is at the base of the block. So 700 Ocean Dr is at 7th St and Ocean, while 1420 Ocean Dr is at 14th St & Ocean.

## Why We Love Deco Design

So what, you may ask, is the big deal about art deco? The term certainly gets thrown around enough in Miami. Given the way this architectural style is whispered about by hotel marketing types, you'd be forgiven for thinking art deco was the pièce de résistance, 'Well, the resort has a lovely deco facade'; 'Our boutique properties incorporate deco porches'; 'Did you notice the deco columns in our lounge?' And so on.

But to be fair, deco has been a sort of renaissance for Miami Beach. It was art deco that made these buildings unique, that caught the eye of Hollywood, which saw something romantically American in the optimism and innovation of a style that blends cubism, futurism, modernism and, most of all, a sense of movement. Beyond that was a nod to, and sometimes even reverence for, the elaborate embellishment of Old World decor. In art deco, we see the link between the lavish design aesthetic of the 19th century and the stripped-down efficiency of the 20th. Unlike a skyscraper, a deco hotel is modern yet accessible, even friendly, with its frescoed walls and shady window eyebrows.

But what's truly great about deco Miami is the example it sets. The Art Deco Historic District of South Beach, a hot tourist destination, is a reminder to city leaders that preserving historic neighborhoods is not just a matter of slavish loyalty to aesthetics, but sometimes the economically practical and innovative way forward. In a city built on fast real estate, it's a bit delicious that the heart of the sexiest neighborhood is the child of preservation and smart planning.

Italians were the first hired to create terrazzo floors, popular in Florida. They'd pour various colors of terrazzo – crushed stones, shells, marble chips or granite, mixed with concrete – into a patterned grid and then polish it. This remarkable marriage of form and function also cools the feet.

## Post-Deco, Miami Modern & Beyond

The tale of Miami architecture is defined by more than deco. As in all cities, Miami's architecture reflects the tastes and attitudes of its inhabitants, who tend to adhere to the aesthetic philosophy espoused by Miami Beach's

### CLASSIC TROPICAL DECO

There are some unifying themes to classical deco structures that are easy enough to spot with a discerning eye. Perhaps most noticeable is a sense of streamlined movement, exemplified by rounded walls, racing stripe details and 'eyebrows,' rounded buttresses that provided shade and visual eye candy to passersby. Porthole windows evoke cruise liners, while lamps and other homewares represent long-past idealizations of a space-age future. Call it 'ray-gun chic'. An intimate (some say cramped) sense of space is offset by terrazzo flooring, often imprinted with the fossils of sea animals, and open verandas, which would naturally cool inhabitants in pre-air-conditioning days. The idea was to venerate technology while seizing on the natural features of the landscape (sea breezes and golden sunlight), adding a dash of organic aesthetic to the overall structure.

## THE CONCH CASTLES OF KEY WEST

Miami this, Miami that; yes, the flashy overstatement of the Magic City's architecture sure is beautiful. But what about Key West? Plenty of gorgeous historical buildings are packed into an easily walkable space and happen to be located on one of the prettiest islands in America. What are we waiting for?

Traditional Keys homes are known as 'Conch houses' for the conch shell that was used as a building material to supplement the traditionally low amounts of stone and wood; today the nickname also references Keys natives, known as Conchs. Conch houses are perhaps the finest example of Caribbean colonial architecture in the US outside New Orleans. They're elegant, recognizably European homes, and while no two dwellings are identical, there are some commonalities across the board. Shuttered windows, wrap-around verandas, sloped roofs and structures built on raised piers – these are all elements that maximized shade and airflow in an era that preceded air-conditioning.

Many Conch houses had fallen into states of total disrepair in the early 20th century, but as in South Beach, a community of artists, gays and lesbians established themselves here, refurbished the neighborhood and saved a bit of American heritage, all the while giving Key West the distinctive aesthetic profile that adds so much to its tourism appeal. You can see plenty of Conch houses in the Key West historic district (the west end of the island); to see a particularly fine assortment in a small space, walk the four blocks along Eaton St from Eaton and William to Eaton and Whitehead.

favorite architect, Morris Lapidus: 'Too much is never enough'. The earliest examples of this homegrown over-embellishment are the Mediterranean-revival mansions of Coral Gables and the Fabergé egg fantasy of the Vizcaya. These residential wedding cakes established Miami's identity as a city of fantasies and dreams, outside the boundaries of conventional tastes, where experimentation was smiled upon as long as it was done with flash. They also spoke to a distinct Miami attitude that is enshrined in city tastes to this day: If you've got it, flaunt it, then shove it back in their faces for a second serving.

The deco movement came about in the early 20th century, when affordable travel became a reality for many. Sea journeys represented the height of luxury, and many deco buildings are decorated with nautical porthole windows.

This penchant for imaginative, decorative flair overlaid the muscular postwar hotels and condos of the 1950s, giving birth to Miami Modernism (or Mimo). Mimo drew off the sleek lines and powerful presence of International Modernism, but led by Lapidus, it also eschewed austerity for grand, theatrical staging. Lapidus himself described his most famous structure, the Fontainebleau, as influenced by the most popular mass media of its time: Hollywood and cinema. The glamour Lapidus captured in his buildings would go on to define Miami's aesthetic outlook; Versace incorporated it into his clothes and Ian Schrager has decked out his hotels with this sense of fairy-tale possibility. Which makes sense: the word 'glamour' originally meant a kind of spell that causes people to see things differently from what they really are, which makes it an appropriate inspiration for the buildings of the 'Magic City'.

There are excellent deco renovations all along Miami Beach which manage to combine modern aesthetic tastes with classical deco details. But in a sense, the modern South Beach school of design is just the natural evolution of principles laid down by deco in the early 20th century. Hoteliers such as Ian Schrager combine a faith in technology – in this case flat-screen TVs, Lucite 'ghost chairs' and computer-controlled lobby displays – with a general air of fantastical glamour. Conceptions of the future (a fantasy of the best the future can be), plus a deep bow to the best of historical decorative arts, still drives the design on Miami Beach. Newer hotels such as the W and Ganservoort South have also expanded the architectural sense of proportion, integrating deco style into Miami Modern (which is to say, enormous) proportions. Whereas in the past deco hotels occupied a lot on a block, the megahotels of Miami Beach's future now stretch for an entire block.

# Survival Guide

## DIRECTORY A–Z ....222

Accommodations....... 222
Discount Cards......... 223
Electricity ............. 224
Food & Drink........... 224
Gay & Lesbian
Travelers .............. 224
Health................. 224
Insurance.............. 225
Internet Access......... 227
Legal Matters .......... 227
Money................. 227
Opening Hours ......... 227
Photography ........... 228
Post.................. 228
Public Holidays......... 228
Safe Travel............. 228
Telephone ............. 228
Tourist Information ..... 229
Travelers with
Disabilities............ 230
Volunteering ........... 230
Women Travelers ....... 230
Work.................. 231

## TRANSPORTATION...232

GETTING THERE
& AWAY ................ 232
Air ................... 232
Land ................. 233
Sea .................. 233
GETTING AROUND....... 233
Air ................... 233
Bicycle ............... 234
Boat ................. 234
Bus .................. 234
Car & Motorcycle....... 235
Hitchhiking ........... 236
Local Transportation .... 236
Taxi .................. 237
Train ................. 237

# Directory A–Z

## Accommodations

Our reviews (and rates) use the following room types:

➡ single occupancy (s)

➡ double occupancy (d)

➡ room (r), same rate for one or two people

➡ dorm bed (dm)

➡ suite (ste)

➡ apartment (apt)

Unless otherwise noted, rates do not include breakfast, bathrooms are private and all lodging is open year-round.

Rates don't include taxes, which vary considerably between towns; in fact, hotels almost never include taxes and fees in their rate quotes, so always ask for the *total rate with tax*. Florida's sales tax is 6%, and some communities tack on more, which can rise to as high as 7.5%. States, cities and towns also usually levy taxes on hotel rooms, which can increase the final bill by 10% to 12%.

Seasonal fluctuations can see rates rise and fall dramatically, especially in Miami, Key West and tourist beach towns. Booking in advance for high-season tourist hot spots (such as Miami and beach towns) can be essential to ensure the room you want. However, inquiring at the last minute, or even same-day, can sometimes yield amazing discounts on available rooms.

Icons in reviews indicate the following:

➡ parking available; used only when parking is an issue

➡ air-conditioning

➡ internet terminal for guest use

➡ wi-fi access in rooms

➡ swimming pool

➡ family-friendly, when particularly notable

➡ pet-friendly

The following are some useful local accommodations websites:

**Florida Bed & Breakfast Inns** (www.florida-inns.com)

**Greater Miami & the Beaches** (www.miamiandbeaches.com/where-to-stay)

**Key West Innkeepers Association** (www.keywestinns.com)

**Florida State Parks Camping** (www.floridastateparks.org/stay-thenight/camping.cfm)

**Everglades National Park Camping** (www.nps.gov/ever/planyourvisit/camping.htm)

### B&Bs & Inns

B&Bs and inns vary from small, comfy houses with shared bathrooms (the least expensive) to romantic, antique-filled historic homes and opulent mansions with private baths (the most expensive).

➡ Accommodations focusing on upscale romance may discourage children.

➡ Inns and B&Bs often require a minimum stay of two or three days on weekends, and sometimes more during major holidays and events.

➡ Advance reservations are pretty much mandatory. Always call ahead to confirm policies (regarding kids, pets, smoking) and bathroom arrangements.

### Camping

Three types of campsites are available: undeveloped ($10 per night), public (around $20) and privately owned ($30 and up). In general, Florida campsites are quite safe. Undeveloped campsites are just that (undeveloped), while most public campsites have toilets, showers and drinking water.

➡ Reserve state-park sites by calling ☎800-326-3521 or visiting www.reserveamerica.com.

➡ Most privately owned campsites are geared to RVs (motor homes) but will also have a small section available for tent campers. Expect tons of amenities such as swimming pools, laundry facilities, convenience stores and bars.

➡ **Kampgrounds of America** (KOA; ☎888-562-0000; www.koa.com) is a national network of private

## SLEEPING PRICE RANGES

The following price ranges refer to a standard double room in high season (unless otherwise noted). Note that 'high season' can mean summer or winter depending on the region.

**$** under $120

**$$** $120 to $240

**$$$** over $240

campsites; their Kamping Kabins have air-con and kitchens. Many KOA sites offer wi-fi.

### Hostels

➡ In most hostels, group dorms are segregated by gender and you'll be sharing a bathroom; occasionally alcohol is banned.

➡ About half the hostels throughout Florida are affiliated with **Hostelling International USA** (HI-USA; ☑301-495-1240, reservations ☑888-464-4872; www.hiusa. org). You don't have to be a member to stay, but non-members pay a slightly higher rate. You can join HI by phone, online or at most youth hostels. From the US, you can book many HI hostels through its toll-free reservations service.

➡ Florida has many independent hostels (www. hostels.com); most have comparable rates and conditions to HI hostels, and some are better.

### Hotels

South Florida is rich in in-dependent accommodation options, but in some towns, such as Homestead, chain hotels are the best (and sometimes, the only) option. If you're looking to spend less than $100 a night on a room in Miami, chain hotels are a decent choice.

The calling-card of chain hotels is reliability: accept-able cleanliness, unremark-able yet inoffensive decor,

and a comfortable bed. A TV, phone, air-conditioning, minirefrigerator, microwave, hair dryer and safe are stand-ard amenities in midrange chains. A developing trend, most evident in Miami, is chain-owned hotels striving for upscale boutique-style uniqueness in decor and design. At these hotels you'll often find rooms that aren't much different to the higher range chains, although the external amenities such as spa and room service will probably be lacking.

High-end hotels over-whelm guests with services: valet parking, room service, newspaper delivery, dry cleaning, laundry, pools, health clubs, bars and other niceties. You'll find plenty of boutique and specialty hotels in places like South Beach and Key West. While all large chain hotels have toll-free reservation numbers, you may find better savings by calling the hotel directly.

Chain-owned hotels in-clude the following:

**Hilton** (☑800-445-8667; www.hilton.com)

**Holiday Inn** (☑888-465-4329; www.holidayinn.com)

**Marriott** (☑888-236-2427; www.marriott.com)

**Radisson** (☑888-201-1718; www.radisson.com)

**Ritz-Carlton** (☑800-542-8680; www.ritzcarlton.com)

**Sheraton** (☑800-325-3535; www.starwoodhotels.com/sheraton)

## Discount Cards

In Miami, check out the **Go Miami** card (www.smartdes-tinations.com). In Key West, there's **Gold Card Key West** (www.goldcardkeywest.com).

In the rest of the Keys:

**Keys Coupons** (www.keyscou-pons.com)

**Keys Kash** (www.fla-keys.com/keyskash)

**Mile Marker Discounts** (www.milemarkerdiscounts.com)

South Florida is a *very* com-petitive tourist destination, so persistence usually pays dividends.

Being a member of certain groups, such as AAA, gives access to discounts, usually about 10%, at many hotels, museums and sights. Simply carry the appropriate ID.

**Auto-club membership** See the Transportation chapter on p235.

**Students** Any student ID is typically honored; international students might consider an **International Student Identity Card** (ISIC; www.isiccard.com).

**Seniors** Generally refers to those 65 and older, but sometimes those 60 and older. Join the **American Association of Retired Persons** (AARP; ☑888-687-2277; www.aarp.org) for more travel bargains.

## BOOK YOUR STAY ONLINE

For more reviews by Lonely Planet authors, check out http://lonelyplanet.com/hotels/. You'll find independent reviews, as well as recommendations on the best places to stay. Best of all, you can book online.

# Electricity

110V/60Hz

110V/60Hz

# Food & Drink

For detailed information about eating and drinking in Miami, see our Food & Drink chapter (p193).

For information on how much to tip, see p227.

# Gay & Lesbian Travelers

Miami, the Keys and Key West are out areas, where homosexuality is practiced openly year-round. Events such as the White Party and Fantasy Fest are major dates in the North American gay calendar. Smaller towns in the Everglades region are more culturally conservative, but gay travelers won't cause much of a stir. In Miami, the gay scene is so integrated it can be difficult to separate it from the straight one; popular hot spots include South Beach, North Beach, and Wynwood and the Design District.

**Damron** (https://damron. com) Damron, an expert in LGBT travel, offers a searchable database of LGBT-friendly and specific travel listings. Publishes popular national guidebooks, including *Women's Traveller, Men's Travel Guide* and *Damron Accommodations.*

**Gay Key West** (www.gaykey-westfl.com) Clearing house for information on LGBT topics in Key West.

**Gay Yellow Network** (www.glyp.com) City-based yellow-page listings include six Florida cities.

**Key West Gay** (www.key-westgay.com) Info on Key West gay topics.

**Miami Gay Travel** (www.miamigaytravel.com) Gay travel guide to Miami.

**Miami-Dade Gay & Lesbian Chamber of Commerce** (www.gogaymi-ami.com) Gay businesses and travel tips.

**Out Traveler** (www.out-traveler.com) Travel magazine specializing in gay travel.

**Purple Roofs** (www.purple-roofs.com) Lists queer accommodations, travel agencies and tours worldwide.

# Health

Florida, and the USA generally, has a high level of hygiene, so infectious diseases are not a significant concern for most travelers.

➡ Vaccines are not required and tap water is safe to drink.

➡ Despite Florida's plethora of intimidating wildlife, the main concerns for travelers are sunburn and mosquito bites.

➡ Ensure you have adequate health insurance in case of accidents. If you experience a major medical emergency in the Everglades, chances are you will end up in Miami for treatment.

➡ Most of the major islands in the Keys, including Marathon, Islamorada and Key Largo, have emergency medical facilities.

## Internet Resources

There is a vast wealth of travel health advice on the internet. Two good sources:

**MD Travel Health** (www. mdtravelhealth.com) Provides complete, updated and free travel-health recommendations for every country.

**World Health Organization** (www.who.int/ith) The superb book *International Travel and Health* is available free online.

Also, consult your government's travel-health website before departure, if one is available:

**Australia** (www.smartraveller. gov.au)

**Canada** (www.hc-sc.gc.ca/index-eng.php)

**UK** (www.fco.gov.uk/en/travel-and-living-abroad)

**United States** (wwwnc.cdc.gov/travel)

## Health Insurance

The United States offers one of the finest levels of health care in the world. The problem is that it can be prohibitively expensive. It's essential to purchase travel-health insurance if your policy doesn't cover you when you're abroad.

➡ If your health insurance does not cover you for medical expenses abroad, obtain supplemental health or travel insurance.

➡ Find out in advance whether your insurance plan will make payments directly to the providers or if it will reimburse you later for any overseas health expenditures.

We have to stress: **A simple visit to the doctor's office can cost hundreds of dollars, and a hospital stay will cost thousands** if you aren't covered by insurance.

## Health Care

➡ If you have a medical emergency, go to the emergency room of the nearest hospital.

➡ If you need any kind of emergency assistance, such as police, ambulance or firefighters, call ☑911. This is a free call from any phone.

➡ If the problem isn't urgent, call a nearby hospital and ask for a referral to a local physician; this is usually cheaper than a trip to the emergency room.

➡ Stand-alone, for-profit urgent-care centers provide good service, but can be the most expensive option.

## Medications

➡ Bring any medications you may need in their original containers, clearly labeled.

➡ A signed, dated letter from your physician that describes all of your medical conditions and medications (including generic names) is also a good idea.

➡ Pharmacies are abundantly supplied. However, some medications that are available over the counter in other countries require a prescription in the US.

➡ If you don't have insurance to cover the cost of prescriptions, these can be shockingly expensive.

## Infectious Diseases

In addition to more-common ailments, there are several infectious diseases that are unknown or uncommon outside North America. Most are acquired by mosquito or tick bites.

**Giardiasis** Also known as traveler's diarrhea. A parasitic infection of the small intestines, typically contracted by drinking feces-contaminated freshwater. Never drink untreated stream, lake or pond water. Easily treated with antibiotics.

**HIV/AIDS** As do all sexually transmitted diseases, HIV infection occurs in the US. Use a

condom for all sexual encounters.

**Lyme Disease** Though more common in the US northeast than in Florida, Lyme disease occurs here. It is transmitted by infected deer ticks, and is signaled by a bull's-eye rash at the bite and flulike symptoms. Treat promptly with antibiotics. Removing ticks within 36 hours can avoid infection.

**Rabies** Though rare, the rabies virus can be contracted from the bite of any infected animal; bats are most common, and their bites are not always obvious. If bitten by any animal, consult with a doctor, since rabies is fatal if untreated.

**West Nile virus** Extremely rare in Florida, West Nile virus is transmitted by culex mosquitoes. Most infections are mild or asymptomatic, but serious symptoms and even death can occur. There is no treatment for West Nile virus. For the latest update on affected areas, see the **US Geological Survey disease maps** (http://disease maps.usgs.gov).

## Animal & Spider Bites

Florida's critters can be cute, but they can also bite and sting. Here are a few to watch out for.

**Alligators and snakes** Neither attack humans unless startled or threatened. If you encounter them, simply back away. Florida has several venomous snakes; immediately seek treatment if bitten.

**Jellyfish and stingrays** Florida beaches can see both; avoid swimming when they're present (lifeguards often post warnings). Treat stings immediately; they hurt but aren't dangerous.

**Spiders** Florida is home to two dangerously venomous spiders – the black widow and the brown recluse. Seek immediate treatment if bitten by any spider.

## Insurance

➡ It's expensive to get sick, crash a car or have things stolen from you in the US.

## INTERNATIONAL VISITORS

### Entering the Region

➡ A passport is required for all foreign citizens. Unless eligible under the Visa Waiver Program, foreign travelers must also have a tourist visa. To rent or drive a car, travelers from non-English-speaking countries should obtain an International Drivers Permit before arriving.

➡ Travelers entering under the Visa Waiver Program must register with the US government's **ESTA program** (https://esta.cbp.dhs.gov) at least three days before arriving; earlier is better, since if denied, travelers must get a visa. Registration is valid for two years.

➡ Upon arriving in the US, all foreign visitors must register in the US-Visit program, which entails having two index fingers scanned and a digital photo taken. For information on US-Visit, see the **Department of Homeland Security** (www.dhs.gov/us-visit).

### Visas

➡ All visitors should reconfirm entry requirements and visa guidelines before arriving. You can get visa information through www.usa.gov, but the **US State Department** (www.travel.state.gov) maintains the most comprehensive visa information, with lists of consulates and downloadable application forms. **US Citizenship & Immigration Services** (www.uscis.gov) mainly serves immigrants, not temporary visitors.

➡ The **Visa Waiver Program** allows citizens of three dozen countries to enter the USA for stays of 90 days or less without first obtaining a US visa. See the ESTA website above for a current list. Under this program you must have a nonrefundable return ticket and 'e-passport' with digital chip. Passports issued/renewed before October 26, 2006, must be machine-readable.

➡ Visitors who don't qualify for the Visa Waiver Program need a visa. Basic requirements are a valid passport, recent photo, travel details and often proof of financial stability. Students and adult males also must fill out supplemental travel documents. The validity period for a US visitor visa depends on your home country. The length of time you'll be allowed to stay in the USA is determined by US officials at the port of entry.

➡ To stay longer than the date stamped on your passport, visit a local **USCIS** (www.uscis.gov) office.

### Customs

For a complete, up-to-date list of customs regulations, visit the website of **US Customs & Border Protection** (www.cbp.gov). Each visitor is allowed to bring into the US duty-free 1L of liquor (if you're 21 or older), 200 cigarettes (if you're 18 or older) and up to $100 in gifts and purchases.

### Embassies & Consulates

To find a US embassy in another country, visit the **US Department of State website** (www.usembassy.gov). Most foreign embassies in the US have their main consulates in Washington, DC, but the below have representation in Miami, except Italy, which is in Coral Gables.

**Brazil** (☎305-285-6200; http://miami.itamaraty.gov.br/en-us; 80 SW 8th St, Suite 2600)

**Canada** (☎305-579-1600; http://can-am.gc.ca/miami/menu.aspx; 200 S Biscayne Blvd, Suite 1600)

**France** (☎305-403-4150; www.consulfrance-miami.org; 1395 Brickell Ave, Suite 1050)

**Germany** (☎305-358-0290; www.germany.info; 100 N Biscayne Blvd, Suite 2200)

**Italy** (☎305-374-6322; www.consmiami.esteri.it/Consolato_Miami; 4000 Ponce de Leon Blvd, Suite 590, Coral Gables)

**Mexico** (☎786-268-4900; http://consulmex.sre.gob.mx/miami; 1399 SW 1st Ave)

**Netherlands** (☎877-388-2443; http://miami.the-netherlands.org; 701 Brickell Ave, Suite 500)

**UK** (☎305-400-6400; http://ukinusa.fco.gov.uk/florida; 1001 Brickell Bay Dr, Suite 2800)

Make sure to have adequate coverage before arriving.

➡ To insure yourself for items that may be stolen from your car, consult your homeowner's (or renter's) insurance policy or consider investing in travel insurance.

➡ Worldwide travel insurance is available at www.lonelyplanet.com/travel_services. You can buy, extend and claim online anytime – even if you're already on the road.

## Internet Access

➡ Nearly every hotel and many restaurants and businesses offer high-speed internet access. In hotel listings, an internet symbol (@) indicates a guest internet terminal and a wi-fi symbol (📶) indicates in-room wi-fi. With few exceptions, all hotels offer in-room plug-in and wi-fi in the lobby. Always ask about connection rates.

➡ Most cafes offer inexpensive internet access, and most transportation stations and city parks are wi-fi hotspots.

➡ Public libraries provide free internet terminals, though sometimes you must get a temporary nonresident library card ($10). For a list of wi-fi hotspots (plus tech and access info), visit **Wi-Fi Alliance** (www.wi-fi.org) and **Wi-Fi Free Spot** (www.wififreespot.com). If you bring a laptop from outside the USA, invest in a universal AC and plug adapter. Also, confirm that your modem card will work.

## Legal Matters

➡ If you are stopped by the police, there is no system for paying traffic tickets or other fines on the spot. The patrol officer will explain your options to you; there is usually a 30-day period to pay fines by mail.

➡ If you're arrested, you are allowed to remain silent, though never walk away from an officer.

➡ You are entitled to have access to an attorney. The legal system presumes you're innocent until proven guilty.

➡ All persons who are arrested have the right to make one phone call. If you don't have a lawyer or family member to help you, call your embassy or consulate. The police will give you the number on request.

### Drinking & Driving

Despite what you sometimes see, it's illegal to walk with an open alcoholic drink on the street. More importantly, don't drive with an open container; any liquor in a car must be unopened or else stored in the trunk. If you're stopped while driving with an open container, police will treat you as if you were drinking and driving. Refusing a breathalyzer, urine or blood test is treated as if you'd taken the test and failed. A DUI (driving under the influence) conviction is a serious offense, subject to stiff fines and even imprisonment.

To purchase alcohol, you need to present a photo ID to prove your age.

## Money

➡ Prices quoted in reviews are in US dollars ($).

➡ Exchange foreign currency at international airports and most large banks in Miami, Orlando, Tampa and other Florida cities.

➡ There is ease and availability of ATMs. Most ATM withdrawals using out-of-state cards incur surcharges of $2 or so.

➡ Major credit cards are widely accepted, and they are required for car rentals.

➡ ATMs have largely negated the need for traveler's checks. However, traveler's checks in US dollars are accepted like cash at most midrange and top-end businesses (but rarely at budget places).

➡ Personal checks not drawn on US banks are generally not accepted.

### Tipping

Tipping is standard practice across America. In restaurants, for satisfactory to excellent service, tipping 15–20% of the bill is expected; less is okay at informal diners. You should only tip below this, or not tip at all (the latter is a very drastic move in American restaurants) if the service was exceptionally bad.

| SERVICE | TIP |
| --- | --- |
| Food | Normal service 15% Good service 18% Great service 20% |
| Bars | $1 per drink $2 or more for complicated cocktails |
| Cafe baristas | Some change in the jar |
| Taxi drivers | 10-15% |
| Hairdressers | 10-15% |
| Skycaps at airports | $1 per bag |
| Porters | $1 per bag |
| Cleaning staff at hotels | A few dollars after a few nights |

## Opening Hours

Unless otherwise noted the standard business hours in reviews are as follows:

**Banks** 8:30am to 5pm Monday to Friday; sometimes 9am to noon or 2pm Saturday.

**Bars** In Miami, most bars 5pm to 3am, in Miami Beach 24 hours, but most bars close for a few hours at 5am, in Key West 5pm to 4am, elsewhere 5pm to 2am.

In all places, some bars close earlier if business is slow.

**Businesses** 9am to 7pm Monday to Friday.

**Restaurants** Breakfast 7am to 11am Monday to Friday, brunch 9am to 2pm Saturday and Sunday; lunch 11am to 2pm Monday to Friday; dinner 5pm to 10pm, later Friday and Saturday.

**Post offices** 9am to 5pm Monday to Friday; sometimes 9am to noon Saturday.

**Shopping** 10am to 6pm Monday to Saturday, noon to 5pm Sunday; shopping malls keep extended hours.

## Photography

➡ All camera supplies (digital memory, camera batteries) are readily available in local drug-stores, which also usually provide inexpensive printing from your memory card (including one-hour service) and burning photo CDs and DVDs.

➡ When photographing people, politeness is usually all that's needed (though street performers appreciate a tip).

➡ For a primer on taking good shots, consult Lonely Planet's *Travel Photography*.

## Post

The **US Postal Service** (USPS; ☎800-275-8777; www. usps.com) is reliable and inexpensive. For 1st-class mail sent and delivered within the USA, postage rates are 44¢ for letters up to 1oz (20¢ for each additional ounce) and 29¢ for standard-size postcards. International airmail rates for postcards and letters up to 1oz are 80¢ to Canada and Mexico, and 98¢ to other countries.

You can have mail sent to you c/o General Delivery at most big post offices (it's usually held for 30 days).

Most hotels will also hold mail for incoming guests.

## Public Holidays

On the following national public holidays, banks, schools and government offices (including post offices) are closed, and transportation, museums and other services operate on a Sunday schedule. Many stores, however, maintain regular business hours. Holidays falling on a weekend are usually observed the following Monday.

**New Year's Day** January 1

**Martin Luther King Jr Day** Third Monday in January

**Presidents Day** Third Monday in February

**Easter** March or April

**Memorial Day** Last Monday in May

**Independence Day** July 4

**Labor Day** First Monday in September

**Columbus Day** Second Monday in October

**Veterans Day** November 11

**Thanksgiving** Fourth Thursday in November

**Christmas Day** December 25

## Safe Travel

Parts of Miami proper, including Little Haiti and nightlife hotspots such as Overtown (just north of Downtown), experience high crime rates. You should be careful in these areas, and as a rule of thumb, avoid hanging out too much in Downtown after dark. Miami Beach on the other hand is safe from a crime perspective, although drunk driving seems depressingly common.

For emergency assistance, such as police, ambulance or firefighters, call ☎911. This is a free call from any phone.

## Hurricanes

Florida hurricane season extends from June through November, but the peak is September and October. Relatively speaking, very few Atlantic Ocean and Gulf of Mexico storms become hurricanes, and fewer still are accurate enough to hit Florida, but the devastation they wreak when they do can be enormous. Travelers should take all hurricane alerts, warnings and evacuation orders seriously.

Hurricanes are generally sighted well in advance, allowing time to prepare. When a hurricane threatens, listen to radio and TV news reports.

**Florida Division of Emergency Management** (www. floridadisaster.org) Hurricane preparedness.

**Florida Emergency Hotline** (☎800-342-3557) Updated storm warning information.

**Hurricane Hotline** (☎305-468-5400)

**National Weather Service** (www.nws.noaa.gov)

## Telephone

➡ Always dial '1' before toll-free (☎800, ☎888 etc) and domestic long-distance numbers. Some toll-free numbers only work within the US.

➡ For local directory assistance, dial ☎411.

➡ To make international calls from the US, dial ☎011 + country code + area code + number. For international operator assistance, dial ☎0.

➡ To call the US from abroad, the international country code for the USA is ☎1.

➡ Pay phones are readily found in major cities, but are becoming rarer. Local calls cost 50¢.

➡ Private prepaid phone cards are available from convenience stores,

## PRACTICALITIES

⇒ **Newspapers** South Florida has a number of major daily newspapers: *Miami Herald* (in Spanish, *El Nuevo Herald*), the *Miami New Times*, the *Key West Citizen* and the *South Dade News Leader*.

⇒ **TV** Florida receives all the major US TV and cable networks. Florida Smart (http://floridasmart.com/news) lists them all by region.

⇒ **DVDs** Video systems use the NTSC color TV standard, not compatible with the PAL system.

⇒ **Electricity** Electrical voltage is 110/120V, 60 cycles.

⇒ **Weights & Measures** Distances are measured in feet, yards and miles; weights are tallied in ounces, pounds and tons.

⇒ **Smoking** Florida bans smoking in all enclosed workplaces, including restaurants and shops, but excluding 'stand-alone' bars (that don't emphasize food) and designated hotel smoking rooms.

⇒ **Time** South Florida is in the US eastern time zone (GMT minus five hours): noon in Miami equals 9am in San Francisco and 5pm in London. During daylight-saving time, clocks move forward one hour in March and move back one hour in November.

---

supermarkets and pharmacies.

⇒ Most of the USA's mobile-phone systems are incompatible with the GSM 900/1800 standard used throughout Europe and Asia. Check with your service provider about using your phone in the US. In terms of coverage, Verizon has the most extensive network, but AT&T, Sprint and T-Mobile are decent. Cellular coverage is generally excellent, except in the Everglades and parts of rural northern Florida.

⇒ The area codes in Miami and the Keys are ☎305 and ☎786; in the Everglades ☎239.

## Tourist Information

There are plenty of chambers of commerce and visitor centers in the region itching to help you make the most of your trip and pass out veritable libraries of pamphlets and coupons.

To order a packet of Florida information prior to coming, contact **Visit Florida** (www.visitflorida.com).

### Miami

**Coconut Grove Chamber of Commerce** (☎305-444-7270; www.coconutgrovechamber.com; 2820 McFarlane Rd, Coconut Grove; ⏱9am-5pm Mon-Fri)

**Coral Gables Chamber of Commerce** (☎305-446-1657; www.coralgableschamber.org; 224 Catalonia Ave, Coral Gables; ⏱9am-5pm Mon-Fri)

**Downtown Miami Welcome Center** (☎786-472-5930; www.downtownmiami.com; 900 S Miami Ave; ⏱9am-5pm Mon-Fri) Provides maps, brochures and tour information for the downtown area.

**Greater Miami & the Beaches Convention & Visitors Bureau** (☎305-539-3000; www.miamiandbeaches.com; 701 Brickell Ave, 27th fl; ⏱8:30am-5pm Mon-Fri) Located in an oddly intimidating high-rise building.

**Miami Beach Chamber of Commerce** (☎305-674-1300; www.miamibeachchamber.com; 1920 Meridian Ave; ⏱9am-5pm Mon-Fri)

### Everglades

**Everglades Area Chamber of Commerce** (☎239-695-

3941; cnr US Hwy 41 & Hwy 29; ⏱9am-4pm)

**Homestead Chamber of Commerce** (☎305-247-2332; www.chamberinaction.com; 455 N Flagler Ave, Homestead; ⏱9am-noon & 1-5pm Mon-Fri)

**Ernest Coe Visitor Center** (☎305-242-7700; www.nps.gov/ever; 40001 State Rd 9336; ⏱8am-5pm)

**Shark Valley Visitor Center** (☎305-221-8776; www.nps.gov/planyourvisit/svdirections; per car/bicycle $10/5; ⏱8:30am-6pm)

**Big Cypress Natural Preserve Visitor Center** (☎239-695-4758; 33000 Tamiami Trail E; ⏱8:30am-4:30pm)

### The Keys

**Key West Chamber of Commerce** (☎305-294-2587; www.keywestchamber.org; 510 Greene St; ⏱8:30am-6:30pm Mon-Sat, to 6pm Sun)

**Lower Keys Chamber of Commerce** (☎305-872-2411; www.lowerkeyschamber.com; MM 31 oceanside; ⏱9am-5pm Mon-Fri, to 3pm Sat)

**Marathon Visitors Center Chamber of Commerce** (☎305-743-5417,

800-262-7284; www.florida-keysmarathon.com; MM 53.5 bayside; ⊙9am-5pm)

**Islamorada Chamber of Commerce** (☑305-664-4503; www.islamoradachamber.com; MM 83.2 bayside; ⊙9am-5pm Mon-Fri, to 4pm Sat, to 3pm Sun)

**Key Largo Chamber of Commerce** (☑305-451-1414; www.keylargochamber.org; MM 106 bayside; ⊙9am-6pm)

## Travelers with Disabilities

Because of the high number of senior residents in Florida, most public buildings are wheelchair accessible and have appropriate restroom facilities. Transportation services are generally accessible to all, and telephone companies provide relay operators for the hearing impaired. Many banks provide ATM instructions in Braille, curb ramps are common and many busy intersections have audible crossing signals.

There are a number of organizations that specialize in the needs of disabled travelers.

**Access-Able Travel Source** (www.access-able.com) An excellent website with many links.

**Flying Wheels Travel** (☑507-451-5005; http://flyingwheelstravel.com) A full-service travel agency specializing in disabled travel.

**Mobility International USA** (www.miusa.org) Advises disabled travelers on mobility issues and runs an educational exchange program.

**Travelin' Talk Network** (www.travelintalk.net) Run by the same people as Access-Able Travel Source; a global network of service providers.

## Volunteering

Volunteering can be a great way to break up a long trip, and it provides memorable opportunities to interact with locals and the land in ways you never would when just passing through. Animal sanctuaries and small parks are always on the lookout for short-term volunteer help.

Florida's state parks would not function without volunteers. Each park coordinates its own volunteers, and most also have the support of an all-volunteer 'friends' organization (officially called Citizen Support Organizations). Links and contact information are on the main **state park website** (http://floridastateparks.org/getinvolved/volunteer.cfm).

**Everglades National Park** (☑305-242-7752; www.nps.gov/ever/supportyourpark/volunteer.htm) Active volunteer program recruits both individuals and groups.

**Florida Keys National Marine Sanctuary** (☑305-292-0311; www.floridakeys.noaa.gov/volunteer_opportunities/welcome.html) Can hook folks up with a plethora of environment-focused volunteer programs across the Keys.

**Miami Habitat for Humanity** (☑305-634-3628; www.miamihabitat.org; 3800 NW 22nd Ave, Miami) Does a ton of work in Florida, building homes and helping the homeless.

**Shake a Leg Miami** (☑305-858-5500; www.shakealegmiami.org; 2620 S Bayshore Dr) A community water-sports complex in Coconut Grove that aims to serve economically and physically disadvantaged children.

**Volunteer Florida** (www.volunteerflorida.org) The primary state-run organization; coordinates volunteer centers across the state. Though it's aimed at Floridians, casual visitors can find situations that match their time and interests.

## Women Travelers

Women traveling by themselves or in a group should encounter no particular problems unique to Florida besides drunken loutishness in Miami and Key West.

There are a number of excellent resources to help traveling women:

➡ Community website www.journeywoman.com facilitates women exchanging travel tips, with links to resources.

➡ The Canadian government (www.voyage.gc.ca) publishes the useful, free, online booklet 'Her Own Way'; look under 'Publications.'

These two national advocacy groups might also be helpful:

**National Organization for Women** (NOW; ☑202-628-8669; www.now.org)

**Planned Parenthood** (☑800-230-7526; www.plannedparenthood.org) Offers referrals to medical clinics throughout the country.

Women need to exhibit the same street smarts as any solo traveler, but they are sometimes more often the target of unwanted attention or harassment. Some women like to carry a whistle, mace or cayenne-pepper spray in case of assault. These sprays are legal to carry and use in Florida, but only in self-defense. Federal law prohibits them being carried on planes.

If you are assaulted, you can call the **police** (☑911) or a rape-crisis hotline; telephone books have lists of local organizations, or contact the 24-hour **National Sexual Assault Hotline** (☑800-656-4673; www.rainn.org). Or, go straight to a hospital. Police can sometimes be insensitive with assault victims, while a rape-crisis center or hospital can advocate on behalf of survivors and act as a link to other services, including the police.

## Work

Seasonal service jobs in tourist beach towns and theme parks are common and often easy to get, if low-paying.

If you are a foreigner in the USA with a standard nonimmigrant visitors visa, you are forbidden to take paid work in the USA and will be deported if you're caught working illegally. In addition, employers are required to establish the bona fides of their employees or face fines. In particular, South Florida is notorious for large numbers of foreigners working illegally, and immigration officers are vigilant.

To work legally, foreigners need to apply for a work visa before leaving home. Student exchange visitors need a J1 visa, which the following organizations will help arrange:

**American Institute for Foreign Study** (AIFS; ☑866-906-2437; www.aifs.com)

**BUNAC** (☑866-220-7771; www.bunac.org)

**Camp America** (☑800-727-8233; www.campamerica.aifs.com)

**Council on International Educational Exchange** (CIEE; ☑800-407-8839; www.ciee.org)

**InterExchange** (☑212-924-0446; www.interexchange.org) Camp and au-pair programs

**International Exchange Programs (IEP): Australia** (☑1300-300-912; www.iep.org.au); **New Zealand** (☑0800-443-769; www.iep.org.nz).

For nonstudent jobs, temporary or permanent, you need to be sponsored by a US employer (who will arrange an H-category visa). These aren't easy to obtain.

# Transportation

## GETTING THERE & AWAY

Nearly all international travelers come to South Florida by air, while most US travelers prefer air or car. Getting to South Florida by bus is a distant third option and by train an even more distant fourth. Miami is a major international airline hub, particularly for American Airlines, and it's the first port of call for many flights from Latin America and the Caribbean. Most flights come into Miami International Airport (MIA), although many are also directed to Fort Lauderdale-Hollywood International Airport (FLL). As it is located at the tip of the USA, Greater Miami is more of a termination of highways and rail lines, rather than a major land-transit interchange area.

Flights, tours and rail tickets can be booked online at www.lonelyplanet.com/bookings.

---

## Air

Unless you live in or near Florida, flying to the region and then renting a car is the most time-efficient option.

### Airports & Airlines

**Miami International Airport** (MIA; ☎305-876-7000; www.miami-airport.com) One of the state's two busiest airports, and one of the nation's most important international gateways.

**Key West International Airport** (EYW; www.keywestinternationalairport.com) A much quieter airport, located off S Roosevelt Blvd on the east side of the island.

**Fort Lauderdale-Hollywood International Airport** (FLL; ☎866-435-9355; www.broward.org/airport; 320 Terminal Dr) A viable gateway airport to the Florida region, located 21 miles north of Downtown Miami.

Air service to Miami is frequent and direct. Flights come from all over the USA, Europe, Latin America and the Caribbean; Key West is served far less often, and often indirectly. A number of international airlines service South Florida.

### Air Passes

International travelers who plan on doing a lot of flying, both in and out of the region, might consider buying an air pass. Air passes are available only to non-US citizens, and they must be purchased in conjunction with an international ticket. Conditions and cost structures can be complicated, but all include a certain number of domestic flights (from three to 10) that must be used within 60 days. Sometimes you must plan your itinerary in advance, but sometimes dates (and even destinations) can be left open. Talk with a travel agent to determine if an air pass would save you money based on your plans.

The two main airline alliances are the **Star Alliance** (www.staralliance.com) and **One World** (www.oneworld.com).

---

### CLIMATE CHANGE & TRAVEL

Every form of transport that relies on carbon-based fuel generates $CO_2$, the main cause of human-induced climate change. Modern travel is dependent on airplanes which might use less fuel per kilometer per person than most cars but travel much greater distances. The altitude at which aircraft emit gases (including $CO_2$) and particles also contributes to their climate change impact. Many websites offer 'carbon calculators' that allow people to estimate the carbon emissions generated by their journey and, for those who wish to do so, to offset the impact of the greenhouse gases emitted with contributions to portfolios of climate-friendly initiatives throughout the world. Lonely Planet offsets the carbon footprint of all staff and author travel.

# Land

## Bus

For bus trips, **Greyhound** (☎800-231-2222; www. greyhound.com) is the main long-distance operator, but **Megabus** (☎877-462-6342; https://us.megabus.com), which can transport you to Tampa and Orlando, is becoming an increasingly viable option. Competition between the two services has helped drop the price of bus transportation. Greyhound serves Florida from most major American metropolitan areas. Greyhound also connects Miami to many major cities in Florida, but you won't be able to access smaller towns.

If you are traveling very long distances (say, across several states) bargain airfares can sometimes undercut buses. On shorter routes, renting a car can sometimes be cheaper. Nonetheless, discounted (even half-price) long-distance bus trips are often available by purchasing tickets online seven to 14 days in advance. Then, once in Florida, you can rent a car to get around. Enquire about multiday passes.

Sample one-way fares (advance-purchase/standard fares) between Miami and some major US cities:

| CITY | FARE | TIME | DAILY |
|------|------|------|-------|
| Atlanta | $59/ 118 | 16- 18hr | 5-6 |
| New Orleans | $92/ 178 | 23- 24hr | 3-4 |
| New York City | $95/ 190 | 33- 35hr | 5-6 |
| Washington, DC | $97/ 190 | 27- 29hr | 5-6 |

## Car & Motorcycle

Driving to Florida is easy; there are no international borders or entry issues. Incorporating Florida into a larger USA road trip is very common, and having a car while in Florida is often a necessity.

Sample distances and times from various points in the US to Miami:

| CITY | ROAD DISTANCE | TIME |
|------|------|------|
| Atlanta | 660 miles | 10½hr |
| Chicago | 1380 miles | 23hr |
| Los Angeles | 2750 miles | 44hr |
| New York City | 1280 miles | 22hr |
| Washington, DC | 1050 miles | 17hr |

## Train

If you're coming from the East Coast, **Amtrak** (☎800-872-7245, 305-835-1222; www. amtrak.com; 8303 NW 37th Ave) makes a comfortable, affordable option for getting here. Amtrak's Silver Service (which includes *Silver Meteor* and *Silver Star* trains) runs between New York and Miami, with services that include major and small Florida towns in between. Unfortunately, there is no longer any direct service to Florida from Los Angeles, New Orleans, Chicago or the Midwest. Trains from these destinations connect to the Silver Service route, but the transfer adds a day or so to your travel time.

Book tickets in advance. Children, seniors and military personnel receive discounts.

| FROM | TO | FARE | TIME |
|------|------|------|------|
| Miami | New York | $141- 185 | 18- 20hr |
| Miami | Orlando | $43- 95 | 5hr |
| Miami | Tampa | $41- 90 | 5hr |

## Sea

Florida is nearly completely surrounded by the ocean, and it's a major cruise-ship port.

If you arrive in Miami via a cruise ship, you'll likely arrive via the **Port of Miami** (☎305-347-4800; www.miamidade.gov/portofmiami), which received nearly four million passengers in 2013 and is known as the 'cruise capital of the world'.

You can boat from Miami to the Keys on the **Key West Express** (☎888-539-2628; www.seakeywestexpress.com; adult/child round trip $147/85, one way $86/60). It departs from Fort Myers Beach and Marco Island daily at 8:30am and does a 3½-hour cruise to Key West. Returning boats depart the seaport at 6pm. You'll want to show up 1½ hours before your boat departs. During winter and fall the Express also leaves from Marco Island.

# GETTING AROUND

Once you reach South Florida, traveling by car is the best way of getting around – it allows you to reach areas not otherwise served by public transportation.

## Air

The US airline industry is reliable, safe and serves Florida extremely well. However, the industry's continuing financial troubles have resulted in a series of high-profile mergers: Midwest joining Frontier, Orlando-based Air Tran merging into Southwest and Continental merging into United.

In general, this has led to fewer flights, fuller airplanes, less perks, more fees and higher rates. Allow extra time for the USA's extensive airport security-screening procedures.

## Airlines in Florida

Main domestic airlines operating in South Florida:

**American** (AA; ☎800-433-7300; www.aa.com) Has a Miami hub and service to and between major Florida cities.

**Delta** (DL;☑800-455-2720; www.delta.com) International carrier to main Florida cities, plus flights from Miami to Orlando and Tampa.

**Frontier** (F9;☑800-432-1359; www.frontierairlines.com) Services Tampa, Orlando and Fort Lauderdale from Denver, Minneapolis and the Midwest.

**Southwest** (WN;☑800-435-9792; www.southwest.com) One of the US's leading low-cost carriers, offering free checked baggage and, at times, extremely low fares.

**Spirit** (NK;☑801-401-2220; www.spiritair.com) Florida-based discount carrier serving Florida cities from East Coast, US, Caribbean, and Central and South America.

**United** (UA;☑800-824-6400; www.united.com) International flights to Orlando and Miami; domestic flights to and between key Florida cities.

**US Airways** (☑800-428-4322; www.usairways.com) Serves Florida from most of US.

## Bicycle

Regional bicycle touring is very popular. Flat topography, ocean breezes on the Overseas Highway and increasing bicycle infrastructure in Miami and Miami Beach make for great itineraries. Just be wary of your surroundings, especially if you go cycling near the north of Downtown. A few blocks north of that area it is especially tense. You may want to target winter to spring; summer is unbearably hot and humid for long-distance cycling.

Renting a bicycle is easy in South Florida. Try the Everglades International Hostel if you want to cycle in the Glades. In Key West there's a plethora of options located on the main drags of Truman Ave and Simonton St; bicycle is probably the easiest way to get around flat Key West. Don't forget that the **Deco-Bike** (☑305-532-9494; www.decobike.com) bike-share program now makes cycling in Miami Beach especially easy.

Some other things to keep in mind:

**Helmet laws** Helmets are required for anyone aged 16 and younger. Adults are not required to wear helmets, but should.

**Road rules** Bikes must obey road rules; ride on the right-hand side of the road, with traffic, not on sidewalks.

**Transporting your bike to Florida** Bikes are considered checked luggage on airplanes, but often must be boxed and fees can be high (over $200).

**Theft** Bring and use a sturdy lock (U-type is best). Theft is common, especially in Miami Beach.

For more information and assistance, visit these organizations:

**League of American Bicyclists** (www.bikeleague.org)

General advice, plus lists of local bike clubs and repair shops.

**International Bicycle Fund** (www.ibike.org) Advice plus a comprehensive overview of bike regulations by airline.

**Better World Club** (☑866-238-1137; www.betterworldclub.com) Offers a bicycle roadside-assistance program.

## Boat

Florida is a huge destination and departure point for cruises of all kind. The **Port of Miami** (www.miamidade.gov/portofmiami) likes to brag that it's the 'cruise capital of the world' with good reason: this is the largest cruise-ship port on Earth.

**Port Everglades** (www.porteverglades.net, www.fort-lauderdale-cruises.com), located near Fort Lauderdale, is also a potential gateway port to the Miami region.

For specials on other multinight and multiday cruises, see the following:

➡ www.cruise.com
➡ www.cruiseweb.com
➡ www.vacationstogo.com
➡ www.cruisesonly.com

Major cruise companies include:

**Carnival Cruise Lines** (☑800-764-7419; www.carnival.com)

**Norwegian Cruise Line** (☑866-234-7350; www.ncl.com)

**Royal Caribbean** (☑866-562-7625; www.royalcaribbean.com)

## Bus

**Greyhound** (☑800-231-2222; www.greyhound.com) is the major carrier in and out of Miami. The major terminals are **Airport terminal** (☑305-871-1810; 4111 NW 27th St); **North Miami terminal** (☑305-945-0801; 16560 NE 6th Ave); and the **Miami Cutler Bay terminal** (Cutler Bay; ☑305-296-9072; Cutler Ridge

### GREEN TRAVEL

**Biking** Good exercise, no gas, fresh air – what's not to love? Try **DecoBikes** in South Beach (see above).

**Metromover** A free way of getting around downtown, but only serves Miami (not Miami Beach).

**Tri-rail** Cheap, fast links between Miami and its outer suburbs.

**Gables Trolley** Fun, nostalgic public transportation through Coral Gables.

**Walking** Especially in South Beach, which is barely 2 miles (2.8km) long.

Mall, 20505 S Dixie Hwy). Megabus picks up from Miami International Airport and 600 NE 1st Ave downtown.

## Car & Motorcycle

The easiest and most popular way to travel around South Florida is by car. While it's possible to avoid using a car on single-destination trips to Miami or Key West, relying on public transit is inconvenient for even limited regional touring. Motorcycles are also popular in Florida, given the flat roads and warm weather (summer rain excepted). In addition, motorized transport is practically a must to explore the Everglades. Greyhound buses run through the Keys, but you can't pull over and smell the roses by the side of the Overseas Highway, which is 90% of the fun.

Roads are well-kept and maintained, with the exception of the occasional pothole and construction site in Miami, and the muddy Loop Rd in the Everglades (which was being improved at the time of research).

### Automobile Associations

The **American Automobile Association** (AAA; ☑800-874-7532; www.aaa.com) has reciprocal agreements with several international auto clubs (check with AAA and bring your membership card). For members, AAA offers travel insurance, tour bookings, diagnostic centers for used-car buyers, a greater number of regional offices, and it advocates politically for the auto industry.

An ecofriendly alternative is the **Better World Club** (☑866-238-1137; www.betterworldclub.com) which donates 1% of earnings to assist environmental cleanup, offers ecologically sensitive choices for services and advocates politically for environmental causes. Better World also has a roadside assistance program for bicycles.

In both organizations, the central member benefit is 24-hour emergency roadside assistance anywhere in the USA. Both clubs offer trip planning and free maps, travel agency services, car insurance and a range of discounts (car rentals, hotels etc).

### Driver's License

Foreign visitors can legally drive in the USA for up to 12 months with their home driver's license. However, getting an International Driving Permit (IDP) is recommended; this will have more credibility with US traffic police, especially if your home license doesn't have a photo or is in a foreign language. Your automobile association at home can issue an IDP, valid for one year, for a small fee. You must carry your home license together with the IDP. To drive a motorcycle, you need either a valid US state motorcycle license or an IDP specially endorsed for motorcycles.

### Insurance

➡ Insurance is legally required; if you don't have it you risk financial ruin if there's an accident.

➡ If you already have auto insurance (even overseas), or if you buy travel insurance, make sure that the policy has adequate liability coverage for a rental car in Florida.

➡ Rental-car companies will provide liability insurance, but most charge extra. Always ask. Rental companies almost never include collision damage insurance for the vehicle. Instead, they offer optional Collision Damage Waiver (CDW) or Loss Damage Waiver (LDW), usually with an initial deductible of $100 to $500. For an extra premium, you can usually get this deductible covered as well.

➡ Most credit cards offer collision damage coverage for rental cars if you rent for 15 days or less and charge the total rental to your card. This is a good way to avoid

paying extra fees to the rental company, but note that if there's an accident, you sometimes must pay the rental-car company first and then seek reimbursement from the credit-card company. Check your credit card policy. Paying extra for some or all of this insurance increases the cost of a rental car by as much as $10 to $30 a day.

### Parking

Parking in Miami is pretty straightforward. Regulations are well signed and meters and street parking is plentiful, with the exception of Downtown by day (and the area by Brickell at most times) and South Beach by night. Downtown, near Bayside Marketplace, parking is cheap but confusing: you must find a place in the head-on parking lots, buy a ticket from a central machine, and display it in your windshield.

**Miami Beach Parking** (☑305-673-7275; www.miamibeachfl.gov/parking) maintains a series of extremely convenient garages across Miami Beach for $1.75 per hour (north of 23rd St it's only $1 although there is a $20 flat rate from 8pm to 5am on Friday, Saturday and Sunday). Look for giant blue 'P' signs at:

➡ Collins Ave at 7th St

➡ Collins Ave at 14th St

➡ Washington Ave at 12th St

➡ Washington Ave at 16th St

➡ 17th St across from the Jackie Gleason Theater of the Performing Arts

If you park illegally or if the meter runs out, parking fines are about $25 to $50, but a tow could cost a lot more. Other useful parking garages can be found in Coral Gables and Coconut Grove.

Street meters in Miami Beach south of 23rd street are $1.50 per hour and need to be fed from 9am to 3am. North of 23rd St meters cost $1 per hour and operate from 8am to 6pm. Most meters allow you to pay for up to three hours, although some have increased that range. Many meter machines include a credit-card option; failing that, you can purchase a Meter Card, available from the **Miami Beach City Hall** (1st fl, 1700 Convention Center Dr); the **Miami Beach Chamber of Commerce** (📞305-674-1300; www.miamibeachchamber.com; 1920 Meridian Ave; ⏰9am-5pm Mon-Fri); any municipal parking lot or any Publix grocery store. Denominations come in $10, $20 and $25 (and meters cost $1 per hour).

## Rental

### CAR

Car rental is very competitive. Most rental companies require that you have a major credit card, that you be at least 25 years old and that you have a valid driver's license (your home license will do but an IDP is recommended). Some national companies may rent to drivers between the ages of 21 and 24 for an additional charge. Those under 21 are usually not permitted to rent at all.

**Car Rental Express** (www.carrentalexpress.com) rates and compares independent agencies in US cities; it's particularly useful for searching out cheaper long-term rentals.

National car-rental companies include the following:

**Alamo** (📞877-222-9075; www.alamo.com)

**Avis** (📞800-331-2112; www.avis.com)

**Budget** (📞800-527-0700; www.budget.com)

**Dollar** (📞800-800-4000; www.dollar.com)

**Enterprise** (📞800-261-7331; www.enterprise.com)

**Hertz** (📞800-654-3131; www.hertz.com)

**National** (📞800-468-3334; www.nationalcar.com)

**Rent-a-Wreck** (📞877-877-0700; www.rentawreck.com)

**Thrifty** (📞800-367-2277; www.thrifty.com)

Rental cars are readily available at all airport locations and many downtown city locations. With advance reservations for a small car, the daily rate with unlimited mileage is about $35 to $55, while typical weekly rates are $200 to $400, plus a myriad of taxes and fees. If you rent from a nonairport location, you save the exorbitant airport fees.

An alternative in Miami is **Zipcar** (www.zipcar.com), a car-sharing service that charges hourly/daily rental fees with free gas, insurance and limited mileage included; prepayment is required.

### MOTORCYCLE

To straddle a Harley across Florida, contact **EagleRider** (📞888-900-9901; www.eaglerider.com) which has offices in Miami. It offers a wide range of models, which start at $150 a day, plus liability insurance. Adult riders (over 21) are not required by Florida law to wear a helmet, but you should.

### MOTORHOME (RV)

Forget hotels. Drive your own. Touring Florida by recreational vehicle can be as low-key or as over-the-top as you wish.

After settling on the vehicle's size, consider the impact of gas prices, gas mileage, additional mileage costs, insurance and refundable deposits; these can add up quickly. Typically, RVs don't come with unlimited mileage, so estimate your mileage up front to calculate the true rental cost.

**CruiseAmerica** (📞800-671-8042; www.cruiseamerica.com) The largest national RV-rental firm has offices across South Florida.

**Adventures On Wheels** (📞800-943-3579; www.wheels9.com) Office in Miami.

**Recreational Vehicle Rental Association** (📞703-591-7130; www.rvda.org) Good resource for RV information and advice, and helps find rental locations.

## Road Rules

If you're new to Florida or US roads, here are some basics:

➡ The maximum speed limit on interstates is 75mph, but that drops to 65mph and 55mph in urban areas. Pay attention to the posted signs. City street speed limits vary between 15mph and 45mph.

➡ Florida police officers are strict with speed-limit enforcement, and speeding tickets are expensive. If caught going over the speed limit by 10mph, the fine is $155.

➡ All passengers in a car must wear seat belts; the fine for not wearing a seat belt is $30. All children under three must be in a child safety seat.

➡ As in the rest of the US, drive on the right-hand side of the road. On highways, pass in the left-hand lane, but anxious drivers often pass wherever space allows.

➡ Unless otherwise signed, you can turn right at a red light as long as you come to a stop first. At four-way stop signs, the car that reaches the intersection first has right of way. In a tie, the car on the right has right of way.

## Hitchhiking

Hitchhiking is never entirely safe in any country, and we don't recommend it. Travelers who decide to hitch should understand that they are taking a small but serious risk. People who do choose to hitch will be safer if they go in pairs and let someone know where they are planning to go. Be sure to ask the driver where he or she is going rather than telling the person where you want to go.

## Local Transportation

### Bus

#### MIAMI

Miami's local bus system is called **Metrobus** (📞305-

891-3131; www.miamidade.gov/transit/routes.asp; tickets $2) and, though it has an extensive route system, service is pretty spotty. Each bus route has a different schedule and routes generally run from about 5:30am to 11pm, though some are 24 hours. Rides cost $2 and must be paid in exact change with a token, coins or a combination of a dollar bill and coins (most locals use the monthly Metropass). An easy-to-read route map is available online.

In South Beach, an excellent option is the **South Beach Local Circulator** (☑305-891-3131; 25¢), a looping shuttle bus with disabled-rider access that operates along Washington between South Pointe Dr and 17th St and loops back around on Alton Rd on the west side of the beach. Rides cost only 25¢ and come along every 10 to 15 minutes between 7:45am and 1am Monday to Saturday and 10am to 1am Sunday and holidays. Look for official bus stops every couple of blocks, marked by posts with colorful Electrowave signs.

Coral Gables has its own new shuttle in the form of a hybrid-electric bus disguised as a trolley. It's free, but only really good for getting around the Gables. The north–south route runs along Ponce de León Blvd from the Douglas Metrorail Station to SW 8th St (between 6:30am and 8pm Monday to Thursday, and 6:30am and 10pm Friday).

**KEY WEST**

**Key West Transit** (☑305-809-3910; www.kwtransit.com; single fare $2) operates a local bus service on Key West. The bus line connects the western, historical half of the island to the residential units and strip malls of eastern Key West. This is primarily a utility service for island residents

who work on the west half of Key West and do not have the means to drive there.

If you're a tourist, KW Transit's more useful service is the **Lower Keys Shuttle**; see www.keywestcity.com and look under departments, then Department of Transportation. This commuter bus service runs between Key West and Marathon nine times a day; fare is just $3. From Marathon you can connect to the **301 Dade-Monroe Express** ($2.35), operated by Dade County, which connects Marathon to Florida City six times a day; see www.miamidade.gov/transit for a detailed schedule. This route works in the opposite direction as well, which means you can feasibly take public buses from Florida City all the way to Key West. Just plan on a long day; for example, if you left from Key West airport at 12:21pm, you'd reach Mile Marker 50 in Marathon at 2pm. Then you'd have to wait till the 301 leaves from MM 50 at 3:45pm, landing you in Florida City at 6pm.

**Metro**

In Miami, the driverless **Metromover** (www.miamidade.gov/transit/mover) circles downtown and connects with **Metrorail** (www.miamidade.gov/transit/rail). It is a 21-mile-long heavy rail system that has one elevated line running from Hialeah through downtown Miami and south to Kendall/Dadeland. Trains run every five to 15 minutes from 6am to midnight. The fare is $2, or $1 with a Metromover transfer. An extension of the Metrorail from Miami proper to the airport is being planned.

The regional **Tri-Rail** (☑800-874-7245; www.tri-rail.com) train connects Dade, Broward and Palm Beach counties. Fares are calculated on a zone basis, and the route

spans six zones. No tickets are sold on the train, so allow time to make your purchase before boarding. All trains and stations are accessible to riders with disabilities. The Tri-Rail website has a list of stations.

## Taxi

Outside MIA, South Beach and the Port of Miami, where taxis buzz around like bees at a hive, you'll likely use a phone to hail a cab. Try **Metro** (☑305-888-8888), **Sunshine** (☑305-445-3333) or **Yellow** (☑305-400-0000) for a ride.

Taxis in Miami have flat and metered rates. You will not have to pay extra for luggage or for extra people in the cab, though you are expected to tip an additional 10% to 15%. Add about 10% to normal taxi fares (or a dollar, whichever is greater). If you have a bad experience, get the driver's chauffeur license number, name and license-plate number and contact the **Taxi Complaints Line** (☑305-375-2460).

In Key West, pick up a metered pink taxi from **Key West Taxis** (☑305-296-6666).

## Train

**Amtrak** (☑800-872-7245, 305-835-1222; www.amtrak.com; 8303 NW 37th Ave) trains run between a number of Florida cities. As a way to get around Florida, Amtrak offers extremely limited service, and yet for certain specific trips their trains can be very easy and inexpensive. In essence, daily trains run between Jacksonville, Orlando and Miami, with one line branching off to Tampa. In addition, Thruway Motorcoach (or bus) service gets Amtrak passengers to Daytona Beach, St Petersburg and Fort Myers.

# Behind the Scenes

## SEND US YOUR FEEDBACK

We love to hear from travelers – your comments keep us on our toes and help make our books better. Our well-traveled team reads every word on what you loved or loathed about this book. Although we cannot reply individually to your submissions, we always guarantee that your feedback goes straight to the appropriate authors, in time for the next edition. Each person who sends us information is thanked in the next edition – the most useful submissions are rewarded with a selection of digital PDF chapters.

Visit **lonelyplanet.com/contact** to submit your updates and suggestions or to ask for help. Our award-winning website also features inspirational travel stories, news and discussions.

Note: We may edit, reproduce and incorporate your comments in Lonely Planet products such as guidebooks, websites and digital products, so let us know if you don't want your comments reproduced or your name acknowledged. For a copy of our privacy policy visit lonelyplanet.com/privacy.

## OUR READERS

**Many thanks to the travelers who used the last edition and wrote to us with helpful hints, useful advice and interesting anecdotes:** Moshe Ash, Heleen Blom, Wren DiGisi, Fredrik Divall, Tim Ozinga, Melanie Steinhoff, Florent Vallespir

## AUTHOR THANKS
### Adam Karlin

To my editors, Jo and Dora, for being understanding, accommodating and supportive; Jaime Levenshon and Bethany Martinez, for an amazing crash-course in Miami dining; my parents, for their unflagging support; Eggy and Gizmo, who have made writing from home more zoo-keeping, cuddling joy than chore; Rachel Houge, my lovely wife, for the same, for her humor, smiles and laughter, and for following me whenever I paddle too close to crocodiles; and to my daughter, who is on the way, and to whom I whisper the hope of new roads, and I promise all the world to explore.

## ACKNOWLEDGEMENTS

Climate map data adapted from Peel MC, Finlayson BL & McMahon TA (2007) 'Updated World Map of the Köppen-Geiger Climate Classification', Hydrology and Earth System Sciences, 11, 163344.

Cover photograph: Ocean Drive, Miami, at twilight, Guido Cozzi / 4Corners ©.

# THIS BOOK

This 7th edition of Lonely Planet's *Miami & the Keys* guidebook was researched and written by Adam Karlin, who also wrote the previous two editions. Earlier editions were written by Beth Greenfield, Kim Grant, Nick Selby and Corinna Selby. This guidebook was commissioned in Lonely Planet's London office, and produced by the following:

**Commissioning Editor**
Jo Cooke
**Destination Editor**
Dora Whitaker
**Product Editor**
Elizabeth Jones
**Book Designer**
Virginia Moreno
**Senior Cartographer**
Alison Lyall

**Assisting Editors** Kellie Langdon, Kate Mathews
**Assisting Cartographers**
Mark Griffiths, Julie Sheridan
**Cover Researcher**
Naomi Parker

**Thanks to** Sasha Baskett, Elin Berglund, Brendan Dempsey, Ryan Evans, Briohny Hooper, Alexander Howard, Indra Kilfoyle, Claire Naylor, Karyn Noble, Anthony Phelan, John Taufa, Juan Winata

# Index

10,000 Islands 132, 139
11th Street Diner 50, 99

## A
A1A 51, 54
accommodations 222-3, *see also individual locations*
activities 18-19, 22-5, 201-5, *see also individual activities*
Adams Key 141
Adrienne Arsht Center for the Performing Arts 64
Ah-Tah-Thi-Ki Seminole Indian Museum 135
air passes 232
air travel 232, 233-4
airboats 129
airports 232
alligator meat 198
alligators 9, 138, 198, 211, 9
amphibians 210-12
animal rights 198
animals 209-12, *see also individual animals*
aquariums 71, 147
architecture 20, 43-50, 217-20
area codes 228-9
Argentinian culture 186-7
Art Basel Miami Beach 25
Art Deco Historic District 9, 39, 42, 43-50, 218-19
art galleries, *see* museums & galleries
art walks 115
art-deco architecture 20, 43-50, 217-20, *see also* Art Deco Historic District
arts 20
ATMs 227
Avalon Hotel 50, **50**

Map Pages **000**
Photo Pages **000**

## B
Bahama Village 161
Bahia Honda 15, 156-8, **15**
baseball 119
basketball 118, 119
bathhouses 84
beaches 18, 32
    Anne's Beach 150
    Fort Zachary Taylor Historic State Park 160
    Haulover Beach Park 61
    Higgs Beach 165
    North Beach (Miami) 11, 59-61, 96-7, 102-3, 112-13, **60**, **11**
    Smathers Beach 165
    Sombrero Beach 154
    South Beach (Key West) 165
    South Beach (Miami) 12, 42, 51-9, 56-7, 90-6, 99-102, 110-12, **52-3**, **56-7**
    Veterans Memorial Park & Beach 157
bears 210
beer 200
Berkeley Shore Hotel 50
bicycling 17, 206, 234
    Florida Keys 148
    Miami 82, 85
Big Cypress 129, 132-3
Big Pine 156-8
Biltmore Hotel 12, 77, 99, **12**
birds 209
bird-watching 147, 157, 209
Biscayne National Park 140-1
Blue Hole 157
boat travel 233, 234
    Everglades, the 133, 141
    Florida Keys 147, 151, 165
Boca Chica Key 158-9
Boca Chita Key 141
books 174
    environment 209, 216
    food 197
    history 181, 182

*botanicas* 70
bowling 82
Brazilian culture 187
Brickell Key 65-6
Britto, Romero 188
budget 17
bus travel 17, 233, 234-5, 236-7
business hours 17, 227
butterflies 160

## C
Calle Ocho 12, 73
camping 204, 222-3
    Everglades, the 132, 139-40, 141, 204
    Florida Keys 15, 148, 153, 158, 204
    Miami 204
canoeing 204-5
    Everglades, the 132, 133, 139
    Florida Keys 150
car travel 17, 233, 235-6
    organizations 235
    rental 236
Cardozo Hotel 45, 95, **44**
Carlyle Hotel 45
Carnaval Miami 23, 73
Castro, Fidel 178, 180
Cavalier South Beach 46, 93, **46**
celebrities 12
cell phones 228-9
cemeteries 69-70, 160
chickees 139
children, travel with 31-4
    Florida Keys 149
    Miami 87
churches
    Coral Gables Congregational Church 79
    Episcopal Church of St Bernard de Clairvaux 80

Miami Beach Community Church 51
    Plymouth Congregational Church 77
cinemas 116
circus arts 86
classical music 118
climate 16, 22-5, *see also individual regions*
cocktails 200
Coconut Grove **76**
    accommodations 98
    drinking & nightlife 115-16
    food 108-9, 196
    sights 74-7
Colombian cuisine 198
Colombian culture 187
Colony Hotel 46, **11**, **46**
Conch Republic, the 160, 185
conservation 130-1, 214-16
consulates 226
Coral Castle 136
Coral Gables 14, **78**
    accommodations 98-9
    drinking & nightlife 116
    food 109-10, 196
    sights 77-9
coyote 210
credit cards 227
Crescent Hotel 46
cricket 119
crocodiles 138
cruises 233, 234
Cuba 180-1
Cuban cuisine 194, 195, 197-8
Cuban culture 73-4, 90, 100, 186
cultural diversity 21, 184-7
culture 174-5
currency 16
customs regulations 226
cycling, *see* bicycling

**D**

dance 117-18
dangers, see safety
day spas 82, 84
DecoBike program 82
deer 157, 210, **21**
Deering, James 75
Delano Hotel 49, 95, **48**
Design District 13, **68**
   accommodations 105-7
   food 114-15, 196
   sights 67-70
digital photography 228
disabilities, travelers
   with 230
discount cards 223
diving 205
   Everglades, the 141
   Florida Keys 147, 156-7,
      165
   Miami 84
dolphins 146, 153, 210
Douglas, Marjory
   Stoneman 130-1, 136
Downtown Miami **62-3**
   accommodations 97-8
   drinking & nightlife
      113-14
   food 103-5, 196
   sights 61-7
drinking & nightlife 18,
   see also individual
   locations
drinks 199-200
driver's licenses 235
driving, see car travel
Dry Tortugas National
   Park 167
Duval Street 159-60
DVDs 229

**E**

economy 175
electricity 224, 229
Elliott Key 141
embassies 226
emergencies 225, 228, 230
environment 208-16
environmental issues
   214-16
   Everglades conservation
      130-1
   lionfish 212
   manatees 140
   swimming with dolphins
      146
Ernest Coe 137, 139-40
Española Way
   Promenade 54

Essex House Hotel 45,
   93, **45**
events 22-5
Everglades, the 9, 36,
   125-41, **126-7**, **14**
   accommodations 125
   camping 132, 139-40,
      141, 204
   climate 125, 138
   conservation 130-1
   environmental issues
      215
   food 125
   highlights 126-7
   hiking trails 203
   itineraries 30
   planning information 125
   travel seasons 125
Everglades City 133-5
Everglades National Park
   128-40
Everglades: River of Grass,
   The 136
exchange rates 17

**F**

Fakahatchee Strand
   Preserve 135
Fantasy Fest 25
fashion 192
festivals 22-5
   food 194
   literary 166
   Miami 88-90
film locations 45, 83, 95,
   114, 147, 157, 164
films 174, 191-2
fishing 207
   Everglades, the 141
   Miami 84
Flagler, Henry Morrison
   178-9
flamenco 191
Floribbean cuisine 196
Florida black bears 210
Florida City 135-7
Florida Keys 36, 142-72,
   **144-5**
   accommodations 142
   camping 15, 148, 153,
      158, 204
   climate 142, 143
   food 142
   highlights 144-5
   hiking trails 203-4
   planning information 142
   travel seasons 142
Florida panthers 138,
   209-10

food 10, 18, 193-9, see also
   individual locations
   alligator meat 198
   Cuban sandwiches 100
   festivals 194
   food trucks 104
   Key lime pie 150, 198
   locavore movement 199
   seafood 194-5, 198, 199
football 118-19
forests 213-14
Fort Jefferson 167
Fort Lauderdale-Hollywood
   International Airport
   122, 123, 232
fossils 151
Freedom Tower 66

**G**

galleries, see museums &
   galleries
gay culture 185
gay travelers 171, 224
gentrification 175
geography 130-1, 208-9
geology 208
giardiasis 225
golf 84-5, 207
Grassy Key 153
Greater Miami 79-82, 99,
   110, 116
Greene, Pardon C 178

**H**

Haitian culture 70, 186
hammocks (groves) 201-2
health 224-5
Hell's Bay 14
Hemingway, Ernest 24,
   160, 161
Hemingway Days 24
heron 157
Heyman, Richard 183
Hiaasen, Carl 189
Hibiscus Island 80
Highway 1 10, 29, **10**
hiking 132-3, 139, 202-4
hip-hop 191
historic buildings & sites 178
   Biltmore Hotel 77, 99
   Black Archives Historic
      Lyric Theater Welcome
      Center 66
   Casa Antigua 161, 164
   Coconut Grove
      Playhouse 75
   Coral Gables City Hall 78
   Dade County
      Courthouse 67

Eden Roc Renaissance
   Miami Beach 61, 97
Fontainebleau 59, 96-7
Fort Jefferson 167
Little White House 161
Merrick House 78
Pigeon Key National
   Historic District 154
San Carlos Institute 161
Strand Building 164
Tower Theater 74
history 176-83
   Bay of Pigs 180
   books 181, 182
   British settlement 176
   crime 181-2
   Cuba, relationship with
      180-1, 182-3
   Great Depression,
      the 180
   Mariel Boatlift 181
   race riots 181
   Seminole wars 176-8
   slavery 176-7
   Spanish settlement 176
hitchhiking 236
HIV/AIDS 225
holidays 228
Holocaust Memorial 54, 58
Homestead 135-7
Hotel Victor 49, 92, **48**
hurricanes 228

**I**

immigration 226
insects 138
insurance 225, 227
   car 235
   health 225
internet access 227
internet resources 17
Islamorada 150-2
itineraries 26-30

**J**

James Royal Palm Hotel
   49, 96, **49**
Japanese culture 187
Jerry's Famous Deli 45, 101
Jewish culture 59, 186

**K**

kayaking 204-5
   Everglades, the 14,
      133, 139
   Florida Keys 150, 152,
      153, 165
   Miami 85

Key Biscayne **72**
accommodations 98
food 107, 196
sights 70-3
Key deer 157, 210, **21**
Key Largo 146-50
Key lime pie 150, 198
Key West 13, 36, 159-72, **162-3**
accommodations 166-9
activities 165
architecture 220
climate 142, 143
drinking & nightlife 13, 170-1
entertainment 171-2
festivals & events 166
food 169-70
gay & lesbian travelers 171
history 143
planning information 142
shopping 172
sights 159-61, 164-5
tours 165-6
transportation 172
travel seasons 142
Key West International Airport 172, 232
Keys, the, *see* Florida Keys
kiteboarding 153, 206

**L**

languages 16
Lapidus, Morris 178, 220
Latin American cuisine 195
Latin American music 190-1
Latino culture 90
legal matters 227
lesbian travelers 171, 224
lifeguard stations 45, 58, **2**, **44**
lighthouses
Cape Florida Lighthouse 71
Key West Lighthouse 164-5
lignum vitae 155
Lincoln Road Mall 42, 51
lionfish 212
literary festivals 166
literature 189-90, *see also* books

Little Haiti **68**
drinking & nightlife 114-15
food 105-7, 196
sights 67-70
Little Havana 12, **74-5**
drinking & nightlife 115
food 107-8, 196
sights 73-4
live music 118
locavore movement 199
Long Key 152-3
Looe Key 156-8
Lower Keys 156-9
Lyme disease 225

**M**

Mallory Square 159, **13**, **19**
manatees 140, 210
mangroves 155, 214
Marathon 153-6
markets
Florida Keys 157
Miami 65
measures 229
medical services 225
merengue 191
metro travel 237
Miami 35, 38-124, **40-1**
accommodations 38, 90-9
activities 82, 84-7
camping 204
children, travel with 87
climate 38
Coconut Grove 74-7, 98, 108-9, 115-16, **76**
Coral Gables 14, 77-9, 98-9, 109-10, 116, **78**
cultural diversity 184, 186-7
Design District 13, 67-70, 105-7, 114-15, **68**
Downtown Miami 61-7, 97-8, 103-5, 113-14, **62-3**
drinking & nightlife 10, 15, 110-16
entertainment 116-19
festivals & events 88-90
food 10, 38, 99-110, 195-6
Greater Miami 79-82, 99, 110, 116
highlights 40-1
hiking trails 202-3
itineraries 27, 28
Key Biscayne 70-3, 98, 107, **72**

Little Haiti 67-70, 105-7, 114-15, **68**
Little Havana 12, 73-4, 107-8, 115, **74-5**
Northern Miami Beach 11, 59-61, 96-7, 102-3, 112-13, **60**, **11**
planning information 38, 55
shopping 119-21
sights 39, 42, 51-82
South Beach 12, 42, 51-9, 56-7, 90-6, 99-102, 110-12, **52-3**, **56-7**
tourist information 122
tours 87-8
travel seasons 38
travel to/from 122-3
travel within 123-4
walking tours 83
Wynwood 67-70, 105-7, 114-15, **68**
Miami Dolphins 118-19
Miami International Airport 122, 123, 232
Miami Marlins 119
Miami River 67
Miami-Dade Public Library 66
Miccosukee culture 129
Miccosukee Village 129
Middle Keys 153-6
MiMo on BiBo (Miami Modern on Biscayne Boulevard) 97
mobile phones 228-9
money 16, 17, 223, 227
Monroe, Eva 77
motorcycle travel 233, 235-6
museums & galleries 13, 32
AC Fine Art 76
Ah-Tah-Thi-Ki Seminole Indian Museum 135
ArtCenter/South Florida 51
Artopia 67
Bass Museum of Art 54
Bay of Pigs Museum & Library 74
Big Cypress Gallery 129, 132
Brisky Gallery 67
Cisneros Fontanal Arts Foundation 66
Coconut Grove Arts Precinct 76
Coral Gables Museum 79
Crane Point Museum 154
Cuba Ocho 73
Florida Keys Eco-Discovery Center 160

Florida Keys History of Diving Museum 151
Fort East Martello Museum & Gardens 161
Gold Coast Railroad Museum 81
HistoryMiami 65
Jewish Museum of Florida 54
Little Haiti Cultural Center 69
Little Havana Art District 74
Lowe Art Museum 77
Marjory Stoneman Douglas Biscayne Nature Center 71
MDC Museum of Art & Design 66
Miami Center for Architecture & Design 66
Miami Children's Museum 81
Miami Museum of Science & Planetarium 75
Miccosukee Village 129
Museum of Art & History at the Custom House 161
Museum of Contemporary Art North Miami 79-80
Museum of the Everglades 133
PanAmerican Art Projects 67
Pérez Art Museum Miami 66
Rubell Family Art Collection 69
Studios of Key West 161
Vizcaya Museum & Gardens 75
Wings Over Miami 81-2
Wolfsonian-FIU 42, 46
World Erotic Art Museum 59
music 19, 190-1

**N**

national & state parks & reserves 214, *see also* parks & gardens
Bahia Honda State Park 156
Barnacle Historic State Park 75
Big Cypress National Preserve 132

Bill Baggs Cape Florida State Park 71
Biscayne National Park 140-1
Curry Hammock State Park 153
Dry Tortugas National Park 167
Everglades National Park 128-40
Fort Zachary Taylor Historic State Park 160
Great White Heron National Wildlife Refuge 157
Indian Key Historic State Park 150
John Pennekamp Coral Reef State Park 147
Lignumvitae Key Botanical State Park 150
Long Key State Recreation Area 152-3
Looe Key National Marine Sanctuary 156-7
National Key Deer Refuge Headquarters 157
Oleta River State Park 61
Pigeon Key National Historic District 154
Windley Key Fossil Reef Geological State Site 151
Native American culture 129, 135, 176-8
newspapers 229
Nicaraguan culture 187
nightclubs 113
nightlife 18, *see also individual locations*
No Name Key 157
Northern Miami Beach 11, **60**, **11**
accommodations 96-7
drinking & nightlife 112-13
food 102-3, 196
sights 59-61

**O**
Ocean Drive 51, **8-9**
Ochopee 129, 132-3
Old Florida 20-1
opening hours 17, 227
orchids 213
outdoor activities 18-19, 201-7, *see also individual activities*

Overseas Highway 10, 29, **10**

**P**
paddleboarding 85
painting 188-9
Palm Island 80
panthers 138, 209-10
parks & gardens, *see also national & state parks & reserves*
Arch Creek Park 61
Bayfront Park 65
Biscayne Community Center & Village Green Park 71, 73
Crandon Park 70-1
Fairchild Tropical Garden 80
Fort East Martello Museum & Gardens 161
Fruit & Spice Park 81
Harry Harris Park 147
Hialeah Park 80
Kampong 75
Matheson Hammock Park 81
Máximo Gómez Park 73
Miami Beach Botanical Garden 58
Nancy Forrester's Secret Garden 161
Pinecrest Gardens 81
South Pointe Park 51
Veterans Memorial Park & Beach 157
Vizcaya Museum & Gardens 75
passports 226
performing arts 116-17
photography 228
planning, *see also individual regions*
budgeting 17
calendar of events 22-5
children, travel with 31-4
internet resources 17
itineraries 26-30
Miami basics 16-17
travel seasons 16, 22-5
plants 212-14
politics 174-5
population 175
postal services 228
public art 189
public holidays 228
public transportation 17, 236-7

**Q**
quirky attractions 20

**R**
rabies 225
recreational vehicles (RVs) 236
reggae 191
religion 175
reptiles 210-12
road rules 227, 234, 236
rodeos 85
Royal Palm 137, 139-40
running 85

**S**
safety 225, 228, 230, 236
Everglades, the 138
Miami 121
sailing 207
salsa 190-1
sculpture 189
sea turtles 212
seafood 194-5, 198, 199
self-catering 197
Seminole culture 135
Seminoles 176-8
senior travelers 223
Shark Valley 128-9
shopping 20, *see also individual locations*
skating 86
Skybar 12, 112, **12**
smoking 229
snakes 138, 211-12
snorkeling 205
Florida Keys 147, 156-7, 157, 165
Miami 84
South Beach 12, 39, **52-3**, **56-7**, **19**
accommodations 90-6
drinking & nightlife 110-12
food 99-102, 195
sights 42, 51-9
Southernmost Point 165
Southern-style cuisine 197
Spanish culture 187
spectator sports 118-19
Star Island 80
Stiltsville 71
stone-crab claws 198
Sugarloaf Key 158-9
Surfcomber 49, 96
surfing 86
swamp buggies 129
swamps 213
swimming 86

synagogues 59

**T**
Tamiami Trail 128-9, 132-5
tango 191
Tavernier 146-50
taxis 237
telephone services 228-9
television 191-2, 229
Tequesta people 177
theater 117
Tides 49, 95, **49**
time 229
tipping 227
tourist information 229-30
tours
Everglades, the 133, 136, 137, 140-1
Florida Keys 150, 151, 154, 165-6
Miami 87-8
train travel 233, 237
transportation 232-7
travel to/from Miami & the Keys 232-3
travel within Miami & the Keys 233-7
trekking, *see hiking*
turtles 154
Tuttle, Julia 178-9
TV 191-2, 229

**U**
University of Miami Hurricanes 119
Upper Keys 143, 146-53

**V**
vacations 228
vegetarian travelers 197, 199
Venetian Pool 77
Versace, Gianni 42
Viernes Culturales 117
Villa by Barton G, The 42, 93
visas 226
volunteering 230

**W**
wakeboarding 206
Waldorf Towers Hotel 46, **47**
walking tours
art walks 115
Miami 83
weather 16, 22-5, 228, *see also individual regions*

websites 17
weights 229
West Nile virus 225
wetlands 213
wi-fi 227
wildlife 209-12
wildlife parks
    & preserves 20, see
    also zoos
Big Cypress National
    Preserve 132
Dolphin Research Center
    153
Everglades Outpost 136
Fakahatchee Strand
    Preserve 135
Florida Keys Wild Bird Re-
    habilitation Center 147

Great White Heron
    National Wildlife
    Refuge 157
John Pennekamp Coral
    Reef State Park 147
Key West Butterfly &
    Nature Conservatory
    160
Looe Key National
    Marine Sanctuary
    156-7
National Key Deer
    Refuge Headquarters
    157
Skunk Ape Research
    Headquarters 132
Turtle Hospital 154

windsurfing
    Everglades, the 141
    Florida Keys 153
    Miami 85
Winter Music
    Conference 23
Wolfsonian-FIU 42, 46
women travelers 230
work 231
Wynwood **68**
    drinking & nightlife
    114-15
    food 105-7, 196
    sights 67-70
Wynwood Walls 69

Y
yoga 86-7

Z
zoos, see also
    aquariums, wildlife
    parks & preserves
Jungle Island 81
Monkey Jungle 81
Sherriff's Animal Farm
    159
Zoo Miami 80-1

NOTES

# Map Legend

## Sights
- Beach
- Bird Sanctuary
- Buddhist
- Castle/Palace
- Christian
- Confucian
- Hindu
- Islamic
- Jain
- Jewish
- Monument
- Museum/Gallery/Historic Building
- Ruin
- Sento Hot Baths/Onsen
- Shinto
- Sikh
- Taoist
- Winery/Vineyard
- Zoo/Wildlife Sanctuary
- Other Sight

## Activities, Courses & Tours
- Bodysurfing
- Diving
- Canoeing/Kayaking
- Course/Tour
- Skiing
- Snorkeling
- Surfing
- Swimming/Pool
- Walking
- Windsurfing
- Other Activity

## Sleeping
- Sleeping
- Camping

## Eating
- Eating

## Drinking & Nightlife
- Drinking & Nightlife
- Cafe

## Entertainment
- Entertainment

## Shopping
- Shopping

## Information
- Bank
- Embassy/Consulate
- Hospital/Medical
- Internet
- Police
- Post Office
- Telephone
- Toilet
- Tourist Information
- Other Information

## Geographic
- Beach
- Hut/Shelter
- Lighthouse
- Lookout
- Mountain/Volcano
- Oasis
- Park
- Pass
- Picnic Area
- Waterfall

## Population
- Capital (National)
- Capital (State/Province)
- City/Large Town
- Town/Village

## Transport
- Airport
- BART station
- Border crossing
- Boston T station
- Bus
- Cable car/Funicular
- Cycling
- Ferry
- Metro/Muni station
- Monorail
- Parking
- Petrol station
- Subway/SkyTrain station
- Taxi
- Train station/Railway
- Tram
- Underground station
- Other Transport

*Note: Not all symbols displayed above appear on the maps in this book*

## Routes
- Tollway
- Freeway
- Primary
- Secondary
- Tertiary
- Lane
- Unsealed road
- Road under construction
- Plaza/Mall
- Steps
- Tunnel
- Pedestrian overpass
- Walking Tour
- Walking Tour detour
- Path/Walking Trail

## Boundaries
- International
- State/Province
- Disputed
- Regional/Suburb
- Marine Park
- Cliff
- Wall

## Hydrography
- River, Creek
- Intermittent River
- Canal
- Water
- Dry/Salt/Intermittent Lake
- Reef

## Areas

- Airport/Runway
- Beach/Desert
- Cemetery (Christian)
- Cemetery (Other)
- Glacier
- Mudflat
- Park/Forest
- Sight (Building)
- Sportsground
- Swamp/Mangrove

## OUR STORY

A beat-up old car, a few dollars in the pocket and a sense of adventure. In 1972 that's all Tony and Maureen Wheeler needed for the trip of a lifetime – across Europe and Asia overland to Australia. It took several months, and at the end – broke but inspired – they sat at their kitchen table writing and stapling together their first travel guide, *Across Asia on the Cheap*. Within a week they'd sold 1500 copies. Lonely Planet was born.

Today, Lonely Planet has offices in Franklin, London, Melbourne, Oakland, Beijing and Delhi, with more than 600 staff and writers. We share Tony's belief that 'a great guidebook should do three things: inform, educate and amuse'.

# OUR WRITER

### Adam Karlin

Coordinating Author Adam's grandmother sheltered him from winter weather in West Palm Beach throughout his childhood, and he worked for a stint at the *Key West Citizen*, covering hyperbolic politicians, Cuban exiles, mosquito-control initiatives and trailer park evictions. It was the sort of journalism gig you supplement with a try at being a local-radio DJ and a few nights' bouncing at Keys bars. After that adventure, Adam went on to Lonely Planet, where he has written or co-authored well over 40 guidebooks, including three editions of *Florida* and *Miami & the Keys*.

**Published by Lonely Planet Publications Pty Ltd**
ABN 36 005 607 983
7th edition – Jan 2015
ISBN 978 1 74220 730 8
© Lonely Planet 2015    Photographs © as indicated 2015
10 9 8 7 6 5 4 3 2 1
Printed in China

Although the authors and Lonely Planet have taken all reasonable care in preparing this book, we make no warranty about the accuracy or completeness of its content and, to the maximum extent permitted, disclaim all liability arising from its use.